Paul and the Image of God

Paul and the Image of God

Chris Kugler
Foreword by N. T. Wright

LEXINGTON BOOKS/FORTRESS ACADEMIC
Lanham • Boulder • New York • London

Published by Lexington Books/Fortress Academic
Lexington Books is an imprint of The Rowman & Littlefield Publishing Group, Inc.
4501 Forbes Boulevard, Suite 200, Lanham, Maryland 20706
www.rowman.com

6 Tinworth Street, London SE11 5AL, United Kingdom

Copyright © 2020 by The Rowman & Littlefield Publishing Group, Inc.

All rights reserved. No part of this book may be reproduced in any form or by any electronic or mechanical means, including information storage and retrieval systems, without written permission from the publisher, except by a reviewer who may quote passages in a review.

British Library Cataloguing in Publication Information Available

Library of Congress Control Number: 2019952837
ISBN 978-1-9787-0738-2 (cloth)
ISBN 978-1-9787-0740-5 (pbk)
ISBN 978-1-9787-0739-9 (electronic)

Contents

Foreword *N. T. Wright*		vii
Acknowledgments		xi
Abbreviations		xiii
1	Framing the Research	1
2	A Century of Studying the *Imago Dei*	19
3	Second-Temple Jewish Monotheism	31
4	The Jewish *Imago Dei* Tradition	61
5	The *Imago Dei* in the Greco-Roman World	89
6	Paul and the Image of God	111
7	2 Corinthians 2.17–4.6	115
8	Romans 7–8	149
9	Colossians 1.15–20; 3.10	179
10	Paul and the Image of God: Conclusion	195
Bibliography		199
Author Index		231
Subject Index		239
Ancient Literature		241
About the Author		249

Foreword

What did Paul believe about Jesus? That question has haunted the study of early Christianity for many generations, especially because Paul's letters are universally recognized as our earliest sources for Christian belief. Theories have come and gone, with some seeing Paul's "Jesus" as merely human, leaving any "divine" implications to a later stage of development, and others insisting that for Paul Jesus embodied the preexistent second person of the Trinity. This question has been bound up with a broader one: How Jewish, or how Hellenized, was Paul's thought in general and his Christology in particular? Until the last generation it was assumed that these questions interlocked, so that the more "Jewish" Paul's thought was the "lower" his Christology, and the more "Hellenized" he was the "higher" the Christology. More recent study, following Martin Hengel's game-changing *Judaism and Hellenism* (1974), has seen this as a false either/or. The Christological debate has once again become wide open, with strong arguments now being made in favor of an "early, high, Jewish" Christology, associated variously with the work of Larry Hurtado, Richard Bauckham, and others.

The question remains complex, however. This is partly because the texts where Paul brings his view of Jesus to rich expression are notoriously dense, packed with quasi-technical terms whose meaning is itself disputed. What's more, these texts regularly form part of larger arguments whose intended drift has likewise been a matter of controversy. Then there is the question of the cultural echo-chamber within which Paul expected his writing to be heard, and at that point we find new versions of the old Judaism/Hellenism divide: Was Paul thinking and writing like a Hellenistic philosopher, or like an apocalyptic Jew? Or is there a *tertium quid*, a middle way in which perhaps he was straddling both? How would we know, and how might that tip the balance of argument one way or the other? At this point the faint-hearted might be tempted to give up the struggle and conclude that we cannot and will not ever know.

The present volume shows that one young scholar at least is not faint-hearted. Dr. Chris Kugler has mastered Paul's writings, particularly the dense and difficult passages about Jesus, and has made himself thoroughly familiar as well with the Jewish and Hellenistic texts and traditions which shimmer, often tantalizingly, in the background. Indeed, he argues here that while Paul's debt to the Jewish "wisdom tradition" is clear, with Jesus in some ways taking the role that "wisdom," *Sophia*, had played in some Jewish texts, this tradition by itself is not enough to explain the subtle way he then expresses the role of Jesus (or, we should say, the mysterious one who "became" the human being Jesus). At this point, Dr. Kugler proposes that Paul drew on the larger world we loosely call "Middle Platonism," which we know in such writers as Philo and Plutarch, to find a way of expressing what he believed had to be said about Jesus: particularly, that Jesus was to be seen as the active agent in the creation of the world itself. For a Jew, that meant that Jesus was doing what only God himself does. Paul was thus addressing debates which had arisen from within the Jewish world; but he was borrowing, for this purpose, the linguistic and philosophical terms of the larger Greek environment.

This, Kugler proposes, had an extra advantage for Paul, over and above the achievement of fresh clarity in articulating Jesus's role. It meant that Paul was not just invoking but actually addressing the wider cultural world of his day, appropriately, of course, for the self-styled "apostle to the Gentiles." And it meant that he was able to sketch a view of himself and his churches, on the one hand, and of various opponents, on the other, in terms of philosophical schools. To see Jesus in the way he was proposing was to attain the ultimate philosophical goal, namely the Image of God. To see things differently was to adopt a deceitful and distorted way of thinking.

The notion of the Divine Image, which forms the main thread running through this thesis, has itself been approached from many angles. My sense of Dr. Kugler's work is that, rather than simply accumulating various meanings of this phrase and ascribing them to Paul, he has performed the more delicate task of seeing how Paul reflected on the massive creative impact of Jesus himself and how, in consequence, he re-expressed existing traditions in a new way and with a fresh angle and emphasis. This ought to make the present study a vital resource for the new generation of Pauline scholars, as we leave behind some of the sterile antitheses of the past and navigate our way, like Paul himself, through a world in which there is now "neither Jew nor Greek." There is much still to do. This book concentrates, rightly, on the three major "image" texts (in 2 Corinthians, Romans, and Colossians), and this invites further exploration of the key Christological statements elsewhere, both inside and outside the Pauline *corpus*. But Dr. Kugler's work provides solid exegetical, philosophical, and theological reasons for pressing on. Like all good scholarship, this book is satisfying in itself and stimulating in its invitation for further research.

N. T. Wright
University of St. Andrews

Acknowledgments

I began the research for this project in the fall of 2014 and completed the writing in the fall of 2018. While the gestation was not extremely long, it was intense, and many shared the labor. I would like especially to mention Drs. Bill Tooman and Scott Hafemann. The former's hermeneutical sophistication and exegetical creativity gave me both guidance and courage along the way. The latter serves as a model of exegetical incisiveness and interpretative patience. He is also the kindest of detractors.

I would also like to mention Drs. David Johnston and Paul Sloan, both of whom entertained innumerable conversations about my topic and offered valuable advice. Special mention should also be made of Dr. Crispin Fletcher-Louis. Not only have I benefited from his published work, but his friendship and kind commitment to read a young scholar's research have been special gifts.

Furthermore, this project benefited from the suggestions of Dr. David Moffitt and Prof. Larry Hurtado. I am particularly grateful for the constant and kind encouragement of the former. Prof. N. T. Wright has routinely gone above and beyond the call of duty. In particular, it was a special pleasure to work with him on Paul so soon after the publication of his massive *Paul and the Faithfulness of God*. Much of what follows has been influenced and indeed greatly enhanced both by innumerable conversations with him and by his all-seeing editorial eye.

I also want to express appreciation to colleagues in my new academic home, the School of Christian Thought at Houston Baptist University (Houston, TX, USA). They have been unfailingly patient in listening to my ideas, in lending to me relevant texts, and generally in creating a wonderfully rich environment in which to conduct research.

Thanks likewise goes to editor extraordinaire, Neil Elliott of Lexington Books/Fortress Academic, without whose kindness and diligence this project would never have come into being.

Without my dad and mom, Larry and Gail Kugler, I would be a very different person who certainly would have embarked on a very different (and less risky) career path. It takes confidence (and, perhaps, some small measure of bravado) to write something meaningful, and any bit of confidence (not to say bravado) reflected in the following pages is due in no small part to their confidence in me.

It has now been four long years (and actually more), several jobs (so well handled), and one beautiful baby boy ("Eli"), and you are somehow more supportive now than you were then. This book, and all of the work and thought which it embodies, is wholly dedicated to you, my gorgeous wife, Katie Rae ("Litty").

P.S: Hank, our dog, insisted that I mention him as well—I think he deserves it.

Abbreviations

DOTP	Alexander, T. Desmond, and David W. Baker, eds. *Dictionary of the Old Testament Pentateuch.* Downers Grove: IVP, 2003.
EDNT	Balz, Horst, and Gerhard Schneider, eds. *Exegetical Dictionary of the New Testament.* 3 vols. Grand Rapids: Eerdmans, 1990 (1978–80).
BAGD	Bauer, W., W. Arndt, F. W. Gingrich, and F. W. Danker, eds. *A Greek-English Lexicon of the New Testament and Other Early Christian Literature.* 3rd edn. Chicago: UCP, 2001.
BDB	Brown, F., S. R. Driver, C. A. Briggs. *Enhanced Brown-Driver-Briggs Hebrew and English Lexicon.* Oxford: Clarendon Press, 1977.
OTP	Charlesworth, James H., ed. *The Old Testament Pseudepigrapha.* 2 vols. Peabody: Hendrickson, 1983.
OGIS	Dittenberger, Wilhelm. *Orientis graeci inscriptiones selectae: supplementum sylloges inscriptionum graecarum.* 2 vols. Leipzig: Hirzel, 1903.
ABD	Freedman, David Noel, ed. *The Anchor Bible Dictionary.* 6 vols. Yale: YUP, 1992.
DPHL	Hawthorne, Gerald F., and Ralph P. Martin. *Dictionary of Paul and His Letters.* Downers Grove: IVP, 1993.
DBI	Hayes, John H. *Dictionary of Biblical Interpretation.* 2 vols. Nashville: Abingdon, 1999.
OCD	Hornblower, Simon, Antony Spawforth, and Esther Eidenow, eds. *The Oxford Classical Dictionary.* 4th edn. Oxford: OUP, 2012 (1968).

TDNT	Kittel, G., G. W. Bromiley, and G. Friedrich, eds. *Theological Dictionary of the New Testament.* 10 vols. Grand Rapids: Eerdmans, 1976 (1932).
DJD	Tov, Emanuel, ed. *Discoveries in the Judaean Desert: The Texts from the Judaean Desert,* 39 vols. Oxford: Clarendon Press, 1951–2002.

Chapter 1

Framing the Research

At the outset of research, one must choose a "route." The particular route which is taken, moreover, not only impacts the presentation of the material but conditions the kinds of question which one asks and the implicit argumentative logic which is thought to be operative at each stage, as well as the specific debate partners which one thinks he or she is engaging. During the early stages of research, I set out better to understand the origins of christology in general and of Pauline christology in particular. Almost immediately, I became fascinated by Paul's *imago Dei* language, not least in relation to Romans 8.29; 2 Corinthians 3.18; 4.4; and Colossians 1.15–20; 3.10. In these latter two texts in particular (2 Cor. 2.17–4.6 and Col. 1.15–20), what puzzled me was the fact that, although they had all the indications of a "divine christology," Paul seemed to compromise the argument with his reference to the *imago Dei*, which I, along with many others, had taken as a reference to the *adam* of Genesis 1.26.[1] This study has convinced me, however, that this was a mistake. Paul's image christology, I will argue, is *not* an "Adam christology" but a "wisdom christology."[2]

Nevertheless, preliminary exegeses of 2 Corinthians 2.17–4.6; Romans 7–8; and Colossians 1.15–20; 3.10 made two things clear: (1) Paul employs his *imago Dei* rhetoric with a stock vocabulary across different texts and within different argumentative contexts, which itself justifies the attempt more fully to understand his "*imago Dei* theology." (2) Moreover, Paul's use of the *imago Dei* in 2 Corinthians 2.17–4.6; Romans 7–8; and Colossians 1.15–20; 3.10 reflects a creative, christological appropriation of the Jewish wisdom tradition and of certain features of Middle Platonic intermediary doctrine. This latter realization impressed upon me the fact that these passages, and the force of the *imago Dei* conception within them, consist of more than is usually considered in debates about Pauline "christology." Hence, the study

1

which follows, though it will certainly participate in the critical christological debates of (roughly) the last one hundred years (e.g., since Bousset's work in 1913), will also consider the historical, theological, and argumentative function of Paul's *imago Dei* theology as it occurs within the larger passages of 2 Corinthians 2.17–4.6; Romans 7–8; and Colossians 1.15; 3.10.[3]

METHODOLOGICAL CONSIDERATIONS

In this section, I intend to do the following: briefly (1) to justify my use of a few key Jewish themes; (2) to clarify a few elements of my hermeneutical method; (3) to explain my larger argumentative approach; and (4) to justify my use of a few terms.

The Jewish Narrative(s)

At certain points, and not least in my discussion of Romans, I make explicit (though limited) use of the sociological notion of "narratives," which are themselves component parts of "worldviews."[4] In my usage, "worldview" refers to the entire, pre-reflective "lens" through which a particular culture, in a particular place and time, encounters and thereby makes sense of all of reality. Worldviews, moreover, are (partly) composed, sustained, and expressed by stories, by larger narratives concerning things like "the divine," "human purpose," and "the ultimate meaning of life." When I sometimes refer, therefore, to certain second-temple Jewish "narratives," I presuppose this larger "worldview" model. Furthermore, though this worldview model tends to highlight the commonalities of a given people group, it need not diminish the force of differences.

We are concerned in particular with "the second-temple Jewish worldview(s)" and "the second-temple Jewish narrative(s)." Of course, "second-temple Judaism" spans several centuries and involves diverse locales and the combined forces of several cultures. In a sense, therefore, it is much more appropriate to speak of second-temple Jewish worldview*s* and second-temple Jewish narrative*s*. However, I only use this worldview model, within which stories have a crucial role, heuristically to refer to what appear to be several common features of *a certain* "second-temple Jewish narrative" which comes to expression in *several* second-temple texts but which is not characteristic of every second-temple text. In any case, my only argument in what follows is that the several features of the Jewish texts which I will highlight *are shared by these texts and by Paul himself, particularly as he expresses himself in Romans*.

These, then, are some of the basic components of the second-temple Jewish narrative which I (and many others) see reflected not only in many second-temple texts (though not all) but also in several of Paul's letters (though not all).[5] (1) YHWH, the God of Israel, is the creator and sustainer of heaven and earth (creational monotheism);[6] (2) this God made human beings so as to steward the *kosmos* in and through them;[7] (3) humans in general have failed at this vocation, resulting in a broken *kosmos*;[8] (4) this vocation devolved onto Israel (election);[9] (5) though called by God, rescued through the exodus, and given the Torah, Israel broke the covenant and went into Babylonian exile;[10] (6) in some as yet unseen way, God will rescue Israel and bring an end to her long exile (eschatology); (7) when this happens, God will reestablish Israel in a position of world sovereignty, making her the means by which he will deal with the nations, for good or for ill.[11] To be sure, this schema is very general, malleable, and not reflective of every second-temple text. Moreover, simply because two or more texts share some of the same features does not mean that these features possess the same meaning and/or perform the same function in each text. Such points have to be argued case by case. Nevertheless, an awareness of this general schema will significantly illuminate our reading of Romans.

N. T. Wright has, however, proposed two further, and controversial, elements to this Jewish "narrative": (1) the postulation that many first-century Jews believed themselves still to be living in a "continuing" exile[12] and (2) the proposal that God had called Israel to be his means of rescuing the world.[13] As to the first point, I agree with Wright: the position should no longer be controversial.[14] To be clear, however, as is evident both from Wright's several discussions of the theme and from the discussions of several others, the proposal that many second-temple Jews believed themselves still to be living in a continuing state of exile *has nothing to do with the fact that many had returned to the land of Israel*.[15] Indeed, it is clear both in the Tanakh and in the relevant second-temple texts that living in the land of Israel is *necessary but insufficient evidence that God and Israel are in good (covenantal) standing*. In fact, most of the relevant texts take foreign hegemony as sure evidence to the contrary.

In this connection, four second-temple texts (though 4 Ezra is to be dated to ca. 100 CE) point us in the right direction.[16] Although Daniel was composed roughly 370 years after the return from Babylon under Cyrus (538 BCE), and although the immediate threat is presented by the Seleucids, the writer places his protagonists *in Babylon*.[17] Nor is this merely a literary convenience. Daniel 9 is particularly instructive in this regard. In 9.4–19, Daniel offers a prayer to the God of Israel in view of Israel's suffering under the Seleucids, on the one hand, and in view of Jeremiah's prophecy that the exile would last seventy years (Dan. 9.1–2; cf. Jer. 25.11-12; 29.10), on the other. The implicit point is that the seventy-year condition Jeremiah predicted has, at least in the eyes of the author, continued to this day. In this vein, the angel Gabriel offers Daniel a response in Daniel 9.24:

4   *Chapter 1*

> (9.24) Seventy weeks are decreed for your people and your holy city: to finish the transgression, to put an end to sin, and to atone for iniquity, to bring in everlasting righteousness, to seal both vision and prophet, and to anoint a most holy place. (NRSV)[18]

On this text, I quote Collins:

> This is taken as seventy weeks of years, or 490 years. Daniel evidently rejected the Chronicler's view that Jeremiah's prophecy was fulfilled by the restoration in the Persian period. . . . Daniel 9 extends the duration of the desolation to seventy weeks of years, or ten jubilees.[19]

For our purposes, the key point is that the author of Daniel interprets the current state of Seleucid oppression as sure evidence that the (covenantal and theological) state of exile continues.

We observe the same phenomenon in Baruch, a pseudepigraphal work probably dating from sometime in the second or first century BCE but fictitiously set "in the fifth year" of the Babylonian exile (1.2).[20] In this connection, I note that several scholars have plausibly proposed that Greek Baruch, as represented by Vaticanus, is actually dependent upon Theodotion Daniel 9.[21] In any case, the book purports to narrate a story in which Baruch "read the words of this book" (1.3) to "all [Jews] who lived in Babylon" (1.4). Upon hearing the words, "(1.6) they wept, and fasted, and prayed before the Lord; (1.7) they collected as much money as each could give, and sent it to Jerusalem" along with a letter. The letter includes a prayer which the Jews in Babylon encouraged those in Jerusalem to pray (1.15–3.8). In particular, the opening of the prayer (1.15–22 [esp. 1.20]) features a clear allusion to Deuteronomy 28.15–68.[22] The prayer's claim is that "the curse that the Lord declared through his servant Moses" (1.20) had come upon Israel, as a result of which, as Deuteronomy 28.15–68 had always promised, Israel had gone into exile. It is precisely within this context, moreover, that Baruch offers an extended praise of *sophia* ("wisdom"; 3.9–4.4):

> (3.29) Who has gone up into heaven, and taken her [*sophia*],
>   and brought her down from the clouds?
> (3.30) Who has gone over the sea, and found her,
>   and will buy her for pure gold? (NRSV)

This text alludes to Deuteronomy 30.11–14.[23] *Sophia*, therefore, has assumed the role of the words of the covenant which, in Deuteronomy 30.14, are "very near to you . . . in your mouth and in your heart for you to observe" (NRSV).[24] However, more pessimistically, rather than emphasizing Israel's (post-covenant renewal; so Deut. 30.1–10) ability to keep Torah, Baruch says of *sophia*: "No one knows the way to her, or is concerned about the path to her" (NRSV 3.31).

In any case, for our purposes, I emphasize that Baruch is operating with a scheme in which the curses of Deuteronomy, curses incurred for breaking the covenant, have come upon Israel and sent her into exile. However, Baruch also holds out the hope that, on the other side of exile, God will send the gift of *sophia* so that Israel might finally be able to keep the covenant. Or, in other words, Baruch holds out the hope that through the gift of *sophia* God might finally bring an end to Israel's state of "exile." For my case, what principally matters is that, because the author of Baruch is writing long after the return under Cyrus, this text provides further evidence that *some* late second-temple Jews—however diverse their reasons might have been—regarded Israel (or some subset thereof) as in a (theological) state of exile.

Fourth Ezra attests to a similar view. This is evident not least in the author's appropriation of the large-scale schema of Daniel 7 in relation to his own day. In particular, in 4 Ezra 11–12.3, the author recounts a dream in which he saw, inter alia, a twelve-feathered, three-headed eagle rising out of the sea (11.1–2). The eagle represents the Roman Empire.[25] When the angel Uriel interprets Ezra's dream (12.4–39), he tells Ezra that the eagle is the fourth beast of Daniel's vision (4 Ezra 12.10–13; cf. Dan. 7.7–8). By constructing a late first-century narrative in which Rome, symbolized by the eagle, is taken as the *last* beast of Daniel 7, the author of 4 Ezra indicates that he regards the exile as a continuing state of affairs.[26]

The Damascus Document is also instructive:

> (1.1) And now, listen, all those who know justice, and understand the actions of (1.2) God; for he has a dispute with all flesh and will carry out judgment on all those who spurn him. (1.3) For when they were unfaithful in forsaking him, he hid his face from Israel and from his sanctuary (1.4) and delivered them up to the sword. But when he remembered the covenant with the forefathers, he saved a remnant (1.5) for Israel and did not deliver them up to destruction. And at the period of wrath, three hundred and (1.6) ninety years after having delivered them up into the hand of Nebuchadnezzar, king of Babylon, (1.7) he visited them and caused to sprout from Israel and from Aaron a shoot of the planting, in order to possess (1.8) his land and to become fat with the good things of his soil.[27]

The writer of this document can claim, (in his calculations) 390 years after the Babylonian sack of Jerusalem, that the exile is finally coming to an end within his own community.[28] The implication is that, despite the return under Cyrus, the rest of Israel remains in a state of exile. Many other texts could make the point, but these will have to suffice.[29]

In closing this discussion, however, I note that this does not mean that *all* Jews believed in a continuing state of exile.[30] Claiming that the first-century state of Roman hegemony was consonant with the idyllic eschatology of the prophets would not have made for very palatable propaganda. However, it is unlikely that the temple authorities and the Herodians would have spoken in such certain terms about a continuing exile. To do so—to intimate that God and Israel were not in good covenantal standing—could (and probably would) de facto undermine their putative divine authorization and position of authority. There were doubtless many and diverse reasons for claiming that Israel remained in a state of exile: foreign hegemony, impure and/or corrupt national leadership, and/or a combination of the latter with a sense that God was acting anew (in an eschatological manner) within one's own community (Qumran and early Christianity). Therefore, when I later propose a reading of Romans 7–8, which suggests that Paul construed Israel's state as one of continuing exile, this does not depend upon the postulation that *every* first-century Jew would similarly have construed Israel's state, or even that, for those who would have, they would have done so for the same reasons.

What should we make, however, of Wright's claim that many second-temple texts construe God's covenant with Israel in fundamentally missiological terms? He has various ways of stating his case:

> [G]ranted the presence of evil in the world, what is the creator going to do about it? The answer given by a wide range of Jewish writers from the redactor of Genesis to the late rabbis is clear: he has called Israel to be his people. "I will make Adam first," says Israel's god [*sic*] in the midrash on Genesis, "and if he goes astray I will send Abraham to sort it all out." The creator calls a people through whom, somehow, he will act decisively within his creation, to eliminate evil from it and to restore order, justice and peace. . . . This belief is a basic assumption throughout the Jewish literature of our period.[31]

> *As far as Paul was concerned, the reason the creator God called Israel in the first place was to undo the sin of Adam and its effects.*[32]

For Wright, therefore, God's covenant with Israel is *fundamentally* missiological; a missional attitude toward the nations is not, then, simply a possible and/or potential implication of the covenant. It is, rather, its original and fundamental purpose.

However, two substantial and relatively recent studies of the primary Jewish material in this connection have not found reason to come to this conclusion. Terence L. Donaldson's careful study, for example, nowhere makes the claim that Jews understood their covenant in missiological terms.[33] Likewise, in Sigurd Grindheim's review essay of Wright's *Paul and the Faithfulness of God*, in which he principally draws upon his earlier monograph *The Crux of Election*, he contends (against Wright) that Israel's "function as witness lies precisely in [their] separateness."[34] In this connection, Grindheim contends of texts like Isaiah 42.6; 49.6; and Psalm 67: "The idea that Israel is the light of the nations must be understood along similar lines."[35] In other words, "Israel's role is not to bring salvation.... They do not even have a missionary function in announcing it."[36]

Therefore, although it is well known, and as Donaldson has demonstrated in detail, that Jews (and Jewish texts) were open to Gentiles—under the right circumstances—participating in Jewish life and even (in some sense) in the eschatological fortunes of faithful Israelites, it is not at all clear that we have a single biblical or second-temple text which construes Israel's election in fundamentally missiological terms.[37]

It seems to me, therefore, that this is what has happened. Wright has, as I will argue below in relation to Romans 2.17–24, *rightly* perceived the way in which, in the polemical contexts (esp.) of Galatians 3–4 and Romans 2–4, Paul has provided a thoroughly missiological construal of Israel's election. In the former text (esp. Gal. 3.8), Paul boldly argues that his mission to the Gentiles, in which he does not prescribe Torah observance, is precisely what the covenant with Abraham originally envisaged. In the latter text, as I will argue below, Paul's conversation with an imaginary Jewish interlocutor features a thoroughly and exclusively missiological construal of Israel's election (Rom. 2.17–24). However, Wright made a mistake in attempting to account for this Pauline construal on the basis of putative Jewish parallels—parallels which the major studies of the Jewish material rightly contend do not exist. Therefore, Paul's missiological construal of Israel's election in these polemical contexts, I suggest, is *not* to be explained on the basis that many (or most) Jews of his day would have construed Israel's election similarly. Rather, Paul's doubtless controversial and polemical construal of Israel's election is to be accounted for on the basis that Paul himself was *compelled* to such a creative reading of the Abraham cycle, and of Israel's election, *because of his unique mission to Gentiles*. This observation will inform our reading of Romans 2.17–24.[38]

Intertextuality

Throughout this book, I will propose readings of several texts, and not least of Paul's letters, which depend upon an appreciation of their intertextual relationships to prior texts (and/or traditions). For this overall hermeneutical strategy, I depend in particular upon Umberto Eco and Richard Hays. Eco argues that any act of interpretation ought to be performed in relation to a given culture's presumed "cultural encyclopedia." By "cultural encyclopedia," Eco refers to what we can suppose to have been the whole body of conventional knowledge of a given people group, or groups, in a given place and time.[39] Words, sentences, paragraphs, symbols, and actions all have their meaning in relation to this encyclopedia.

Furthermore, coming to the work of Hays, I proceed on the assumption that Paul's letters take for granted the cultural encyclopedia of the Jewish scriptures and their reception.[40] Much of my treatment of Paul, therefore, will be an exercise in intertextual (and sometimes intratextual) interpretation. In this regard, I have found Hays's seven criteria useful:[41]

(1) Availability: "Was the proposed source of the echo available to the author and/or original readers?";[42]
(2) Volume: "The volume of an echo is determined primarily by the degree of explicit repetition of words or syntactical patterns, but other patterns may also be relevant: how distinctive or prominent is the precursor text within Scripture?";[43]
(3) Recurrence: "How often does Paul elsewhere cite or allude to the same scriptural passage?";[44]
(4) Thematic Coherence: "How well does the alleged echo fit into the line of argument that Paul is developing?";[45]
(5) Historical Plausibility: "Could Paul have intended the alleged meaning effect? Could his readers have understood it?";[46]
(6) History of Interpretation: "Have other readers, both critical and pre-critical, heard the same echoes?";[47] and
(7) Satisfaction: "With or without clear confirmation from the other criteria listed here, does the proposed reading make sense? Does it illuminate the surrounding discourse?"[48]

I regard criteria 1 through 4, along with 7, as important components of any proposed echo and/or allusion. However, as to the criterion of "Historical Plausibility" (5), I do not regard it as necessary that all or even most of Paul's audience should have been able to detect such allusions.[49] I will return to this below. Point 6, likewise, is desirable but not necessary.[50]

At this point, while not wishing to wade too deeply into the debates about intertextuality, a few points of clarification are in order. Hays speaks—sometimes interchangeably—of "allusion" and "echo." He is capable, however, of a sharper delineation: "*allusion* is used of obvious intertextual references, *echo* of subtler ones."[51] Furthermore, Hays conceives of "[q]uotation, allusion and echo ... as points along a spectrum of intertextual reference, moving from the explicit to the subliminal."[52] These distinctions provide a helpful way of proceeding.[53]

We must also briefly address the question of authorial "intent" in relation to proposed echoes and allusions. This question also relates intimately to the criterion of "Historical Plausiblity," particularly in terms of whether or not it is reasonable to suppose both that a given author "intended" an echo or allusion and that a given audience would have been able to detect it. The usually implicit question goes something like this. Is it reasonable to suppose that Paul would have "intended" this or that echo or allusion in letters written to audiences at least partly composed of Gentiles, many of whom doubtless would not have "heard" extremely subtle scriptural echoes? In this connection, even if—excluding the case of the Roman church (which Paul had not founded: cf. Rom. 1.10–15; 15.22–9)—we assume that Paul and his associates, and perhaps locals within his congregations, capably and frequently taught the scriptures, many proposed scriptural allusions are still sufficiently subtle for us to conclude that many Gentiles would not have heard them.

Nevertheless, I submit, this line of questioning betrays a serious failure to think historically about the first-century, ex-Pharisaic Jew, Paul. In effect, it simply assumes that Paul was quite capable of thinking and writing about God, about God's people and about God's past, present, and future activity *in "ascriptural" terms*. In other words, this line of questioning proceeds on the assumption that Paul could think and write about "theology" in terms which were *not* fundamentally shaped, colored, and informed by the Jewish scriptures. On this point, I follow Hays:

> The vocabulary and cadences of Scripture—particularly of the LXX—are imprinted deeply on Paul's mind, and the great stories of Israel continue to serve for him as a fund of symbols and metaphors that condition his perception of the world, of God's promised deliverance of his people, and of his own identity and calling. His faith, in short, is one whose articulation is *inevitably* intertextual in character, and Israel's Scripture is the "determinate subtext that plays a constitutive role" in shaping his literary production.[54]

A Note on Terms

Throughout, I make use of certain, convenient shorthands. For instance, I routinely use the word "Christian" as the least cumbersome way of referring to someone who is a participant in the early Christian movement. I do not hereby, however, intend to indicate that such a person is marked off from something called "Judaism." When I use the expression "early Christianity," furthermore, this is simply a convenient shorthand for "an ancient movement characterized by devotion to Jesus of Nazareth." Similarly, when I use the word "Judaism," this is the least cumbersome shorthand known to me for "the ancient Jewish tradition/way of life."[55] Likewise, without intending any pejorative connotation, I sometimes indiscriminately refer to Gentiles as "pagans."[56] Furthermore, my use of the label "philosophical tradition(s)" is especially general and necessarily so. Because, as we will see in due course, our period (ca. 100 BCE–200 CE) was characterized by an extreme philosophical "eclecticism," it is at times either unhelpful and/or strictly inaccurate to refer to something as, for example, a "Stoic" or "Middle Platonic" tradition. For instance, in the case of Philo's *logos* speculation, it is widely acknowledged that Philo—here as elsewhere—is deeply influenced by Middle Platonism.[57] However, it is also widely acknowledged that Philo's *logos* ultimately derives from classic Stoicism.⁵⁸ Does Philo's *logos* speculation, therefore, constitute a "Middle Platonic" or a "Stoic" tradition? It seems to me best in this and similar cases to refer in general to "philosophical traditions" and to attempt to achieve more specificity by exposition rather than by labeling. Moreover, for the personified "Wisdom" of the Jewish wisdom tradition, I consistently use the Greek transliteration *sophia*.

Furthermore, even though I occasionally refer to the early Christians as "converts," it should be borne carefully in mind that the modern meaning of the term can mislead when applied to the first century.⁵⁹ In the ancient world, most people believed in many gods and taking on the worship of other gods was not seen as a "conversion." Gods were intimately associated with ethnicities, people groups, locales, and, therefore, peoples' sense of ethnic identity. To "convert" meant to renounce all such associations—the associations by which the gods held together and sustained the very fabric of society—and to forge totally new ones. In other words, in the ancient world "conversion" was not a shorthand for "the interior transformation of one's life."

Moreover, unless I am citing another source, I refrain from using the word "Christ." Rather, I consistently translate Χριστός as "Messiah." I do so particularly in light of Matthew Novenson's sea-change work in which he convincingly demonstrates that the older (false) distinction between a name, on the one hand, and a title, on the other, is misleading. Rather, so Novenson argues, Χριστός belongs to the linguistic-onomastic category "honorific."⁶⁰ Examples of other ancient honorifics include Alexander "the Great," "Augustus," and Antiochus "Epiphanes."⁶¹ At the linguistic-onomastic level, these designations began as colorful ways of expressing something about the figure to whom they refer: "the great king," "the most exalted" or "the one who is worthy of worship," and "the one who manifests god." In the course of use, however, at the *semantic* level, context became the determinative factor. In any case, for our purposes, the key point is that honorifics always retain the semantic *potential* of expressing the latent meaning of the designation, but such semantic meaning can only be determined by contextual use. Therefore, in order to indicate that Χριστός retains such semantic potential, I translate it as "Messiah" throughout. However, I do not hereby intend to indicate that it belongs to the linguistic-onomastic category of a "title."

In a later section, I will define what I do and do not mean by "second-temple Jewish monotheism." At this point, however, I offer brief comment about the various expressions I use to designate what is often called a "high christology." N. T. Wright characteristically uses the language of "christological monotheism."⁶² Larry Hurtado speaks of a "binitarian mutation" or a "variant form" of first-century Jewish monotheism, though he has long referred to "Christ devotion" and also to "Jesus devotion."⁶³ Bauckham developed the notion of "divine identity christology."⁶⁴ Crispin Fletcher-Louis coined the phrase "Jesus monotheism" and Chris Tilling simply speaks of "divine christology."[65] While certainly not wishing to imply the homogeneity of these scholars' work, each in his own way is attempting to indicate that, insofar as the proper context of early christology is exclusivist Jewish monotheism and its characteristic demarcation of "the unique divine identity" (so esp. Bauckham), a wide array of early Christian texts and practices present Jesus as divine. Therefore, while I will make particular use of Bauckham's model of "the unique divine identity," I will also employ "high christology," "christological monotheism," "divine christology," and "Jesus devotion."

NOTES

1. It is not that I assumed then or would argue now that an allusion to the *adam* of Gen. 1.26 would automatically rule out a "divine christology," as though Paul and other early Christians who held to the divinity of Jesus could not also and simultaneously hold to his full humanity. It is that, rather, I regarded it as surprising then and think it simply incorrect now to read the image christology of Rom. 8.29; 2 Cor. 3.18; 4.4; and Col. 1.15 as though Paul were *predicating* the divinity of Jesus—which he is indeed predicating and in many ways assuming in these passages—on his association with the Adam-as-God's-created-image of Gen. 1.26. Being fully divine *and* fully human is not the same thing as being fully divine *because* of being fully human.

2. Throughout, though I will argue that Paul's image christology is a wisdom christology *rather than* an Adam christology per se, I presuppose that Paul regarded the divine Jesus *also* as a genuine, historical, and publicly executed human being of the very recent past and that this component of Jesus's person was an indispensable element of Paul's christology.

3. Unfortunately, Haley Goranson Jacob, *Conformed to the Image of His Son: Reconsidering Paul's Theology of Glory in Romans* (Downers Grove: IVP, 2018); and Matthew E. Gordley, *New Testament Christological Hymns: Exploring Texts, Contexts, and Significance* (Downers Grove: IVP, 2018), appeared too late for me substantially to engage them. I have, however, read Gordley's book with attention (my *RBL* review is forthcoming) and it will feature in some of the footnotes.

4. On this, see esp. Paul Marshall, Sander Griffioen, and Richard Mouw, eds., *Stained Glass: Worldviews and Social Science* (Lanham: University Press of America, 1989); Clifford Geertz, *The Interpretation of Cultures* (New York: Basic Books, 2000 [1973]); and the classic study of Peter Berger and Thomas Luckmann, *The Social Construction of Reality: A Treatise in the Sociology of Knowledge* (Garden City: Doubleday, 1966). More recently, see J. W. Sire, *Naming the Elephant: Worldview as a Concept* (Downers Grove: IVP, 2004); and David Naugle, *Worldview: The History of a Concept* (Grand Rapids: Eerdmans, 2002).

5. On these basic points, see, e.g., E. P. Sanders, *Judaism: Practice and Belief, 63 BCE—66CE* (Minneapolis: Fortress, 2016 [1992]), 397–494; N. T. Wright, *The New Testament and the People of God*, vol. 1 of *Christian Origins and the Question of God* (Minneapolis: Fortress, 1992), 145–338 (esp. 215–338), hereafter *NTPG*; Idem, *Paul and the Faithfulness of God*, 2 vols., vol. 4 of *Christian Origins and the Question of God* (Minneapolis: Fortress, 2013), 75–196, hereafter *PFG*; and J. D. G. Dunn, *The*

Parting of the Ways Between Christianity and Judaism and Their Significance for the Character of Christianity, 2nd edn. (London: SCM, 2006 [1991]), 24–58.

6. For a list of texts in this connection, see Richard Bauckham, *Jesus and the God of Israel: "God Crucified" and Other Studies on the New Testament's Christology of Divine Identity* (Milton Keynes: Paternoster, 2008), 9, nn. 8–9. For YHWH as sole creator: "Isa. 40:26, 28; 42:5; 44:24; 45:12, 18; 48:13; 51:16; Neh. 9:6; (LXX) Hos. 13:4; 2 Macc. 1:24; Sir. 43:33; Bel 5; Jub. 12:3–5; Sib. Or. 3:20–35; 8:375–76; Sib. Or. frg. 1:5–6; Sib. Or. frg. 3; Sib. Or. frg. 5; 2 En. 47:3–4; 66:4; Apoc. Ab. 7:10; Jos. Asen. 12:1–2; T. Job 2:4." For YHWH as sole ruler: "Dan. 4:34–5; Bel 5; Add. Esth. 13:9–11; 16:18, 21; 3 Macc. 2:2–3; 6:2; Wis. 12:13; Sir. 18:1–3; Sib. Or. 3:10, 19; Sib. Or. frg. 1:7, 15, 17, 35; 1 En. 9:5; 84:3; 2 En. 33:7; 2 Bar. 54:13; Josephus, *Ant.* 1:155–6." Though I cite all of the texts from Bauckham, the provenance of some of them is contested. See esp. James R. Davila, *The Provenance of the Pseudepigrapha: Jewish, Christian, or Other?*, JSJSupp 105 (Leiden: Brill, 2005), and esp. the conclusions on pp. 230–31.

7. On this point, see the discussion of the Jewish *imago Dei* tradition.

8. Cf., most obviously, Gen. 3.17–19. The point is implicit in Ezek. 36.33–36 and Isa. 55.13, though there it is (unsurprisingly) focused upon Israel. Instructive too is the speech which Pseudo-Baruch puts onto the lips of personified Jerusalem in Bar. 4–5. Furthermore, that the animals are insubordinate to humans following Adam and Eve's sin in the Apocalypse of Moses (hereafter "Greek LAE") 12 and 14 makes a similar point. We will see that this general line of thought is crucial for an appreciation of Rom. 8.

9. See esp. N. T. Wright, *The Climax of the Covenant: Christ and the Law in Pauline Theology* (Minneapolis: Fortress, 1991), 21–26, citing the echoes of Gen. 1.28 at Gen. 12.2; 17.2, 6, 8; 22.16; 26.3; 28.3; 35.11; 47.27; and 48.3. He also notes the Edenic themes connected to Israel's restoration in Jer. 3.16; 23.3; Ezek. 36.11; and Zech. 10.8; and the way in which Adam and Israel are linked in Jub. 2.23; 3.30; 15.27; 16.26; 19.23–31; 22.11–13; T. Lev. 18.10; 1 En. 90.19, 30, 37; Wis. 2.23; 3.8; 4 Ezra 3.4–36; 6.53–59; 9.17; 2 Bar. 14.17–19; 1QS 4.23; CD 3.20; and 1QH 17.15. Cf. also John M. G. Barclay, "*Paul and the Faithfulness of God*" *SJT* 68.2 (2015): 235–43; and Sigurd Grindheim, "Election and the Role of Israel" in Christoph Heilig, J. Thomas Hewitt, and Michael F. Bird, eds., *God and the Faithfulness of Paul*, WUNT 2.413 (Tübingen: Mohr Siebeck, 2016), 329–46 (hereafter *GFP*), both of whom accept the point. However, Barclay rightly rejects Wright's further contention that many second-temple texts provide evidence of a thoroughly missiological construal of Israel's election—that is, that God's covenant with Israel *fundamentally* envisaged the rescue of the nations. On this, see immediately below.

10. The theme is obviously ubiquitous in the Tanakh and in second-temple literature. Most obviously, cf. 2 Kgs 24–25; 2 Chr. 36; Ezek. 8–10; Dan. 1.1–2; 9; the whole of Bar.; and CD 1.1–8.

11. For points 6 and 7, see the discussion in Sanders, *Judaism*, 473–74, with texts cited on pp. 475–77. I would add, in particular, Dan. 7.27; 1 En. 38; and 4 Ezra 6.55–59.

12. The proposal concerning the continuing exile goes all the way back to Wright, *Climax*, esp. 140–41 and *passim*. See also Idem, *NTPG*, 199–301 and *passim*; Idem, *Jesus and the Victory of God*, vol. 2 of *Christian Origins and the Question of God* (Minneapolis: Fortress, 1996), *passim*; Idem, *PFG*, 139–63; and Idem, "Yet the Sun Will Rise Again: Reflections on the Exile and Restoration in Second Temple Judaism, Jesus, Paul, and the Church Today" in James M. Scott, ed., *Exile: A Conversation with N. T. Wright* (London: IVP, 2017), 19–82.

13. On this proposal, see esp. Wright, *Climax*, 21–25; Idem, *NTPG*, 259–67; Idem, *PFG*, 783–814; and Idem, *Pauline Perspectives: Essays on Paul 1978–2013* (Minneapolis: Fortress, 2013), 489–509. See also the reviews of Wright by Barclay, "*Paul*," 235–43; and Grindheim, "Election," 329–46. The most important studies include Harold H. Rowley, *The Biblical Doctrine of Election* (London: Lutterworth, 1950); Theodorus C. Vriezen, *Die Erwählung Israels nach den Alten Testament*, ATANT 24 (Zürich: Zwingli, 1953); Robert Martin-Achard, *A Light to the Nations: A Study of the Old Testament Conception of Israel's Mission to the World*, trans. by J. P. Smith (Edinburgh: Oliver and Boyd, 1962); Seock-Tae Sohn, *The Divine Election of Israel* (Grand Rapids: Eerdmans, 1991); Ellen Juhl Christiansen, *The Covenant in Judaism and Paul: A Study of Ritual Boundaries as Identity Markers*, AGJU 27 (Leiden: Brill, 1995); Sigurd Grindheim, *The Crux of Election: Paul's Critique of the Jewish Confidence in the Election of Israel*, WUNT 2.202 (Tübingen: Mohr Siebeck, 2005); Christopher J. H. Wright, *The Mission of God: Unlocking the Bible's Grand Narrative* (Downers Grove: IVP, 2006); Joel Kaminsky, *Yet I Loved Jacob: Reclaiming the Biblical Concept of Election* (Nashville: Abingdon, 2007); Terence L. Donaldson, *Judaism and the Gentiles: Jewish Patterns of Universalism (to 135 CE)* (Waco: Baylor University Press, 2008); and David C. Sim and James S. McLaren, eds., *Attitudes to Gentiles in Ancient Judaism and Early Christianity*, LNTS (London: T & T Clark, 2015).

14. See Wright, *PFG*, 139: "All this brings us back to another point which in my view ought by now to be non-controversial." Wright provides an impressive list of scholars who now take this position on pp. 139–40, nn. 262–64. Note esp. his emphasis on the "Deuteronomic scheme" behind many of the primary texts on pp. 139–63. See also O. H. Steck, *Israel und das gewaltsame Geschick der Propheten: Untersuchungen zur Überlieferung des deuteronomistischen Geschichtbildes im Alten Testament, Spätjudentum und Urchristentum* (Neukirchen-Vluyn: Neukirchener Verlag, 1967); Idem, "Das Problem theologischer Strömungen in nachexilischer Zeit" *ET* 28 (1968): 445–58; James M. Scott, "'For as Many as Are of Works of the Law Are under a Curse' (Gal 3:10)" in C. A. Evans and J. A. Sanders, eds., *Paul and the Scriptures of Israel* (Sheffield: JSOT Press, 1993), 187–221; Idem, ed., *Exile: Old Testament, Jewish & Christian Conceptions* (Leiden: Brill, 1997); and most recently, Idem, ed., *Exile*. James C. VanderKam, "Exile in Apocalyptic Jewish Literature" in Scott, ed., *Exile: Old Testament*, 89–109 (94, italics added), comments, "A common portrait of exile in the apocalyptic literature envisages it as a state of affairs that began at some point near the end of the kingdom of Judah *and continued to the author's day and even beyond*." For a recent review of scholarship on this issue, see esp. Nicholas G. Piotrowski, "The Concept of Exile in Late Second Temple Judaism: A Review

of Recent Scholarship" *CBR* 15.2 (2017): 214–47, who concludes, "Even if scholars cannot currently agree upon a specific working definition of 'exile' in late Second Temple Judaism, it must nonetheless be conceded that surely *something* was in the air" (239, italics original). Robert Kugler, "Continuing Exile among the People of the Dead Sea Scrolls" in Scott, ed., *Exile*, 163–82, accepts Wright's thesis with the caveat that the hope for the end of exile was more variously expressed in the Scrolls than Wright has acknowledged. Jörn Kiefer, "Not All Gloom and Doom: Positive Interpretations of Exile and Diaspora in the Hebrew Bible and Early Judaism" in Scott, ed., *Exile*, 119–34 (esp. 128–34), while agreeing with Wright's basic emphasis, rightly insists that not all Jews regarded their dispersion as a social, political, and/or theological disaster. Steven M. Bryan, "The End of Exile: The Reception of Jeremiah's Prediction of a Seventy-Year Exile" *JBL* 137.1 (2018): 107–26, appeared too late for me to engage it.

15. See Wright, *PFG*, 140 and n. 265. Cf. also Martien A. Halvorson's case that this metaphorical/theological use of "exile" is actually rooted in preexilic literature: *Enduring Exile: The Metaphorization of Exile in the Hebrew Bible*, VTSup 141 (Leiden: Brill, 2011).

16. Bruce M. Metzger, "The Fourth Book of Ezra" in *OTP* 1.520: "According to most scholars, the original Jewish document known today as 4 Ezra was composed about A.D. 100."

17. Cf. John J. Collins, *Daniel: A Commentary on the Book of Daniel*, Hermeneia (Minneapolis: Fortress, 1993), 26: "By the end of the nineteenth century . . . there was an established consensus in favor of the Maccabean dating." See pp. 62–64 with literature cited therein. Cf. also Louis F. Hartman and Alexander A. Di Lella, *The Book of Daniel: A New Translation with Notes and Commentary*, AB23 (New York: Doubleday, 2005 [1978]), 9–18; and the short overview of the "Antiochene Crisis" in Sanders, *Judaism*, 23–34. For Josephus's account, see *Ant.* 12.248–56.

18. All translations of ancient and modern texts are my own unless otherwise noted.

19. Collins, *Daniel*, 352, italics original. Cf. also the helpful discussion in John Goldingay, *Daniel*, WBC 30 (Dallas: Word Books, 1989), 257–60. However, I note the interesting proposal of John S. Bergsma, "The Persian Period as Penitential Era: The 'Exegetical Logic' of Daniel 9.1–27" in Knoppers, Grabbe, and Fulton, eds., *Exile and Restoration Revisited: Essays on the Babylonian and Persian Periods in Memory of Peter R. Ackroyd*, LSTS (London: T & T Clark, 2009), 50–64 (60, italics original): "It would be better to recognise that Dan. 9.24 announces a 70-week penitential period that does not start with Jeremiah's prophecy of '70 years' but rather is *subsequent* to the Jeremianic period."

20. On the dating of Baruch, see now esp. Sean A. Adams, *Baruch and the Epistle of Jeremiah: A Commentary Based on the Texts in Codex Vaticanus*, SCS (Leiden: Brill, 2014), 4–6, who provides a helpful chart of opinions on p. 5. Cf. also Davila, *Provenance*, 225. Adams, *Baruch*, 7, further argues, "[T]he dominant theme of exile and restoration provides a cohesive vision throughout the book and binds the work together."

21. So esp. Adams, *Baruch*, 60–93, *passim*, and the scholars listed on pp. 64–65; O. H. Steck, *Das Apokryphe Baruchbuch: Studien zu Rezeption und Konzentration*

"kanonischer" Überlieferung, FRLANT 160 (Göttingen: Vandenhoeck & Ruprecht, 1993), 80; and Emmanuel Tov, *The Greek and Hebrew Bible: Collected Essays on the Septuagint*, VTSup 72 (Leiden: Brill, 1999), 519–26.

22. So also Adams, *Baruch*, 68.

23. So also Ibid., 110–11.

24. Cf. the very suggestive comparison between the wisdom speculation in Bar. 3.29–30, with its allusion to Deut. 30.11–14, and the christological formulation of Paul in Rom. 10.6–10, with its allusion to the same passage: J. D. G. Dunn, *Christology in the Making: A New Testament Inquiry Into the Origins of the Doctrine of the Incarnation*, 2nd edn. (Grand Rapids: Eerdmans, 1996 [1980]), 184–87; and Idem, *The Theology of Paul the Apostle* (Grand Rapids: Eerdmans, 1998), 280–81. It is, therefore, all the more surprising that Dunn rejects wisdom christology just a few passages earlier in Rom. 8.3: so Dunn, *Christology*, 44–46, 111–12; and Idem, *Paul*, 277–79.

25. So, e.g., Michael E. Stone and Matthias Henze, *4 Ezra and 2 Baruch: Translations, Introductions, and Notes* (Minneapolis: Fortress, 2013), 2–3.

26. The same point could be made in relation to 2 (Syriac) Baruch. I cite Matthias Henze, *Jewish Apocalypticism in Late First Century Israel: Reading Second Baruch in Context*, TSAJ 142 (Tübingen: Mohr Siebeck, 2011), 119: "By choosing the Babylonian invasion of Jerusalem as the setting for his book, the author of 2Bar suggests, albeit implicitly, that the root cause for Israel's demise under the Romans dates back to 587 BCE. . . . In a way, Israel never completely overcame the blow she suffered from the hand of Nebuchadnezzar, so that Titus's devastating advances should be interpreted as a recrudescence of the old wounds, wounds that never healed."

27. As reconstructed and translated in F. García Martínez and E. J. C. Tigchelaar, *The Dead Sea Scrolls Study Edition*, 2 vols. (New York: Brill, 1997–1998), 1.551.

28. I note the comment of Kugler, "Continuing Exile," 170: "That the people of the Dead Sea Scrolls once considered themselves in particular to be enduring a continuing exile is a virtual commonplace among students of the Scrolls."

29. Wright's case concerning 4QMMT; 1QS; 1QH 11; 11QT; Tob.; 1 En.; T. Levi; and T. Jud. is also convincing (*PFG*, 139–63).

30. E.g., Wright, *PFG*, 157–58, notes Sirach as an exception.

31. *NTPG*, 251–2.

32. *PFG*, 784, italics original.

33. Donaldson, *Judaism and the Gentiles*.

34. Grindheim, "Election," 336.

35. Ibid.

36. Ibid.

37. Wright, *Climax*, 21–26, largely makes his case on the basis of the following: the echoes of Gen. 1.28 at Gen. 12.2; 17.2, 6, 8; 22.16; 26.3; 28.3; 35.11; 47.27; and 48.3; the edenic themes connected to Israel's restoration in Jer. 3.16; 23.3; Ezek. 36.11; and Zech. 10.8; and the association between Adam and Israel in Jub. 2.23; 3.30; 15.27; 16.26; 19.23–31; 22.11–13; T. Lev. 18.10; 1 En. 90.19, 30, 37; Wis. Sol. 2.23; 3.8; 4 Ezra 3.4–36; 6.53–59; 9.17; 2 Bar. 14.17–19; 1QS 4.23; CD 3.20; and 1QH 17.15. However, in their different ways, these texts make the point that Israel is now God's true humanity, not that Israel is now God's means of *rescuing* humanity.

38. Unfortunately, this text is not treated in Grindheim, *The Crux of Election*.

39. Umberto Eco, *A Theory of Semiotics* (Indiana: IUP, 1976), 110.

40. See esp. Richard B. Hays, *Echoes of Scripture in the Letters of Paul* (New Haven: YUP, 1989), ix–33; Idem, *Echoes of Scripture in the Gospels* (Waco: Baylor University Press, 2016), 1–14; though the larger approach goes all the back to his doctoral thesis, *The Faith of Jesus Christ: The Narrative Substructure of Galatians 3.1—4.11*, 2nd edn. (Grand Rapids: Eerdmans, 2002 [1983]) (esp.) xi–71. Craig A. Evans, "Listening for Echoes of Interpreted Scripture" in Craig A. Evans and James A. Sanders, eds., *Paul and the Scriptures of Israel*, BSEC (New York/London: Bloomsbury, 2015 [1993]), 47–51, is right to emphasize not only echoes of scripture but echoes of scripture's *reception* in the second-temple period.

41. For these criteria, see Hays, *Letters of Paul*, 29–33. Moreover, Hays is clear that intertextual and intratextual readings are, like most historical readings, hardly ever *indisputably* certain: "The foregoing discussion suggests that we must reckon with varying degrees of certainty in our efforts to identify and interpret intertextual echoes" (29). Furthermore, like Hays, I "do not use these criteria explicitly in my readings of the texts, but they implicitly undergird the exegetical judgments" (29).

42. Ibid. 29–30.

43. Ibid. 30.

44. Ibid.

45. Ibid.

46. Ibid.

47. Ibid. 31.

48. Ibid. 31–32.

49. So also Ibid. 30: "We should always bear in mind, of course, that Paul might have written things that were not readily intelligible to his actual readers."

50. So Ibid. 31: "The readings of our predecessors can both check and stimulate our perception of scriptural echoes in Paul. While this test is a possible restraint against arbitrariness, it is also one of the least reliable guides for interpretation, because Gentile Christian readers at a very early date lost Paul's sense of urgency about relating the gospel to God's dealings with Israel."

51. Ibid. 29, italics original.

52. Ibid. 23.

53. For appreciative but critical engagements with Hays, see esp. Craig Evans, "Listening for Echoes of Interpreted Scripture," 47–51; William A. Tooman, *Gog of Magog: Reuse of Scripture and Compositional Technique in Ezekiel 38–39*, FAT 2.52 (Tübingen: Mohr Siebeck, 2011), 8 and n. 26, who criticizes Hays's lack of terminological precision; and Paul Foster, "Echoes without Resonance: Critiquing Certain Aspects of Recent Scholarly Trends in the Study of the Jewish Scriptures in the New Testament" *JSNT* 38.1 (2015): 96–111, who largely criticizes Hays for systematically screening out possible influences from the larger Greco-Roman world.

54. Hays, *Letters of Paul*, 16, citing Thomas Green, *The Light in Troy: Imitation and Discovery in Renaissance Poetry* (New Haven: YUP, 1982), 50, italics added.

55. On the dangers of anachronism with respect to these terms, see esp. Wayne A. Meeks, "Judaism, Hellenism, and the Birth of Christianity" in Troels Engberg-Pedersen, ed., *Paul Beyond the Judaism/Hellenism Divide* (Louisville: John Knox Press,

2001), 17–28; and Dale B. Martin, "Paul and the Judaism/Hellenism Dichotomy: Toward a Social History of the Question" in Ibid. 29–62. In this connection, I translate Ἰουδαῖος throughout as "Jew" rather than "Judean," simply because of common convention. On this question, see, e.g., Philip F. Esler, "Giving the Kingdom to an *Ethnos* That Will Bear Its Fruit: Ethnic and Christ-Movement Identities in Matthew" in Daniel M. Gurtner, Grant Macaskill, and Jonathan T. Pennington, eds., *In the Fullness of Time: Essays on Christology, Creation, and Eschatology in Honor of Richard Bauckham* (Grand Rapids: Eerdmans, 2016), 177–96.

56. For a defense of this convention by classical scholars, see, e.g., Polymnia Athanassiadi and Michael Frede, eds., *Pagan Monotheism in Late Antiquity*, repr. (Oxford: OUP, 2008 [1999]), 5–7.

57. A classic discussion can be found in John Dillon, *The Middle Platonists: 80 B.C to A.D. 220*, rev. edn. with a new afterword (Ithaca: Cornell University Press, 1996 [1977]), esp. 139–83. Cf. also the recent discussions in Maren R. Niehoff, *Philo of Alexandria: An Intellectual Biography* (New Haven: YUP, 2018), 93–108, 192–241.

58. So Dillon, *The Middle Platonists*, 159: "[T]he Logos . . . [is] a concept borrowed from the Stoics."

59. On this, see esp. Paula Fredriksen, "Judaizing the Nations: The Ritual Demands of Paul's Gospel" *NTS* 56 (2010): 232–52; and, with respect to Paul, Wright, *PFG*, 1418–26.

60. So Matthew V. Novenson, *Christ among the Messiahs: Christ Language in Paul and Messiah Language in Ancient Judaism* (New York: OUP, 2012), esp. 87–97. Novenson's case has been endorsed by, e.g., Wright, *PFG* 817, n. 127; and Larry W. Hurtado, "Paul's Messiah Christology" in Gabriele Boccaccini and Carlos A. Segovia, eds., *Paul the Jew: Rereading the Apostle as a Figure of Second-Temple Judaism* (Minneapolis: Fortress, 2016), 107–32, now found in and cited from Idem, *Ancient Jewish Monotheism and Early Christian Jesus Devotion: The Context and Character of Christological Faith*, LEC (Waco: Baylor University Press, 2017), 539–58 (esp. 540–43), hereafter *AJM*. See now also Matthew V. Novenson, *The Grammar of Messianism: An Ancient Jewish Political Idiom and Its Users* (Oxford: OUP, 2017).

61. See Novenson, *Christ*, 87–97.

62. E.g., Wright, *Climax*, 99 and *passim*.

63. Larry W. Hurtado, *One God, One Lord: Early Christian Devotion and Ancient Jewish Monotheism*, 3rd edn. (New York: Bloomsbury T & T Clark, 2015 [1988]), 93–128, hereafter *OGOL*; Idem, *Lord Jesus Christ: Devotion to Jesus in Earliest Christianity* (Grand Rapids: Eerdmans, 2003), 1–78, hereafter *LJC*; and Idem, *AJM*, xiii: "I have also come to use 'Jesus-devotion' or 'devotion to Jesus,' in place of 'Christ-devotion,' to give due emphasis to the treatment of a historical figure as rightful recipient of cultic devotion."

64. Bauckham, *Jesus*, 18.

65. So the titles of their respective monographs: Crispin Fletcher-Louis, *Jesus Monotheism: Volume I—Christological Origins: The Emerging Consensus and Beyond* (Eugene: Cascade Books, 2015); and Chris Tilling, *Paul's Divine Christology* (Grand Rapids: Eerdmans, 2015 [2012]).

Chapter 2

A Century of Studying the *Imago Dei*

In order to contextualize my case concerning Paul's *imago Dei* theology, I provide a brief survey of roughly the last century of critical study of the *imago Dei*. In this regard, though I have included the discussion of Larsson and Marques within the discussion of the "Bultmann *Schule*," I have otherwise agreed with Stefanie Lorenzen's demarcation of (roughly) three separate stages of modern research on the *imago Dei*: (1) the *religionsgeschichtliche Schule* to Bultmann; (2) the Bultmann *Schule*; and (3) the (what I call) "Merkabah *Schule*."[1] While the studies in each respective category bear a clear "family resemblance," the categorization is by no means designed to imply the homogeneity of the studies in each category. The categories are broad and cover diverse scholars and agendas. However, they are particularly helpful for analyzing larger scholarly movements.

THE *IMAGO DEI* IN THE *RELIGIONSGESCHICHTLICHE SCHULE*

Especially characteristic of the Göttingen *Schule* was the tendency to explain Christian origins by recourse to putative parallels or precedents in the Greco-Roman world in general and in ancient Gnosticism in particular.[2] The case was no different with study of the *imago Dei*. For Bousset, Paul's *imago Dei* conception principally derived from the Gnostic "Heavenly Redeemer myth," though one could also discern resonances of the imperial cult, in relation to which the emperor was often conceived of as *imago Dei*.[3] As to the background of Gnosticism, Carsten Colpe demolished this and similar hypotheses roughly sixty years ago, demonstrating (among other problems) the late date of most of the relevant material.[4] In this connection, Colpe's criticisms prove irreparably damaging to virtually every study of the *imago Dei* until the work of Larsson and Marques, which we will consider below. With respect to the imperial cult hypothesis, in which Paul's *imago Dei* christology is to be (at least partly) explained as Paul's or certain early Christians' deliberate christological adaptation of imperial rhetoric, I will argue below that the Jewish wisdom tradition and Middle Platonic intermediary speculation provide a much more thorough and satisfying background for Paul's image christology.

Richard Reitzenstein proposed two different kinds of influence on what he regarded as two different kinds of *imago Dei* conception in Paul.[5] On the one hand, he argued that the background of the *imago Dei* conception embedded within 1 Corinthians 15.49 could be found in "early Iranian Death-Texts" from traditions like the so-called "Hymn of the Souls" from the Acts of Thomas and the so-called Mandaean "songs of the dead."[6] On the other hand, Reitzenstein explained 2 Corinthians 3.18; 4.4; and Romans 8.29 against the background of "Hellenistic Mysticism." The former proposal concerning the background of 1 Corinthians 15.49 appears not to have influenced many. The latter proposal, as I will demonstrate in due course, depends upon a misjudgment about the probable background of 2 Corinthians 3.18, which does not lie in Jewish mysticism but rather in Paul's christological appropriation of a Jewish exegetical tradition concerning Moses's vision of God.

Bultmann's proposal, I think, represents a small step forward, though he regrettably recapitulated the Gnostic hypothesis.[7] In particular, he rightly recognized the way in which cosmology and soteriology are joined both in Philo's *logos* speculation and in the Jewish wisdom tradition more generally and the way in which this conceptual milieu served as the principal background for 2 Corinthians 4.4 and Colossians 1.15.

THE *IMAGO DEI* IN THE BULTMANN *SCHULE*

With respect to the *imago Dei*, Käsemann largely followed Bultmann.[8] In 1958, however, Friedrich-Wilhelm Eltester provided a major contribution to the question in his *Eikon im Neuen Testament*. Eltester rightly argued that the *imago Dei* conception should be traced back to Plato in particular—as well as to Genesis—and that this Platonic tradition was positively adapted in Hellenistic Judaism, not least in the Philonic *corpus* and the Wisdom of Solomon. Moreover, operating with the then-common, strict division between Palestinian- and Hellenistic-Christian *Urgemeinden*, Eltester postulated that Paul borrowed the conception from the latter.[9] However, in terms of the history of scholarship to this point, of crucial significance is Eltester's rejection of the Gnostic hypothesis and his postulation of the influence of Middle Platonism mediated *via* Hellenistic Judaism.

A mere two years later Jacob Jervell produced a major study of the topic, *Imago Dei: Gen. 1,26f. im Spätjudentum, in der Gnosis und in den paulinischen Briefen*.[10] Jervell's contribution is threefold. (1) He provided the most extensive treatment of the Jewish material up to that point. (2) He also performed a form-critical analysis of Paul's *imago Dei* texts in which he concluded that Paul had borrowed the conception from the baptismal theology of the Hellenistic-Christian *Urgemeinden*, a tradition which itself had been influenced by Gnosticism. (3) Jervell then applied this theory to several Pauline texts. Romans 8.29 betrays, so he argued, Paul's theology of baptism as proleptic resurrection.[11] In 1 Corinthians 15.49, Paul "eschatologizes" this baptismal tradition, and here one can detect both Gnostic and Philonic influence.[12] Second Corinthians 3.18 is understood similarly.[13] However, according to Jervell, the deutero-Paulines reflect an "ethicyzing" of this baptismal tradition (Col. 3.10; and Eph. 4.22–24).[14] In the same vein, 2 Corinthians 4.4; Philippians 2.6; and Colossians 1.15 are all explained as adaptations of the early baptismal theology of the Hellenistic-Christian *Urgemeinden*.[15]

As to Jervell's case, though I too allow for the *possibility* that the *imago Dei* conception held a place in the baptismal ritual of the Pauline communities, I do not think that we can recover some pre-Pauline baptismal ritual of the Hellenistic-Christian *Urgemeinden* via a form-critical analysis of Paul's *imago Dei* texts. Furthermore, not only is Jervell's restatement of the Gnostic hypothesis untenable but so is his acceptance of the then-common, sharp distinction between Jewish-Christian and Hellenistic-Christian *Urgemeinden*—a distinction on the basis of which some scholars have postulated that Paul was solely influenced by, and solely held a relationship with, the latter.[16]

Ten years later, Peter Schwanz published his major work, *Imago Dei als christologisch-anthropologisches Problem in der Geschichte der Alten Kirche von Paulus bis Clemens von Alexandria*, in which—though he helpfully traced the question into the early Fathers—he largely followed Jervell.[17] The principal background for Paul's *imago Dei* theology is Gnosticism.[18]

Edvin Larsson was the first scholar to make a serious attempt to understand Paul's *imago Dei* theology against the background of the Old Testament.[19] In this regard, he stands out rather sharply from the Bultmann *Schule*. He contended that, although the actual language of צלם אלהים (or εἰκών θεοῦ) is nowhere found in the Tanakh outside of Genesis, related motifs were associated with God, with God's people, and particularly with Israel's king.[20] Furthermore, Larsson connected this supposed Jewish imperial *imago Dei* theology with the "son of man" tradition of Daniel 7, whence it came, so he argued, into Paul's *imago Dei* theology.[21] This historical and exegetical move allowed Larsson to deny the possible influence of the Philonic and Gnostic material.[22] As we will see below, however, and as suggestive as some of Larsson's connections are, the parallels with the Jewish wisdom and Middle Platonic intermediary traditions are much stronger.

Valdir Marques, on the other hand, committed himself to a semantic analysis of εἰκών in the LXX.²³ Therein, he distinguished two kinds of *imago Dei* tradition. (1) He took Genesis 1.26 as an instance of a "spiritual" appropriation of the *imago Dei*. In that text, therefore, as well as in Genesis 5.1, 3; 9.6; Sirach 17.3; Wisdom 2.23; and 7.26, the "image" is to be identified with something incorporeal *within* the human being rather than with the total, corporeal human being herself. He takes all of the instances in Paul, too, to reflect this "spiritual" appropriation of the *imago Dei*. (2) Marques did concede, however, that certain texts attest to a "physical" interpretation of the *imago Dei*.

THE *IMAGO DEI* IN THE MERKABAH *SCHULE*

In large part, it was the 1981 dissertation of Seyoon Kim, *The Origin of Paul's Gospel*, which inaugurated a new phase of research into the *imago Dei*. Kim's proposal, moreover, found further supporters in, for example, Segal, Newman, and Vollenweider.²⁴ I refer to this phase of research as the "Merkabah *Schule*" principally for the convenience of the comparison with the earlier *Schulen*. In actual fact, these scholars represent less of a unified program and more of a noticeable trend in understanding the background of Paul's use of the *image Dei*.

In their different ways, they offer a similar reconstruction. Jewish apocalyptic or "Merkabah Mysticism" was the *religionsgeschichtliche* context within which Paul interpreted the "Damascus christophany."²⁵ As a result of this contextual interpretation, Paul concluded that the glorified Jesus was also the "image of God." Two major points, however, stand against this proposal: (1) All four scholars take 2 Corinthians 3–4, a text in which Paul refers to Jesus as "the image of God" (4.4), as a semiautobiographical account of the Damascus christophany.²⁶ As I will argue below, however, this text is better explained in other terms. (2) As Lorenzen has noted, we have no evidence that the *imago Dei* language was *ever* used in any of the merkabah traditions.²⁷ Therefore, though I agree that such traditions are important for an appreciation of the so-called "Damascus christophany," they do not of themselves explain the christological designation "image of God."

OTHER RELEVANT STUDIES

Stefanie Lorenzen

We now come to the study of Stefanie Lorenzen. A particularly valuable feature of her treatment lies in the fact that it so thoroughly highlights and convincingly critiques the long scholarly tradition of "internalizing" or "spiritualizing" the *imago Dei* conception.[28] Against this tendency, Lorenzen rightly argues that "the body for Paul has a crucial meaning: it is the medium of the Christ event and the bearer of God—more particularly, the bearer of the image of Christ."[29] Indeed, for Paul, the whole human being, rather than some spiritual or anatomical part thereof (e.g., the "soul," "spirit," or "mind"), will be conformed to the image of the Messiah (cf. esp. Rom. 8.23 with 8.29; cp. Phil. 3.21).

Her overall methodology, however, is questionable. It seems to represent an overreaction to a traditional *religionsgeschichtliche* analysis.[30] *Religionsgeschichtlichen* analyses, so Lorenzen contends, are less "controllable" than "word-oriented" (i.e., "lexical") approaches.[31] Therefore, she proposes to use sources for comparison with Paul's letters which are close in date, locale, and thought.[32] Quite reasonably, she selects Philo's writings and the Wisdom of Solomon. Then, for each of these three bodies of work, she performs a semantic analysis, deliberately bracketing out religion-historical questions.[33] She is, therefore, not concerned with the apparently less controllable question of the texts and traditions which might have influenced Paul or the Alexandrians' *imago Dei* theology. This represents, I suggest, an overreaction. Of course, religion-historical approaches are always in danger of inappropriately transporting the apparent meaning of a unit from an earlier text into a later text. The proper control on this danger, however, is a closer reading of the later text, a reading which respects its unique (and different) *Sitz im Leben*. The correct strategy is not to read Paul or the Alexandrians as though their clear dependence upon earlier *imago Dei* traditions is irrelevant to their interpretation.

George H. van Kooten

George H. van Kooten's book *Paul's Anthropology in Context* is both innovative and wide-ranging.[34] While the title suggests that it fundamentally consists of an assessment of Paul's anthropology as it relates to the anthropologies of Judaism and the larger Greco-Roman world, van Kooten focuses in particular upon two related issues: (1) the *imago Dei* conception in ancient Judaism and the Greco-Roman world and (2) the way in which the philosophical *imago Dei* tradition in particular illuminates the writings of Philo and Paul.[35]

I note the positive gains of the book. While there is little originality to his treatment of the Jewish *imago Dei* tradition (a treatment which is, nonetheless, strong), van Kooten's survey of the philosophical *imago Dei* tradition is extremely illuminating.[36] For example, he demonstrates that the concept of the *imago Dei* was pervasive in the philosophical tradition, not least in Middle Platonism.[37] He further demonstrates, following the classic study of

Dillon, that the philosophical *imago Dei* tradition was largely dependent upon Plato's *Timaeus*.[38] His survey of this tradition, moreover, significantly illuminates his reading of Philo and Paul, even though his reading of the former is much more convincing.[39]

There are several features of the book, however, which do not convince. For example, I am unpersuaded by van Kooten's postulation, made solely on the basis of 1 Thessalonians 5.23, that Paul works with a clear and consistent tripartite anthropology.[40] Relatedly, in agreement with Lorenzen, I reject van Kooten's proposal that Paul *equates* the *imago Dei* with the human "mind" (νοῦς).[41] Rather, Lorenzen is correct to contend that Paul regards the entire, embodied human being as God's image rather than some anatomical part thereof.[42] Most problematic, however, is the fact that van Kooten fails both to perceive the significance of the Jewish wisdom tradition and to indicate the crucial ways in which Paul's *imago Dei* theology differs radically from the philosophical *imago Dei* traditions. In any case, van Kooten will serve as a constant debate partner throughout.

J. D. G. Dunn

Because I will argue that Paul's image christology is essentially a "wisdom christology," I have decided here to engage J. D. G. Dunn's well-known and controversial construal of such.[43] In *Christology in the Making*, and later in *The Theology of Paul the Apostle*, Dunn argued that Adam christology, on the one hand, and wisdom christology, on the other, were the fundamental categories of Pauline christology. This is one of his clearest statements, along with, at least to his mind, the obvious implication:

> That there is no clear thought of Christ's preexistence independent of such imagery (Wisdom and Adam) is a factor of considerable importance in determining the significance to be given to subsequent statements of Christ's preexistence. . . . In assessing Paul's christology at this point and in theologizing further on the basis of it, a central fact remains primary: that Paul's christology was not seen as a threat to Israel's inherited monotheism by his Jewish contemporaries, nor was it intended by Paul himself as a complete redefinition of that monotheism.[44]

Below I will contest the view that Paul did not intend a "reworking" of Jewish monotheism.[45] In this connection, it is hard to see how Dunn could not have perceived the implications of Paul's (or some other early Christian's) christological adaptation of the *Shema* in 1 Corinthians 8.6. Or, as he later changed his view on this point, perhaps he *did* come to see the implications.[46] In any case, here I am principally concerned with his reductionistic construal of wisdom christology.

As a part of our engagement with Dunn, it will prove helpful briefly to consider Gordon D. Fee's bold position, a position articulated not least in relation to Dunn's construal of wisdom christology. Fee argues, "In the light of the evidence, therefore, both in Paul's letters and in the Wisdom literature, we must conclude that Wisdom christology is *not* found in Paul's letters and thus has no role in the reconstruction of Paul's christology."[47] Fee's negative case can be summarized as follows: (1) The wisdom tradition is variegated; (2) Jesus is never "identified" with *sophia* in Paul; (3) Paul does not appear to be particularly indebted to the major wisdom texts (e.g., Prov.; Sir.; Bar.; and Wis.); (4) there are no *major* linguistic connections between any of the wisdom texts and Paul's letters; (5) and, finally, Paul's Χριστός assumes a role in his theology and practice which *sophia* never held in any Jewish wisdom tradition.[48] One can, however, fundamentally agree with most of these points and nevertheless reject the conclusion.

Fee is likely reacting to these kinds of statement from Dunn: "Paul does have a conception of the preexistent Christ. But it is the preexistence of Wisdom now identified by and as Christ."[49] To be sure, Fee is correct to contend (against Dunn) that Paul nowhere simply *identifies* Jesus with the *sophia* of the Jewish wisdom tradition. Moreover, Fee is right to argue both that Paul does not demonstrate *extensive* linguistic dependence upon any one Jewish wisdom text and that Paul's Χριστός assumes a position in his theology and *praxis* which *sophia* never held in any Jewish wisdom tradition. However, none of this is an argument against the following points. (1) Jesus, like *sophia/logos* in the Wisdom of Solomon and the writings of Philo, plays an intermediary role in cosmology, a role articulated by means of "prepositional metaphysics" ("by whom/through whom"; 1 Cor. 8.6; Col. 1.15–20; cp. John 1.3, 10; and Heb. 1.2).[50] (2) In Romans 8.29 and Colossians 1.15, Paul refers to Jesus with the language of the *imago Dei* and then immediately calls him πρωτότοκος. As I will demonstrate below, this is clearly formulaic, semi-technical cosmological language which reflects the influence of Middle Platonism, possibly mediated *via* the Jewish wisdom tradition. Therefore, while Fee is correct to contend that Paul's christology of preexistence does not depend upon any one wisdom *text*, he is wrong to conclude that Paul, therefore, made no use of Jewish wisdom *speculation*.[51]

With this brief engagement with Fee behind us, we are now in a better position to consider Dunn's construal of the relationship between Jesus and *sophia*. Commenting upon the image christology of Colossians 1.15, Dunn writes,

> [Paul] is identifying this divine Wisdom with Christ, just as ben Sira and Baruch identified divine Wisdom with the Torah. . . . The effect is the same: not to predicate the actual (pre)existence of either Torah or Christ prior to and in creation itself, but to affirm that Torah and Christ are to be understood as the climactic manifestations of the preexistent divine wisdom.[52]

The putative parallels with Sirach 24 or Baruch 3.9–4.4, however, are not as strong as Dunn supposes. In both texts, notwithstanding the striking association—indeed, perhaps equation—of *sophia* and Torah, the association/equation is nevertheless *dialectical*. Both texts speak first and less ambiguously of the preexistence of *sophia* and only then of *sophia*'s association and perhaps equation with Torah. *But no such dialectic exists in Paul's texts*. Rather, Paul seems unambiguously to speak *only and exclusively* of the preexistence of the one who was in "the form of God" (Phil. 2.6) and who was and is "the image of God" (Col. 1.15), without any dialectical reference to *sophia*.[53] Therefore, that Paul christologically reworked Jewish *sophia* speculation demands neither that he ambiguously "associated" Jesus with preexistent *sophia* nor that he understood Jesus to have a complex, dialectical relationship with her. Rather, and on the contrary, the lack of any such dialectic suggests that, at least for Paul, Jesus had *personally replaced the impersonal sophia of the Jewish wisdom tradition*.

NOTES

1. So Stefanie Lorenzen, *Das paulinische Eikon-Konzept: Semantische Analysen zur Sapientia Salomonis, zu Philo und den Paulusbriefen*, WUNT 2.250 (Tübingen: Mohr Siebeck, 2008), 1–16, hereafter *EK*. The survey of D. J. A. Clines, "The Image of God in Man" *TB* 19 (1968): 53–103, is still important, particularly for the comments on the Fathers (54–55). However, despite the great value of this survey, he wrongly concludes that Paul's image christology is simply one component of his Adam christology, against which interpretation I will argue throughout.

2. On this, see esp. Larry W. Hurtado, "A New Introduction" in Wilhelm Bousset, *Kyrios Christos: A History of the Belief in Christ from the Beginnings of Christianity to Irenaeus* (Waco: Baylor University Press, 2013 [1913]), v–xx, with literature cited therein. On the theological proclivities of certain members of the Göttingen *Schule*, see esp. Karsten Lehmkühler, *Kultus und Theologie: Dogmatik und Exegese in der religionsgeschichtliche Schule* (Göttingen: Vandenhoeck & Ruprecht, 1996). For insightful analyses of the historical and philosophical context of the *Schule*, see esp. Suzanne L. Marchand, *German Orientalism in the Age of Empire: Religion, Race, and Scholarship* (Cambridge: CUP, 2009); and Susannah Heschel, *The Aryan Jesus: Christian Theologians and the Bible in Nazi Germany* (Princeton: PUP, 2008).

3. Bousset, *Kyrios Christos*, 206. Bousset's imperial cult hypothesis partly anticipates the position of George H. van Kooten, *Paul's Anthropology in Context: the Image of God, Assimilation to God and Tripartite Man in Ancient Judaism, Ancient Philosophy and Early Christianity*, WUNT 232 (Tübingen: Mohr Siebeck, 2008), 204–06, hereafter *PA*. On the reception of *Kyrios Christos* in general, see esp. Hurtado, "A New Introduction" in *Kyrios Christos*, x–xx; and Idem, "New Testament

Christology: A Critique of Bousset's Influence" *TS* 40.2 (1979): 306–17, now found in and cited from Idem, *AJM*, 11–24.

4. Carsten Colpe, *The religionsgeschichtliche Schule: Darstellung und Kritik ihres Bildes vom gnostischen Erlösermythus* (Göttingen: Vandehoeck & Ruprecht, 1961). Martin Hengel, *The Son of God*, trans. by J. Bowden (Eugene: Wipf and Stock, 1976 [1975]), 33–35, credits Colpe with bringing "this hypothetical reconstruction crashing down" (33). See also the helpful discussion in Seyoon Kim, *The Origin of Paul's Gospel*, repr. (Eugene: Wipf and Stock, 2007 [1981]), 159–62.

5. Richard Reitzenstein, *Die Hellenistischen Mysterienreligionen: nach ihren Grundgedanken und Wirkungen*, mit 2 Bildtafeln, Gebundene Ausgabe (Darmstadt: Miss. Buchgesellschaft, 1956), 350–51. Also arguing for distinct *imago Dei* conceptions in Paul, see H. Kuhli, "εἰκών, όνος, ἡ" in *EDNT* 1.388–91 (390): "Three conceptual motifs can be distinguished in Paul's metaphorical usage. . . . This state of affairs should provide—esp. in view of the striking independence of these conceptions from each other—a warning against attempts both to harmonize and to derive all from one cause." However, as my treatment of Paul will demonstrate, to say that these three conceptions—"a) mankind as God's *image*, b) Christ as God's *image*, c) believers in their relationship to Christ's *image*" (390)—betray a "striking independence" is a serious overstatement.

6. Reitzenstein, *Die Hellenistischen Mysterienreligionen*, 357.

7. Rudolf Bultmann, *Theology of the New Testament*, trans. by Kendrick Grobel, with a new introduction by Robert Morgan, 2 vols. (Waco: Baylor University Press, 2007), 132.

8. See Ernst Käsemann, *Leib und Leib Christi: eine Untersuchung zur paulinischen Begrifflichkeit*, BHTh 9 (Tübingen: 1933), 81–87.

9. So Friedrich-Wilhelm Eltester, *Eikon im Neuen Testament*, BZNW 23 (Berlin: 1958), esp. 113–20.

10. Jacob Jervell, *Imago Dei: Gen. 1,26f. im Spätjudentum, in der Gnosis und in den paulinischen Briefen*, FRLANT 2.58 (Göttingen: Vandenhoeck & Ruprecht, 1960).

11. Ibid. 272–75.

12. Ibid. 260–68.

13. Ibid. 173–97.

14. Ibid. 232–33, 239–40, 243, and 246.

15. Ibid. 197–218.

16. The best critique of this position in relation to Pauline christology is Hurtado, *LJC*, 79–97, 155–76, who strongly argues that it was precisely *Judean* Christian circles with whom Paul hoped to maintain a strong connection.

17. Peter Schwanz, *Imago Dei als christologisch-anthropologisches Problem in der Geschichte der Alten Kirche von Paulus bis Clemens von Alexandria*, AGR 2 (Halle: 1970).

18. Ibid. esp. 270.

19. Edvin Larsson, *Christus als Vorbild: Eine Untersuchung zu den paulinischen Tauf- und Eikontexten*, ASNU 23.19 (Uppsala: 1962).

20. Ibid. 115–27.

21. Ibid. 128–71.
22. So Ibid. 137–38, 165–71.
23. Valdir Marques, *"Eikón" em Paulo. Investigação teológica e bíblica à la luz da LXX* (Rome: Pontificia Università Gregoriana, 1986).
24. Kim, *Paul's Gospel*, 193–239; Alan F. Segal, *Paul the Convert: The Apostolate and Apostasy of Saul the Pharisee* (New Haven: YUP, 1990), 34–71; Carey Newman, *Paul's Glory Christology: Tradition and Rhetoric* (Köhn: Brill, 1992), 92–104, 164–85, 241–47; and Samuel Vollenweider, "Zwischen Monotheismus und Engelchristologie: Überlegungen zur Frühgeschichte des Christusglaubens" *ZThK* 99 (2002): 21–44. Lorenzen's discussion and critique is to the point: *EK*, 11–15.
25. On Paul and merkabah mysticism, see Dale Allison, "Acts 9:1–9, 22:6–11, 26:12–18: Paul and Ezekiel" *JBL* 135.4 (2016): 807–26.
26. So Kim, *Paul's Gospel*, 193–239; Segal, *Paul*, 34–71; Newman, *Glory Christology*, 164–85, 229–34; Vollenweider, "Zwischen," 21–44; and also, e.g., Christian Dietzfelbinger, *Die Berufung des Paulus als Ursprung seiner Theologie*, WMANT 58 (Neukirchen-Vluyn: Neukirchener Verlag, 1985), 62–64; Christian Wolff, *Der zweite Brief des Paulus an die Korinther*, THKNT 8 (Berlin: Evangelische Verlagsanstalt, 1989), 8–9; Martin Hengel and Roland Deines, eds., *The Pre-Christian Paul*, trans. by John Bowden (Philadelphia: Trinity Press International, 1991), 79; Margaret Thrall, *The Second Epistle to the Corinthians*, 2 vols., ICC (Edinburgh: T & T Clark, 1994), 1.298; Paul Barnett, *The Second Epistle to the Corinthians*, NICNT (Grand Rapids: Eerdmans, 1997), 211; Murray J. Harris, *The Second Epistle to the Corinthians: A Commentary on the Greek Text*, NIGTC (Grand Rapids: Eerdmans, 2005), 336; and Udo Schnelle, *Apostle Paul: His Life and Theology*, trans. by M. Eugene Boring (Grand Rapids: Baker, 2005 [2003]), 90–91. Note Victor P. Furnish, *II Corinthians: Translated with Introduction, Notes, and Commentary*, AB32A (New York: Doubleday, 1984), 250: "According to many interpreters, Paul is referring here to his own conversion experience," who, however, dissents from this position.
27. So Lorenzen, *EK*, 12, n. 75, and 14.
28. Lorenzen, *EK*, 2–16 (esp. 3–4).
29. Ibid. 2.
30. See Ibid. 15–19.
31. Ibid. 15.
32. Ibid.
33. For her treatment of Wisdom of Solomon, Philo, and Paul, cf. respectively *EK*, 25–69; *EK*, 69–138; *EK*, 139–256.
34. George H. van Kooten, *Paul's Anthropology in Context: the Image of God, Assimilation to God and Tripartite Man in Ancient Judaism, Ancient Philosophy and Early Christianity*, WUNT 232 (Tübingen: Mohr Siebeck, 2008), hereafter *PA*.
35. Cf. the pointed review of Joel B. Green in *RBL* 1 (2011): "Indeed, one might be forgiven for imagining that, in van Kooten's view, Paul's chief conversation partner and influence in the construction of his anthropology was Philo—or, at least, Philonic thought—since we learn repeatedly what Paul must have thought by way of comparison with Philo."
36. On the Jewish *imago Dei* tradition, see van Kooten, *PA*, 1–47. On the philosophical *imago Dei* tradition, see Ibid. 122–69.

37. See esp. Ibid. 122–69.

38. *PA*, 93–94; and Dillon, *The Middle Platonists*, 8 and *passim*.

39. On Philo, see van Kooten, *PA*, 220–44, and 269–312. On Paul, see Ibid. 176–219, 245–412.

40. *Contra* Ibid. 269–312 (esp. 270, 294–95, and 308). Rather, cf. Udo Schnelle, *The Human Condition: Anthropology in the Teachings of Jesus, Paul, and John*, trans. by O. C. Dean (Minneapolis: Fortress, 1996 [1991]), esp. ch. 3 (104, italics mine): "The trichotomous sounding phrase τὸ πνεῦμα καὶ ἡ ψυχὴ καὶ τὸ σῶμα reflects no Hellenistic anthropology according to which a person is divided into body, soul, and spirit. Paul is merely emphasizing that the sanctifying work of God concerns *the whole person*."

41. *Contra* van Kooten, *PA*, 370–92. See also Joel B. Green, "Why the *Imago Dei* Should Not Be Identified with the Soul" in Joshua R. Farris and Charles Taliaferro, eds., *Theological Anthropology*, ARCTA (Surrey: Ashgate Publishing, 2015), 179–90.

42. See Lorenzen, *EK*, 139–276 (esp. 272–76).

43. On wisdom christology in Paul, see esp. Dunn, *Christology*, 163–212; and Idem, *Paul*, 266–93. For important engagements with Dunn, see esp. Hurtado, *OGOL*, 163–64; *LJC*, 44–46, 118–26; Wright, *Climax*, 90–98; Gordon D. Fee, *Pauline Christology: An Exegetical-Theological Study* (Peabody: Hendrickson, 2007), *passim*; and Bauckham, *Jesus*, 182–232 (*passim*).

44. Dunn, *Paul*, 292–93. That Dunn feels the need to say that Paul did not intend a "*complete* redefinition" betrays the concession that Paul did, indeed, intend *some kind of* redefinition, however we account for it. After all, in his Romans commentary, Dunn himself says that "the process [of early christological reflection] seems rather to have consisted in more careful and subtle *redefining* of Jewish monotheism" (*Romans 1–8*, vol. 38A [Dallas: Word, 1998], 421, italics mine). This is why, e.g., Hurtado righty speaks of a "mutation" or "variant form" of Jewish monotheism: so *OGOL*, 93–128; *LJC*, 1–78; and "The Binitarian Shape of Early Christian Worship" in Newman, Davila, and Lewis, eds., *The Jewish Roots of Christological Monotheism*, LEC (Waco: Baylor University Press, 2017 [1999]), ch. 11, now found in and cited from *AJM*, 301–26. On the question of the "zeal-driven," Jewish-monotheistic opposition to early Jesus devotion, see esp. Idem, "Pre-70 CE Jewish Opposition to Christ Devotion" *JTS* 50.1 (1999): 35–58, now found in and cited from *AJM*, 185–210; and, with respect to Paul's own monotheistic zeal, *LJC*, 93–6.

45. Oddly, Dunn cites Wright's language of "christological monotheism" (referring to Wright, *Climax*, 117 and *passim*) in support of his position. However, on the very page of *Climax*, Wright states, "It is now, I believe, necessary to assert that, although the writers of the New Testament did not themselves formulate the doctrine of the Trinity, they bequeathed to their successors a manner of speaking and writing about God which made it, or something very like it, almost inevitable." See also Wright, *PFG*, 609–773.

46. Dunn held this view in *Christology*, e.g., 180; and *Paul*, e.g., 253 but changed his view in Idem, *Did the First Christian Worship Jesus? The New Testament Evidence* (Louisville: Westminster John Knox, 2010), 108–09, in light of his student's argument: James McGrath, *The Only True God: Early Christian Monotheism in Its*

Jewish Context (Urbana: University of Illinois Press, 2009), 38–44. For a convincing refutation of McGrath on this point, see Fletcher-Louis, *JM*, 33–92; and the remarks in Hurtado, *OGOL*, 160–62. For the view that Paul christologically reworks the *Shema* in 1 Cor. 8.6, see esp. Wright, *Climax*, 120–36; Idem, *PFG*, 661–70; Bauckham, *Jesus*, 210–18; and Fletcher-Louis, *JM*, 39–60.

47. Fee, *Christology*, 619, italics original; and Ibid. esp. 595–619 (597–98, n. 12).

48. For these basic points, see Ibid. 618–19.

49. Dunn, *Paul*, 292.

50. On "prepositional metaphysics," see below.

51. Cf. also my case below regarding Paul's use of wisdom speculation in Col. 1.15–20.

52. J. D. G. Dunn, *The Epistles to the Colossians and to Philemon: A Commentary on the Greek Text*, NIGTC (Grand Rapids: Eerdmans, 1996), 89.

53. Dunn's case in which Phil. 2.6 does *not* refer to Jesus's preexistent state has not convinced many: so Dunn, *Christology*, 114–28; and Idem, *Paul*, 281–93. For response, cf. esp. Hurtado, *LJC*, 118–25.

Chapter 3

Second-Temple Jewish Monotheism

IS MONOTHEISM EVEN AN
APPROPRIATE CATEGORY?

As I will argue that Paul's image christology represents a deliberate and creative attempt to include Jesus within the "unique divine identity" as creator, and as I will argue that this cosmogonical and "divine christology" means what it means in relation to exclusivist Jewish monotheism, it is necessary to consider whether Jewish "monotheism" is an appropriate historical category at all.[1] For instance, Nathan MacDonald's study *Deuteronomy and the Meaning of "Monotheism"* demonstrated that the word itself originated among seventeenth-century Cambridge Platonists and was often utilized so as to present the philosophical belief in one "God" as the fitting intellectual (and ethical) *telos* of an evolutionary development from a morally inferior polytheism.[2] MacDonald further argued that this post-Enlightenment, morally charged, and evolutionary model of "monotheism" has often been read back into ancient Israelite religion by specialists of the Old Testament.[3] Along with this linguistic challenge to the use of the term "monotheism" could be added the archaeological studies which have thoroughly demonstrated the ubiquity both of the worship of Asherah and of idols in Israelite abodes from the preexilic period.[4] This evidence has led to the following conclusions from several different studies:

> From these inscriptions . . . it is evident that Asherah was still known and venerated as a goddess in and around Judah and Israel. In Judah and Israel *before the Babylonian Exile*, a goddess Asherah or a cultic object called "asherah" was closely associated with the cult of YHWH.[5]

> Texts dating to the Exile or shortly beforehand are the first to attest to unambiguous expressions of Israelite monotheism.... Not only are the other deities powerless; they are nonexistent.... *Down to the Babylonian captivity*, Israelite religion tolerated some cults within the larger framework of the national cult of Yahweh. While some illicit practices persisted into the Persian period (Isa. 65:3; 66:17), these religious phenomena do not appear to have been tolerated in the central cult of Yahweh.[6]
>
> From the archaeological point of view, we know almost nothing about the cult of the Babylonian period.... In the beginning of the Persian period, however ... the archaeological picture is completely different.... From now all the figurines are only found in areas outside the region settled by the returning Judean exiles ... [and] in the areas of the country occupied by Jews, not a single cultic figurine has been found! ... *To sum up: the change from many gods to one god in Judah was established by the Jews in Babylon, and from there it was brought back to Judah.*[7]

Therefore, whatever might have been true either of "popular" religion in preexilic Israelite abodes or even in the first temple, things were markedly different after the Babylonian exile.[8] This coordinates well with the scriptural evidence in which texts usually dated to the exile or shortly thereafter (e.g., Isa. 40–55) often express—in ways which most earlier texts do not—a resolute and exclusivist Jewish monotheism.[9] On the basis of the archaeological and textual evidence, therefore, it seems reasonable to deduce that the resolute, polemical, and aniconic Jewish monotheism of exilic and postexilic Jewish traditions was forged precisely in the crucible of the Babylonian exile.[10]

Notwithstanding the particular points outlined above, however, there have been two further contentions in recent scholarship. (1) Some have suggested that there is evidence of a loose and "inclusive" Jewish monotheism in the later second-temple period. (2) Picking up MacDonald's point, others have argued that use of the term "monotheism" at all is inappropriate as a descriptor either of second-temple Jews or of the early Christians (many of whom were second-temple Jews).[11] With both of these points in mind, Paula Fredriksen has made the following case:

> [W]hat do we mean by "monotheism?" In the modern context of its origin, the word denotes belief in a single god who is the only god. When modern scholars transpose the term to antiquity, the definition remains constant. And that is a large part of the problem.[12]
>
> Big books and long articles have appeared analyzing the sudden and early development of high christological claims by imputing an austere and exclusive monotheism to late Second Temple Judaism.[13]
>
> Some scholars rightly note that a) Jews were monotheists and b) some Christian Jews, such as Paul or the author of the Gospel of John, imputed divinity to Jesus.

The correct inference from these observations is not, I think, the tortured Chalcedonianism *avant la lettre* that we now see assigned to first-century figures, who supposedly "identified" Christ with the Father in some unique, binitarian way. Multiple divine personalities are native to ancient monotheism.[14]

With a similar though not equivalent point, William Horbury has argued,

> It is argued overall that the interpretation of Judaism as a rigorous monotheism, "exclusive" in the sense that the existence of other divine beings is denied, does less than justice to the importance of mystical and messianic tendencies in the Herodian age—for these were bound up with an "inclusive" monotheism, whereby the supreme deity was envisaged above but in association with other spirits and powers.[15]

What should we make of these challenges to the use of the category of "second-temple Jewish monotheism?" As to the definitional issue, I will continue without apology to use the word "monotheism," as well as the adjectives "exclusive" and "resolute," to describe the following second-temple situation.[16] (1) In the central cult of the Jerusalem temple, "worship," particularly in terms of sacrifice, was exclusively reserved for Israel's God, YHWH.[17] Nor was this cultic veneration an arbitrary marker. Sacrifices were the specific means by which one "recognized" or "acknowledged" the existence and power of a deity. Not to offer any other "god" sacrifices effectively communicated that any other suprahuman being and/or force in the *kosmos* was not on the same level as the "God" to whom one was in fact offering sacrifices.[18] (2) Upon close examination, the view of, and devotional actions toward, Jesus of Nazareth—as both are reflected in many early Christian sources—provide our *only* evidence from this period of Jews *both* firmly maintaining the characteristically exclusive monotheism of the Jewish tradition *and* ascribing divinity to a separate, distinguishable figure. The closest the Jewish tradition comes to anything like this—and this is not very close—is the *sophia/logos* speculation of Philo and the Wisdom of Solomon, both of which we will consider below.

Nevertheless, it is certainly the case that many second-temple texts reflect a fascination with a whole host of exalted "figures," some of whom are quite closely associated with YHWH and his activity.[19] In this connection, Hurtado helpfully distinguishes between three types of what he calls "divine agency" speculation: "personified divine attributes" (e.g., *sophia*, *logos*, Glory);[20] "exalted patriarchs" (e.g., Enoch and Moses);[21] and "principal angels."[22] While I do not wish to dispute that certain second-temple texts and, indeed, certain second-temple practices intended to portray these figures in exalted terms, I do wish to challenge the inference that these texts and/or practices thereby intended to portray these figures as "divine."[23]

Let us consider the most pertinent evidence. Taking the categories demarcated above in reverse order, what should we make of the "principal angel" speculation most often adduced as evidence that some second-temple Jews were prepared to regard certain angels as divine?[24] Loren Stuckenbruck, whose studies are still some of the most careful and detailed, notes the following evidence in particular: a second-century-BCE epigraph from Rheneia; T. Lev. 5.5–6; Jos. Asen. 15.11–12; Tob. 11.14–15; 11Q14, frg. 1, col. 1.2–6; 4Q400, frg. 2.1–9; 4Q403 frg. 1, col. 1.31b–33a; 4Q418, frg. 81.1–15; and Ps. Phil. 15.6.[25] However, as Stuckenbruck himself concluded in an earlier study, none of these pieces of evidence indicates that the Jewish practices reflected in these texts—in which angels are either intermediaries or prayerfully (and sometimes "apotropaically") invoked alongside the one God—are somehow less rigorously monotheistic.[26]

In each of these cases, angels, sometimes portrayed in very exalted terms, are either "invoked" and/or "praised" alongside (often) "God Most High." They are, therefore, clearly and consistently portrayed as subservient to the one God. Moreover, their glorious depiction is not so much designed to indicate that they stand in for, replace, or compete with the one God of Israel but that they are, indeed, the glorious and authorized intermediaries of this even more glorious God. Angels, in this regard, seem to serve two principal purposes in second-temple thought.[27] (1) Second-temple Jews conceived of their sovereign God as having a massive and extremely impressive host of heavenly servants (so, e.g., Dan. 7.10 and 1 En. 14.22), servants which embodied and thereby demonstrated their master's even greater glory.[28] (2) Moreover, because second-temple Jews were monotheists, the conception of innumerable angelic servants allowed them graphically to conceive of, and to express, their one God's immanent activity in the world—*via* his angelic servants—while simultaneously holding onto his transcendent sovereignty over the world.[29] Points 1 and 2, far from diminishing the glorious depiction of angels, demanded it. But it would be a mistake on this basis to conclude that second-temple Jews regarded these angels as "divine."

In this same connection, in his study of Colossians, Clinton Arnold has adduced the evidence of the Jewish, apotropaic invocation of angels.[30] On the basis of this evidence, he argues that Jews of the late second-temple period lived with an ever-increasing sense of the transcendent inaccessibility of their God.[31] Therefore, these same Jews began "turning to angels *instead of God*";[32] indeed, the meager evidence of the invocation of angels supposedly demonstrates that "[t]he relationship of Yahweh with his people was displaced for a manipulative relationship with his angels."[33] However, all that, for example, Lorenzen (who acknowledges as much) and Arnold have demonstrated is that some Jews were prepared to invoke angels *alongside* of YHWH and *in his service*. But, however much we should learn from this about the cosmolog(ies) of second-temple Jews, this is not at all evidence that these same Jews regarded these angels as separate, divine beings. Indeed, I cite one of the pieces of evidence adduced by Arnold to make the point. This evidence comes from the so-called "Prayer of Jacob":

(1.1) Father of (the) Patria[rch]s,
 Father of al[l] (things),
 [Fathe]r of (the) powe[rs (δυνάμεων) of the co]sm[os]
(1.2) *Cr[e]ato[r* of a]l[l . . .],
 Creator of the angels and archang[e]l[s],
 the *Creator* of (the) re[deeming] nam[es];
(1.3) I invoke you . . .[34]

This example well illustrates a point which we will discuss subsequently. Even though this text provides evidence of a Jewish prayer in which angels feature prominently, the angels are unambiguously distinguished from the one God as *creatures from creator*. This is a classic example of the way in which cosmogonical activity serves as the clearest conceptual category by which second-temple Jews demarcated "the unique divine identity."

In my treatment of Colossians, I will consider in more detail Arnold's objective-genitive construal of θρησκεία τῶν ἀγγέλων in Colossians 2.18, a construal which he coordinates with his claim that some (syncretistic) Jews indeed worshipped angels. In this regard, though I think it more likely that the author intended a subjective genitive with his use of θρησκεία τῶν ἀγγέλων, I note a crucial point. Even if the author of Colossians intended to refer to the human worship *of angels*, this would only be evidence of a *polemical characterization* of one group by another. In other words, even this would not be evidence that those so characterized would have understood their actions similarly.

However, if none of the above traditions are evidence that the Jews in question were "compromising" their monotheism, how do we explain the "angelic refusal of worship" traditions or the outright polemical charge that some Jews indeed worshipped angels?[35] Some suppose the former to imply that, in fact, some Jews and/or Christians did worship angels.[36] Two points, however, urge caution in this regard. (1) While the "angelic refusal" tradition is variegated, it is also a stereotypical feature of visionary texts, such that it would be unwise to assume that every instance of this tradition betrays a historical situation in which angels were actually being worshipped as and/or alongside the God of Israel.[37] (2) As pertains both to the "angelic refusal" tradition and to the outright charge of angel worship in some rabbinic and early Christian sources, we should bear in mind that these are *polemical characterizations* made by one group against "the other."[38] In other words, these traditions are not direct evidence that Jews and/or Jewish Christians actually worshipped angels.

In this connection, we should also note the several pieces of New Testament evidence which indicate that at least some early Christians were at pains to present Jesus as totally superior to angels (esp. Rom. 8.38; Eph. 1.20–21; Phil. 2.10; Col. 1.16; Heb. 1–2; and 1 Pet. 3.22).[39] This is part of the point of Paul saying that Jesus had been exalted above every "angel" (ἄγγελος), "ruler" (ἀρχή), "power" (δύναμις) (Rom. 8.38), "authority" (ἐξουσία), and "dominion" (κυριότης) (Eph. 1.20–21); that to him every "heavenly" (ἐπουράνιος) knee would bow (Phil. 2.10); and that he created "everything visible and invisible, whether thrones or dominions or rulers or authorities (εἴτε θρόνοι εἴτε κυριότητες εἴτε ἀρχαὶ εἴτε ἐξουσίαι)—all things were created through him and for him" (Col. 1.16 NRSV). It is also widely agreed that, whatever else should be said of Hebrews 1–2, the author is arguing that Jesus is far superior to angels.[40] First Peter 3.22, likewise, is closely parallel to Romans 8.38 and Ephesians 1.20–21. We should also add the "angelic refusal" tradition of Revelation (19.10; 22.8–9)—a text in which Jesus *is* worshipped (5.8–14)—as further evidence of Jesus's superiority to angels in early Christian texts.[41] In this regard, are these christological traditions implicit evidence that some ancient Jews or Jewish Christians worshipped angels? I think not. At the very most, rather, these traditions provide evidence that at least some early Christians wanted to be clear that, in case the christological point were to be misunderstood, Jesus belonged in a category altogether different from angels.

With this clarification, we return to the question of the "angelic refusal" tradition. I make the following two points. (1) On the one hand, it is possible that the "angelic refusal" tradition is simply so stereotypical of Jewish visionary traditions that it is usually included in such.[42] (2) On the other hand, though these are not mutually exclusive, it is also possible that the tradition serves in Jewish and Christian texts as an implicit polemic against a perceived overemphasis upon and/or fascination with angelic beings and/or the heavenly world. However, even this would not prove that those on the receiving end of such polemics viewed *their own interest* in angels as some kind of "loosening" of their strict monotheism. Indeed, because our best evidence for ancient Jewish angel worship is both indirect and polemical, I think it is at least as likely that the Jews and Christians who made such accusations were thereby *deliberately mischaracterizing* the widespread Jewish interest in angels. Particularly with respect to the polemic against putative Jewish practices in rabbinic writings (so esp. Mek. Ex. 20.4, 20; Tg. Ps. J. Ex. 20.20; t. Hul. 2.18; b. Avod. Zar. 42.b; and m. Hul. 2.8), I think it is at least as likely that, in view of what the rabbis perceived as the dangerous and increasingly widespread *novum* of early Jesus devotion, on the one hand, and (to a lesser extent) early Gnosticism, on the other, some of them polemicized against what they otherwise would have regarded as the perfectly acceptable, still strictly monotheistic interest in God's subordinate heavenly entourage.[43] But, in an attempt to (re)define themselves over against early Christianity and early Gnosticism, the rabbis rejected what they otherwise would have regarded as perfectly monotheistic.

This position informs, furthermore, the particular criticism which I would level at the controversial construal of Daniel Boyarin, who insists that some form of ditheism, generated and sustained not least by the vision of Daniel 7.9–14 (and traditions precipitated by this vision), characterized much of late second-temple Judaism before it was anathematized by the fresh construction of rabbinic orthodoxy, with the result that the older, "orthodox" Jewish position consisted of worship both of YHWH and of "one like a son of man."[44] This is one of the ways in which he states his case:

> This suggests to me that in their project of producing an orthodoxy for Judaism, the Rabbis were disowning a common (how common, I think, we will never know) Jewish practice of *worship* of the second God, actually named within mystical texts, the lesser YHWH [My name is in him], Metatron, who is Enoch, the Son of Man.[45]

I note immediately that, for Boyarin, over against the well-known construal of Segal, the so-called "Two Powers Heresy" is precisely not "extrinsic" to rabbinic Judaism but characteristic of an older "orthodoxy" which, in an attempt to define themselves over against early Christianity and early Gnosticism, the rabbis anathematized, thereby rejecting what had long been acceptable.[46] In this, I *partly* agree with Boyarin, though I reject his characterization of this older "orthodoxy" as a kind of ditheism. Rather, what was acceptable "orthodoxy" was, as in, for example, the cases of the one like a son of man (Dan. 7), the Elect One (1 En. 37–71), and certain kinds of "principal angel speculation," the exalted depiction of certain "figures" alongside *and subordinate to* the one God. However, with the increasing pervasiveness of early Jesus devotion and early Gnosticism—in which both traditions went *far beyond* the speculation of Daniel 7; the Similitudes; and "principal angels"—the rabbis rejected even this previously acceptable, latter speculation *so as all the more clearly to define themselves over against the former movements*. This rabbinic polemic is not at all evidence, however, that those Jews participating in such speculation understood it as a kind of diminishing of their rigorous monotheism. Below I will consider in more detail the particular figures (one like a son of man and Enoch) to which Boyarin's citation refers.

But before we turn to "exalted patriarchs," it will prove helpful to consider Bauckham's heuristic category for synthesizing Jewish monotheistic thought of the second-temple period: the "unique divine identity." This is how Bauckham employs this language:

> The God of Israel had a unique divine identity. . . . Since the biblical God has a name and a character, since this God acts, speaks, relates . . . the analogy of human personal identity suggests itself as the category with which to synthesize the biblical and Jewish understanding of God. . . . This is not to say [however] that the human analogy is adequate.[47]

To summarize Bauckham's case in my own words, the Jewish monotheistic tradition comprises (1) "creational monotheism": YHWH is the creator and sustainer of all things; (2) "covenantal monotheism": YHWH is the God of Israel; (3) "eschatological monotheism": YHWH will be the central agent of Israel's (and perhaps the world's) redemption; and (4) "cultic monotheism": in view of points 1 to 3, YHWH alone is to be worshipped. In this connection, Bauckham is right to give a *logical* priority to points 1 to 3: "[T]he exclusive worship of the God of Israel is *precisely a recognition of and response to his unique identity*."[48] However, I note that, even though Israel's belief in YHWH's unique divine identity was *logically* prior to their cultic devotion to this God, it was cultic devotion which in practice most clearly indicated YWH's sole divinity.[49]

Bauckham further argues that "God's unique identity . . . was carefully framed so as to indicate the absolute distinction between God and all other reality."[50] One could put the matter this way. In religion-historical terms, cultic worship most clearly demarcated YHWH's sole divinity. In theological-conceptual terms, cosmogonical activity most clearly demarcated YHWH's sole divinity. He is the "creator" and everything else is a "creature" (cf., e.g., Isa. 44.24; 45.18; 48.12–13; Neh. 9.6; 2 Macc. 1.24–29; Bel 5; Jub. 12.3–5; Sib. Or. 3.20–35; 8.375–76; Sib. Or. frg. 1.5–6; Sib. Or. frg. 3; Sib. Or. frg. 5; 2 En. 47.3–4; 66.4; Apoc. Ab. 7.10; Jos. Asen. 12.1–2; and T. Job 2.4). Note in particular the "exclusive monotheism" of some of these texts:[51]

> Thus says YHWH, your Redeemer,
> who formed you in the womb:
> "I am YHWH, who made all things,
> who alone (Heb. לבדי; Gr. μόνος) stretched out the heavens,
> who by myself spread out the earth . . ." (Isa. 44.24 NRSV)

"And Ezra said: 'You are YHWH, you alone (Heb. לבדך; Gr. μόνος); you have made heaven, the heaven of heavens, with all their host, the earth and all that is on it, the seas and all that is in them. To all of them you give life, and the host of heaven worships you.'" (Neh. 9.6 NRSV)

(1.24) "'O Lord, Lord God, Creator of all things, you are awe-inspiring and strong and just and merciful, you alone (μόνος) are king and are kind, (1.25) you alone (μόνος) are bountiful, you alone (μόνος) are just and almighty and eternal.'" (2 Macc. 1.24–25)

In characterizing the "unique divine identity," however, Bauckham made one crucial mistake. While the conception of YHWH's high and exalted throne certainly functions in some texts as an indication of his total sovereignty (so esp. Isa. 6.1; 1 En. 14.18–22; and 2 En. 20.3), this conception is *not* a reliable criterion by which to judge a figure's "divinity" (or otherwise) in Jewish texts.[52] But, supposing this to be the case, Bauckham was forced to conclude, on the basis that the Elect One of the Similitudes appears to sit upon the throne of God in several texts (cf. 1 En. 45.3; 51.3; 55.4; 61.8; 62.2–5; and 69.27), that this figure is indeed—even if *the only* such figure in second-temple Jewish thought—portrayed as divine. Further buttressing his case that a figure sitting upon God's throne is necessarily divine, Bauckham argues that this is precisely the logic because of which the Elect One receives the worship befitting the one God of Israel (so 1 En. 46.5; 48.5; 62.6, 9).[53] One wonders, however, if Bauckham's decisive criterion of "enthronement" is so much derived from an inductive study of Jewish texts as necessarily inferred from his reconstruction of christological origins, in which Jesus's enthronement *à la* an interpretation of Psalm 110.1 is *the* decisive factor.[54] In any case, not least because I consider Bauckham's model of "the unique divine identity" useful, it is necessary to demonstrate the weakness of making "enthronement" or "obeisance" the key criterion by which to judge a figure's divinity (or otherwise) in second-temple texts.[55]

We turn first to consider a few texts from Daniel. Obviously, the crucial material comes from chapter 7; however, because of a few interesting features of chapter 2, we begin here. In Daniel 2, immediately following Daniel's interpretation of Nebuchadnezzar's dream, "King Nebuchadnezzar fell on his face, worshipped Daniel (Ara. לדניאל סגד / OG. προσεκύνησε τῷ Δανιηλ), and commanded that a grain offering and incense be offered to him" (Dan. 2.46).[56] Of this text, Josephus writes,

> When King Nebuchadnezzar had heard these things and recognized his dream, he was amazed at Daniel's nature and, falling on his face, hailed him in the manner in which men worship God (ᾧ τρόπῳ τὸν θεὸν προσκυνοῦσι, τούτῳ τὸν Δανίηλον ἠσπάζετο). He also commanded that they should sacrifice to him as to a god.[57]

The crucial question is, however, this: Are we to take this text as evidence that some second-temple Jews regarded Nebuchadnezzar's actions as *exemplary*? In other words, is it meant to imply the appropriateness—*even for faithful Israelites*—of worshipping certain human beings? Or, as is far more likely, is this text simply designed to do the following: (1) to exalt Daniel as a paradigmatic Israelite and (2) to humiliate Nebuchadnezzar as a paradigmatic, idolatrous pagan?

We now come to the fascinating case of Daniel 7, for which, as with the rest of Daniel, we have three principal textual traditions: MT; the Old Greek (OG); and Theodotion (Th).[58] It is usually assumed that the OG represents a "free" translation(s) of a Hebrew-Aramaic *Vorlage*—sometimes reflecting readings older than proto-MT—and that the Theodotionic version represents a corrective recension of the OG in the direction of a better translational reflection of proto-MT.[59] It is not part of my case, however, to discern whether or not Theodotion Daniel represents a recension of the OG, or, as McLay argues, an independent translation of a proto-MT *Vorlage*.[60] For my case, all that matters is that OG Daniel 7 and Theodotion Daniel 7 reflect different, though similar, attempts to safeguard against the possible (and incorrect) ditheistic construal of proto-MT Daniel 7. Here, in large part, I follow the careful study of Loren Stuckenbruck.[61]

We now turn to the details of the textual traditions of Daniel 7.[62] In MT and Th Daniel 7.13–14, the one like a son of man comes "*with* the clouds of heaven (MT: עִם־עֲנָנֵי שְׁמַיָּא/ Th: μετὰ τῶν νεφελῶν τοῦ οὐρανοῦ)" and "*unto* the Ancient of Days (MT: וְעַד־עַתִּיק יוֹמַיָּא/ Th: ἕως τοῦ παλαιοῦ τῶν ἡμερῶν)."[63] Furthermore, this "son of man," like "the people of the holy ones of the Most High" in MT 7.27 or simply "the holy ones of the Most High" in Th 7.27, is offered the submissive obeisance of conquered peoples (MT: פְּלַח/ Th: δουλεύω). However, in the Old Greek of Daniel 7.13–14, 27, (1) the "one like a son of man" comes "*upon* the clouds of heaven (ἐπὶ τῶν νεφελῶν τοῦ οὐρανοῦ)";[64] (2) "*as* [rather than '*unto*'] the Ancient of Days (ὡς παλαιὸς ἡμερῶν)"; and (3) the verbs used to describe the actions required of conquered peoples in 7.14 and 7.27 are *not* the same.[65] In 7.14, "all the nations of the earth, according to their ethnicities, and every glory (πάντα τὰ ἔθνη τῆς γῆς κατὰ γένη καὶ πᾶσα δόξα)" is expected "to *worship*" (λατρεύω) the "son of man," while in 7.27 "all authorities (πᾶσαι αἱ ἐξουσίαι)" are simply "subjected (ὑποτάσσω)" and "obedient (πειθαρχέω)" to "the holy people of the Most High."

A closer look at these three textual traditions across the rest of Daniel, particularly with respect to MT's פְּלַח, Th's δουλεύω and OG's λατρεύω, is instructive.[66] The verb פְּלַח appears nine times in MT Daniel (3.12, 14, 17, 18, 28; 6.17, 21; 7.14, and 27) and, leaving aside the cases of 7.14 and 7.27 for the moment, always refers to cultic worship. Furthermore, aside from the case of 3.17, in which Th offers φοβέομαι ("to fear") as a translation, פְּלַח is rendered in all of these cases in Th and OG by some form of λατρεύω. However, though in 7.14 and 7.27 MT provides two further instances of פְּלַח, Th instead offers δουλεύω in *both instances* and OG provides λατρεύω and ὑποτάσσω (and πειθαρχέω), respectively.

Therefore, we have a scenario in which the MT of Daniel makes use of a verb in seven instances from Daniel 3 to Daniel 6, all of which denote cultic worship, and then makes use of the same verb two more times in 7.14 and 7.27. But, does this of itself indicate that the verb *must* carry the connotation of cultic worship in MT 7.14 and 7.27? I think not. Rather, not only can the Aramaic פלח—like (for instance) the Hebrew שחה and עבד and the Greek προσκυνέω—denote reverential prostration *without* the connotation of cultic worship, but that MT uses פלח with reference *both* to "one like a son of man" (7.13) and to "the people of the holy ones of the Most High" (7.27) suggests that פלח does *not* refer to cultic worship in 7.14. However, even if one should take MT's פלח in 7.14 to denote the cultic worship of the one like a son of man—however this figure should be understood—this still would not indicate that the worship so offered by the conquered peoples was *exemplary* for the true people of God.[67] In other words, even if—and I do not think that this is the correct construal—MT's פלח at 7.14 denotes "cultic worship," this would still not be evidence that some second-temple Jews either practiced or endorsed the worship of another figure as or alongside the one God of Israel.

But what of the case of Theodotion Daniel? I recall from above that, although Th had provided λατρεύω *in every instance* for MT's פלח in 3.12, 14, 18, 28; 6.17, and 21—leaving only the case of 3.17, in which Th had provided φοβέομαι—in 7.14 and 7.27, Theodotion uncharacteristically offered δουλεύω in both cases. In this connection, though δουλεύω *can* mean "cultic worship," this change of vocabulary likely reflects a deliberate attempt to indicate that cultic worship is *not* in view in Daniel 7.14, 27.

We are left, then, to consider the Old Greek of Daniel. Like Theodotion, the Old Greek provides λατρεύω in every instance for MT's פלח in 3.12, 14, 17, 18, 28; 6.17, and 21. *However*, in chapter 7, OG Daniel makes a lexical distinction between the kind of reverence offered to the one like a son of man (7.13–14), on the one hand, and to "the holy people of the Most High," on the other. The former is offered, I contend, worship (λατρεύω) befitting the one God of Israel, while the latter are offered the subjugation (ὑποτάσσω) and obedience (πειθαρχέω) of conquered peoples.

Does Old Greek Daniel 7, therefore, provide us with unique evidence in which a Jewish text clearly portrays a figure distinguishable from the one God as divine? Again, I think not. This is, I suggest, what has happened.[68] Even though I do not even take MT Daniel 7 as a scene in which the son of man figure—however this figure should be understood—is presented as divine, I suggest that Old Greek and Theodotion Daniel 7 represent different attempts to safeguard against such a misunderstanding. In this regard, the Theodotionic textual tradition of Daniel 7.14, 27 reflects an early and crucial translational decision, preferring δουλεύω for MT's פלח instead of Th's much more characteristic λατρεύω. The OG, on the other hand, *conflates* the one like a son of man with the Ancient of Days, thereby producing little more than the kind of theophanic tradition found in Ezekiel 1.26–28.[69] Indeed, it is *possible* in this regard that Ezekiel 1.26–28, in which the Glory of the LORD appears "like the appearance of a human being (דמות כמראה אדם)," partly facilitated this conflation of the two "figures," with the result that the one God of Israel simply appears *both* as one like a son of man and as the Ancient of Days.[70]

With the consideration of the textual traditions of Daniel 7 behind us, we are in a better position to consider the interpretations of, for example, Rowland and Fletcher-Louis. Rowland takes OG Daniel 7 as evidence that the author intended to portray the son of man as "the embodiment of the person of the Ancient of Days" and as one who "takes upon himself the form and character of God himself."[71] Fletcher-Louis argues that in the OG the son of man "is somehow *identified with, expresses,* or *shares in* the divine identity."[72] In this regard, however, I suggest that Rowland and Fletcher-Louis are guilty of precisely the interpretative mistake against which the tradents of the OG were trying to safeguard.

None of this is to deny, however, that the "one like a son of man" of MT Daniel 7.13–14 is remarkably exalted within the context of second-temple Judaism, nor that the creative works of OG and Th Daniel 7.13–14 do not also make this clear. I am only contesting the view that any of the three principal textual traditions of Daniel 7 portrays the "one like a son of man" as a properly divine being who is distinguishable from the God of Israel and worthy of the worship of faithful, monotheistic Israelites.

Having treated the relevant features of Daniel, we now turn to the case of the Elect One of the Similitudes. As I mentioned above, this figure is often depicted as enthroned (cf. 1 En. 45.3; 51.3; 55.4; 61.8; 62.2–5; and 69.27) and as receiving some kind of obeisance (1 En. 46.5; 48.5; 62.6, 9). He is also portrayed as preexisting the creation of the *kosmos* (esp. 48.2–7; cf. also 4 Ezra 13.25–32; and 2 Bar. 29.3). Therefore, that he is a remarkably august figure within the context of second-temple literature is incontestable. To conclude that he is "divine," however, is a mistake. Of absolutely decisive importance here, as in the case of Daniel 7.13–14, is the fact that he is only ever offered obeisance *by the "nations" whom he has presumably subjugated*. There is not one unambiguous instance of the faithful offering worship.

For example, even if we should take the case of 46.5 as "worship" ("they did not *exalt* or *praise* him"), this would still be the (pagan) worship offered by the conquered "kings . . . and their kingdoms" (46.5). The case of 48.5, however, requires a bit more comment:

> All who dwell on the earth will fall down and worship before him, and they will glorify and bless and sing hymns to the name of the Lord of Spirits.[73]

Are Nickelsburg and VanderKam right to translate Ethiopic *sagada* ("to prostrate oneself") as "to worship"? In this regard, I cite the recent and apposite comments of Maurice Casey:

At both *1 En.* 48.5 and 62.9 the Ge'ez word is *sagada*, which normally represents the Greek προσκυνεῖν, the Aramaic סגד or the Hebrew השתהוה. All these words have a range of meaning which includes not only worship, but also respectful behaviour to human beings of superior status. For example, at Ruth 2.10, וישתחו is used of Ruth bowing down before Boaz: Targum סגידת, Peshitta *sgdt*, LXX προσεκύνησεν, Ge'ez *sagadat*.[74]

Context, then, is the determinative factor. Against a reading in which proper worship befitting the Lord of Spirits (YHWH) is offered to the Elect One in 48.5, I make two related points. (1) If the author intended to depict what is offered to the Elect One as identical to that which is offered to the Lord of Spirits, it is odd that both are not recipients of *all* of the actions; furthermore, in this regard, it is surely striking that, while *wadqa* ("to fall down") and *sagada* ("to prostrate oneself") need *not* refer to cultic worship, the language of "glorifying" (*sabehha*) and "blessing" (*baraka*) and "singing hymns" *must* refer to worship.

(2) The case of 62.6–9 further strengthens the above point. Pagans and the actions required of them are italicized, while the faithful and the actions required of them are underlined. The text maintains a clear distinction:

(62.6) And *the kings and the mighty and all who possess the land will bless and glorify and exalt* [perhaps "worship"] *him who rules over all, who was hidden.*
(62.7) For from the beginning the Son of Man was hidden, and the Most High preserved him in the presence of his might, and he revealed him to the chosen.
(62.8) And <u>the congregation of the chosen and holy will be sown; and all the chosen will stand in his presence</u> on that day.
(62.9) And *all the kings and the mighty and the exalted and those who rule the land will fall on their faces* in his presence; and *they will worship and set their hope* [perhaps "worship"] *on that Son of Man, and they will supplicate and petition for mercy from him.*

If the text intended to present the Son of Man as divine and/or to depict the faithful offering him the worship befitting the Lord of Spirits, it is very difficult to explain why the author has so clearly distinguished the actions required of the conquered peoples, on the one hand, and the actions required of the faithful, on the other. On this basis, I propose, what is actually depicted here is the humiliated and ultimately idolatrous worship of conquered peoples. Even the Similitudes, therefore, do not provide us with evidence of a second-temple text in which a figure other than YHWH is worshipped and/or portrayed as genuinely divine.

I now briefly consider the cases adduced by Fletcher-Louis in which, so he argues, "in one way or another a human figure ... is worshipped."[75] We begin with the relevant portion of the Latin Life of Adam and Eve:

(12.1) And the devil sighed and said, "O Adam, all my enmity and envy and sorrow concern you, since because of you I am expelled and deprived of my glory which I had in the heavens in the midst of the angels, and because of you I was cast onto the earth. . . . (13.2) When you were created, I was cast out from the presence of God. . . . (13.3) When God blew into you the breath of life and your countenance and likeness were made in the image of God (*ad imaginem Dei*), Michael brought you and made us worship you in the sight of God, and the LORD God said, 'Behold Adam! I have made you in our image and likeness (*ad imaginem et similitudinem nostram*).' (14.1) And Michael went out and called all the angels, saying, 'Worship the image of the LORD God (*adorate imaginem Domino Dei*)' . . . (14.2) And Michael himself worshipped first, and called me [the devil] and said, 'Worship the image of God (*adora imaginem Dei*) . . . !' (14.3) And I [the devil] answered, 'I do not worship Adam!'. . . 'He ought to worship me!' . . . (16.1) And the LORD God was angry with me [the devil] and sent me with my angels out from our glory."[76]

This text narrates the tradition of satan's fall from heaven and offers an etiology.[77] It is possible, furthermore, that at least part of this tradition—namely, satan's jealousy at the creation of humanity in God's image—is presupposed in Wisdom 2.23–24.[78] Essentially, the enmity between satan and his company and the rest of humanity is explained by recourse to the *imago Dei*: it must be, so the text reasons, that satan and his company begrudged humanity's unique, exalted, and special relation to the one God. But, as interesting as this tradition is, and as much as it might tell us about the theological anthropology of some second-temple Jews, does the text intend to present Adam as an independent, divine figure? It seems to me that the answer must be, "No." Aside from the fact that this text serves the particular etiological purpose outlined above, the point seems not so much to be that the angels are directed to worship Adam *qua* Adam, as a distinct, divine being, but that, rather, the angels are enjoined *to worship the one God* through the *medium* of his image. It would be a mistake to conclude on this basis, however, that this text provides evidence that some second-temple Jews were prepared to countenance the worship of humanity in general or of Adam (or any other righteous or exalted human) in particular as a divine being.[79]

We now briefly consider together Fletcher-Louis's case concerning the traditions of reverent prostration before the high priest. One tradition is preserved by Hecataeus of Abdera in Diodorus Siculus (*Bib. Hist.* 40.3.3–8), another in Sirach 50, and still another regarding Alexander the Great's prostration in Josephus (*Ant.* 11.331) and elsewhere (b. *Yoma* 69a).[80] The first case is a simple instance of prostration; the second involves an extended and laudatory panegyric at the climax of which is the people's prostration before the high priest; and the last involves the amazing prostration of Alexander the Great himself. Though doubtless there is much here to learn about the nature and theological logic of temple worship in general and of the high priestly office in particular, we have no reason to take any of these traditions as evidence that some second-temple Jews believed in the distinct divinity of the high priest. That he was viewed, at least in his cultic office, as uniquely and intimately associated with YHWH is not in dispute; that he was regarded, therefore, as "divine," however, is much to be doubted.

We now turn briefly to consider the final category of "divine agency": "personified divine attributes." In this regard, because I have argued that the sole theological-conceptual criterion of divinity in second-temple Jewish monotheism is cosmogonical activity, I contend that the *sophia/logos* speculation of Wisdom and the Philonic *corpus* is the closest we come in second-temple literature to a "figure" which is portrayed as divine. But even this claim needs immediate clarification and qualification. Though it is routinely thought, and too casually stated, that the *sophia* of Proverbs 8 and of Sirach 1 and 24 plays a role in the creation of the *kosmos*, this is simply not the case. Rather, in these texts (Prov. 8.22; Sir. 1.4, 9; and 24.8), *sophia* is a privileged *witness* to, rather than a *participant* in, the creation of the *kosmos*.[81] Moreover, in neither of these cases is *sophia* an actual "hypostasis."[82] Rather, this speculation principally served the following purposes. (1) As in the case of angel speculation, it allowed Jewish monotheists to hold together God's transcendent sovereignty over the world with his dynamic interaction within that world.[83] (2) It graphically made the point that the creator God is uniquely wise and that the whole created order reflects and is in some sense imbued with his unique wisdom.

Therefore, in terms of the Jewish wisdom tradition, it is not until the *sophia* speculation of the Wisdom of Solomon (esp. 9.1–2) that *sophia* unambiguously assumes a role in the creation of the *kosmos*.[84] Accordingly and crucially—unlike the cases of Proverbs 8.22 and Sirach 1.4, 9; 24.8–9—in the Wisdom of Solomon *sophia* is precisely *not* created by God. Rather, in this text, *sophia* stands on the "creator side" of the Jewish distinction between the creator and the creature.

Much the same can be said of Philo's complex and multifaceted doctrine of the *logos*.[85] As is the case with the nature of *sophia* in Wisdom 7.22–8.1, much of the character of Philo's *logos* owes to Middle Platonic intermediary doctrine.[86] In one place, however, Philo is careful to indicate that the *logos*—unlike the true God—is not an "uncreated creator" but that, rather, it straddles the line between the creator and the creature:

(205) He [the *logos*] glories in this prerogative and proudly (206) describes it in these words "and I stood between the Lord and you" (Deut. v. 5), that is neither uncreated as God, nor created as you, but midway between the two extremes (οὔτε ἀγένητος ὡς ὁ θεὸς ὢν οὔτε γενητὸς ὡς ὑμεῖς, ἀλλὰ μέσος τῶν ἄκρων).[87]

This text is quite revealing because it provides evidence of the way in which a philosophically inclined first-century Jew might conceive of the nature and logic of first-century Jewish monotheism. The conceptual demands of Jewish monotheism, in which cosmogonical activity indicates "divinity," pushed Philo (among other reasons) to ascribe "divinity" to the *logos*, while the influence of philosophical intermediary doctrine pushed him to maintain a strict distinction between the "uncreated God" and his *logos*. In any case, this text reflects the assumption that for first-century Jewish monotheism cosmogonical activity was the chief criterion of divinity.[88]

However, as fascinating as the *sophia/logos* speculation of Wisdom and the Philonic *corpus* is, we should not regard it as even a *partial* "precedent" for early christology. In this regard, we must distinguish between the theological and conceptual resources which were catalyzed in early christological reflection and the notion of "precedents" for early christology.[89] For anything like the latter, we would need (at least) evidence of actual second-temple Jews both actively expressing a characteristically exclusivist Jewish monotheism and also venerating an actual human being in ways which paralleled their veneration of the one God. In this vein, I am aware of no scholar who would postulate a strong "precedent" for early christology.

I make two final points before I conclude my case concerning ancient Jewish monotheism. (1) That certain angelic beings in the Scrolls, reflecting earlier biblical traditions (e.g., Job 1.6; and Ps. 82.1), are sometimes call *El, Elym*, or *Elohym* is not evidence that the tradents of these traditions were "loose" monotheists and/or regarded these angels as on a level with the one God.[90] Maxwell J. Davidson in particular has persuasively argued that in these very same traditions "there is never a cosmic dualism in which God stands opposite his equal or near-equal."[91] (2) Though the issue requires much more thought and space, it is not clear than any variation of so-called "pagan monotheism" provides a strong parallel to exclusivist Jewish monotheism. To be sure, Michael Frede's case concerning the monotheistic tendencies issuing from the cosmologies of Plato, Aristotle, and Zeno into later philosophical cosmology is suggestive, as is his reminder that the Jewish and Christian polemic against all others as "pagan polytheists" sometimes oversimplifies and thus obscures the matter.[92] Likewise, Stephen Mitchell's case concerning the widespread cult of Theos Hypsistos in the ancient Mediterranean deserves much more attention from scholars of second-temple Jewish monotheism.[93] However, and crucially, it is still generally the case that the widespread second-temple Jewish practice of *exclusive cultic worship* of one God alone, the God of Israel, was unique and objectionable in its ancient context. Whatever else might have been true of "pagan monotheists," most seem to have been perfectly happy with the cultic worship of many and diverse gods.[94]

CONCLUSION

With three caveats, I now summarize my case concerning the nature and shape of second-temple Jewish monotheism. My case does not rest upon the supposition that (1) *all* second-temple Jews were strict monotheists; and/or that (2) *all* second-temple texts characterize the "unique divine identity" in exactly the same way; and/or (3) that some Jewish texts (e.g., the Similitudes) did not, from the perspective of other Jews, present a "figure" in offensively august terms. Rather, my larger case is as follows. (1) The above Jewish material indicates that a rigorous and exclusivist Jewish monotheism characterized second-temple (a) cultic practice and (b) thought. (2) In relation to (b), an inductive study of second-temple texts demonstrates that cosmogonical activity was taken to be the clearest theological and conceptual criterion of divinity. (3) Following from point (2), and duly noting the *sophia/logos* speculation in Wisdom and the Philonic *corpus*, I contend that early christology provides us with our *only* evidence from this period of exclusivist Jewish monotheists holding in belief and *praxis* to "the unique divine identity" and also including a distinct, separate, and (therefore) divine figure within that identity. In relation to point (3), I note both (a) "cultic activity" and (b) the belief that the preexistent Jesus created the *kosmos*.[95] In this regard, it is particularly in relation to (b) that our study of image christology takes on its proper significance.

(a) As to "cultic activity," I simply note what Hurtado noted in his 1988 study, against the significance of which evidence, taken together as a composite whole, there has been no successful refutation. (1) In early Christian literature, Jesus is the subject of poetical/hymnic material (esp. Phil. 2.6–11; and Col. 1.15–20), though God "the father" is perhaps the ultimate addressee. (2) The exalted Jesus is the corecipient of prayer (esp. 1 Cor. 16.22; cf. also Acts 1.24; 2 Cor. 12.2–10; and 1 Thess. 3.11–13). (3) Converts are baptized in or with reference to Jesus and/or his "name" (so esp. Acts 22.16; and 1 Cor. 6.11), thereby reflecting both a cultic ritual and the christological adaptation of the Old Testament theme of calling upon "the name of YHWH" (so, e.g., Gen. 12.8; 13.4; 21.23; 26.25; Ps. 99.6; 105.1; and Joel 2.32).[96] (4) The Eucharist, another early Christian liturgical rite, is held in Jesus's honor and with reference to him (so 1 Cor. 11.23–26). (5) Jesus's name figures in key early Christian liturgical confessions (esp. Rom. 10.9; 1 Cor. 12.3; and Phil. 2.11). And, finally, (6) Revelation 1.17–3.22 provides evidence that at least some early Christians accepted prophetic oracles as coming through Christian prophets and ultimately from the exalted Jesus, thereby indicating that, at least insofar as the prophetic practices of the Tanakh serve as a paradigm, such Christians hereby treated oracles coming from the exalted Jesus in the same manner as ancient Israelites had treated oracles coming from the one God himself.⁹⁷ Following Hurtado, therefore, I contend both that we do not have anything like a full precedent for this composite picture of early Christian practices in second-temple Judaism and that these practices clearly indicate that, for these early Christians, Jesus had been included within the unique divine identity.

(b) Returning to the above point that, by ascribing to Jesus cosmogonical activity in his preexistent state, the early Christians deliberately and unambiguously included him within the unique divine identity, I note the following key texts: John 1.1–3; 1 Corinthians 8.6; Colossians 1.15–16; and Hebrews 1.2. In this regard, though I have found Bauckham's heuristic category of "the unique divine identity" useful, I have refined it by contending that, at the theological-conceptual level, cosmogonical activity *alone* is the key marker of the unique divine identity. This observation, furthermore, gives us unique insight as to why it is precisely within the above christological traditions (John 1.1–3; 1 Cor. 8.6; Col. 1.15–16; and Heb. 1.2) that we find the use of "prepositional metaphysics" (e.g., "through/by whom"). As I will argue in due course, it is precisely because cosmogonical activity was the key indicator of divinity in the Jewish tradition that, within early christological traditions in which such activity had been ascribed to the preexistent Jesus, early Christians made use of the prepositional metaphysics of the philosophical tradition *in order to safeguard against a collapsing of the two distinct figures within the one unique divine identity*. For this study of the *imago Dei*, this observation is of crucial importance because, as I will argue, Paul's image christology is a wisdom christology (and not an Adam christology) in which he christologically adapts both Jewish *sophia* speculation and (perhaps *via* the latter) Middle Platonic intermediary doctrine so as to present Jesus as thoroughly included within the unique divine identity as *creator* and yet as distinguishable from God ("the father") and as his paradigmatic "image."⁹⁸

Excursus: **Wesley Hill's *Paul and the Trinity***

Before moving on from our discussion of Jewish monotheism, we should note the quite different challenge offered by Wesley Hill's *Paul and the Trinity*.⁹⁹ This is the overall purpose of his project:

> [T]he readings of Paul I will offer . . . will be self-consciously *historical* readings. . . . Second, trinitarian theologies [particularly of "relations"] will be employed as hermeneutical *resources* and, thus, mined for conceptualities which may better *enable* a genuinely historical exegesis.¹⁰⁰

There is, of course, nothing straightforwardly problematic about mining fourth- and fifth-century theological thinkers for conceptual resources which might assist in an essentially historical exegesis of Paul. One might discover that these writers perceptively read and appropriately explicated Paul's christology within a different conceptual universe. What *is* problematic, however, is Hill's dismissive rhetoric concerning the context of second-temple Jewish monotheism. In a few short lines, Hill discounts all of the painstaking work which has been done on first-century Jewish monotheism as the historical context within which one should appreciate Paul's christology.[101] He contends that the Jewish category of "monotheism" is only a "supposedly more historical" category than an explicit conception of trinitarian relations.[102] Hill apparently "substantiates" this point by a simple reference to the definitional difficulty highlighted by MacDonald.[103] Moreover, the christological work of scholars as diverse as Dunn, Casey, McGrath, Bauckham, and Hurtado is explained as the decidedly anti-creedal attempt, owing particularly to sixteenth-century biblical rationalism, on the one hand, and to Protestantism's "pronounced Christocentricity," on the other, to expound "christology as a distinct area of inquiry from trinitarian theology" largely by inventing a "newly minted term—'monotheism.'"[104]

An emphasis upon trinitarian relations is Hill's primary concern:

> The main task . . . is to suggest a way of discussing Paul's theology and christology that does *not* begin with the vertical question . . . but rather with the question of *relations*. The conceptuality of "low" or "high" christology threatens to obscure the way in which, for Paul, the identities of God, Jesus, and the Spirit are constituted by their relations with one another.[105]

Instead of the question of "low" and "high" christologies, therefore, Hill would have us pay attention to "the mutually conditioning, mutually constitutive relations between these categories/ 'persons' [Father, Son, and Spirit]."[106]

With respect to Hill's overall case, I make a few points. He is right to redress the neglect of the relational dynamics between "father," "son," and "Spirit" in Paul's letters.[107] He is wrong, however, as a matter of historical method, to ignore the nature, shape, and logic of second-temple Jewish monotheism. His method reflects a failure to distinguish between different kinds of question. For instance, whether a later trinitarian theology of relations faithfully explicates the "deep structure" of Paul's theology is not the same question as to what Paul himself, as a first-century Jewish monotheist, thought about his own monotheism, nicene, and pneumatology. Perhaps Paul would have looked down at the Nicene Creed and recognized a penetrating analysis of the deep structure of his theology, but he would not straightforwardly have recognized his own christologically reworked Jewish monotheism. I suggest, therefore, that if we have more to learn about the "relational" nature of Paul's theology, and perhaps more to learn from an explicit trinitarian theology of relations, it is not because first-century Jewish monotheism was a bad historical and conceptual starting point.

NOTES

1. On second-temple Jewish monotheism, the following have been particularly instructive: Hurtado, *OGOL*, 1–96; Idem, "First-Century Jewish Monotheism" *JSNT* 71 (1998): 3–26, now found in and cited from Idem, *AJM*, 115–35; Idem, "'Ancient Jewish Monotheism' in the Hellenistic and Roman Periods" *JAJ* 4 (2013): 379–400, now found in and cited from Idem, *AJM*, 137–61; Idem, "Monotheism, Principal Angels, and the Background of Christology" in Timothy H. Lim and John J. Collins, eds., *Oxford Handbook of the Dead Sea Scrolls* (Oxford: OUP, 2012), 546–64; now found in and cited from Idem, *AJM*, 163–84; Wright, *NTPG*, 248–58; Idem, *PFG*, 619–33; Johannes Woyke, *Götter, 'Götzen,' Götterbilder: Aspekte einer paulinischen 'Theologie der Religionen'* (Berlin: de Gruyter, 2005), 163–79; Bauckham, *Jesus*, 1–181; Tilling, *Christology*, 63–74; Fletcher-Louis, *JM*, 293–316; and Andrew Chester, *Messiah and Exaltation: Jewish Messianic and Visionary Traditions and New Testament Christology*, WUNT 207 (Tübingen: Mohr Siebeck, 2007), esp. 45–79. On the characteristic rhetoric of ancient Jewish monotheism, see esp. Paul A. Rainbow, "Monotheism and Christology in 1 Corinthians 8:4–6" PhD Diss. (Oxford University, 1987); and Darina Staudt, *Monotheistische Formeln im Urchristentum und ihre Vorgeschichte bei Griechen und Juden*, NTOA 80 (Göttingen: Vandenhoeck & Ruprecht, 2012), the latter of which also considers Greek and early Christian traditions. Still relevant in this regard are Samuel S. Cohen, "The Unity of God: A Study in Hellenistic and Rabbinic Theology" *HUCA* 26 (1955): 425–79; and Ralph Marcus, "Divine Names and Attributes in Hellenistic Jewish Literature" *PAAJR* (1931–1932): 43–120, the latter of which demonstrates that, at least on linguistic grounds, there is little evidence of a lax Jewish monotheism among diaspora Jews. On Josephus's monotheistic rhetoric, still valuable are Adolf Schlatter, *Wie sprach Josephus von Gott?* BFCT 1.14 (Gütersloh: Bertelsmann, 1910); and Idem, *Die Theologie des Judentums nach dem Bericht des Josephus*, BFCT 2.26 (Gütersloh: Bertelsmann, 1932).

2. Nathan MacDonald, *Deuteronomy and the Meaning of "Monotheism,"* 2nd corrected edn. (Tübingen: Mohr Siebeck, 2012 [2003]), 1–20.

3. Ibid. 21–58. See, however, Bauckham's compelling criticisms of MacDonald: *Jesus*, 62–71.

4. See esp. Bob Becking, Meindert Dijkstra, Marjo C. A. Korpel and Karel J. H. Vriezen, eds., *Only One God? Monotheism in Ancient Israel and the Veneration of the Goddess Asherath* (New York: Sheffield Academic Press, 2001); Ephraim Stern, "From Many Gods to the God: The Archaeological Evidence" in Reinhard G. Kratz and Hermann Spieckermann, eds., *One God, One Cult, One Nation: Archaeological and Biblical Perspectives*, BZAW 405 (New York: de Gruyter, 2010), 395–403; and the *Forschungsgeschichte* in Robert Gnuse, *No Other Gods: Emergent Monotheism in Israel*, OTS 241 (New York: Bloomsbury T & T Clark, 1997), 62–128.

5. Meindert Dijkstra, "I Have Blessed You by YHWH of Samaria and His Asherah: Texts with Religious Elements from the Soil Archive of Ancient Israel" in Becking et al, eds., *Only One God*, 44, italics added.

6. Mark S. Smith, *The Early History of God: Yahweh and the Other Deities in Ancient Israel*, 2nd edn. (Grand Rapids: Eerdmans, 2002 [1990]), 191–92, italics added.

7. Stern, "One God," 401–02, italics added.

8. On the "monotheism" of the Tanakh and/or the preexilic period, see esp. R. G. Kratz and H. Spieckermann, eds., *Götterbilder, Gottesbilder, Weltbilder: Polytheismus und Monotheismus in der Welt der Antike*, 2 vols., FAT 2.17, 18 (Tübingen: Mohr Siebeck, 2006); M. Oeming and K. Schmid, eds., *Der eine Gott und die Götter: Polytheismus und Monotheismus im antiken Israel* (Zürich: Theologischer, 2003); Smith, *The Early History of God*; Idem, *The Origins of Biblical Monotheism: Israel's Polytheistic Background and the Ugaritic Texts* (Oxford: OUP, 2001); J. Day, *Yahweh and the Gods and Goddesses of Canaan*, JSOTSup 265 (Sheffield: SAP, 2000); and Gnuse, *No Other Gods*.

9. On the "consensus status" of this position, see esp. Gnuse, *No Other Gods*, 62–128; and Mark S. Smith, *God in Translation: Deities in Cross-Cultural Discourse in the Biblical World* (Grand Rapids: Eerdmans 2010 [2008]).

10. Cf. similarly Hurtado, *LJC*, 29–31 (esp. 30): "[I]t may have been precisely in the forcible encounter with the many gods of other nations and peoples, indeed, an encounter on the 'home turf' of these gods in lands of Israelite/Judean exile, that the rather pugnaciously monotheistic claims that came to characterize religious Jews were explicitly formulated"; and Gnuse, *No Other Gods*, 62–128. Hurtado, *AJM*, 146, rightly emphasizes that the Seleucid Crisis, which itself precipitated the Maccabean Revolt, only served further to increase the intensity with which second-temple Jews held to and expressed their exclusivist Jewish monotheism.

11. Cf., e.g., Peter Hayman, "Monotheism—A Misused Word in Jewish Studies?" *JJS* 42 (1991): 1–15.

12. Paula Fredriksen, "Mandatory Retirement: Ideas in the Study of Christian Origins Whose Time Has Come to Go" *SR* 35 (2006): 231–46, now found in and cited from David B. Capes, April D. DeConick, Helen K. Bond, and Troy Miller, eds., *Israel's God and Rebecca's Children: Christology and Community in Early Judaism and Christianity*, LEC (Waco: Baylor University Press, 2007), 25–38 (35).

13. Ibid.

14. Ibid.

15. Horbury, "Jewish and Christian Monotheism in the Herodian Age" in Loren T. Stuckenbruck and Wendy E. S. North, eds., *Early Jewish and Christian Monotheism*, JSNTSup 263 (London: Continuum, 2004), 16–44 (17).

16. I here follow the stated approach of Hurtado, *AJM*, 117: "The first methodological point to emphasize is the importance of proceeding inductively in forming and using analytical categories such as 'monotheism.'" Cf. also Hurtado, *AJM*, 142–43: "[I] propose that 'ancient Jewish monotheism' (n.b., not 'monotheism' *simpliciter*) can serve to label the sort of exclusive religious outlook and practice advocated and reflected in Jewish sources of the same [second-temple] period. Granted . . . 'ancient

Jewish monotheism' does not fit the typical definition of 'monotheism' in modern dictionaries."

17. Hurtado offers this useful definition of "worship": *AJM*, 116, n. 4: "I use the word 'worship' here to designate open, formal, public, and intentional actions of invocation, adoration, appeal, praise, and communion."

18. So also Hurtado, *LJC*, 29–53; Idem, *AJM*, 151–56; Yehoshua Amir, "Die Begegnung des biblischen und des philosophischen Monotheismus als Grundthema des jüdischen Hellenismus" *ET* 38 (1978): 2–19 (esp. 4); and Sanders, *Judaism*, 311–12 (italics mine): "'Religion' . . . was defined *primarily* as cultic worship. What was the worship of Zeus? Temples, purifications, *sacrifices* and festivals. The same is true of all the other gods of antiquity." On the clear monotheism of second-temple prayers, see esp. T. M. Jonquiere, *Prayer in Josephus* (Leiden: Brill, 2007); E. G. Chazon, "Hymns and Prayers in the Dead Sea Scrolls" in Peter W. Flint and James C. VanderKam, eds., *The Dead Sea Scrolls After Fifty Years: A Comprehensive Assessment* (Leiden: Brill, 1998), 244–70; D. K. Falk, *Daily, Sabbath, and Festival Prayers in the Dead Sea Scrolls* (Leiden: Brill, 1998); A. Enermalm-Ogawa, *Un langage de prière juif en grec: Le témoignage des deux premiers livres des Maccabées*, ConBNT 17 (Uppsala: Almquist & Wiksell, 1987); and N. B. Johnson, *Prayer in the Apocrypha and Pseudepigrapha: A Study of the Jewish Concept of God*, SBLMS 2 (Philadelphia: SBL, 1948).

19. Michael Mach, *Entwicklungsstadien des judischen Engelglaubens in vorrabinischer Zeit*, TSAJ 34 (Tübingen: Mohr Siebeck, 1992), in particular demonstrates the growing Jewish interest in angels in the Persian and Hellenistic periods.

20. See Hurtado, *OGOL*, 41–52.

21. See Ibid. 53–72.

22. See Ibid. 73–98.

23. Use of the adjective "divine" is governed by the presumed metaphysical context in relation to which it is used. Throughout, it is used in relation to a contested but widely affirmed account of second-temple Jewish monotheism in which most Jews both believed in and worshipped only Israel's God YHWH; hereby, so this account goes, they expressed their belief that YHWH was supreme not only in degree but in kind from all other reality. I further note that the adjective "divine" in this sense functions as a linguistic-analytical tool with which we might better historically, philosophically, and theologically understand and articulate phenomena true to the historical and conceptual features of the traditions under discussion *while not always "parroting"—and sometimes apparently contradicting—the language usage of those same traditions*. For example, it is well known that the Scrolls sometimes refer to what appear to be angelic beings as "gods"; however, it is also clear that, despite this linguistic usage (which cannot, however, be theologically inconsequential), the very same texts and traditions do not appear to regard these "gods" as on the same metaphysical level as the one God of Israel. It seems to me, therefore, analytically useful and historiographically legitimate to refer to the latter being alone as "divine" and the former beings otherwise. On this, see esp. Maxwell J. Davidson, *Angels at Qumran: A Comparative Study of 1 Enoch 1–36, 72–108 and Sectarian Writings from Qumran* (Leiden: Brill, 1992), esp. 309.

24. So, e.g., Clinton E. Arnold, *The Colossian Syncretism: The Interface between Christianity and Folk Belief at Colossae* (Grand Rapids: Baker, 1996), 8–89 (esp. 32–89); and Peter Schäfer, *Rivalität zwischen Engeln und Menschen: Untersuchungen zur rabbinischen Engelvorstellung*, Studia Judaica, FWJ 8 (Berlin: de Gruyter, 1975), 67–72. On this whole question, see Kevin P. Sullivan, *Wrestling with Angels: A Study of the Relationship between Angels and Humans in Ancient Jewish Literature and the New Testament*, AGJU 55 (Leiden: Brill, 2004); and Darrell D. Hannah, *Michael and Christ: Michael Traditions and Angel Christology in Early Christianity*, WUNT 2.109 (Tübingen: Mohr Siebeck, 1999), both of whom also consider the possible influence of angel speculation on early christology. On Jewish angel speculation in general, see esp. Saul Olyan, *A Thousand Thousands Served Him: Exegesis and the Naming of Angels in Ancient Judaism*, TSAT 36 (Tübingen: Mohr Siebeck, 1993); and Mach, *Entwicklungsstadien*. On angel speculation in the Scrolls, Davidson, *Angels at Qumran*, 309, concludes that, despite the well-known "dualism" in many of these texts, "there is never a cosmic dualism in which God stands opposite his equal or near-equal."

25. So Loren T. Stuckenbruck, "'Angels' and 'God': Exploring the Limits of Early Jewish Monotheism" in Stuckenbruck and North, eds., *Early Jewish and Christian Monotheism*, 45–70 (53–70). Cf. also Idem, *Angel Veneration and Christology: A Study in Early Judaism and in the Christology of the Apocalypse of John*, LEC (Waco: Baylor University Press, 2017 [1995]).

26. So Stuckenbruck, *Angel Veneration and Christology*, 200–03.

27. I am not claiming, however, that they *only* serve these two purposes.

28. So also Hurtado, *OGOL*, 26: "Do you see how great our God is, who has such a vast and powerful retinue to do nothing but serve him?"

29. See esp. the discussions in Wright, *NTPG*, 258–59; and Hurtado, *OGOL*, 22–36, 41–51, 73–95. Much the same could be said of Jewish *sophia* speculation.

30. So Arnold, *Syncretism*, 8–89 (esp. 32–89). On this, see now G. Bohak, *Ancient Jewish Magic: A History* (Cambridge: CUP, 2008), who states, "Nowhere in the ancient Jewish magical texts will we find any divine being which would rival the Jewish God. . . . Thus, there is nothing that would show that the Jews behind these texts abandoned the basic monotheistic principle of worshipping One God only" (52).

31. In this regard, I provide a lengthy quotation from Cecilia Wassen, "Angels and Humans: Boundaries and Synergies" in Peter W. Flint, Jean Duhaime, and Kyung S. Baek, eds., *Celebrating the Dead Sea Scrolls: A Canadian Contribution*, EJL 30 (Atlanta: SBL, 2011), 523–39 (537, italics mine): "[I]n line with many Jewish texts from the Second Temple period, which elaborated on the nature and role of angels, many Qumran documents reflect developed speculations about angels. Still, we need to think about why angels played such an important role in the sectarian imagination. The focus on angels in Second Temple Judaism in general is often understood as a way of bridging the distance between an increasingly transcendent God and humanity, perhaps influenced by the structure of huge empires in which royal officials were in charge in dealing with the king's subjects whereas the king was hardly ever seen. The angels in the scrolls are certainly doing God's work by maintaining the cosmos and executing judgment. *But this overall image does not fit very well with the pattern of*

angelic functions in the scrolls. Rather than intermediaries who operate between the human and heavenly realms, the angels form a fellowship with the faithful elect. . . . Furthermore, we do not find strong evidence of angels as mediators of revelations in the sectarian literature, at least not in a direct role as heavenly guides or interpreters of dreams and visions. . . . The scrolls at Qumran also testify to a rather optimistic view of humans' ability to reach the divine sphere in a direct way, and, conversely, *to a belief in God's direct, unmediated revelation to humans*. This circumstance challenges us to rethink the reasons for the developed speculations about angels in the Qumran literature; there are likely many factors that contribute to this interest."

32. Arnold, *Syncretism*, 33, italics mine.

33. Ibid. 59.

34. Reconstruction and translation are from J. H. Charlesworth, "Prayer of Jacob" in *OTP* 2.715–23 (720, italics added), who argues that, though we possess only a single fourth-century papyrus, we "have no reason to doubt" that the original composition was in Greek and of ca. second- to fourth-century provenance (715).

35. On the "angelic refusal" tradition (cf. Apoc. Zeph. 6.15; Asc. Isa. 7.21–22; Rev. 19.10; and 22.8–9), see Mach, *Entwichlungsstadien*, 291–300; Stuckenbruck, *Angel Veneration and Christology*, 75–103; Hurtado, *OGOL*, 30–36, 86–88; and Richard Bauckham, "The Worship of Jesus in Apocalyptic Christianity" *NTS* 27.3 (1981): 322–41.

36. So esp. Schäfer, *Rivalität*, 67–72 (67): "Hinweise auf eine solche Praxis finden sich zwar nur indirekt, nämlich in der Polemik der Rabbinen gegen die Engelverehrung; doch ist diese Polemik Beweis genug für das tatsächliche Vorhandensein eines Engelkultes im rabbinischen Judentum." More cautiously, see Mach, *Entwichlungsstadien*, 291–300.

37. See the comments in Philip Alexander, "'The Agent of the King Is Treated as the King Himself': Does the Worship of Jesus Imply His Divinity?" in Gurtner et al, eds., *In the Fullness of Time*, 97–114 (98).

38. This crucial point is well appreciated in Hurtado, *OGOL*, 28–36. On the rabbinic sources, see Mek. Ex. 20.4, 20; Tg. Ps.-J. Ex. 20.20; t. Hul. 2.18; b. Avod. Zar. 42.b; and m. Hul. 2.8. On the Christian sources, see Celsus's accusation, preserved in Origin, *Cels.* 5.6; Idem, *Comm. Jo.* 13.17; Clement of Alexandria, *Strom.* 6.5.39; and Apol. Arist. 14; with the brief but helpful discussion in Hurtado, *OGOL*, 34–36.

39. This does not mean, of course, that angel speculation could not have played some role in the rise and/or subsequent shape of christology. See, e.g., Sullivan, *Wrestling with Angels*; Hannah, *Michael and Christ*, esp. 137–39 on Hebrews 1–2; Stuckenbruck, *Angel Veneration and Christology*, 205–74; Charles A. Gieschen, *Angelmorphic Christology: Antecedents and Early Evidence*, LEC (Waco: Baylor University Press, 2017 [1995]); Christopher Rowland, "The Vision of the Risen Christ in Rev. i. 13 ff.: the Debt of an Early Christology to an Aspect of Jewish Angelology" *JTS* 39.1 (1980): 1–11; Idem, *The Open Heaven: A Study of Apocalyptic in Judaism and Early Christianity* (Eugene: Wipf & Stock, 2002 [1982]), *passim*; Crispin Fletcher-Louis, *Luke-Acts: Angels, Christology, and Soteriology*, WUNT 2.94 (Tübingen: Mohr Siebeck, 1997), *passim*. On the problem which the christology of Hebrews 1–2 is supposedly addressing, Stuckenbruck, *Angel Veneration and*

Christology, 137, concludes, "It is impossible to decide between argument [*sic*] against a veneration of angels and an 'angel Christology.'"

40. See, e.g., David M. Moffitt, *Atonement and the Logic of Resurrection in the Epistle to the Hebrews*, NovTSup 141 (Leiden: Brill, 2011), 45–53, 118–44, with literature cited therein. Moffitt, *Atonement*, 47–53 (esp. 47–48, n. 2), rightly emphasizes that, at least for the author of Hebrews, the "son's" present superiority to angels, while not unrelated to his divinity, is principally predicated on the basis of his *now-exalted humanity*.

41. Cf. esp. Bauckham, "The Worship of Jesus," 327–31.

42. So Alexander, "'The Agent of the King Is Treated as the King Himself,'" (98).

43. So also Hurtado, *OGOL*, 34–36; Idem, *AJM*, 134; Wright, *NTPG*, esp. 259; and E. E. Ellis, *The Old Testament in Early Christianity* (Grand Rapids: Baker, 1992), 115–16.

44. So esp. Daniel Boyarin, "Beyond Judaisms: Metatron and the Divine Polymorphy of Ancient Judaism" *JSJ* 41 (2010): 323–65. Cf. also his *Border Lines: The Partition of Judaeo-Christianity*, DRLAR (Philadelphia: University of Pennsylvania Press, 2004); and "Two Powers in Heaven; or, the Making of a Heresy" in H. Najman and J. Newman, eds., *The Idea of Biblical Interpretation: Essays in Honor of James L. Kugel*, JSJSup 83 (Leiden: Brill, 2004), 331–70. For not dissimilar positions, see, e.g., Margaret Barker, *The Great Angel: A Study of Israel's Second God* (London: SPCK, 1992); Rowland, "The Vision of the Risen Christ," 1–11; Idem, *The Open Heaven*, 94–113; and J. E. Fossum, *The Name of God and the Angel of the Lord: Samaritan and Jewish Concepts of Intermediation and the Origin of Gnosticism*, LEC (Waco: Baylor University Press, 2017 [1985]), *passim*. For a critique of the latter two scholars in particular, see esp. Hurtado, *OGOL*, 88–95.

45. Boyarin, "Beyond Judaisms," 335, italics mine. Though I disagree with much of Boyarin's essay, his discussion of the rabbinic material is extremely illuminating and his conclusion regarding the derivation of the name "Metatron"—namely, that it derives from a combination of the Greek words μετά ("with") and θρόνος ("a throne")—in which he follows Hugo Odeberg, *3 Enoch or the Hebrew Book of Enoch* (New York: Ktav, 1973), 125–36, is quite convincing (cf. pp. 356–39).

46. On the rabbinic "Two Powers" heresy, see esp. the classic study of Alan F. Segal, *Two Powers in Heaven: Early Rabbinic Reports about Christianity and Gnosticism* (Waco: Baylor University Press, 2012 [1977]). Boyarin, "Beyond Judaisms," is at pains to demonstrate that, very much unlike Segal's construal in which the Two Powers heretics were *extrinsic* to rabbinic Judaism (so Christians and Gnostics), the Two Powers "heresy" actually represents a case in which, in the fresh construction of rabbinic "orthodoxy," the rabbis were attempting to define themselves over against "the other" by anathematizing as a "heresy" something which to that point had represented completely acceptable "ditheistic" tendencies in rabbinic (and other kinds of) Judaism.

47. Bauckham, *Jesus*, 6–17 (6).

48. Ibid. 12, italics original.

49. Bauckham himself argued this in "The Worship of Jesus," 322: "[I]t was worship which was the real test of monotheistic faith in religious practice." However,

he seems subsequently to have backed away from this emphasis: "In more recent publications Bauckham seems to back away a bit from his earlier emphasis on worship as the crucial criterion and manifestation of Jewish monotheism . . . preferring to characterize both Jewish monotheism and early Christ-devotion mainly in conceptual/doctrinal terms" (Hurtado, *LJC*, 47, n. 66). See also Larry W. Hurtado, "Worship and Divine Identity: Richard Bauckham's Christological Pilgrimage" in Gurtner et al., eds., *In the Fullness of Time*, 82–96 (esp. 83–87). Here we must rigorously distinguish between the *logical* priority of beliefs and the *religion-historical* priority of cultic devotion.

50. Bauckham, *Jesus*, 12.

51. On the rhetoric of second-temple monotheism, see esp. Rainbow, "Monotheism and Christology."

52. On the throne of God, see esp. Bauckham, *Jesus*, 152–81. Also making the enthronement of Jesus a crucial factor in the origins of christology, see esp. Timo Eskola, *Messiah and the Throne*, WUNT 2.142 (Tübingen: Mohr Siebeck, 2001), esp. 295–374. Relatedly, on the influence of Psalm 110 in early christology, see esp. David M. Hay, *Glory at the Right Hand: Psalm 110 in Early Christianity*, SBLMS (Atlanta: Scholars Press, 1973).

53. Bauckham, *Jesus*, 16. On this text, see the discussions in Hurtado, *OGOL*, 53–58; Bauckham, *Jesus*, 169–72; Tilling, *Christology*, 206–33; and Fletcher-Louis, *JM*, 167–205.

54. Bauckham, *Jesus*, 172–81. Psalm 110.1 is the most quoted and/or alluded to text in all of the New Testament. The apparatus of NA[28] provides Matt. 22.44; 26.64; Mark 12.36; 14.62; [16.19]; Luke 20.42; 22.69; Acts 2.34; Rom. 8.34; 1 Cor. 15.25; Eph. 1.20; Heb. 1.3, 13; 8.1; and 10.12. To this should be added 1 Pet. 3.22.

55. While I find Bauckham's heuristic category of "the unique divine identity" useful, it should not be played off against the category of "divine agency": so Larry W. Hurtado, "Worship and Divine Identity," esp. 89.

56. Collins, *Daniel*, 171, states, "The specifically religious character of the veneration is underlined by the mention of sacrifice and incense." See also Hartman and Di Lella, *Daniel*, 150.

57. *Ant.* 10.211–12 (Marcus, LCL, slightly revised).

58. For the OG of Daniel 7, the principal witness is the ca. early 3C CE P967. As Emanuel Tov, *Textual Criticism of the Hebrew Bible*, 3rd edn., rev. and exp. (Minneapolis: Fortress, 2012), notes, "[E]xcept for the late Hexaplaric manuscripts . . . [a]ll other manuscripts contain the revision of the *kaige*-Theodotion" (133). However, that the OG of Daniel 7.9–14 at least predates Revelation 1.13–16 is likely confirmed by the fact that the latter text appears to presuppose a textual tradition of Daniel 7.9–14 in which the son of man and the Ancient of Days are conflated (e.g., cf. particularly the description of the son of man's hair [rather than the Ancient of Day's hair; so OG Dan. 7.9] as "white wool" [ἔριον λευκὸν/ Rev. 1.14]).

59. See esp. Tim McLay, *The OG and Th Versions of Daniel*, SBLSCS 43 (Atlanta: Scholars Press, 1996), who concludes that, contrary to the *communis consensus*, Theodotion Daniel represents an *independent* translation of a Hebrew *Vorlage* rather than a recension of the OG. For a classic, brief, but well-documented statement of the more traditional view, in which "Kaige-Theodotion" represents a recension

of the OG toward a more "formal" reflection of proto-MT, see esp. Tov, *Textual Criticism*, 142–43, with literature cited therein. On the reasons for this Th recension toward proto-MT, see Ibid. 141, with literature cited therein.

60. So McLay, *The OG and Th Version*.

61. Loren T. Stuckenbruck, "'One like a Son of Man as the Ancient of Days' in the Old Greek Recension of Daniel 7,13: Scribal Error or Theological Translation" *ZNW* 86 (1995): 268–76.

62. All translations of MT, Th, and OG Daniel are here my own.

63. For μετά in this connection, see Mark 14.62; and Rev. 1.7.

64. For ἐπί in this connection, see Matt. 24.30; 26.64; and Rev. 14.14–16.

65. So also Stuckenbruck, "'One like a Son of Man,'" 270–73.

66. On the wide range of connotation which these words can have, cf. for פלח, e.g., the entry in *BDB* 1108; and, for δουλεύω and λατρεύω respectively, e.g., the entries in *BAGD* 259; and 597; and also the citation from Maurice Casey, "Method in Our Madness, and Madness in Their Methods: Some Approaches to the Son of Man in Recent Scholarship" in Benjamin E. Reynolds, ed., *The Son of Man Problem: Critical Readings*, CRBS (London/New York: Bloomsbury T & T Clark, 2018), 97–116 (112), below.

67. On the question of the "son of man," particularly as it relates to Christian origins, see, e.g., Larry W. Hurtado and Paul L. Owen, eds., *Who is This Son of Man? The Latest Scholarship on a Puzzling Expression of the Historical Jesus*, LNTS 208 (New York/London: Bloomsbury T & T Clark, 2011).

68. So also, to a degree, Stuckenbruck, "'One like a Son of Man,'" 270–73.

69. Cf. also Stuckenbruck, "'One like a Son of Man,'" 275: "It is thus tempting to attribute a monotheizing tendency to the translator"; J. Lust, "Daniel 7,13 and the Septuagint" *ETL* (1978): 68–69; and Segal, *Two Powers*, 202, who takes the textual tradition of the OG to reflect a deliberate attempt to safeguard against any kind of "Two Powers" heresy. I, therefore, reject the attempt of Benjamin E. Reynolds, made solely on the basis of the fact that the figure in OG Dan. 7.13–14 is "given authority," to argue that the son of man and the Ancient of Days are *not* conflated: "The 'One Like a Son of Man' According to the Old Greek of Daniel 7, 13–14" *Biblica* 89 (2008): 70–80 (74).

70. So also Stuckenbruck, "'One like a Son of Man,'" 275.

71. Rowland, *Open Heaven*, 98.

72. Fletcher-Louis, *JM*, 196.

73. Translation taken from George W. E. Nickelsburg and James C. VanderKam, *1 Enoch 2: A Commentary on the Book of Enoch Chapters 37—82*, Hermeneia (Minneapolis: Fortress, 2012), 166.

74. Casey, "Method in Our Madness," 112. Cp., e.g., the use of προσκυνέω in Revelation 3.9: "I will make those of the synagogue of Satan who say that they are Jews and are not, but are lying—I will make them come and bow down before your feet (προσκυνήσουσιν ἐνώπιον τῶν ποδῶν σου), and they will learn that I have loved you" (NRSV).

75. Crispin Fletcher-Louis, "The Worship of Divine Humanity as God's Image and the Worship of Jesus" in Carey C. Newman, James R. Davila, and Gladys S. Lewis, eds., *The Jewish Roots of Christological Monotheism*, LEC (Waco: Baylor

University Press, 2017 [1999]), ch. 6 (112–13). For a response to Fletcher-Louis, see esp. Hurtado, *LJC*, 37–42; and Larry W. Hurtado, "*Jesus Monotheism Volume 1: Christological Origins: The Emerging Consensus and Beyond*" *RBL* 8 (2016).

76. A synopsis and translation of the different versions of LAE (Greek, Latin, Armenian, Georgian and Slavonic) can be found in Gary A. Anderson and Michael E. Stone, *A Synopsis of the Books of Adam and Eve*, 2nd rev. edn. (Atlanta: Scholars Press, 1999). The translation is taken from M. D. Johnson, "Life of Adam and Eve" in *OTP* 2.262. I provide the Latin from the critical reconstruction of W. Meyer, "Vita Adae et Evae" in *Abhandlungen der königlich bayerischen Akademie der Wissenschaften, Philosophische-philologische Klasse*, vol. 14 (Munich: 1878), of which Johnson, "Life of Adam and Eve," is a translation. The principal Latin witnesses upon which Meyer relied were S (9C); T (10C); and M (12C). To my mind, Fletcher-Louis has demonstrated the following. (1) A tradition in which angels worship (or are asked to worship) Adam is pre-Christian (Fletcher-Louis, *JM*, 250–63); and (2) LAE 12–16 goes back to a Hebrew original and is ultimately of Jewish provenance (Ibid. 263–66). Joel Marcus, "Son of Man as Son of Adam" *RB* 110 (2003): 38–61 (54), notes other possible texts which might presuppose this tradition; and Moffitt, *Atonement*, 133–38, contends that a tradition very like it is presupposed by the author of Hebrews.

77. Cf. Johnson, "Life of Adam and Eve" in *OTP* 2.262, n. 12a; and now Loren T. Stuckenbruck, *The Myth of Rebellious Angels: Studies in Second Temple Judaism and New Testament Texts* (Grand Rapids: Eerdmans, 2017 [2014]). On this tradition's etiological purpose, see esp. John Levison, *Portraits of Adam in Early Judaism: from Sirach to 2 Baruch* (New York: Bloomsbury, 2015 [1988]), 185.

78. So also Marcus, "Son of Man," 54.

79. *Contra* Fletcher-Louis, *JM*, 269–76.

80. For his case concerning the report of Hecataeus of Abdera in Diodorus Siculus, *Bib. Hist.* 40.3.3–8, see esp. his *Luke-Acts*, 120–29. On Sirach 50, see his "The Temple Cosmology of P and Theological Anthropology in the Wisdom of Jesus ben Sira" in Craig A. Evans, ed., *Of Scribes and Sages: Early Jewish Interpretation and Transmission of Scripture*, LSTS 50, SSEJC 9 (Sheffield: SAP, 2004), 69–113. On the tradition of Alexander the Great's prostration, see his "The Worship of the Jewish High Priest by Alexander the Great" in Stuckenbruck and North, eds., *Early Christian and Jewish Monotheism*, 71–102.

81. See esp. Ronald Cox, *By the Same Word: Creation and Salvation in Hellenistic Judaism and Early Christianity*, BZNW 145 (Berlin: de Gruyter, 2007), 10–11 (esp. 10, n. 28, noting other texts in the Tanakh), with literature cited therein. On the difficult Hebrew word אָמוֹן in Prov. 8.30, cf. Richard J. Clifford, *Creation Accounts in the Ancient Near East and the Bible*, CBQ 26 (Washington: CBA, 1994), 101. On the Wisdom tradition more generally, see the classic studies of Gerhard von Rad, *Wisdom in Israel* (Nashville: Abingdon, 1972); and J. L. Crenshaw, *Old Testament Wisdom: An Introduction* (Atlanta: John Knox Press, 1981).

82. So esp. Cox, *By the Same Word*, 10, n. 28: "While these passages may have contributed to the development of the notion of cosmological agency in Hellenistic Judaism and Christianity, they do not appear to provide any concrete evidence of a personified (or hypostatic) cosmological agent."

83. With respect to the Philonic *corpus* and Wisdom in particular, cf. esp. all of Ibid. 6–12 and esp. 22: "However, for Diaspora Jews seeking to preserve the transcendence of their God and yet articulate his relevance to their Hellenistic world, the Middle Platonic system would have been considerably more amenable then [*sic*] the monism of the Stoics. The Jews even had a ready-to-hand vehicle in personified Wisdom for co-opting the Platonic intermediary doctrine."

84. So Ibid. 12–16.

85. For a good, succinct introduction to Philo's *logos* doctrine, cf. Thomas Tobin, "Logos" in *ABD* 4.348–56.

86. So esp. Cox, *By the Same Word*, 12–16, 20–25, 56–140; and Dillon, *The Middle Platonists*, 139–83 (esp. 155–61).

87. Philo, *Heir* 205–06 (Colson and Whitaker, LCL, slightly revised).

88. While the point is not crucial for our purposes, Cox, *By the Same Word*, 12–25, 56–140, argues strongly that, for the author of Wisdom and Philo, *sophia/logos* is properly hypostatic. Cp. Hurtado, *OGOL*, 41–51, and esp. 210–11, n. 25.

89. For *sophia* speculation as a crucial background for early christology, see, e.g., U. Wilkens, *Weisheit und Torheit*, BHT 26 (Tübingen: J. C. B. Mohr, 1959); H. Hegermann, *Die Vorstellung vom Schöpfungsmittler im hellenistischen Judentum und Urchristentum*, TU 82 (Berlin: Akademie-Verlag, 1961); H. -F. Weiss, *Untersuchungen zur Kosmologie des hellenistischen und palästinischen Judentum*, TU 97 (Berlin: Akademie-Verlag, 1966); Berton L. Mack, *Logos und Sophia: Untersuchungen zur Weisheitstheologie im hellenistischen Judentum* (Göttingen: Vandenhoeck & Ruprecht, 1973); B. A. Pearson, "Hellenistic-Jewish Wisdom Speculation and Paul" in R. L. Wilken, ed., *Aspects of Wisdom in Judaism and Early Christianity* (Notre Dame: UNDP, 1975), 43–66; and Wright, *Climax*, 107–14; and Idem, *PFG*, 619–773.

90. See esp. Heiser, "Monotheism," 1–30; and Idem, "The Divine Council." Heiser, "Monotheism," 3, notes ~ 185 such instances in Qumran sectarian texts.

91. Davidson, *Angels at Qumran*, 309.

92. So Michael Frede, "Monotheism and Pagan Philosophy in Later Antiquity" in Athanassiadi and Frede, eds., *Pagan Monotheism*, 41–67.

93. Stephen Mitchell, "The Cult of Theos Hypsistos among Pagans, Jews, and Christians" in Athanassiadi and Frede, eds., *Pagan Monotheism*, 81–148.

94. So also Hurtado, *AJM*, 132: "Moreover, in pagan versions [of monotheism], beliefs about a high god were not characteristically taken as demanding or justifying a cultic neglect of the other divine/heavenly beings." I note, furthermore, this crucial concession at the beginning of Athanassiadi and Frede, eds., *Pagan Monotheism*, "[T]o describe such pagans as monotheists needs a serious qualification of the term, since they believed in many divine beings *and perhaps even worshipped them, or at least condoned and perhaps encouraged their worship*" (2, italics mine). An earlier study, J. Teixidor, *The Pagan God: Popular Religion in the Graeco-Roman Near East* (Princeton: PUP, 1977), 13–17, noted this point. See the careful discussion of John P. Kenney, "Monotheistic and Polytheistic Elements in Classical Mediterranean Spirituality" in A. H. Armstrong, ed., *Classical Mediterranean Spirituality* (New York: Crossroad, 1986), 269–92. See also S. Mitchell and P. van Nuffelen, *One God: Pagan Monotheism in the Roman Empire* (Cambridge: CUP, 2010).

95. It is not that cosmogonical activity is the *only* remarkable christological conception in early Christian literature but that this activity is *the key conceptual criterion* by which ancient Jews demarcated the unique divine identity. For instance, especially remarkable is the ascription of "YHWH-texts" to Jesus: so esp. David B. Capes, *Old Testament Yahweh Texts in Paul's Christology*, LEC (Waco: Baylor University Press, 2017 [1992]).

96. On baptism "into the name of Jesus," see Lars Hartman, *"Into the Name of the Lord Jesus": Baptism in the Early Church*, SNTW (Edinburgh: T & T Clark, 1997), esp. 37–50.

97. On these six features of early Jesus devotion, see Hurtado, *OGOL*, 105–19.

98. I will not argue separately that Paul was an exclusivist Jewish monotheist, a claim which is rarely doubted (so esp. Rom. 1.18–23; 3.30; 11.36; 1 Cor. 8.4–6; Gal. 3.20; and 1 Thes. 1.9–10). On this, see esp. Wright, *PFG*, 619–43; Tilling, *Christology*, 63–74; Woyke, *Götter*, 163–79; Wolfgang Schrage, *Unterwegs zur Einzigkeit und Einheit Gottes: Zum 'Monotheismus' des Paulus und seiner alttestamentliche-frühjudischen Tradition*, BTS 48 (Neukirchen-Vluyn: Neukirchener, 2002); Hurtado, *LJC*, 79–93; and Schnelle, *Paul*, 70–75: "All Jewish theology, including that of the Jewish Christian Paul, proceeds from its basis in monotheism" (70).

99. Wesley Hill, *Paul and the Trinity: Persons, Relations and the Pauline Letters* (Grand Rapids: Eerdmans, 2015).

100. Ibid. 45.

101. Ibid. 23–25.

102. Ibid. 24.

103. Ibid. 24, referencing Nathan MacDonald, "The Origin of 'Monotheism'" in Stuckenbruck and North, eds., *Early Jewish and Christian Monotheism*, 204–15.

104. Hill, *Paul*, 21–24.

105. Ibid. 25.

106. Ibid. 31.

107. Throughout, the language of "father" and "son" is lowercase while the language of "Spirit" is uppercase when it denotes "the Spirit of God."

Chapter 4

The Jewish *Imago Dei* Tradition

Throughout I have referred, and will continue to refer, to the "Jewish *imago Dei* tradition." However, this is simply a convenient shorthand. It is not intended to imply the homogeneity of every instance of the *imago Dei* in second-temple sources. Rather, the shorthand stands in for the more cumbersome, though more accurate, expression "instances of the *imago Dei* in Jewish texts from the second-temple period." After all, to take one prominent example, it explains very little to refer to instances of the *imago Dei* in Philo as instances of the "Jewish *imago Dei* tradition." By this, we should mean little more than that Philo is a Jew who prizes the Jewish scriptures and engages Genesis 1.26–27.[1]

THE BIBLICAL *IMAGO DEI* TRADITION[2]

The *imago Dei* language itself is rare in the Tanakh, appearing exclusively in the book of Genesis and then exclusively in texts usually assigned to the so-called Priestly Source or Priestly Redaction (Gen. 1.26, 27; 5.3; and 9.6).[3] With regard to Genesis 5.3 and 9.6, we will not consider either text in much detail. The former is fundamentally designed to assure the reader of the perpetuation of the *imago Dei* from Adam to his son Seth (and beyond), while the latter makes the *imago Dei*—and the close association with the deity which it implies—the basis of human dignity: "Whoever sheds the blood of a human, by a human shall that person's blood be shed; for in his own image God made humankind" (NRSV).

We turn, therefore, to the foundational instance of Genesis 1.26–27:

(1.26) Then God said, "Let us make humankind in our image (Heb. בצלמנו; Gr. κατ' εἰκόνα ἡμετέραν), according to our likeness (Heb. כדמותנו; Gr. καθ' ὁμοίωσιν);⁴ and let them have dominion over the fish of the sea, and over the birds of the air, and over the cattle, and over all the wild animals of the earth, and over every creeping thing that creeps upon the earth."

(1.27) So God created humankind in his image (Heb. בצלמו), in the image of God he created them (Heb. בצלם אלהים; Gr. κατ' εἰκόνα θεοῦ); male and female he created them. (NRSV)

The consensus of Old Testament scholarship is that Genesis 1.26–27 reflects a "democratization" ("universalization" is to be preferred) of a wider ANE royal ideology.⁵ The royal ideologies of Egypt, Assyria, and Mesopotamia are usually deemed especially relevant.⁶ Whereas in these ideologies the king and the king alone serves as an image of a god, in Genesis 1.26–27 *all of humanity* is created to be an image of the one and only God.⁷ Moreover, as will be relevant to our later discussion, the consensus is that Genesis 1.26–27 regards the whole human being, rather than some anatomical part thereof, as God's image. In any case, because this text should likely be dated either during or shortly after the Babylonian exile, and because—as I argued above—it was precisely at this time that certain Jewish traditions began forcefully to express a resolute and aniconic Jewish monotheism, we should consider one particular possibility: namely, that the *imago Dei* theology of the so-called Priestly Source represents a bold adaptation of Jewish idol polemics.⁸ After all, צלם routinely refers to a cult "idol" in roughly contemporary biblical literature (e.g., Num. 33.52; 2 Kgs. 11.18; 2 Chr. 23.17; Ezek. 7.20; 16.17; 23.14; and Amos 5.26). In this regard, Andreas Schüle has convincingly argued:

> Yet, the end of these cultic images did not put an end altogether to the idea of the "Image of God." It is remarkable that very much at the same time when prophets like Deutero-Isaiah and Ezekiel poured scorn on the *idols*, the idea of the "Image of God" was very much alive in another strand of biblical tradition that is probably about contemporaneous with these prophets.⁹

This state of affairs, moreover, goes some way toward a historical explanation of the relative paucity of the expression in the Tanakh. Why is it, in other words, that the *imago Dei* is so rare in the Tanakh but occurs with relative frequency, as we will see below, in later second-temple literature? In this regard, Curtis has convincingly argued, "It seems likely that the danger presented to Israel's religion by idolatry precluded that [positive, anthropological] use *until after the Exile had eliminated idolatry as a major problem.*"¹⁰

In any case, especially relevant for our purposes is the contextual meaning of the *imago Dei* in Genesis 1.26. Though the details are certainly not spelled out, the conception seems at least to imply humanity's close relationship to the deity, a deity whose sovereign rule, furthermore, humanity was created precisely to instantiate. However, how are we to understand the two expressions בצלמנו and כדמותנו? Particularly, (1) are the two nouns roughly interchangeable and (2) what is the sense of the prepositions ב and כ? As to the interchangeability of the nouns, Genesis 5.1 and 5.3 point in the direction of the affirmative.[11] Whereas Genesis 1.26 states that humanity was created "*in* the image" (בצלמנו) and "*as* the likeness" (כדמותנו) of God, Genesis 5.1 and 5.3, respectively, reverse this phraseology when they say that God made humanity "*in* the likeness of God" (בדמות אלהים) and then "*in* his likeness, *as* his image" (בדמותו כצלמו). This also suggests the interchangeability of the prepositions.[12]

However, what is the specific force of the ב and the כ in Genesis 1.26–27?[13] Does the text imply that God was in fact "image-less" before the creation of humanity, in which case humanity was created simply *as* God's image? Or, on the other hand, does the text imply that God *already had an image* according to which humanity itself was made? Genesis 5.3 seems significantly to illuminate the issue: "When Adam had lived one hundred thirty years, he became the father of a son in his likeness, according to his image (בדמותו כצלמו), and named him Seth" (NRSV). In this text, the prepositions indicate that Seth was somehow "patterned" after Adam. It seems best, therefore, to take Genesis 1.26–27 similarly. In MT Genesis 1.26–27, God *already has an image* after which humanity is patterned.[14]

This is, in any case, certainly the meaning of LXX. The use of κατά as the consistent translation of ב in 1.26, 27; 5.1, and 3 makes the point unambiguous.[15] However, interestingly, the instance of בצלם in 9.6 is translated ἐν εἰκόνι θεοῦ. Nevertheless, all of the instances in LXX Genesis imply that God already had an image before he created humanity. This interpretative possibility, moreover, as we will see below, was later appropriated—though in quite different ways—by Philo, the author of Wisdom, and Paul himself.

I further note, though the question is somewhat beyond our purview, that some studies have drawn attention to the fact that the theophany of Ezekiel 1.26–28 might presuppose the anthropogonical tradition of Genesis 1.26–28.[16] In the former text, the prophet writes that "the appearance of the likeness of the Glory of LORD (מראה דמות כבוד יהוה)" appeared to him "like the appearance of a human being (דמות כמראה אדם)." In other words, this theophany in which the God of Israel looked something like אדם might be an obverse way of saying that אדם was created in the "image" and "likeness" of כבוד יהוה. Whatever we make of Ezekiel 1.26–28, it is possible that 4Q504, frag. 8, col. 1.4 reflects this logic when it perhaps provides a reading of Genesis 1.26 *via* Ezekiel 1.26–28: "[Adam,] our father, you fashioned in the likeness of [your] Glory . . ."[17]

In any case, to conclude this brief discussion of the *imago Dei* in the Tanakh, I summarize the following points. (1) The *imago Dei* conception is extremely rare in the Tanakh, occurring only in Genesis (1.26, 27; 5.3; and 9.6). (2) The explanation for the paucity of the conception likely lies in the fact that this *image Dei* anthropology was only ever going to gain traction in the postexilic period, during a time in which there was little threat of large-scale Jewish idolatry. (3) Genesis 1.26–27, the key text to which the Jewish *imago Dei* tradition looks back, reflects a universalization of a wider ANE royal ideology. All of humanity functions as an image of the one God and is, therefore, given the task of ruling God's world on his behalf. (4) Finally, both MT and LXX Genesis 1.26–27 indicate that God already had an image according to which he made humanity.

SECOND-TEMPLE *IMAGO DEI* TRADITIONS

In this section, leaving aside the many occurrences in Philo for the moment, I note every instance of the *imago Dei* in Jewish sources ranging roughly from the exile to the end of the second century CE. In this regard, however, not every instance of the *imago Dei* merits extended consideration, not least as some of these occurrences are mere quotations of Genesis 9.6. Naturally, placing the *terminus ante quem* at the end of the second century CE raises difficult questions of provenance. For simplicity's sake, I largely follow James Davila's influential analysis unless, of course, he does not consider a particular text.[18] Occurrences of the *imago Dei* in obviously Christian sources—as in, for example, the early Fathers—will not receive consideration.[19] The reason for this is partly practical and partly methodological. On the one hand, this would have greatly increased the size of the project. On the other hand, I am attempting to identify possible influences *on* the apostle Paul rather than influences *from* the apostle Paul *on* later writers.

I here provide a brief listing of all instances of the *imago Dei* in second-temple Jewish sources: Jubilees 6.8; Sirach 17.3; 1 Enoch 106.10; Sibylline Oracles 1.23; 3.8; 8.266, 402; Liber Antiquitatum Biblicarum 3.11; 50.7; Wisdom 2.23; 7.26; Testament of Naphtali 2.5; Life of Adam and Eve 10 (2x); 12 (2x); 33; 35; Pseudo Phocylides 1.106; 4 Ezra 8.44; 2 Enoch 65.2; and Pirke Avoth 3.14 (3x).[20] The conception is ubiquitous in Philo, with 118 occurrences of the lexeme εἰκών, many of which are in this connection. Sibylline Oracles 8, however, clearly betrays Christian redaction and is too late to be considered here.[21] Moreover, Davila expresses doubts about the provenance of the Testaments, Pseudo-Phocylides, and LAE.[22] Second Enoch should also be treated with caution.[23] Nevertheless, so long as we bear carefully in mind that not all of these texts are *certainly* of non-Christian, Jewish provenance, there is no harm in examining the ways in which they might illuminate Paul's use of the *imago Dei*.

This gives us, then, these statistics for the Jewish *imago Dei* tradition. We have five instances in the Tanakh, all confined to Genesis (Gen. 1.26, 27; 5.1, 3; and 9.6). There are no instances in the Scrolls or in Josephus. The Mishnah, moreover, boasts only three instances, all occurring within the same passage (Pir. Av. 3.14 [3x]). For second-temple literature which is almost certainly of Jewish origin and likely of Palestinian provenance, we have nine occurrences (Jub. 6.8; Sir. 17.3; 1 En. 106.10; LAB 3.11; 50.7; 4 Ezra 8.44; and Pir. Avo. 3.14 [3x]). For second-temple literature which is possibly of Jewish origin and/or of Palestinian provenance, we have eight instances (T. Naph. 2.5; LAE 10 [2x]; 12 [2x]; 33; 35; and 2 En. 65.2). If we exclude Philo's *corpus*, we have five occurrences from the diaspora which are likely of Jewish origin (Wis. 2.23; 7.26; Sib. Or. 1.23; 3.8; and Ps. Phoc. 1.106). Therefore, leaving aside Philo's *abundant* use of the conception, while also excluding Genesis and including literature down to the Mishnah, we have twenty-two occurrences of the *imago Dei* conception in second-temple Jewish literature, eight of which are of uncertain provenance. Paul adds another seven instances (Rom. 8.29; 1 Cor. 11.7; 15.49 [2x]; 2 Cor. 3.18; 4.4; Col. 1.15; and 3.10).[24] Though the question is beyond our scope, it is noteworthy and deserving of more consideration as to why, within the large, combined *corpora* of the Scrolls and Josephus, we do not have a single instance of the *imago Dei*.

In any case, not all of the above occurrences are of equal importance. Jubilees 6.8 and LAB 3.11, for instance, offer mere quotations of Genesis 9.6 within their larger rewritings of Genesis. These texts, therefore, will not receive consideration.

Sirach 17.3[25]

According to his own strength, he clothed them, and according to his own image, he made them (καθ' ἑαυτὸν ἐνέδυσεν αὐτοὺς ἰσχὺν καὶ κατ' εἰκόνα αὐτοῦ ἐποίησεν αὐτούς).

With respect to this text, whose likely provenance is Palestinian and whose likely date is ca. 200 BCE, I make the following points. (1) Within a context in which the writer refers to the *imago Dei*, he speaks also of being "clothed" (ἐνδύω). Interestingly, Philo and Paul make a similar connection (cf. *Conf.* 144–47; and Col. 3.10).[26] Whatever the provenance and ultimate meaning of this notion, it was clearly taken for granted by all three of these writers. It is possible—though by no means demonstrable—that all three depend, at least in part, upon a notion found in the Greek Life of Adam and Eve: namely, that Adam was "clothed" with glory before his fall (GLAE 20.2; cp. 3 Bar. 4.16). Similar traditions can also be found in later rabbinic literature.[27] (2) Moreover, as the next verse goes on to say that God "gave them dominion over beasts and birds" (17.4), we should probably understand the *imago Dei* theology of this text along the same lines as that of Genesis 1.26–27.²⁸ In other words, serving as the *imago Dei* involves ruling God's world on God's behalf. (3) Beyond this, however, the *imago Dei* conception does not appear to be particularly load-bearing for Sirach.

1 Enoch 106.1–10

(106.1) And after some days my [Enoch] son, Methuselah, took a wife for his son Lamech, and she became pregnant by him and bore him a son. (106.2) And his body was white as snow and red as a rose; the hair of his head as white as wool and his *demdema* beautiful; and as for his eyes, when he opened them the whole house glowed like the sun—(rather) the whole house glowed even more exceedingly. . . . (106.4) And his father, Lamech, was afraid of him and fled and went to Methuselah his father; (106.5) and he said to him, "I have begotten a strange son: He is not like an (ordinary) human being, but he looks like the children of the angels of heaven to me (οὐχ ὅμοιον τοῖς ἀνθρώποις ἀλλὰ τοῖς τέκνοις τῶν ἀγγέλων τοῦ οὐρανοῦ). . . . (106.7) So I am beseeching you now, begging you in order that you might go to his (grand)father Enoch, our father, and learn from him the truth, for his dwelling place is among the angels." . . . (106.8) And when Methuselah heard the words of his son, he came to me [Enoch] to the ends of the earth; for he had heard that I was there, and he cried aloud, and I heard his voice and I came to him. . . . (106.10) "Now, my father, hear me [Methuselah]: For unto my son Lamech a son has been born, one whose *form and image* are not like unto the characteristics of human beings (καὶ ὁ τύπος αὐτοῦ καὶ ἡ εἰκὼν αὐτοῦ οὐχ ὅμοιος ἀνθρώποις)."²⁹

The above text ultimately derives from the so-called book of Noah, parts of which have apparently been inserted into the composite text of 1 Enoch. For the original composition, Isaac provides the date of "late pre-Maccabean."³⁰ First Enoch is, furthermore, preserved in toto only in late Ethiopic manuscripts; however, we do possess one Hebrew (1Q19, frag. 3; covering 106.2–6) and two Aramaic (4Q204, frag. 5, col. 1; and 4204, frag. 5, col. 2; covering 106.1–2; and 106.13–19, respectively) fragments from Qumran.³¹ And although 1 Enoch 106.7–10 is not preserved in the Scrolls, we possess one fourth-century Greek manuscript of 1 Enoch 97.6–104; and 106–07, a critical reconstruction of which has been provided by Black and Denis.³² It is from this critical reconstruction that I provide elements of the Greek into Isaac's translation of a fifteenth-century Ethiopic manuscript, a translation which was "not influenced" by the Aramaic fragments.³³ Naturally, the following discussion presupposes that an original Hebrew צלם stood behind the Greek εἰκών.³⁴

Within the Enochic literature in general and within the tradition of the Watchers in particular, this text seems to serve a particular etiological purpose. Of special concern to this tradition is the devastating effects wrought when "the sons of God" (i.e., angels) slept with "the daughters of humans" (Gen. 6.4) and the latter bore children (cf. 1 En. 1–36 and esp. 1 En. 6; 15.8–9).[35] Within this broader tradition, the concern that Noah might have been begotten of angels is, as van Kooten says, "very serious."[36] However, in 1 Enoch 106.13–18, Enoch assures Methuselah that Noah is indeed Lamech's son and that he is not the result of a union between the Watchers and human women. It seems to be implicit that Noah's remarkable appearance owes instead to the remarkable purpose which God was to accomplish through him.[37] Though the rest of the *kosmos* will be destroyed, Noah and his family (along with the animals) will be preserved (1 En. 106.13–18).

Nevertheless, we are still left with the question: Is Noah patterned after the image of the angels or not? To be sure, 2 Enoch 22.8–10 rather unambiguously indicates that Enoch, upon his assumption, somehow became indistinguishable from "the holy ones." However, in this particular case, I agree with van Kooten.[38] In relation to the Watchers tradition, this text contends that Noah, unlike so much of the rest of humanity, was precisely *not* patterned after the angels. Indeed, this is part of the text's etiological explanation of Noah's superior righteousness within the context of Genesis 6–9 (cf. esp. Gen. 7.1). Therefore, I contend that the text makes use of the *imago Dei* tradition of Genesis 1–9 in relation to the tradition of the Watchers (Gen. 6) in order to provide an etiological explanation as to why Noah was chosen to "restart" the human race. Noah, so the text implicitly reasons, does not, like so much of the rest of now-wicked humanity after Genesis 6, bear the "image" of fallen angels but rather the "image" of God.

Pseudo Philo 50.7

I am the wife of Elkanah; and because God has shut up my womb, I have prayed before him that I do not go forth from this world without fruit and that I do not die without having my own image.

Pseudo Philo's LAB is preserved only in a Latin translation from the Greek, which itself was translated from an original Hebrew. Of course, this discussion presumes that the Latin *imago* translates the Greek εἰκών which itself translated the Hebrew צלם. The text is likely of ca. first-century Palestinian provenance.[39] Interestingly, in the retelling of Hannah's discussion with Eli the priest (1 Sam. 1.9–18), Pseudo Philo has Hannah echo the language of Genesis 5.3, a text which reads, "When Adam had lived one hundred thirty years, he became the father of a son in his likeness, according to his image, and named him Seth" (NRSV). Beyond this interesting point, however, this text adds little more to our ongoing investigation.

Sibylline Oracles 1.22–24[40]

And then later he again fashioned an animate object, making a copy from his own image (εἰκόνος ἐξ ἰδίης ἀπομαξάμενος), youthful man, beautiful, wonderful.

With respect to this text, whose date is not precisely determinable and whose provenance is possibly Phrygian, I make one simple point.[41] The text simply presupposes that God already had an image according to which he made Adam ("making a copy from his own image").

Sibylline Oracles 3.8–10

Humans, who have the form which God molded in his image
(ἄνθρωποι θεόπλαστον ἔχοντες ἐν εἰκόνι μορφήν),
why do you wander in vain, and not walk the straight path
ever mindful of the immortal creator?

For this text (Sib. Or. 3.1–96), Collins provides the *terminus post quem* of 70 CE and the provenance of Alexandria.[42] I make the following points. (1) By combining the language of "God molded" (θεόπλαστος) with the language of the *imago Dei*, the writer has hereby combined the accounts of the creation of human beings from Genesis 2.7 (καὶ ἔπλασεν ὁ θεὸς τὸν ἄνθρωπον . . .) and Genesis 1.26–27.[43] (2) Furthermore, within a context in which the writer vehemently castigates idolatry (3.10–34; esp. v. 31) and insists upon worship of "the one God" (3.11: εἷς θεός ἐστι)—the latter of which reflects an allusion to the *Shema*—it is striking that the same writer refers to humans with language which is routinely used of idols in the biblical tradition (e.g., [all LXX] Deut. 4.16; 4 Kgs. 11.18; 2 Chr. 33.7; Ezek. 7.20; 16.17; 23.14; Isa. 40.19, 20; Hos. 13.2; Dan. 2.31 [3x], 34, 35; 3.1, 2, 3, 5, 7, 10, 12, 14, 15, 18; cf. also Wis. 13.13, 16; 14.15, 17; 15.5).[44] Therefore, whatever we make of the possibility that instances of the *imago Dei* in Genesis reflect a bold adaptation of idol polemics, this is likely the case here.

Ezra 8.44

But man, who has been formed by your hands and is called your own image (*est et tuae imagini nominatus*) because they are made like you, and for whose sake you have formed all things—have you also made him like the farmer's seed?

Four Ezra is best preserved in Latin manuscripts which represent a translation from the Greek, which itself was probably translated from an original Hebrew text of late first-century date and Palestinian provenance.[45] The original document seems to have been occasioned, inter alia, by the Roman destruction of Jerusalem and the resulting sense that God had finally and forever abandoned his people. The text features a dialogue wherein Pseudo Ezra questions God *via* the angel Uriel and God responds *via* Uriel. Within a larger context in which Pseudo Ezra questions the justice of God for (apparently) allowing so few eschatological salvation (7.45–8.36), Uriel responds with a parable. "For just as," so Uriel reasons, "the farmer sows many seeds upon the ground and plants a multitude of seedlings, and yet not all that have been sown will come up in due season . . . so all those who have been sown in the world will not be saved" (8.41). It is to this parable that Pseudo Ezra provides the above indignant response. In Pseudo Ezra's view, it is totally inappropriate, particularly in view of the *imago Dei* theology of Genesis 1.26–27, to liken humanity simply to the seed of the farmer. Rather, so Pseudo Ezra argues, it was for humanity's sake that God made all things. In this regard, we should note the way in which this passage intimately relates to the similar passage of 6.35–59. In this latter text, Pseudo Ezra reflects upon God's creation of the *kosmos* in general and of Adam in particular and states,

> "[A]nd over these [parts of the *kosmos*] you placed Adam . . . and from him we have all come, the people whom you have chosen.
> All this I have spoken before you, O Lord, because you have said that it was *for us that you created this world*" (6.54–56).

In other words, Israel is God's true humanity, called, as Adam originally was, to rule over God's creation. Beyond this point, however, the author's use of the *imago Dei* appears designed to do little more than to indicate humanity's close relationship to the deity and their consequent value (cp. e.g., Greek LAE 33.5; and 35.2).[46]

Wisdom 2.23; 7.26[47]

> (2.23) [F]or God created humanity for incorruption and he made them in his own eternal image (ὅτι ὁ θεὸς ἔκτισεν τὸν ἄνθρωπον ἐπ' ἀφθαρσίᾳ καὶ εἰκόνα τῆς ἰδίας ἀϊδιότητος ἐποίησεν αὐτόν),[48] (2.24) but through the devil's jealously death entered the world (φθόνῳ δὲ διαβόλου θάνατος εἰσῆλθεν εἰς τὸν κόσμον), and those who belong to his [the devil's] lot tested them. (NRSV)

As I noted earlier in another connection, it is possible that this text presupposes certain elements of a tradition now found most fully in LAE, a text to which we will turn below.[49] Indeed, because the author brings the idea of the devil's jealousy into such close proximity to the idea of the *imago Dei*, it is possible that he presupposes an etiological tradition in which it was precisely God's creation of humanity in his image which precipitated the devil's jealousy.⁵⁰ In this connection, I am unpersuaded by Levison's case that this text does not refer to a tradition similar to the one now found in LAE but, rather, to Genesis 4.⁵¹ Levison argues that we should take διαβολός as a reference to Cain rather than to the supreme, heavenly opponent of God. While it is true that διαβολός *can* refer to an ordinary human adversary (cf., e.g., LXX Est. 7.4; 8.1, with reference to Haman), we have no evidence of this designation with reference to Cain and a preponderance of roughly contemporary evidence with reference to the supreme, demonic opponent of God (e.g., Jub. 10.8; 3 Bar. 4.8; T. Naph. 3.1; 8.4, 6; T. Job 3.3; 17.1; 26.6; T. Sol. 15.11; Jos. As. 12.9; Greek LAE 15; 16 [3x]; 17; 21; and 37x in the New Testament). Therefore, while I do not deny that the "death" which entered the world (Wis. 2.24) might be a reference to Cain and Abel, I persist in reading the "jealousy of διαβολός" as a reference to the tradition in which God's creation of humanity in his image made the devil jealous.

However, before we turn to the question of what precisely constitutes the "image" in 2.23, we should consider 7.26:

For she [*sophia*] is a breath of the power of God,
and a pure emanation of the glory of the Almighty;
therefore nothing defiled gains entrance into her.
For she is a reflection of eternal light,
a spotless mirror of the working of God,
and an image of his goodness (εἰκὼν τῆς ἀγαθότητος αὐτοῦ). (NRSV)

With respect to this text, I make the following points. (1) As several scholars have argued, though Wisdom betrays both Stoic and Middle Platonic influence, the sequence of "breath," "emanation," "reflection," "mirror," and "image" is distinctively Middle Platonic.⁵² (2) In 9.1, furthermore, we *might* have evidence—though the formulation was also well known in biblical and second-temple traditions putatively uninfluenced, or at least much less influenced, by philosophical cosmology (e.g., Ps. 33.6; Jub. 12.4; 2 Bar. 21.4; 14.17; T. Abr. 9.6; and 4 Ezra 6.38)—that the author of Wisdom understood Jewish *sophia* and the philosophical *logos* in quite similar terms: "O God of my ancestors and Lord of mercy, who have made all things by your *logos* (ἐν λόγῳ σου), and by *sophia* you have formed humans (καὶ τῇ σοφίᾳ σου κατασκευάσας ἄνθρωπον)" (9.1).⁵³

(3) This *sophia*, moreover, which is clearly a cosmogonical agent in (e.g.) 7.22; and 9.1, is an "image of his [God's] goodness (εἰκὼν τῆς ἀγαθότητος αὐτοῦ)." I take this, furthermore, following Sterling in particular, as an allusion to Genesis 1.26, in which the author thereby takes *sophia/logos* to be the cosmogonical "image" of God according to which (so LXX Gen. 1.26: κατ' εἰκόνα ἡμετέραν) Adam himself was made.⁵⁴ Indeed, keeping with the other

circumlocutions in 7.26, the only reason the author has not simply written "an image of God" but, rather, "an image of *his goodness*" is to be explained by the fact that the author as a whole reflects a distinctively Middle Platonic *Tendenz* in which the transcendence of the deity is all-important.[55] We should take the phrase "an image of his goodness," therefore, as a direct allusion to Genesis 1.26.

(4) Therefore, when we take 7.26 together with 2.23, we are right to conclude that the author of Wisdom took *sophia* to be the cosmogonical image of God according to which humanity was made. Or, to be more specific, because the reference to the *imago Dei* in 2.23 follows so closely upon the reference to "blameless souls" in 2.22 (ψυχή ἀμωμή), we are probably right to conclude that the author of Wisdom, like Philo (e.g., *Creation*, 69) and Pseudo Phocylides (1.106), took the human "soul" to constitute God's image.[56] Indeed, this association between the *imago Dei* and the human soul, and the association of the latter with the Middle Platonic doctrine of "immortality" (so esp. Wis. 1.12–15; 2.22–3.6; 8.19; 9.15; and 15.8), seems designed as a distinctively Middle Platonic argument against the kind of Epicurean materialism in view in Wisdom 1.16–2.24.[57] In this case, therefore, Wisdom 2.23–24 reflects a fascinating combination of features: (1) the Jewish tradition of the devil's jealousy at the creation of humanity in God's image and (2) the Middle Platonic argument, over against Epicurean materialism, that the human "soul-as-God's-image" is immortal and will (therefore) outlast physical death. To this should also be added the fact that the author of Wisdom appears to combine belief in the immortality of the soul with the characteristically Jewish belief in bodily resurrection (cf. esp. 3.7–8).[58]

Life of Adam and Eve

(12.1) And the devil sighed and said, "O Adam, all my enmity and envy and sorrow concern you, since because of you I am expelled and deprived of my glory which I had in the heavens in the midst of the angels, and because of you I was cast onto the earth. . . . (13.2) When you were created, I was cast out from the presence of God. . . . (13.3) When God blew into you the breath of life and your countenance and likeness were made in the image of God (*ad imaginem Dei*), Michael brought you and made us worship you in the sight of God, and the LORD God said, 'Behold Adam! I have made you in our image and likeness (*ad imaginem et similitudinem nostram*).' (14.1) And Michael went out and called all the angels, saying, 'Worship the image of the LORD God (*adorate imaginem Domino Dei*). . . . (14.2) And Michael himself worshipped first, and called me [the devil] and said, 'Worship the image of God (*adora imaginem Dei*) . . .!' (14.3) And I [the devil] answered, 'I do not worship Adam!' . . . 'He ought to worship me!' . . . (16.1) And the LORD God was angry with me [the devil] and sent me with my angels out from our glory."

As we have already considered this text in another connection, I only restate the main points. (1) This text offers an etiology for the tradition of satan's fall from heaven based upon the *imago Dei* theology of Genesis 1.26–27. (2) In relation to its etiological function, I suggest, it expresses an exalted view of humanity in view of which those producing and reading the text can take courage in their current "cosmic warfare."[59] (3) Furthermore, it seems to be implicit that, before the creation of Adam, God was in fact "image-less." In this sense, therefore, the text represents a distinct Jewish *imago Dei* tradition in which, rather than God creating humanity *according to* his image, humanity itself simply *is* the image of God.[60]

There are also important references to the *imago Dei* in Greek LAE (the Apocalypse of Moses) in 10 (2x); 12 (2x); 33; and 35.[61] In 10, Eve upbraids a wild animal for "attacking" (πολεμέω) her son and exclaims:

O you evil beast, do you not fear to attack the image of God (τὴν εἰκόνα τοῦ θεοῦ)? . . . How did you not remember your subjection, for you were once subjected to the image of God (ὅτι πρότερον ὑπετάγης τῇ εἰκόνι τοῦ θεοῦ/ 10.3)?

This text represents part of a myth in which, following Eve's disobedience to God's commandment (10.2), the animals over which humanity were originally set begin to rebel. Indeed, this rebellion is interpreted precisely as the animal kingdom's improper insubordination to the vicegerents of God: the *imagines Dei*. The instances of the *imago Dei* in 12 (2x), moreover, depend entirely upon this story and do not add materially to our investigation.

In 33.5, following Adam and Eve's sin, the angels beseech the God of Israel on behalf of Adam and pray: "Holy Jael, forgive, for he is your image, and the work of your holy hands (ὅτι εἰκών σου ἐστὶν καὶ ποίημα τῶν χειρῶν σου τῶν ἁγίων)." In relation to this text, I make two points. (1) Here, as in the case of 4 Ezra 8.44, the *imago Dei* seems principally to convey the supreme value of human beings.[62] (2) It is *possible*, furthermore, that the expression "the work of your holy hands" forms a deliberate contrast with the stereotypical characterization of idols in the biblical tradition, which are "the work of *human* hands" (e.g., 2 Kgs. 19.18; 2 Chr. 32.19; Ps. 115.4; 135.15; Isa. 37.19; and cp. Wis. 13.10). With respect to the text of 35.2, it merely refers back to this episode.

2 Enoch 65.2[63]

And then he put together man in his own image, and put into him eyes to see and ears to hear, the heart to reflect and the mind to deliberate.

While the above is the only instance of the actual *imago Dei* language in 2 Enoch, it probably looks back to 2 Enoch 44.1–3:

The LORD with his own two hands created mankind; in a facsimile of his own face, both great and small, the LORD created them. And whoever insults a person's face, insults the face of a king, and treats the face of the LORD with repugnance.

The texts begins with a probable allusion to Genesis 2.7 ("with his own two hands"; cp. e.g., Ps. 119.73; 138.8; and Isa. 64.8) and then to Genesis 1.26 ("a facsimile of his own face").[64] Indeed, the immediate connection with kingship ("insults the face of a king") possibly reflects an interpretation of the *imago Dei* in Genesis 1.26: that is, that serving as the *imago Dei* entails ruling the world on God's behalf.[65]

In any case, I make the following points. (1) Though 2 Enoch will go on explicitly to refer to the *imago Dei* (65.2), it is likely that the language of "a facsimile of his [God's] own face" was chosen so as more graphically to depict the theological and ethical implications of the *imago Dei*. Indeed, to insult a human "face" is to insult the "face" of God.[66] (2) Relatedly, the point of the *imago Dei* theology of 65.2 seems to be that humans were created with unique capacities—"eyes to see and ears to hear, the heart to reflect and the mind to deliberate"—so as both to be uniquely associated with the one God and to be his unique instruments in the world.

Testament of Naphtali 2.2–5[67]

(2.2) For just as a potter knows the pot, how much it holds, and brings clay for it accordingly, so also the Lord forms the body in correspondence to the spirit (οὕτω καὶ ὁ Κύριος πρὸς ὁμοίωσιν τοῦ πνεύματος ποιεῖ τὸ σῶμα), and instills the spirit corresponding to the power of the body. (2.3) And from one to the other there is no discrepancy, not so much as a third of a hair, for all the creation of the Most High was according to height, measure, and standard. (2.4) And just as the potter knows the use of each vessel and to what it is suited, so also the Lord knows the body to what extent it will persist in goodness, and when it will be dominated by evil. (2.5) For there is no form or conception (πᾶν πλάσμα καὶ πᾶσα ἔννοια) which the Lord does not know since he created every human being according to his own image (πάντα γὰρ ἄνθρωπον ἔκτισε κατ' εἰκόνα ἑαυτοῦ).

As Kee notes, this is not the only evidence of the Testament of Naphtali's interest in "physiognomy."[68] In particular, the text argues that, when God creates human beings, he is especially concerned with the fitting correspondence between the physical body and the spirit which imbues that body. Indeed, the way in which the author expresses this point, and the way in which this itself reflects a remarkably creative adaptation of Genesis 1.26, is striking. As in the cases of 4Q504, frag. 8, col. 1.4; 4Q417, frag. 2, col. 1.15–18; LAE 13.3; and Sibylline Oracles 3.8–10, Testament of Naphtali 2.5 reflects a conflated reading of Genesis 1.26 and 2.7, a conflation which is evident in the close combination of πλάσμα (so LXX Gen. 2.7: καὶ ἔπλασεν ὁ θεὸς τὸν ἄνθρωπον . . .) and the clear allusion to Genesis 1.26 (so LXX Gen. 1.26: κατ' εἰκόνα). When we join this observation with the fact that in 5.2 the author states that "the Lord forms the body in correspondence to the spirit (οὕτω καὶ ὁ Κύριος πρὸς ὁμοίωσιν τοῦ πνεύματος ποιεῖ τὸ σῶμα)"—particularly noting the use of πρὸς ὁμοίωσιν—we are right to see this latter text as another allusion to Genesis 1.26 (so LXX Gen. 1.26: καθ' ὁμοίωσιν) and so to see the whole passage as a creative adaptation of this biblical tradition. Particularly noteworthy are the following points. (1) In this text, the "correspondence" (ὁμοίωσις) is no longer between God and humanity but between each individual person's body and spirit. (2) I contend, following van Kooten's suggestion, that the reflexive pronoun in the phrase "πάντα γὰρ ἄνθρωπον ἔκτισε κατ' εἰκόνα ἑαυτοῦ" refers *not* to *God's* own image but to some (semi-Platonic ideal?) "image" of each individual person.[69]

Pseudo Phocylides 1.100–06[70]

(1.100) Do not dig up the grave of the deceased, nor expose to the sun
(1.101) what may not be seen, lest you stir up the divine anger.
(1.102) It is not good to dissolve the human frame;
(1.103) for we hope that the remains of the departed will soon come to the light
(1.104) out of the earth; and afterward they will become gods (ὀπίσω δὲ θεοὶ τελέθονται).
(1.105) For the souls (ψυχαὶ) remain unharmed among the deceased.
(1.106) For the spirit is a loan of God to mortals, and (his) image (πνεῦμα γάρ ἐστι θεοῦ χρῆσις θνητοῖσι καὶ εἰκών).

Davila cautions that we cannot be certain of the Jewish provenance of this text. It might well come from a Gentile who is simply sympathetic to certain aspects of the Jewish tradition.[71] In any case, the reader is certainly jarred by the combination of apparently disparate themes. On the one hand, the first few verses ground a concern over the treatment of corpses upon the specifically Jewish belief in bodily resurrection.[72] On the other hand, vv. 105–06 betray a belief in the immortality of soul, which is here synonymous with God's spirit and conceived of as his image (cp. Wis. 2.22–23; and Philo, *Creation* 69).[73] Indeed, it is precisely because the soul/spirit is God's "image" that it will "remain unharmed among the deceased." Likewise, because the soul/spirit ultimately comes from, and belongs to, God, it is assured of an eventual reunification with God.[74] This seems to be the logic of 1.104: "afterward they will become gods."[75]

The text as a whole, therefore, betrays the influence of the Middle Platonic tradition.[76] It should also be noted, however, that the concept of the soul as a loan from the divine is also reflected in a few Jewish texts of the diaspora, which are themselves, at this point, influenced by Middle Platonism.[77] Moreover, as I have already indicated, the clear notion of bodily resurrection is of specifically Jewish provenance.[78] In any case, van Kooten is right to draw a comparison with the doctrine of the soul-as-God's-image in Wisdom 2.23-24.[79] However, he is wrong not to note the way in which these two texts combine the doctrine of the immortality of the soul (in the present) with the doctrine of a (future) bodily resurrection (so Wis. 3.7–8; and Ps. Phoc. 1.103–04).[80] Indeed, both texts ground *present* comfort in the doctrine of the immortality of the soul-as-God's-image (Wis. 2.23–24; Ps. Phoc. 1.105–06); however, both ground *future* hope in the doctrine of eventual bodily resurrection (Wis. 3.7–8; and Ps. Phoc. 1.103–04).

Pirke Avoth 3.14[81]

A He [Rabbi Akiba] would say, "Precious is the human being, who was created in the image [of God].
B he was created in the image [of God],
C as it is said, 'For in the image of God he made man.'"

As this is the only reference to the *imago Dei* in the Mishnah, and as it appears here within a string of other (apparently unrelated) traditions and without comment, it is not possible to offer detailed analysis of its meaning. I simply note the text for the sake of comprehensiveness.[82]

4Q504, frag. 8, col. 1.4[83]

[... Adam,] our father, you fashioned in the likeness of [your] Glory (יצרתה בדמות כבודכה) . . .

We have already noted this text above as possible evidence of a reading of Genesis 1.26 *via* Ezekiel 1.26–28. In this case, the author would be taking the Glory of the LORD (1.28)—which appeared in Ezekiel as "the likeness of the appearance of a human being (דמות כמראה אדם/ 1.28)"—as the "likeness" (דמות) according to which Adam was made. I also noted that the combination of the language of "likeness" (דמות) and "formed" (יצר), as in the cases of LAE 13.3; Sibylline Oracles 3.8–10; and Testament of Naphtali 2.5 (and 4Q417, frag. 2, col. 1.15–18 below), reflects a conflated reading of Genesis 1.26-27 and 2.7.

But now we consider the way in which this theme might relate to the well-known hope in the Scrolls of attaining "all the glory of Adam" (CD 3.20; 1QS 4.22–23; and 1QH 4.14–15/ כול כבוד אדם). Fletcher-Louis argues:

> [T]he notion of Adam's glory is best understood as an affirmation of a particular theological anthropology, rooted, not in the *Endzeit*, but in the *Urzeit*: because the true Israel are the true Adam and the Qumran community are the true Israel they possess all that Adam possessed before his departure from paradise. . . . [I]t is not simply a human "honour" or "dignity" that is in view, but a Glory which is God's own. The Qumran community believed, then, that it was their vocation to fulfil the responsibility given to Adam *to embody God's own Glory.*[84]

Fletcher-Louis further argues, because of the use of the language of "the likeness of [your] Glory" in an exposition of the creation of Adam, "[I]n 4Q504 frag. 8 Adam is identified in some way with the Glory occupying God's throne in Ezekiel 1."[85] Van Kooten likewise speaks of a "fusion" of these two figures.[86] This is all the more likely, so Fletcher-Louis and van Kooten claim, because Ezekiel describes the "likeness of the Glory of YHWH" as "the likeness of the appearance of *'ādām*" (1.26).[87]

Fletcher-Louis and van Kooten, however, have subtly but significantly misconstrued 4Q504, frag. 8, col. 1.4. The author has not "identified" or "fused" Adam with the enthroned figure of Ezekiel 1.26–28. Rather, reading Ezekiel 1.26–28 together with Genesis 1.26–27, the author has not unnaturally concluded that the enthroned figure of Ezekiel 1.26–28—"the likeness of the Glory of the LORD" (1.28)—must have been the figure *in whose image and likeness Adam himself was made in Genesis 1.26–28*.

But what should we make of the expression "all the glory of Adam" (CD 3.20; 1QS 4.22–23; and 1QH 4.14–15/ כול כבוד אדם)? Is Fletcher-Louis correct to suggest that it refers to Adam's responsibility "to embody God's own Glory." Or, is van Kooten right to argue that it primarily denotes a glorious luminosity: "this phrase, 'all the glory of Adam,' is indeed the contracted form of the view that Adam's glory reflects the brilliance of God's glory"?[88] The former proposal, I suggest, while not completely wrong, overdetermines the meaning of the phrase, while the latter does not well account for the texts in which it occurs.

Rather, in all three instances, the phrase "all the glory of Adam" functions as a convenient synecdoche, referring comprehensively to the whole range of features which many second-temple Jews would have associated with prelapsarian life in the garden of Eden, not the least of which were the enjoyment of God's presence and the sovereignty over the *kosmos*:

> Those who remained steadfast in it [the new covenant inaugurated by the advent of the Teacher of Righteousness; cf. CD 1.1–11] will acquire eternal life, and all the glory of Adam (כול כבוד אדם) is for them (CDª, col. 3.20).
>
> (4.18) God, in the mysteries of his knowledge and in the wisdom of his glory, has determined an end to the existence of injustice and on the appointed time
> (4.19) of the visitation he will obliterate it forever . . .

(4.20) Then God will refine, with his truth, all of humanity's deeds, and will purify for himself the structure of human beings, ripping out all spirit of injustice from the innermost part

(4.21) of their flesh, and cleansing them with the spirit of holiness from every wicked deed . . .

(4.22) For those God has chosen for an everlasting covenant

(4.23) and to them shall belong all the glory of Adam (כול כבוד אדם). . . . Until now the spirits of truth and injustice feud in the heart of human beings.

(4.25) For God has sorted them into equal parts until the appointed end and the new creation . . . (1QS, col. 4.18–25).[89]

(4.14) You [protect] the ones who serve you loyally, [so that] their posterity is before you all the days. You have raised an [eternal] name,

(4.15) [forgiving] offense, casting away all their iniquities, giving them as a legacy all the glory of Adam (כול כבוד אדם) [and] abundance of days (1QH, col. 4.14–15).[90]

Clearly, in these documents the phrase "all the glory of Adam" is stereotyped and formulaic. However, nothing in the immediate or larger context of these passages suggests that the phrase denotes an Adamic vocation "to embody God's own Glory."[91] Rather, as I stated above, the phrase seems to serve as a synecdoche for something like, "the glorious existence which God originally intended for Adam." In 1QS, however, there is a particular nuance to, if not an outright qualification of, this notion. In this text, "all the glory of Adam" functions within the larger schema of a dualistic anthropology and eschatology. As 1QS, col. 3.17–19 states, "(3.17) He created humanity to rule (3.18) the world and placed within him two spirits so that he would walk with them *until the moment of his visitation*: they are the spirits (3.19) of truth and of deceit." In other words, in 1QS "all the glory of Adam" is an eschatological glory which, in a sense, was not even available to Adam. It is a glory, rather, which will solely characterize those from whom God has ripped "all spirit of injustice from the innermost part" (1QS, col. 4.20) of their being. In this very specific sense, there will be a "new creation" (col. 4.25) in which the monistic anthropology of a humanity characterized solely by the "spirit of truth/holiness" (col. 4.21) will become a reality.[92]

4Q417, frag. 2, col. 1.15–18

(1.15) [A]nd a book of remembrance is written in his presence (1.16) for those who keep his word. And this is the vision of meditation and a book of remembrance. And he will give it as an inheritance to Adam/humanity/Enosh (אנוש) together with a spiritual people (רוח עם),[93] f[o]r (1.17) according to the pattern of the holy ones is his fashioning (כתבנית קדושים יצרו), but he did not give meditation (as) a witness to the spirit of flesh (רוח בשר), for it does not know the difference between (1.18) [goo]d and evil.[94]

Though this text nowhere refers to the "image" (or even to the "likeness") of God, I consider it here because the phrase "according to the pattern of the holy ones is his fashioning" betrays clear allusions to Genesis 1.26 (so כתבנית קדושים) and to 2.7 (so יצר).⁹⁵ However, not only is the text very lacunose but it possesses several contested features.⁹⁶ For instance, what is the meaning of אנוש (Adam/humanity/Enosh?); a "spiritual people"; תבנית ("pattern"?); קדושים ("holy ones"; "angels"?); and "the spirit of flesh"? Lange and Brooke, for instance, take אנוש to refer to the Enosh of Genesis 4.26; however, as the *DJD* editors note, this is quite improbable.⁹⁷ On the other hand, Collins and Goff prefer to see a reference to the Adam of Genesis 1–3.⁹⁸ Elgvin, however, followed by Wold, takes אנוש as a reference to humanity in general.⁹⁹ In this regard, I have found Collins and Goff most persuasive.¹⁰⁰ אנוש is best taken as a reference to the Adam of Genesis 1.26–27, who was, according to this text, "fashioned" (יצר) "according to the pattern of the holy ones (כתבנית קדושים)," the latter of which, furthermore, we should take as a reference to angels.¹⁰¹

In this regard, as Collins argues, this would mean that this text provides evidence of a reading of the plural pronouns of Genesis 1.26 ("*our* image"; "*our* likeness") in which they refer to God's heavenly court.¹⁰² This observation, as Collins, Goff, and van Kooten argue, provides us with a guide by which to interpret the rest of the fragment.¹⁰³ The text, therefore, expresses a dualistic anthropology grounded in the two creation accounts of Genesis 1 and 2. According to this construal, the "Adam" of Genesis 1.26, in whose inheritance "a spiritual people" (עם רוח) are promised a share, was "fashioned" (יצר) "according to the pattern of the holy ones/angels (כתבנית קדושים יצרו)." Clearly, "a spiritual people" is a reference to members of the community in good standing. They are, like the Adam of Genesis 1.26, patterned after the angels.¹⁰⁴ On the other hand, the "spirit of flesh" (רוח בשר) that "does not know the difference between [goo]d and evil" reflects an allusion to the creation account of Genesis 2.4–9.¹⁰⁵ Hereby, the author portrays those outside of the community as created not after the pattern of the angels but, rather, *à la* the second creation account of Genesis 2.4–3.24, an anthropogonical tradition in which humans do *not* have the crucial knowledge of "good and evil."¹⁰⁶

CONCLUSION: THE JEWISH *IMAGO DEI* TRADITION (APART FROM PHILO)

We leave our study of Philo for a later section, particularly because his thorough appropriation of philosophical cosmology and teleology is greatly illuminated by its contextualization within and in relation to the philosophical tradition. For now, I summarize our findings with respect to Jewish *imago Dei* tradition (apart from Philo). (1) The Tanakh provides us with only five instances of the *imago Dei*, all confined to Genesis (Gen. 1.26, 27; 5.1, 3; and 9.6). These texts are usually assigned to the so-called Priestly Source and/or Redaction, a tradition which, along with the Deuteronomistic tradition, was notoriously antipathetic toward polytheism, iconism, and various kinds of divine anthropomorphism.[107] In other words, although the instances in Genesis are cases of what we might call "theomorphism" (humans characterized with divine language) and only implicitly cases of anthropomorphism (gods characterized with human language), it is still likely to be the case that these instances of the *imago Dei* in the Priestly Tradition reflect a deliberate and audacious anthropological adaptation of Jewish idol polemics. Furthermore, following the general consensus, I have argued that the *imago Dei* theology of Genesis 1.26–27 reflects a universalization of ANE royal ideology. Moreover, the cases of the *imago Dei* in Genesis (Gen. 1.26, 27; 5.1, 3; and 9.6) presuppose that God already had an image according to which he then made Adam. Finally, following Curtis in particular, I have suggested that the paucity of the conception in the Tanakh might be explained by the fact that it was deemed too risky and too audacious to expound an "image anthropology" during a time period (preexilic) in which the large-scale threat of Jewish idolatry was ever present.

(2) Surprisingly, and despite important discussions of and allusions to the creation account (esp. 4Q504, frag. 8, col. 1.4; and 4Q417, frag. 2, col. 1.15–18), neither the Scrolls nor Josephus provide us with a single instance of the *imago Dei* language. Though the question is beyond our scope, it deserves consideration. (3) When and where the conception is attested, it is attested nine times in sources almost certainly of Jewish origin and likely of Palestinian provenance (Jub. 6.8; Sir. 17.3; 1 En. 106.10; LAB 3.11; 50.7; 4 Ezra 8.44; and Pir. Av. 3.14 [3x]), eight times in sources possibly of Jewish origin and/or of Palestinian provenance (T. Naph. 2.5; LAE 10 [2x]; 12 [2x]; 33; 35; and 2 En. 65.2), and (apart from Philo) five times in sources almost certainly from the diaspora (Wis. 2.23; 7.26; Sib. Or. 1.23; 3.8; and Ps. Phoc. 1.106). This gives us, then, excluding Genesis and the Philonic *corpus*, twenty-two explicit references to the *imago Dei* in second-temple Jewish literature. As I stated above, the lexeme εἰκών occurs 118 times in Philo, and many of the occurrences are in this connection. Paul, furthermore, adds another seven instances (Rom. 8.29; 1 Cor. 11.7; 15.49 [2x]; 2 Cor. 3.18; 4.4; Col. 1.15; and 3.10).

(4) Here I note the texts in which we can be reasonably confident that the *imago Dei* receives a "physical" or "spiritual" interpretation. In 1 Enoch 106.10, the *imago Dei* appears unambiguously to refer to a physical likeness, though this is probably presupposed in several other texts (Sib. Or. 1.22–24; LAE 10 [2x]; 12 [2x]; 33; and 35). Wisdom 2.22–23 and Pseudo-Phocylides 1.106, however, clearly give the *imago Dei* a nonphysical interpretation, the

former equating it with the "soul" and the latter with the "spirit." Though we will consider Philo in more detail below, here I note that he explicitly endorses a nonphysical interpretation of the *imago Dei*, thereby indicating that such an interpretation was well known:

> After all the rest, as I have said, Moses tells us that humanity was created according to the image and likeness of God (κατ' εἰκόνα θεοῦ καὶ καθ' ὁμοίωσιν). Right well does he say this, for nothing earth-born is more like God than man. Let no one represent the likeness as one to a bodily form (τὴν δ' ἐμφέρειαν μηδεὶς εἰκαζέτω σώματος χαρακτῆρι); for neither is God in human form, nor is the human body God-like (οὔτε γὰρ ἀνθρωπόμορφος ὁ θεός, οὔτε θεοειδὲς τὸ ἀνθρώπειον σῶμα.). But it is in respect of the mind, the sovereign element of the soul, that the word "image" is used (ἡ δὲ εἰκὼν λέλεκται κατὰ τὸν τῆς ψυχῆς ἡγεμόνα νοῦν).[108]

In this connection, I further note that unambiguously nonphysical interpretations of the *imago Dei all* come from diaspora sources, while unambiguously physical interpretations *all* come from what are likely Palestinian sources. This is unlikely to be coincidental. Rather, it probably reflects the fact that in Palestine and its immediate environs any theological-anthropological reflection—and no less reflection on the *imago Dei*—was less likely (than would have been the case in the diaspora) to come under the pressure of Greek anthropology, which almost certainly would have pushed toward an equation of the *imago Dei* with the "highest element" of humanity: the "soul" or "spirit." We now turn to consider instances of the *imago Dei* in the wider Greco-Roman world.

NOTES

1. Throughout this section, van Kooten, *PA*, 7–47, is a constant debate partner.
2. By "biblical," I refer to the Tanakh as represented by the Masoretic tradition, though I will at times consider versional evidence.
3. On the *imago Dei* in the Priestly Source/Redaction, see esp. Andreas Schüle, "Made in the 'Image of God': The Concepts of Divine Images in Gen 1–3" *ZAW* 117 (2005): 1–20; B. Janowski, "Die lebendige Statue Gottes: zur Anthropologie der priesterlichen Urgeschichte" in M. Witte, ed., *Gott und Mensch im Dialog: Festschrift für Otto Kaiser zum 80, Geburstag*, BZAW 345.1, vol. 1 (New York: de Gruyter, 2004), 183–214; W. R. Garr, *In His Own Image and Likeness: Humanity, Divinity and Monotheism*, CHANE 15 (Leiden: Brill, 2003); E. B. Firmage, "Genesis 1 and the Priestly Agenda" *JSOT* 82 (1999): 97–114; R. Hinschberger, "Image et ressemblance dans la tradition sacerdotale: Gen 1:26–8; 5:1–3; 9:6b" *RSR* 59 (1985): 185–99; W. Gross, "Die Gottebenbildlichkeit des Menschen im Kontext der Priesterschrift" *TQ* 161 (1981): 244–64; and Edward M. Curtis, "Image of God" in *ABD*

3.389: "all [references to the *imago Dei*] . . . are assigned to the Priestly source of the Pentateuch as proposed by most modern scholars."

4. The famously contested question of the use of the first-person plural pronouns here ("*our* image" and "*our* likeness") is beyond our scope. For the three major options—(1) the trinitarian explanation (so, e.g., Ep. Bar. 6.12; and Justin Martyr, *Dial.* 62); (2) the grammatical explanation (i.e., the so-called "majestic plural"); and (3) the heavenly court/angelic explanation—cf., e.g., John H. Walton, *Genesis*, NIVAC (Grand Rapids: Zondervan, 2001), 128–32; Gordon J. Wenham, *Genesis 1–15*, WBC 1 (Grand Rapids: Zondervan, 1987), 27–28; and Gerhard von Rad, *Genesis*, rev. edn., OTL (Philadelphia: Westminster John Knox, 1973 [1972]), 44–66. In the context of Genesis 1.26, Walton, *Genesis*, 129–30, is correct to prefer the "heavenly court/angelic" option, an interpretation which was, as we will see below, known in second-temple Judaism (cf. 4Q417, frag. 2, col. 1.15–18). On one occasion (*Flight* 68–69), Philo takes the plural to imply that, while God himself created governing reason (ὁ λογικός) within the human soul, he allowed his "powers" (δύναμις) to make "the mortal" (ὁ θνητός) portion of the soul. On another occasion (*Names* 30–31), the plurality allows Philo to explain the distinction between the good and the wicked, taking only the former to have been created by the one God.

5. So, e.g., Edward M. Curtis, *Man as the Image of God in Genesis in the Light of Ancient Near Eastern Parallels* (Ann Arbor: University of Michigan Microfilms International, 1984); Idem, "Image of God" in *ABD* 3.389–91; E. H. Merrill, "Image of God" in *DOTP* 441–45 (442–44); and G. Wittenberg, "The Image of God: Demythologization and Democratization in the Old Testament" *JTSA* 13 (1975): 12–23. More recently, see J. Richard Middleton, *The Liberating Image: The Imago Dei in Genesis 1* (Grand Rapids: Brazos Press, 2005), esp. chs. 3–5. For a history of research up to 1993, see esp. W. Gross, "Die Gottebenbildlichkeit des Menschen nach Gen 1,26.27 in der Diskussion des letzten Jahrzehnts" *BN* 68 (1993): 35–48.

6. So the references in the previous note.

7. For the monotheism of the Priestly Source, see, e.g., Jacob Milgrom, "Priestly ('P') Source" in *ABD* 5.454–61.

8. On the dating of P, on which there is wide consensus, see, e.g., Jan Christian Gertz, "The Partial Compositions," trans. by P. Altmann, in Jan Christian Gertz, Angelika Berlejung, Konrad Schmid, and Markus Witte, eds., *T & T Clark Handbook of the Old Testament: An Introduction to the Literature, Religion and History of the Old Testament* (New York: T & T Clark, 2012 [2008]), 293–382 (301).

9. Schüle, "Made in the 'Image of God,'" 2, italics original.

10. Curtis, "Image of God" in *ABD* 3.391, italics mine.

11. So also Ibid. 3.389; and Wenham, *Genesis*, 29–32, with a helpful discussion of opposing views.

12. So Curtis, "Image of God" in *ABD* 3.389; and Wenham, *Genesis*, 28–29.

13. On the possible range of meanings for ב and כ, cf. esp. P. Joüon & T. Muraoka, *A Grammar of Biblical Hebrew*, 2 vols. (Roma: Pontificio Istituto Biblico, 2003), 2.486–87, 490–91.

14. In this connection, not least on the basis of the similar function of ב and כ in these texts, I note Joüon & Muraoka, *A Grammar of Biblical Hebrew*, 2.487, n. 4: "כ is never used with the meaning *as* of ב *essentiae*." Cf. also, e.g., Wenham, *Genesis*,

29, italics original: "Thus Clines can argue that man was not created as an imitation of the divine image but to *be* the divine image. However, the interchangeability of the preposition ב and כ in Gen 5:1, 3, especially in connection with the words 'image' and 'likeness' makes this view untenable . . . ב here means 'according to, after the pattern of.'"

15. Cf. T. Muraoka, *A Greek-English Lexicon of the Septuagint* (Louvain: Peeters, 2009), 365.

16. For this suggestion, see esp. John F. Kutsko, "Ezekiel's Anthropology and Its Ethical Implications" in M. S. Odell & J. T. Strong, eds., *The Book of Ezekiel: Theological and Anthropological Perspectives*, SSSBL 9 (Atlanta: SBL, 2000), 119–41; and Idem, *Between Heaven and Earth: Divine Presence and Absence in the Book of Ezekiel*, BJSUCSD 7 (Winona Lake: Eisenbrauns, 2000), ch. 4; and van Kooten, *PA*, 2–5, with others cited in 3–5, nn. 6–7.

17. Noting Ezekiel 1.26–28 in this connection, see also Baillet in *DJD* 7, 162–63, from whom I take the reconstruction and translation. However, unlike Baillet, I have capitalized "Glory" so as to indicate that כבוד here refers to the manifest presence of Israel's God. Furthermore, I note the text's combination of יצר and דמות, a combination which likely reflects a conflated reading of Genesis 1.26 and 2.7 (cp. 4Q417, frag. 2, col. 1.15–18; LAE 13.3; Sib. Or. 3.8–10; and T. Naph. 2.5).

18. James R. Davila, *The Provenance of the Pseudepigrapha: Jewish, Christian, or Other?*, JSJSupp 105 (Leiden: Brill, 2005).

19. However, in this regard, Schwanz, *Imago Dei*, is still very valuable. Cf. also the classic treatment of Vladimir Lossky, *In the Image and Likeness of God*, new edn., trans. by Thomas E. Bird, eds. by Thomas E. Bird and John H. Erickson (New York: St Vladimir's Seminary Press, 2001 [1974]).

20. The instances in Syn. Pr. 7.34.6 and Apoc. Sed. 13.1–3 are likely too late to be included here. Cf. the discussions in D. A. Fiensy, "Hellenistic Synagogal Prayers" in *OTP* 2.671–76; and S. Agourides, "Apocalypse of Sedrach" in *OTP* 1.605–08, respectively.

21. So John J. Collins, "Sibylline Oracles" in *OTP* 1.415–7.

22. So Davila, *Provenance*, 232–33.

23. See the options listed by F. I. Andersen in *OTP* 1.95–97.

24. I note, however, the language of "likeness" (ὁμοίωσις) in Eph. 4.24 and Jam. 3.9 in likely allusions to Genesis 1.26.

25. There is no extant Hebrew text for this portion of Sirach. On the ancient Hebrew and versional evidence, cf. Patrick W. Skehan and Alexander A. Di Lella, *The Wisdom of Ben Sira: A New Translation with Notes, Introduction, and Commentary*, AB39 (New York: Doubleday, 1987), 51–62.

26. Neither Skehan and Di Lella, *Ben Sira*, 281–82; nor van Kooten, *PA*, 8–9, appear to notice this.

27. Cf. esp. Gary A. Anderson, *The Genesis of Perfection: Adam and Eve in Jewish and Christian Imagination* (Louisville: Westminster John Knox, 2001), 117–34.

28. So Skehan and Di Lella, *Ben Sira*, 282; van Kooten, *PA*, 8; and Levison, *Portraits*, 36–37, 47–48.

29. Without further comment, I note that τύπος is quite rare in LXX, occurring only four times and only once as a translation of צלם (LXX Amos 5.26).

30. E. Isaac, "1 (Ethiopic Apocalypse of) Enoch" in *OTP* 1.5–8 (1.7). Cf. also Loren T. Stuckenbruck, *1 Enoch 91–108*, CEJL (New York/Berlin: De Gruyter, 2007), 616; and George W. E. Nickelsburg, *1 Enoch 1: A Commentary on the Book of Enoch Chapters 1–36; 81–108*, ed. K. Baltzer, Hermeneia (Minneapolis: Fortress, 2001), 14.

31. So Isaac, "1 (Ethiopic Apocalypse of) Enoch" in *OTP* 1.6; Stuckenbruck, *1 Enoch 91–108*, 614–16; Nickelsburg, *1 Enoch 1*, 9–20. On 1Q19, see Barthélemy and Milik in *DJD* 1, 84–85. On 4Q204, frag. 5, col. 1; and 4Q204, frag. 5, col. 2, cf. esp. J. T. Milik with M. Black, *The Books of Enoch: Aramaic Fragments of Qumran Cave 4* (Oxford: Clarendon Press, 1976), 206–17, 352–53.

32. Matthew Black and Albert Marie Denis, *Apocalypsis Henochi Graece: fragmenta pseudepigraphorum quae supersunt graeca*, vol. 3 of *Pseudepigrapha veteris testamenti graece* (Leiden: Brill, 1970).

33. So Isaac, "1 (Ethiopic Apocalypse of) Enoch" in *OTP* 1.86–87.

34. On the text-critical issues at 1 Enoch 106.9–12, see esp. Stuckenbruck, *1 Enoch 91–108*, 644–54.

35. So e.g., Ibid. 607: "[T]he account presupposes the story of the fallen angels from heaven as found in the *Book of Watchers* (106:12; cf. 6:1–7:1)." Cf. also his *The Myth of Rebellious Angels*, 12–77, 103–19, and 281–326. This tradition served in some Jewish texts as an (at least partial) explanation of the problem of evil: so Stuckenbruck, *The Myth of Rebellious Angels*, 1–35.

36. van Kooten, *PA*, 12. Indeed, it is precisely the "impregnation of women on earth by the rebellious angels and the resulting births of giants [which] explains why the unusual appearance of Noah leads his father Lamech to suspect that he was fathered by one of these angels" (Stuckenbruck, *1 Enoch 91–108*, 607).

37. So Stuckenbruck, *1 Enoch 91–108*, 607–08; and Nickelsburg, *1 Enoch 1*, 539–40. However, Stuckenbruck rightly emphasizes that "Noah's significance is symbolic. . . . For the readers, then, the figure of Noah is a symbol of the righteous few who, in the course of eschatological events, will be rescued from divine destruction when it comes upon the wicked" (608).

38. So van Kooten, *PA*, 13.

39. On all of this, see D. J. Harrington, "Pseudo-Philo" in *OTP* 2.297–303.

40. The original language of the Sibyllina is Greek: so John J. Collins, "Sibylline Oracles" in *OTP* 1.317–22. Ibid. states that the "present collection of Sibylline oracles is composed of two distinct collections in manuscript" (320–01). For our purposes, we are only concerned with "the two manuscript groups usually referred to as φ and ψ [which] contains books 1–8" (321). Essentially, these two groups comprise four codices a piece, all of which date to ca. 15C. I cite the Greek from the critical reconstruction of J. Geffcken, *Die Oracula Sibyllina*, GCS 8 (Leipzig: 1902), of which Collins, "Sibylline Oracles," is a translation.

41. On the possible dates, see Collins, "Sibylline Oracles" in *OTP* 1.331–32; and on the provenance, see Idem, 1.332, who follows J. Geffcken, *Komposition und Entstehungszeit der Oracula Sibyllina*, repr., TU 23, NF 8.1 (Leipzig: 1967 [1902]), 50.

42. So Collins, "Sibylline Oracles" in *OTP* 1.360.

43. Cp. 4Q504, frag. 8, col. 1.4; 4Q417, frag. 2, col. 1.15–18; LAE 13.3; and T. Naph. 2.4–5.

44. So also van Kooten, *PA*, 27–28, though without noticing either the conflated reading of Genesis 1.26–27 and 2.7 or the clear allusion to the *Shema* in 3.11.

45. On all of this, see B. M. Metzger, "The Fourth Book of Ezra" in *OTP* 1.517–24. The earliest and principal Latin witness is Codex Sangermanensis, which dates to 822 CE. I depend upon the reconstruction of the Latin of R. L. Bensly, *The Fourth Book of Ezra, the Latin Version Edited from the MSS*, T&S 3.2 (Cambridge: 1895), of which Metzger, "The Fourth Book of Ezra" is a translation.

46. So also Levison, *Portraits*, 186.

47. For the date of the Wisdom of Solomon, David Winston, *The Wisdom of Solomon: A New Translation with Introduction and Commentary*, AB43 (New York: Doubleday, 1979), 20–25 (20), writes: "[V]arious scholars have placed it anywhere between 220 BCE and 50 CE." Greek was, furthermore, certainly the original language.

48. Some manuscripts read ἰδιότητος ("himself") instead of ἀϊδιότητος ("eternality"): cf. Winston, *Wisdom*, 121; and Joseph Ziegler, ed., *Sapientia Salomonis*, Septuaginta: Vetus Testamentum Graecum, Band 12.1 (Göttingen: Vandenhoeck & Ruprecht, 1981), 101–02, for the evidence. For our purposes, the distinction is not very significant. I note, furthermore, that the distinction involves a single α and could, therefore, be explained as a simple scribal blunder.

49. So also Marcus, "Son of Man as Son of Adam," 54.

50. The idea that the devil's jealous at least partly explains the enmity between him and humans is reflected in, e.g., 2 En. 31.3–6; 3 Bar. 4.8; t. Sot. 4.17; bt. Sot. 9b; br. 18.6; bt. Sanh. 59b; and Josephus, *Ant.* 1.41. However, none of these traditions explicitly ground this jealousy—as does LAE 12–16 and possibly Wis. 2.23–24—in the *imago Dei* tradition.

51. So Winston, *Wisdom*, 121; and *contra* Levison, *Portraits*, 51–52.

52. On Wisdom's appropriation of the philosophical tradition in general, see esp. Winston, *Wisdom*, 172–90; John J. Collins, *Jewish Wisdom in the Hellenistic Age*, OTL (Louisville: Westminster John Knox Press, 1997), 196–232; and Gregory Sterling, "The Role of Philosophy in the Thought of Paul" in Heilig et al., eds., *GFP*, 235–53 (243): "The point is that Wisdom used not only Stoic concepts but also Middle Platonic thought. It is important to remember this when thinking about Paul's appropriation of philosophy"; Idem, "The Love of Wisdom: Middle Platonism and Stoicism in the Wisdom of Solomon" in Troels Engberg-Pedersen, ed., *From Stoicism to Platonism: The Development of Philosophy 100 BCE—100 CE* (Cambridge: CUP, 2017), 198–213; and Cox, *By the Same Word*, 58–87. On the distinctively Middle Platonic character of 7.26, see Winston, *Wisdom*, 184–90; Collins, *Jewish Wisdom*, 199–200; Sterling, "The Love of Wisdom"; and Cox, *By the Same Word*, 64–69.

53. So Winston, *Wisdom*, 200–01; and Cox, *By the Same Word*, 71.

54. So Sterling, "The Role of Philosophy," 243.

55. So esp. Cox, *By the Same Word*, 66 (italics mine): "It may just be poetic embellishment or it may be an effort, in the midst of a cosmically immanent Sophia, *to preserve the transcendence of God*." Indeed, "Pseudo-Solomon keeps the physical world at arm's length from the deity, with the figure of Sophia very much in the middle" (66).

56. So Winston, *Wisdom*, 29–30; and van Kooten, *PA*, 36.

57. So Winston, Wisdom, 25–32; and van Kooten, *PA*, 36.

58. So esp. N. T. Wright, *The Resurrection of the Son of God*, vol. 3 of *Christian Origins and the Question of God* (Minneapolis: Fortress, 2003), 162–75.

59. On the tradition's fundamentally etiological function, see esp. Levison, *Portraits*, 185.

60. So also van Kooten, *PA*, 28–32; and Levison, *Portraits*, 174–84.

61. For the Greek text, I have used the critical edition of J. L. Sharpe, *Prolegomena to the Establishment of the Critical Text of the Greek Apocalypse of Moses*, Diss. (Duke University: 1969), from which Johnson, "Life of Adam and Eve," provides a translation. Sharpe works with sixteen Greek manuscripts, the earliest of which dates to ca. 11C.

62. So also Levison, *Portraits*, 186.

63. Second Enoch is preserved exclusively in Old Slavonic, with the oldest manuscript dating to ca. fourteenth century. It was likely originally composed in Hebrew, whence it was translated into Greek and then into Old Slavonic. The date is contested but F. I. Andersen, "2 (Slavonic Apocalypse of) Enoch" in *OTP* 1.91–100 (91), offers ca. late first-century CE. See Ibid. 91–100, for the previous information.

64. So Andersen, "2 (Slavonic Apocalypse of) Enoch" in *OTP* 171, nn. b and c; and van Kooten, *PA*, 32–35.

65. Neither in the previous note seem to notice this possibility.

66. So also Andersen, "2 (Slavonic Apocalypse of) Enoch" in *OTP* 171, n. b; and van Kooten, *PA*, 32–33.

67. For the Greek of the Testaments, we have five principal witnesses, the earliest of which is dated to ca. tenth century. For the Greek, I have made use of the critical edition of R. H. Charles, *The Greek Versions of the Testaments of the Twelve Patriarchs* (Oxford: 1908), of which H. C. Kee, "Testaments of the Twelve Patriarchs" in *OTP* 1.782–828, is a translation. Kee contends that the Testaments were originally composed in Greek and that the Aramaic fragments of the Testament of Levi and the Hebrew fragments of the Testament of Naphtali found at Qumran, as well as the demonstrably "much later Hebrew testaments of Judah and Naphtali," represent independent developments (776–77). Furthermore, Kee provides the date of ca. "the Maccabean period" (778). I note again, however, that Davila, *Provenance*, 5, 232, expresses doubts about the pre-Christian, Jewish provenance of this text. For the apparently independent Hebrew Testament of Naphtali found at Qumran (4Q215), cf. Michael E. Stone in *DJD* 22, 73–82.

68. So Kee, "Testaments of the Twelve Patriarchs" in *OTP* 1.811, n. 2a. On physiognomy in second-temple Jewish texts in general, see esp. M. Popovic, *Reading the Human Body: Physiognomics and Astrology in the Dei Sea Scrolls and Hellenistic-Early Roman Period Judaism*, STDJ 67 (Leiden: Brill, 2007).

69. So also van Kooten, *PA*, 40–41.

70. Pseudo-Phocylides is a pseudonymous Greek poem composed in Greek (Ionic) hexameter. Five principal Greek manuscripts survive, the earliest of which dates to ca. tenth century. It was likely composed sometime between 200 BCE and 200 CE in Alexandria. On all of this, see P. W. van der Horst, "Pseudo-Phocylides"

in *OTP* 2.565–73. I have made use of the critical edition of D. Young, *Theognis, Ps-Pythagoras, Ps.-Phocylides, Chares, Anonymi aulodia, fragmentum teleiambicum* (Leipzig, 1971), of which van der Horst, "Pseudo-Phocylides," is a translation.

71. So Davila, *Provenance*, 36–37, 232, 234. van der Horst, "Pseudo-Phocylides" in *OTP* 2.578, n. g., notes that some have taken the reference to "becoming gods" in 1.104 to betray either Christian authorship or redaction. On "deification" in early Christian soteriology, see esp. Ben C. Blackwell, *Christosis: Engaging Paul's Soteriology with his Patristic Interpreters* (Grand Rapids: Eerdmans, 2016 [2011]), esp. xix–114; and Norman Russell, *The Doctrine of Deification in the Greek Patristic Tradition* (Oxford: OUP, 2004).

72. So van der Horst, "Pseudo-Phocylides" in *OTP* 2.757–58, nn. c–f; and Walter T. Wilson, *The Sentences of Pseudo-Phocylides*, CEJL (Berlin: de Gruyter, 2005), 144.

73. On the synonymity of ψυχή and πνεῦμα in second-temple diaspora literature, see e.g., Wis. 16.14; Philo, *Spec.* 1.295; and Josephus, *War* 3.374; and Idem, *Ant.* 11.240.

74. Wilson, *Pseudo-Phocylides*, 146–47, reasonably proposes that the conception of the soul as a "loan" from God might ultimately depend upon a passage from Plato's *Timaeus*: "His [the Supreme Principle's] children [lesser divinities] gave heed to their father's command and obeyed it. They took the immortal principle of the mortal living creature, and imitating their own maker, they borrowed from the *kosmos* portions of fire and earth and water and air, *as if meaning to pay them back*" (42E–43A).

75. Wilson, *Pseudo-Phocylides*, 146, cites Seneca, *Marc.* 23.1–2, in this connection: "[T]he souls that are quickly released from intercourse with men find the journey to the gods above most easy; . . . they fly back more lightly to the source of their being.. . ." This too likely looks back to Plato's famous discussion in the *Theaetetus* 176A–B: "[A]nd they [evils] cannot have their place among the gods, but must inevitably hover about mortal nature and this earth. Therefore we ought to try to escape from earth to the dwelling of the gods as quickly as we can; and to escape it to become like a god, so far as this is possible" (H. N. Fowler, LCL, slightly revised).

76. So Wilson, *Pseudo-Phocylides*, 3–39; and van der Horst, "Pseudo-Phocylides" in *OTP* 2.565–73.

77. Cf., e.g., Wis. 15.8; Philo, *Cher.* 117–18; Idem, *Giants* 12–13; Idem, *Heir.* 104–05; Idem, *Spec.* 1.295; Josephus, *War* 3.372–75. A similar though not equivalent point can be found in Philo, *Post.* 5; 1 En. 51.1; LAB 3.10; and 33.3.

78. So Wilson, *Pseudo-Phocylides*, 145: "This is one of the few sections of the poem that clearly reveals its Jewish origins"; and van der Horst, "Pseudo-Phocylides" in *OTP* 2.578, n. f.

79. So van Kooten, *PA*, 37.

80. *Contra* Ibid. Cf. E. Peuch, *La croyance des Esséniens en la vie future: immortalité, résurrection, vie éternelle? Histoire d'une croyance dans le Judaisme ancien*, 2 vols. (Paris: Cerf, 1993), 158–62. Cf. also n. 277.

81. The translation is taken from Jacob Neusner, *The Mishnah: A New Translation* (New Haven: YUP, 1988), 680.

82. The text is not noted in van Kooten, *PA*.

83. Reconstruction and translation are from Baillet in *DJD* 7, 162–63. However, unlike Baillet, I have capitalized "Glory" so as to indicate that כבוד here refers to the manifest presence of Israel's God.

84. Fletcher-Louis, *All the Glory of Adam: Liturgical Anthropology in the Dead Sea Scrolls*, STDJ 42 (Leiden: Brill, 2002), 97, italics mine.

85. Ibid. 92–93.

86. van Kooten, *PA*, 16.

87. So Fletcher-Louis, *All the Glory of Adam*, 92–93; and Ibid.

88. van Kooten, *PA*, 21.

89. The textual and tradition-history of CD and 1QS, as well as the communities which they might reflect, is complex and contested. See esp. John J. Collins, *Beyond the Qumran Community: The Sectarian Movement of the Dead Sea Scrolls* (Grand Rapids: Eerdmans, 2010), 1–87.

90. The reconstruction and translation of all of these texts are from Martínez and Tigchelaar, eds., *The Dead Sea Scrolls*.

91. *Contra* Fletcher-Louis, *All the Glory of Adam*, 97.

92. So also van Kooten, *PA*, 18–20. On the dualistic anthropology of the Scrolls more generally, see e.g., Géza G. Xeravitis, *Dualism in Qumran*, LSTS 208 (New York/London: T & T Clark, 2010), esp. chs. 5–8.

93. I have here reproduced a superscripted עם to reflect the manuscript: so Martínez and Tigchelaar, *The Dead Sea Scrolls*, 2.858.

94. On this text, see also J. Strugnell, D. Harrington, T. Elgvin, and J. Fitzmyer in *DJD* 34, 143–210, whose translation, though not reconstruction, differs slightly from Martínez and Tigchelaar, *The Dead Sea Scrolls*, 2.859.

95. So also B. G. Wold, *Women, Men, and Angels: The Qumran Wisdom Document Musar leMevin and Its Allusions to Genesis Creation Traditions*, WUNT 2.201 (Tübingen: Mohr Siebeck, 2005), 124–49 (148); hereby, as in the cases of 4Q504, frag. 8, col. 1.4; LAE 13.3; Sib. Or. 3.8–10; and T. Naph. 2.5, the text reflects a conflated reading of Gen. 1.26–27 and 2.7.

96. See esp. Wold, *Women, Men, and Angels*, 97–102, 124–49. On angels more generally in the Scrolls, cf., e.g., Maxwell Davidson, *Angels at Qumran: A Comparative Study of 1 Enoch 1–36, 72–108 and Sectarian Writings from Qumran* (Leiden: Brill, 1992).

97. A. Lange, *Weisheit und Prädestination: Weisheitliche Urordnung und Prädestination in den Textfunden von Qumran*, STDJ 18 (Leiden: Brill, 1995), 87–88; and George J. Brooke, "Biblical Interpretation in the Wisdom Texts from Qumran" in C. Hempel, A. Lange, and H. Lichtenberger, eds., *The Wisdom Texts from Qumran and the Development of Sapiential Thought: Studies in the Wisdom at Qumran and Its Relationship to Sapiential Thought in the Ancient Near East, the Hebrew Bible, Ancient Judaism and the New Testament*, BETL 159 (Louvain: Peeters, 2001), 201–20 (213). Cf. Strugnell, Harrington, Elgvin, & Fitzmyer in *DJD* 34, 164.

98. So John J. Collins, "In the Likeness of the Holy Ones: The Creation of Humankind in a Wisdom Text from Qumran" in D. W. Parry and E. C. Ulrich, eds., *The Provo International Conference on the Dead Sea Scrolls: Technological Innovations, New Texts, and Reformulated Issues*, STDJ 30 (Leiden: Brill, 1999), 609–18

(610–12); and M. J. Goff, *The Worldly and Heavenly Wisdom of 4QInstruction*, STDJ 50 (Leiden: Brill, 2003), 95–99.

99. So T. Elgvin, "The Mystery to Come: Early Essene Theology of Revelation" in Cryer and Thompson, eds., *Qumran between the Old and New Testaments*, JSOT-Sup 290 (Sheffield: SAP, 1998), 113–50 (142–43); and Wold, *Women, Men, and Angels*, 138–49.

100. So also van Kooten, *PA*, 32–37.

101. So also Wold, *Women, Men, and Angels*, 145–49; Lange, *Weisheit und Prädestination*, 86; Collins, "In the Likeness of the Holy Ones," 613–14; and *contra* Elgvin, "The Mystery to Come," 142, who takes קדושים, on a parallel with רוח עם, as a reference to the community as "holy people."

102. So Collins, "In the Likeness of the Holy Ones," 615; and van Kooten, *PA*, 23.

103. So Collins, "In the Likeness of the Holy Ones," 616–17; Goff, *The Worldly and Heavenly Wisdom*, 94–99; and van Kooten, *PA*, 23–27.

104. On the community's very close association with, and imitation of, angels, see esp. Cecilia Wassen, "Angels and Humans: Boundaries and Synergies" in Flint, Duhaime, and Baek, eds., *Celebrating the Dead Sea Scrolls*, 523–39 (533–37); and Devorah Dimant, "Men as Angels: The Self-Image of the Qumran Community" in A. Berlin, ed., *Religion and Politics in the Ancient Near East*, STJHC (Potomac: University Press of Maryland, 1996), 93–103, both of which cite the key texts. On angels as priests within the heavenly temple in the Scrolls, see esp. the critical edition: Carol Newsom, *Songs of the Sabbath Sacrifice: A Critical Edition*, HSS 27 (Atlanta: Scholars Press, 1985); and Idem, "'He Has Established for Himself Priests': Human and Angelic Priesthood in the Qumran Sabbath Shirot" in L. Schiffman, ed., *Archaeology and History in the Dead Sea Scrolls: The New York University Conference in Memory of Yigael Yadin*, JSPSup 8 (Sheffield: JSOT Press, 1990), 101–20.

105. I, therefore, disagree with Wold, *Women, Men, and Angels*, 131–49; and van Kooten, *PA*, 25–27, when they argue that 4Q417, frag. 2, col. 1.15–18, expresses a dualistic anthropology in which humanity is *eventually*, though not from their creation, divided into "a spiritual people" and a "fleshly people." In this regard, I note a crucial distinction with 1QS, col. 4.18–25. This latter text expresses an anthropology in which *every* human being is created with the "spirit of truth" and the "spirit of injustice," such that individual human beings might follow the one or the other. Contrastively, in 4Q417, frag. 2, col. 1.15–18, we find a much more deterministic anthropogony in which *some* are created *à la* Gen. 1.26–27 and *others* are created *à la* Gen. 2.4–9. So also Goff, *The Worldly and Heavenly Wisdom*, 99.

106. On all of this, see Collins, "In the Likeness of the Holy Ones," 616–17; Goff, *The Worldly and Heavenly Wisdom*, 94–99; and van Kooten, *PA*, 23–27.

107. Cf., e.g., Jacob Milgrom, "Priestly ('P') Source" in *ABD* 5.454–61.

108. Philo, *Creation*, 69 (Colson and Whitaker, LCL, slightly revised).

Chapter 5

The *Imago Dei* in the Greco-Roman World

ANCIENT PHILOSOPHY

The last thirty years or so has witnessed a proliferation of work on the question of Paul's relationship to ancient philosophy.[1] This study, however, is principally concerned with the *imago Dei*. As such, any contribution that I might make to this larger debate is welcome but ultimately indirect.

In what follows, I provide a brief survey of the relevant components of the ancient philosophy of ca. 100 BCE to ca. 200 CE so as better to situate my analysis of the *imago Dei* tradition(s). As is routinely recognized, the period under discussion is very difficult to characterize. While some scholars speak of "the Middle Platonic" period, others prefer the labels "The Eclectic Period" or "the Transitional Period."[2] Engberg-Pedersen well describes the complex situation:

> One thing particularly striking about the Transitional Period is that almost all philosophers within the period to some degree adopted ideas from philosophies other than their own. . . . What we find is that many philosophers who were basically Stoics . . . also drew on ideas that had a specifically Platonic pedigree. Conversely, many philosophers who were basically Platonists . . . also drew on ideas that had a specifically Stoic pedigree.[3]

John Dillon goes as far as to say:

> In fact, a wide range of terms and concepts had already by the beginning of the first century B.C. become virtually common currency, and in later times there was really no sense of their ultimate provenance.[4]

Michael Frede explains the historical phenomenon which precipitated this situation:

> It seems that Sulla's conquest of Athens in 87 BC had a devastating effect on philosophy in Athens. . . . The consequences of this are easy to see. The diffusion of philosophers and the emergence of a variety of centres of philosophical study encouraged a proliferation of philosophical positions, fostered separate and independent developments, and undermined the unity of the position of the school. . . . This goes some way to explain the absence of clear contours in the history of the philosophy done in the period from 125 BC to 250 AD. . . . To some extent it was arbitrary how somebody was classified.[5]

In light of this complex state of affairs, Engberg-Pedersen rightly captures a crucial feature of the philosophy of this period:

> [W]hat he [D. Sedley] actually shows is that such syncretism should be understood not as an act of blending or bringing ideas together in a great melting pot, but in a rather more specific manner as a strategy of "reclaiming" or "absorbing" ideas from a philosophy other than one's own into one's own philosophy. The syncretism does not erase the differences between any two philosophies. Nor does it in any way imply that a given philosopher is no longer either a Stoic or a Platonist (or again, a Christian). On the contrary, it is precisely while being either this or that that one may also "reclaim" or "absorb" foreign ideas into one's own philosophy.[6]

While I prefer the language of "appropriation" or "adaptation" to the language of "syncretism" or "absorption," the point is well stated. For our purposes, the crucial thing to note is that when an author of this period appears to make use of a tradition which is ultimately of, for example, Middle Platonic provenance, this does not straightforwardly indicate that the author in question is a Middle Platonist. Each author's position must be appreciated on its own terms. Therefore, even though I myself will argue that Paul made use of certain features of Middle Platonism, I will also argue that his use of these features is quite unlike the use of the same features by *any author* in that tradition.

We should also bear in mind that the "philosophy" of this period was not only an academic discipline but a popular topic with which many would have been reasonably conversant.[7] This philosophy was, moreover, regularly divided into three separate, but related, branches: "physics," "ethics," and "logic."[8] Of particular concern to us is "physics." In this regard, Dillon states,

> The distinction [in our period] is between a completely transcendent . . . and an active demiurgic one ["god"]. The later Platonists adopted the Stoic Logos into their system as the active force of God in the world. . . . In Philo, partly,

no doubt, because of his strongly monotheistic inclinations, we have a contrast rather between God and his Logos than between a first and second God.[9]

Furthermore, it is important to note the way in which the "physics" of this period, which also included what we call "metaphysics," related to philosophical teleology. In the regard, Sterling's summary is especially illuminating:

> [T]he Hellenistic schools formulated different goals that can be quite revealing. . . . The Stoics argued that an individual should live "according to nature" (κατὰ φύσιν), understanding nature in panentheistic terms.[10] Middle Platonists picked up a phrase from Plato's *Theaetetus* and made "likeness to god" (ὁμοίωσις θεῷ) the ultimate aim.[11] Neopythagoreans had a similar although different formulation; they made the tag "follow God" (ἕπου θεῷ) their goal.[12] Epicureans made "pleasure" (ἡδονή) the ultimate aim, although it was pleasure in the sense of freedom from disturbance. . . .[13] In this way the Epicureans made the goal likeness to the gods who were unperturbed. *The point is that the Stoics, Middle Platonists, Neopythagoreans, and Epicureans all made life in harmony with god(s) the basic goal of their systems. There was a common ground between Paul and the Hellenistic philosophical systems that should not be missed.*[14]

Below we will focus particularly upon the Middle Platonic *telos* of "likeness to god" and the way in which this became associated with the *imago Dei*.

THE *IMAGO DEI* IN THE GRECO-ROMAN WORLD

In the survey which follows, I have four particular aims,[15] (1) to demonstrate that the *imago Dei* conception was a well-known feature of Greco-Roman imperial and philosophical thought; (2) to show that the conception was sometimes especially associated with Plato's teleological doctrine of "likeness to god," as is the case in Philo and Plutarch (and Clement of Alexandria); (3) to demonstrate that Philo (like the author of Wisdom) reflects a particular reading of Genesis 1.26 in which he takes the cosmogonical *logos* to be the protological image according to which Adam himself was made; and, finally, (4) in this latter connection, to demonstrate that Philo's *logos* speculation and Wisdom's *sophia* speculation, not least in the way in which they both reflect the appropriation of Middle Platonic intermediary doctrine, significantly illuminate Paul's *imago Dei* theology.

The Imago Dei and Cosmology

We begin with Plato's *Timaeus*, a text which proved to be the most formative in subsequent discussions of philosophical cosmology,[16]

> Now the whole Heaven, or Cosmos (πᾶς οὐρανὸς ἢ κόσμος) ... which has come into existence must necessarily, as we say, have come into existence by reason of some Cause. ... Again, if these premises be granted, it is wholly necessary that this Cosmos should be an image of something (Τούτων δὲ ὑπαρχόντων αὖ πᾶσα ἀνάγκη τόνδε τὸν κόσμον εἰκόνα τινὸς εἶναι).[17]

Here I only note that Plato calls the *"kosmos"* an εἰκών ("image"), something which he states even more explicitly near the end of the *Timaeus*:

> And now at length we may say that our discourse concerning the All (περὶ τοῦ παντός) has reached its termination. For this our Cosmos (ὁ κόσμος) has received the living creatures both mortal and immortal and been thereby fulfilled; it being itself a visible Living Creature embracing the visible creatures, an image of the Intelligible, a perceptible god (εἰκὼν τοῦ νοητοῦ θεὸς αἰσθητός), most great and good and fair and perfect in its generation—even this one Heaven sole of its kind (εἷς οὐρανὸς ὅδε μονογενὴς ὤν).[18]

Here we see that Plato's *"kosmos,"* which he also calls "Heaven," is "an image of the Intelligible, a perceptible god." It is also, furthermore, and for this very reason, μονογενής ("unique"; cf. also *Tim.* 31). In other words, this is an "intermediary doctrine" in which the *kosmos*, as an image of Plato's "Intelligible" (the "ideal world" beyond sense perception), is the "unique" (μονογενής) intermediary between Plato's ideal world (beyond sense perception) and the world of sense perception. That is why it is called "an image of the Intelligible, a *perceptible* god (θεὸς αἰσθητός)."[19] The basic structure of this formulation, by a route which is now untraceable to us, made its way not only into Philo's writings and the Wisdom of Solomon but also into the prologues of the Gospel of John (1.14, 18) and the letter to the Hebrews (1.6), as well as into two of Paul's letters (Rom. 8.29; Col. 1.15).[20]

In *On the Confusion of Tongues*, after referring to the *logos* as God's πρωτόγονος ("firstborn"), Philo states that "the ancient *logos* is God's image (θεοῦ γὰρ εἰκὼν λόγος ὁ πρεσβύτατος)" (146–47). Furthermore, in Wisdom's exposition of *sophia*, just before referring to *sophia* as "an image of his goodness (εἰκὼν τῆς ἀγαθότητος αὐτοῦ)" (7.26), the text states, "There is in her a spirit that is intelligent, holy, μονογενές ..." (7.22).[21] As a part of the famous *logos* theology of John's prologue, John states that the *logos* had a "glory as of μονογενοῦς παρὰ πατρός" (1.14), and he then goes on to call this *logos* "μονογενὴς θεός" (1.18). At the beginning of the letter to the Hebrews, after referring to Jesus as the "reflection of his [God's] glory" (ἀπαύγασμα τῆς δόξης/ cp. Wis. 7.26), the writer shortly after calls him the πρωτότοκος ("firstborn"). Similarly, in Romans 8.29 and Colossians 1.15, Paul refers to Jesus as the "image" of God and then immediately as the πρωτότοκος ("firstborn"). The instance of Colossians 1.15–16 is particularly telling because

Paul provides an explanatory clause which explains the appropriateness of the designation: "*because* by him all things were created (ὅτι ἐν αὐτῷ ἐκτίσθη τὰ πάντα)" (1.16). Of course, these texts all have their particular nuances, the careful study of which is beyond our scope.[22] I simply note that, as Cox in particular has demonstrated, all of these texts, in their different ways, reflect adaptations of Middle Platonic intermediary doctrine.[23]

Now, with this question behind us for the moment, I quote the text in which Plato put forward his famous doctrine of "likeness to god":

> Therefore, we ought to try to escape from earth to the dwelling of the gods as quickly as we can; and to escape is to become like god, so far as this is possible (φυγὴ δὲ ὁμοίωσις θεῷ κατὰ τὸ δυνατόν); and to become like god is to become righteous and holy, with wisdom (ὁμοίωσις δὲ δίκαιον καὶ ὅσιον μετὰ φρονήσεως γενέσθαι).[24]

As Dillon in particular has demonstrated and as we will see below, Plato's doctrine of "likeness to god" was accepted by many in the subsequent philosophical traditions as the proper *telos* of true philosophy.[25]

The *Imago Dei* and the King

We now turn to consider the imperial *imago Dei* tradition. The idea that the king, and the king alone, served as God's image was a well-known feature of ancient imperial thought. In fact, what is possibly our earliest evidence of the *imago Dei* language reflects this usage. The text is preserved in Plutarch, who claims that his material comes from the fourth-century-BCE philosopher and tutee of Aristotle, Phaenias of Eresus:

> [T]hemistocles, thus at the threshold of the dreadful ordeal, had audience first with Artabanus the Chiliarch, or Grand Vizier, and said that he was a Hellene, and that he desired to have an audience with the King on matters which were of the highest importance and for which the monarch entertained the most lively concern. Whereupon the Chiliarch replied: "O Stranger, men's customs differ; different people honor different practices; but all honor the exaltation and maintenance of their own peculiar ways. Now you Hellenes are said to admire liberty and equality above all things; but in our eyes, among many fair customs, this is the fairest of all, to honor the King, and to pay obeisance to him as the image of that god who is the preserver of all things (τιμᾶν βασιλέα, καὶ προσκυνεῖν ὡς εἰκόνα θεοῦ τοῦ τὰ πάντα σώζοντος)."[26]

Of particular note here is the way in which this text associates the *imago Dei* with the preservation and maintenance of "all things." Just as in Genesis 1.26–28 and several other of the Jewish texts we have surveyed, there is a tight connection between serving as God's image and exercising sovereignty over the *kosmos*.

We also possess epigraphic evidence of the imperial *imago Dei* tradition. For example, coming within a long succession of reverential epithets, Ptolemy V Epiphanes (210–180 BCE) is referred to as "εἰκόνος ζώσης τοῦ Διός ('living image of Zeus')."²⁷

For our purposes, one of the most crucial texts comes from Plutarch, in which he demonstrates that the imperial *imago Dei* tradition and the philosophical *imago Dei* tradition could be joined and that the latter could be associated with Plato's teleological doctrine of likeness to god:

> Now justice is the aim and end of law, but law is the work of the ruler, and the ruler is the image of god who orders all things (δίκη μὲν οὖν νόμου τέλος ἐστί, νόμος δ' ἄρχοντος ἔργον, ἄρχων δ' εἰκὼν θεοῦ τοῦ πάντα κοσμοῦντος). Such a ruler needs no Pheidias nor Polycleitus nor Myron to model him, but by his virtue he forms himself in the likeness of god (εἰς ὁμοιότητα θεῷ) and thus creates a statue most delightful of all to behold and most worthy of divinity (αὐτὸς αὑτὸν εἰς ὁμοιότητα θεῷ δι' ἀρετῆς καθιστὰς καὶ δημιουργῶν ἀγαλμάτων τὸ ἥδιστον ὀφθῆναι καὶ θεοπρεπέστατον). . . . [The ruler is] one who, possessing god's *logos* (θεοῦ λόγον ἔχων), establishes, as his likeness and luminary, intelligence in place of sceptre.²⁸

We note two features of this remarkable text.²⁹ (1) Pheidias, Polycleitus, and Myron were all well-known sculptors here associated with the construction of cult images.³⁰ Therefore, this is another example of the tradition of comparing human "images" with cult "idols." (2) Furthermore and more importantly, this text demonstrates that Plutarch understood the possibility of becoming the image of god as synonymous with attaining "likeness to god" (εἰς ὁμοιότητα θεῷ), the latter of which involves a clear allusion to Plato's *Theaetetus* 176B. We will see that this connection is at least as old as Philo and, so I will argue, presupposed by Paul as well.

Humans as Images

I also note a text which, though coming sometime after Paul (ca. 2C), suggests that *imago Dei* traditions were widespread and well known. In an earlier writing titled *Essays in Portraiture*, Lucian of Samasota discussed the appropriateness of comparing human beings with the gods. Then, having apparently received criticism for such a discussion, he defended his views as follows:

> It is not incumbent upon you, then, to be thus timorous in respect of praise. If any offense at all has been perpetrated against divinity in that essay, you are not

accountable for it—unless you think that to listen makes one accountable; it is I whom the gods will punish, after first punishing Homer and the other poets! But to this day they have not punished the best of the philosophers for saying that man was God's image (ἀλλ' οὐδέπω οὐδὲ τὸν ἄριστον τῶν φιλοσόφων ἠμύναντο εἰκόνα θεοῦ τὸν ἄνθρωπον εἰπόντα εἶναι)![31]

Though we should allow for the element of hyperbole, this text indicates that "image anthropology" was probably widespread and well known.

Philo[32]

We now come to the *imago Dei* speculation of Philo of Alexandria, a Jewish writer whose use of the *imago Dei* sheds more light on Paul's than any writer we have so far considered. I note in particular that I am not especially concerned to expound Philo for his own sake, nor will I attempt to reconcile apparently disparate elements of his thought. As we will see, Philo has reading*s* of Genesis 1.26 and not simply *a* reading. Nevertheless, the reading which we will focus upon is no less illuminating for that. However, to be clear, in what follows I am *not* arguing that Philo's thought *in general* is illuminating for Paul's thought *in general*. Nor am I arguing that the particular Philonic texts which we will consider are characteristic of Philo's thought as a whole. That might or might not be the case; but, for our purposes, it is beside the point. Rather, I consider the Philonic texts below because they provide evidence of *possible* appropriations of the *imago Dei* in a writer roughly contemporary with Paul.

The Imago Dei *and the* Logos[33]

In the exposition of his intermediary *logos* doctrine, Philo refers to the *logos* as God's εἰκών a number of times.[34] In this connection, we begin by considering a few key texts in which he explicates elements of his cosmology in relation to Genesis 1.

> God's shadow is his *logos*, which he made use of like an instrument, and so made the world. But this shadow, and what we may describe as the representation, is the archetype (ἀρχέτυπον) for further creations. For just as God is the paradigm for the image (ὥσπερ γὰρ ὁ θεὸς παράδειγμα τῆς εἰκόνος), to which the title of Shadow has just been given, even so the image becomes the paradigm of other beings (οὕτως ἡ εἰκὼν ἄλλων γίνεται παράδειγμα), as the prophet made clear at the very outset of the Law-giving by saying, "And God made humanity according to the image of God (κατ' εἰκόνα θεοῦ)," implying that the image had been made such as representing God, but that the man was made according to the image when it had acquired the force of a paradigm (τοῦ δὲ ἀνθρώπου κατὰ τὴν εἰκόνα λαβοῦσαν δύναμιν παραδείγματος).[35]

Here we see several key elements of Philo's cosmology. He takes God himself as the archetype or paradigm of the *logos*, and he takes the *logos*—as an "image" of the archetypal God—as the archetype or paradigm of further things. He then reads Genesis 1.26 to the effect that God made humanity according to the paradigm of the *logos*.

In *Questions and Answers on Genesis*, Philo writes,

> Why does (Scripture) say, as if (speaking) of another God, "in the image of God he made man" [Gen. 9.6] and not "in his own image"? Most excellently and veraciously this oracle was given by God. For nothing mortal can be made in the likeness of the most high One and Father of the universe but (only) in that of the second god (δεύτερος θεός), who is his *logos*.[36]

Philo here wrestles with what he takes to be a certain peculiarity of Genesis 9.6. In that text, God speaks of "God" ("in the image of *God*") in the third person, as if, so Philo reasons, he were referring to "another God." However, so Philo assumes, this text certainly does not expound pagan polytheism. Therefore, he reasons, this text must refer to the *logos*. However, because (in his reading) the one God calls the *logos* "god/God" (Gr.: θεός), Philo concludes that the "most high One and Father" must have been referring to "the second god (δεύτερος θεός), who is his *logos*." Nevertheless, even though the language of (or similar language for) the "second god" for the "intermediate principal" is also attested in other Middle Platonic thinkers (so, e.g., Numenius, frag. 11–12; and Alcinous, *Epit.* 10),[37] and even though Philo here perhaps betrays a debt to that linguistic convention, we probably should not take this Philonic language as an infraction of his Jewish monotheism. Rather, Philo's use of θεός with reference to the *logos* is to be explained mainly on the basis that he is expounding his source text (Gen. 9.6).

"Form" and "Image"

We now come to three Philonic texts which are of enormous value in the assessment of Paul's *imago Dei* theology.[38] In *Special Laws* 1.327–29, Philo defends Plato's theory of Forms/Ideas:

> Some aver that the incorporeal Forms (ἀσωμάτους ἰδέας) are an empty name devoid of any real substance of fact, and thus they abolish in things the most essential element of their being, namely the archetypal paradigms (ἀρχέτυπον παράδειγμα) of all qualities in what exists, and on which the form and dimensions of each separate thing was modeled.... Could anything be more preposterous than this? For when out of that confused matter God produced all things, He did not do so with His own handiwork, since His nature, happy and blessed as it was, forbade that He should touch the limitless chaotic matter. Instead He

made full use of the incorporeal potencies well denoted by their name of Forms (αἱ ἰδέαι) to enable each kind to take its appropriate shape (μορφήν).³⁹

According to this text, the "Forms," as "archetypal paradigms," give to each thing its "shape."

Earlier in *Special Laws* (1.171), furthermore, Philo had argued that our "rational spirit (λογικός πνεῦμα)" was "formed according to the archetypal Form of the divine image (ἐμορφώθη πρὸς ἀρχέτυπον ἰδέαν εἰκόνος θείας)."⁴⁰ And the "divine image," moreover, not only elsewhere in Philo (*Creation* 25; *All. Int.* 3.96; *Heir* 231; *Quest.* 2.62; *Tong.* 97; 147; *Flight* 101; and *Dreams* 1.239) but also in *Special Laws* (1.81; 3.83, 207), is the *logos*: "And the image of God is the *logos* (λόγος δ' ἐστὶν εἰκὼν θεοῦ) through which the whole universe was framed" (*Spec. Laws* 1.81).⁴¹ Therefore, we have the following scenario in book 1 of Philo's *Special Laws*. (1) Because the one God could not "touch the limitless chaotic matter" (1.328), "He made full use of the incorporeal.... Forms to enable each kind to take its appropriate shape (μορφήν)" (1.329). In this sense, the one God is transcendent and beyond even (Philo's adaptation of) Plato's Forms. (2) The "archetypal" and "paradigmatic" (1.171, 327) "Form," moreover, is none other than the "divine image" (1.171), which is the *logos* (1.81; 3.83, 207). The paradigmatic *logos*-as-God's-image, therefore, as a cosmological and teleological adaptation of Plato's Forms, "forms" everything which comes into existence (1.171, 329).

That this reading is on target is confirmed by a similar passage in *Flight* (12):

> For the world has come into being, and assuredly it has done so under the hand of some cause;⁴² and the *logos* of him who makes it is himself the seal, by which each thing that exists has received its shape (μεμόρφωται). Accordingly from the outset form in perfection accompanies the things that come into being, for it is an impress and image of the perfect *logos* (εἰκὼν τελείου λόγου).⁴³

This cosmology, I suggest, in which the divine "image" functions as the pattern according to which other things are "formed" (μορφόω), provides the most plausible context within which to appreciate the logic and combination of Paul's εἰκών and μορφή language:

2 Cor. 3.18: "τὴν δόξαν κυρίου κατοπτριζόμενοι τὴν αὐτὴν εἰκόνα μεταμορφούμεθα ἀπὸ δόξης εἰς δόξαν."
Rom. 8.29: "προώρισεν συμμόρφους τῆς εἰκόνος τοῦ υἱοῦ αὐτοῦ."

In these texts, I contend, Paul reflects a similar adaptation of Middle Platonic intermediary doctrine. Jesus, the divine image, functions as the paradigmatic "form" for the rest of humanity. In Romans 8.29, to which we will come below, Paul states that God "predestined [humans] to share the same form as the image (συμμόρφους τῆς εἰκόνος) of his son." In 2 Corinthians 3.18, on the other hand, to which we will also come below, Paul contends that those in the Messiah are presently being "*trans*formed (μεταμορφούμεθα) into the same image [as the son]." This change, however, from συμμορφ- to μεταμορφ-, is less likely to be explained in religion-historical terms and more likely to be explained as Paul's own creative adaptation. In Romans 8.29, Paul looks back into God's premundane creative purposes and contends that, from before the beginning, the one God predestined humans to be wholly patterned after the pattern/"image"/likeness of his son. Whereas, in 2 Corinthians 3.18, Paul *assumes* that, at present, all of humanity—and no less the Corinthian Christians—are at least partially "mis-formed" and "misshaped" and require "*trans*formation" (μεταμορφόω).[44] In any case, I contend that, on the basis of the strength of the above Philonic parallels and the total lack of parallels anywhere else in the Jewish or pagan world, Middle Platonic intermediary doctrine serves as the principal background of the logic and combination of εἰκών and μορφ- in 2 Corinthians 3.18 and Romans 8.29.

Prepositional Metaphysics

Following the above consideration of the combination of "form" and "image" language in Philo and of the way in which this suggests that Paul christologically adapted certain elements of Middle Platonic intermediary doctrine, we now turn to the related evidence of the early Christian use of "prepositional metaphysics."[45] Prepositional metaphysics refer to the use of "prepositional shorthand" in the articulation of different types of cosmological causation. However these shorthands made their way from technical philosophical speculation into early Christianity, they certainly did so in the case of five New Testament texts: John 1.3 (also 1.10); Romans 11.36; 1 Corinthians 8.6; Colossians 1.15–16; and Hebrews 1.2. As I have already suggested, it is possible that this kind of metaphysical shorthand was mediated to early Christianity *via* Hellenistic Judaism.[46] In any case, like the authors of John (1.3, 10) and Hebrews (1.2), Paul regarded Jesus as the one "through whom" (δι' ⸀οὗ/ δι' αὐτοῦ) the *kosmos* came into being (1 Cor. 8.6; and Col. 1.16). Moreover, because in the case of Romans 11.36 we see that Paul was quite capable of ascribing all of the prepositions to "God" (the κύριος of v. 34; probably "the father"), it is clear that the christologically reworked *Shema* of 1 Corinthians 8.6 reflects a careful division of the metaphysical prepositions *between* the "one God" and the "one Lord":

ἀλλ' ἡμῖν εἷς θεὸς ὁ πατὴρ
ἐξ οὗ τὰ πάντα καὶ ἡμεῖς εἰς αὐτόν,

καὶ εἷς κύριος Ἰησοῦς Χριστὸς
δι' οὗ τὰ πάντα καὶ ἡμεῖς δι' αὐτοῦ.⁴⁷

Interestingly, however, in the case of Colossians 1.15–16, all of the metaphysical prepositions (including the unique ἐν αὐτῷ) refer exclusively to "the son" (1.13):

(1.15) ὅς ἐστιν εἰκὼν τοῦ θεοῦ τοῦ ἀοράτου,
πρωτότοκος πάσης κτίσεως,
(1.16) ὅτι ἐν αὐτῷ ἐκτίσθη τὰ πάντα . . .
τὰ πάντα δι' αὐτοῦ καὶ εἰς αὐτὸν ἔκτισται.

But before we can appreciate the christological implications of these texts, we need a basic understanding of the history of this tradition.⁴⁸ The tradition began with Aristotle's distinction between four "causes" (αἴτια): the material (τὸ ἐξ οὗ), the formal (τὸ εἶδος ἢ τὸ παράδειγμα), the efficient (ἡ ἀρχὴ τῆς μεταβολῆς ἡ πρώτη ἢ τῆς ἠρεμήσεως), and the final (τὸ οὗ ἕνεκα).⁴⁹ However, Aristotle apparently did not systematize the use of prepositions in relation to each cause.⁵⁰ In any case, and though we cannot draw clear lines for the subsequent development of prepositional metaphysics, we can be sure that they were well known in the first century. For example, in Alcinous's *Didaskalikos*, which, although it dates to the ca. second century CE, is basically a revised version of the work of one of Augustus's court philosophers (Arius Didymus), we read,

> If the world is not such as it is by accident, it has not only been generated from something (ἔκ τινος), but also by something (or someone) (ὑπό τινος), and not only this, but also with reference to something (πρός τι). But what could that with reference to which it is generate be other than form (ἰδέα)? So forms (αἱ ἰδέαι) exist.⁵¹

Seneca attests to the tradition in Latin. He first indicates the Stoic position: "Accordingly, there must be, in the case of each thing, that from which it is made (*unde fiat aliquid*), and, next, an agent by which it is made (*deinde a quo fiat*). The former is its material, the latter its cause."⁵² Then, having commented upon the Peripatetic tradition, Seneca goes on to examine the Platonic tradition:

> Accordingly, there are five causes, as Plato says: that "from which" (*id ex quo*), that "by which" (*id a quo*), that "in which" (*id in quo*), that "toward which" (*id ad quod*), and that "for which" (*id propter quod*).⁵³

Similarly, in Philo we read:

For to bring anything into being needs all these conjointly, the "by which" (τὸ ὑφ' οὗ), the "from which" (τὸ ἐξ οὗ), the "through which" (τὸ δι' οὗ), and the "for which" (τὸ δι' ὅ).⁵⁴

These first-century authors list these metaphysical prepositions as though they were well known.

What, however, should we make of such evidence in relation to Paul? Gregory Sterling has argued that the attribution of all three prepositions—ἐξ αὐτοῦ, δι' αὐτοῦ, and εἰς αὐτόν—to one "cause" in Romans 11.36 reflects Stoic influence.⁵⁵ However, he regards 1 Corinthians 8.6 as a "mixed text," in which characteristically Stoic formulations are used for "God the father"—ἐξ οὗ and εἰς αὐτόν—while characteristically Platonic ("intermediary") language is used for the "son"—δι' οὗ are all things.⁵⁶ According to Sterling, the force of Colossians 1.15–20 is even more difficult to ascertain both because it attributes all of the prepositions to the son and because it includes another phrase: ἐν αὐτῷ ("in/by him"; Col. 1.16, 17, 19).⁵⁷

Did Paul know, as Sterling asks near the beginning of his essay, "the technical meanings of these phrases"?⁵⁸ If Paul did know the technical meanings, I suggest, he put them to very limited if astonishing use. I contend much the same for Paul's reworking of Jewish *sophia* speculation and of Middle Platonic intermediary doctrine more generally. Paul's intention is particularly evident because of the context within which—and not coincidentally the context within which the authors of John (1.3, 10) and Hebrews (1.2) as well—make use of these metaphysical prepositions. In each case, cosmogonical activity, which is characteristically rigorously and exclusively ascribed to the one God alone in second-temple Jewish tradition, is ascribed to the preexistent Jesus. Therefore, I contend, these early christological traditions reflect a deliberate inclusion of Jesus in the unique divine identity.⁵⁹ The ascription of cosmogonical activity to the preexistent Jesus, however, ran the theological-conceptual risk of implying that the preexistent and divine Jesus now constituted the one God worshipped by the early Christians in toto. In this regard, I suggest, the prepositional metaphysics of the philosophical tradition were deemed useful in articulating *a distinction within the one divine identity between God "the father" and Jesus "the son."*

In this regard, however, van Kooten is wrong to draw a comparison either with Philo or with Middle Platonism:

> Philo appears here to be part of the development in contemporary Middle Platonism in which, as Dillon has shown, the Demiurge is no longer regarded as the highest God, as was still the case in Plato's *Timaeus*. Instead the function of Creator is increasingly thought to be fulfilled by a second God.... In passing, I note that this is also the view of Paul, as we can deduce from 1 Corinthians 8.6.⁶⁰

It is, however, not the case that Paul exclusively ascribes cosmogonical activity to the son, the "second god" in this conception. Indeed, that Paul can ascribe all of the prepositional metaphysics to God "the father" (Rom. 11.36), divide them between "God the father" and the "Lord Jesus the Messiah" (1 Cor. 8.6), and/or ascribe all of them to "the son" (Col. 1.13), suggests that, at least for Paul, these prepositions did not serve to demarcate different kinds and/or levels of divinity. In this regard, I further note that Paul regarded not only Jesus the son (1 Cor. 8.6; and Col. 1.15) but also God the father as the creator (Rom. 1.25; and 11.36) of the *kosmos*.

This is, then, a partial answer to Sterling's question. The Pauline evidence adduced suggests that Paul was not particularly concerned with the clear, consistent, and "ontological" use of the prepositions whereby he might articulate different levels/kinds of divinity. Rather, as I have just argued, the prepositions allowed Paul both to include Jesus within the unique divine identity as a cosmogonical agent and yet still to express a distinction within that unique divine identity. Furthermore, and particularly in relation to Paul's view of Jesus as the paradigmatic and cosmogonical image of God, this element of christologically adapted Middle Platonic intermediary doctrine allowed Paul to present Jesus as the protological and teleological paradigm of human beings. Beyond this, however, and whether or not Paul had an intimate knowledge of the different meanings of the metaphysical prepositions, he appears only to have put them to these limited if astonishing purposes.

I emphasize one further point. Though I have already argued and will argue in greater detail below (esp. in relation to Rom. 8.3; and Col. 1.15–30) that Paul's image christology reflects the influence of Jewish *sophia* speculation, I here emphasize that this speculation by itself does not account for the above christological traditions.[61] In particular, Paul's use of prepositional metaphysics (esp. 1 Cor. 8.6; and Col. 1.15–20), his collocation of εἰκών and πρωτότοκος (Rom. 8.29; and Col. 1.15), and his collocation of εἰκών and μορφ- language all suggest the influence of Middle Platonic intermediary doctrine, even if the influence of the latter were ultimately mediated *via* Hellenistic Judaism.

The Imago Dei and "Likeness to God"

As I have already mentioned, Philo, like Plutarch (*Un. Rul.* 780E–F), equates the *imago Dei* with Plato's *telos* of "likeness to god":

> We have known some of the image-makers offer prayers and sacrifices to their own creations though they would have done much better to worship each of their two hands. . . . Surely to persons so demented we might well say boldly, "Good sirs, the best of prayers and the goal of happiness is to become

like God (ὦ γενναῖοι, καὶ τέλος εὐδαιμονίας τὴν πρὸς θεὸν ἐξομοίωσιν). Pray you therefore that you may be made like your images (εὔχεσθε οὖν καὶ ὑμεῖς ἐξομοιωθῆναι τοῖς ἀφιδρύμασιν)".[62]

I note immediately that, unlike in the case of Plutarch (*Un. Rul.* 780E–F), Philo does not actually use the word εἰκών, though the sentiment is obviously the same. I make the following points. (1) This is another instance of the contrast between cult "idols" and human "images" of God. (2) The phrase "τέλος εὐδαιμονίας τὴν πρὸς θεὸν ἐξομοίωσιν" is an unambiguous allusion to Plato's teleological doctrine of ὁμοίωσις θεῷ. (3) In this latter connection, the fact that Philo uses the cognate verb to refer to becoming an image of God (ἐξομοιόω) suggests that he saw the two conceptions as interchangeable ways of referring to the same eudaemonistic *telos*. Even though, therefore, Philo's exhortation to "be made like your images" appears to be dripping with sarcasm, the sarcasm nevertheless presupposes the association between images of God and Plato's eudaemonistic *telos* of "likeness to god."

Before we move to the next section, I mention a particular possibility. It seems not unreasonable to suppose that at least some readers of LXX Genesis 1.26 might have thought that they had "found" Plato's famous doctrine in that text and there associated with the *imago Dei*: "εἶπεν ὁ θεός, Ποιήσωμεν ἄνθρωπον κατ' εἰκόνα ἡμετέραν καὶ καθ' ὁμοίωσιν." According to this text, God made humanity "according to his likeness (καθ' ὁμοίωσιν)," an idea which is here closely associated with being made "according to his image." This *might* have facilitated, at least for some of those familiar with LXX Genesis 1.26, a connection between the *imago Dei* and Plato's doctrine of ὁμοίωσις θεῷ. In this regard, and as far as I have been able to tell, the first writer *explicitly* to make this connection is Clement of Alexandria (ca. 150–215 CE):[63]

> It is time, then, for us to say that the pious Christian alone is rich and wise, and of noble birth, and thus call him, and believe him to be, God's image, with his likeness (εἰκόνα τοῦ θεοῦ μεθ' ὁμοιώσεως), having become "righteous and holy, with wisdom" (δίκαιον καὶ ὅσιον μετὰ φρονήσεως), by Christ Jesus, and so far already like God (ὅμοιν ἤδη καὶ θεῷ).[64]

This text provides us with a fascinating angle of vision on Clement's reading of Genesis 1.26 *via* his interpretation of Plato's teleological doctrine. Indeed, he explicitly quotes from the *Theaetetus* (176B) in the second half of the passage. We recall the text: "[A]nd to become like god is to become righteous and holy, with wisdom (ὁμοίωσις δὲ δίκαιον καὶ ὅσιον μετὰ φρονήσεως γενέσθαι)."[65] Clement claims that "the Christian alone" has attained this likeness to God "by Christ Jesus." I note, moreover, that Clement has tellingly revised LXX Genesis 1.26 for two reasons (instead of κατ' εἰκόνα ἡμετέραν καὶ καθ' ὁμοίωσιν, we read εἰκόνα τοῦ θεοῦ μεθ' ὁμοιώσεως). (1) Changing "according to the likeness" to "*with* the likeness" allowed him more clearly to allude to the wording of *Theaetetus* 176B (cf. μετὰ φρονήσεως); (2) and this same alteration allowed Clement to make the distinction, a distinction widely made in Patristic writers, between "image" and "likeness," the former of which is simply endemic to humanity while the latter of which can be more or less realized.[66]

Therefore, I put forward the following case which will be crucial for my treatment of Paul. On the basis of the evidence from Philo (*Dec.* 72–74); Plutarch (*Un. Rul.* 780E–F), and Clement of Alexandria (*Prot.* 12.122.4), I contend that Paul's *imago Dei* theology too reflects an association with Plato's teleological doctrine of "likeness to god." This is evident from the following two factors, the first of which subdivides into three points. (1) Paul's image christology reflects a creative christological appropriation of Middle Platonic intermediary doctrine, an appropriation which is evident in the following: (a) the formulaic and semi-technical collocation of εἰκών and πρωτότοκος (Rom. 8.29; and Col. 1.15–16) (b) and of μορφ- and εἰκών (2 Cor. 3.18; and Rom. 8.29), (c) as well as the use of prepositional metaphysics (1 Cor. 8.6; and Col. 1.15–16). (2) Furthermore, below we will see the rhetorical and argumentative coherence which 2 Corinthians 2.17–4.6; Romans 7–8; and Colossians 1.15–20; 3.10 possess when we perceive that Paul's *imago Dei* theology is deliberately designed to evoke Plato's teleological doctrine of likeness to god. Hereby, Paul casts essentially inner-Jewish issues in philosophical dress, thereby presenting his opponents and/or opposing views as bound up with a shallow and deceitful philosophy and presenting himself and his sympathizers as those who attain to the *telos* of true philosophy: the image of God (2 Cor. 3.18; Rom. 8.29; and Col. 3.10).

THE *IMAGO DEI* IN THE GRECO-ROMAN WORLD: CONCLUSION

Throughout this survey, I have made the following case. (1) The *imago Dei* conception was a well-known feature of Greco-Roman imperial and philosophical thought. (2) The conception, moreover, was sometimes particularly associated with Plato's famous doctrine of "likeness to god," as is clear from the cases of Philo (*Dec.* 72–74); Plutarch (*Un. Rul.* 780E–F), and Clement of Alexandria (*Prot.* 12.122.4.) (3) Several features of Paul's image christology—that Jesus is the cosmogonical image of God (esp. Col. 1.15); that he is the pattern to which believers will be conformed (2 Cor. 3.18; Rom. 8.29; cp. Phil. 3.21); that the language of μορφ-, εἰκών, and πρωτότοκος all occur within Paul's *imago Dei* discourse (2 Cor. 3.18; Rom. 8.29; and Col. 1.15–16); and that Paul articulates the cosmogonical role of Jesus *via* prepositional metaphysics—indicate that he has deliberately and christologically adapted Middle Platonic intermediary doctrine. (4) Furthermore, it appears that Paul's christological use of Middle Platonic intermediary doctrine fundamentally served two purposes: (a) it allowed him to include Jesus within the unique divine identity by including him within the one theological-conceptual category (cosmogonical activity) which most clearly and exclusively demarcated that identity in second-temple Jewish monotheism while also expressing a distinction within that identity; (b) moreover, Middle Platonic intermediary doctrine allowed Paul to present Jesus as the archetypal pattern to which believers will ultimately be conformed. (5) Finally, and in relation to point (2), we will see that the rhetorical arguments of 2 Corinthians 2.17–4.6; Romans 7–8; and Colossians 1.15–20; 3.10 all reflect the fact that Paul intends his *imago Dei* theology to evoke Plato's teleological doctrine of "likeness to god."

NOTES

1. Most obviously, Abraham Malherbe, *Paul and the Popular Philosophers* (Minneapolis: Fortress, 1989); Troels Engberg-Pedersen, *Paul and the Stoics* (Edinburgh: T & T Clark, 2000); Idem, ed., *Paul Beyond the Judaism/Hellenism Divide* (Louisville: Westminster John Knox Press, 2001); Idem, *Cosmology and Self in the Apostle Paul: The Material Spirit* (Oxford: OUP, 2010); Tuomas Rasimus, Troels Engberg-Pedersen, and Ismo Dunderberg, eds., *Stoicism in Early Christianity* (Grand Rapids: Baker, 2010). More recently, see Wright, *PFG*, 197–245, 1354–407, with the critique of Gregory Sterling, "The Role of Philosophy," 235–53; C. Kavin Rowe, *One True Life: The Stoics and Early Christians as Rival Traditions* (New Haven: YUP, 2016); and esp. the essays by Gregory Sterling: "Hellenistic Philosophy and the New Testament" in Stanley Porter, ed., *Handbook to Exegesis of the New Testament*, NTTS 25 (Leiden: Brill, 1997), 313–58; Idem, "'The Jewish Philosophy': The Presence of Hellenistic Philosophy in Jewish Exegesis in the Second Temple Period" in Carol Bakhos, ed., *Ancient Judaism in Its Hellenistic Context*, JSJSS 95 (Leiden: Brill, 2005), 131–53; and Idem, "The Love of Wisdom: Middle Platonism and Stoicism in the Wisdom of Solomon" in Troels Engberg-Pedersen, ed., *From Stoicism to Platonism: The Development of Philosophy 100 BCE—100 CE* (Cambridge: CUP, 2017), 198–213.

2. Cf. the discussion in John Dillon, *The Middle Platonists: 80 B.C. to A.D. 220*, rev. edn. (Ithaca, NY: Cornell University Press, 1996 [1977]), xiv. Engberg-Pedersen, "Setting the Scene: Stoicism and Platonism in the Transitional Period in Ancient Philosophy" in Rasimus et al., eds., *Stoicism in Early Christianity*, 1–15, prefers "The Transitional Period." Wright, *PFG*, 197–245, 1354–407, provides an illuminating

discussion, though he underestimates the importance of Platonism in the period: see Sterling, "The Role of Philosophy," 235–53; and the ready concession of this point in Wright, "The Challenge of Dialogue: A Partial and Preliminary Response" in Heilig et al., eds., *God and the Faithfulness of Paul*, 711–67 (754–57).

3. Engberg-Pedersen, "Setting the Scene," 4–5, who goes on correctly to note: "But then . . . no early Christian writer was either a Platonist or a Stoic *per se*" (5). It is, therefore, odd to read a few pages later: "the worldview of the apostle Paul was basically a Stoic one" (11). For a compelling critique of Engberd-Pedersen's Stoic construal of Paul, see esp. Wright, *PFG*, 1383–407. E.g., Sterling, "The Role of Philosophy," 249, finds Wright's critique convincing.

4. Dillon, *The Middle Platonists*, xv.

5. Michael Frede, "Epilogue" in Keimpe Algra, Jonathan Barnes, Jaap Mansfeld, and Malcolm Schofield, eds., *The Cambridge History of Hellenistic Philosophy* (Cambridge: CUP, 2005), 790, 792.

6. Engberg-Pedersen, "Setting the Scene," 7.

7. See esp. Wright, *PFG*, 204; and the discussions in Johan C. Thom, "Paul and Popular Philosophy" in Cilliers Breytenbach, ed., *Paul's Greco-Roman Context*, BETL 277 (Leuven: Peeters, 2015), 47–74; and Sterling, "The Role of Philosophy," 240.

8. See the discussion in Dillion, *The Middle Platonists*, 43–51; and Sterling, "The Role of Philosophy," 239–42, noting on p. 239, "The order was apparently not fixed." Dillon contends that Xenocrates (396–314 BCE) should be credited with the tripartite division (pp. 22–39), although he notes that "Aristotle does seem to make the distinction in *Topics* I 14 (p. 22)." On the whole question, see Augustinus C. J. Habets, "Geschiedenis van de indeling van de filosofie in de oudheid" PhD Diss. (University of Utrecht, 1983). Cicero, *Acad.* 1.19, however, credits Plato with the threefold distinction, while *Diog. Laert.* 3.56 credits Plato with *adding* the third branch, which Diogenes calls διαλεκτικός.

9. Dillon, *The Middle Platonists*, 46–48.

10. Citing *Ar. Did.* 5B3; *Diog. Laert.* 7.87–89; and *Stobaeus* 2.77.16–27, 2.75.11–76.8.

11. Citing Plato, *Theaet.* 167B; Philo, *Flight* 63, 82; Alcinous, *Did.* 181, 19–182, 14. See also the discussion in Dillion, *The Middle Platonists*, 122–3.

12. Citing Plutarch, *Superst.* 169B, who reports Pythagoras as saying "that we are at our best when we approach the gods (πρὸς τοὺς θεοὺς βαδίζοντες)"; and Iamblichus, *Life Pyth.* 86 and 137, who wrote that "their entire way of life is arranged to follow god (πρὸς τὸ ἀκολουθεῖν τῷ θεῷ)."

13. Citing *Diog. Laert.* 10.127–32; and Cicero, *Fin.* 1.29–30.

14. Sterling, "The Role of Philosophy," 240–1, italics added. See also the discussion in Dillon, *The Middle Platonists*, 43–4.

15. Although many of these texts are discussed in van Kooten, *PA*, 122–69, they are little known in this connection. In any case, van Kooten's survey is quite indiscriminate at points, homogenizing texts with quite different conceptions. As one example, van Kooten, *PA*, 72–73, takes Epictetus's (*Dis.* 2.8.11–13) essentially Stoic (panentheistic) claim that humans are "portions of Divinity (μέρη θεῶν)" as an

example of the *imago Dei* tradition. Clearly, however, the logic of the *imago Dei* tradition, in which there is (1) an image, (2) that of which it is an image, and (3) that for which the image is a paradigm, is quite different from the logic of Stoic panentheism in which humans are simply "portions of divinity."

16. Dillon, *The Middle Platonists*, 8. Cf. also Cox, *By the Same Word*, 29, n. 5: "A substantial impetus in this emphasis on physics is Plato's dialogue *Timaeus*. Already in the second century we see signs of renewed interest in this cosmopoetic discourse, namely by Stoics. Eudorus himself wrote a commentary on the dialouge [sic] and it is [sic] serves as the foundational text for subsequent generations of later Platonists." On the *Timaeus* in general, see, e.g., Gretchen J. Reydams-Schils, *Demiurge and Providence: Stoic and Platonist Readings of Plato's Timaeus* (Turnhout: Brepols, 1999); A. E. Taylor, *A Commentary on Plato's Timaeus* (New York: Garland, 1987); and Richard D. Mohr, *The Platonic Cosmology* (Leiden: Brill, 1985).

17. *Tim.* 28A–29B (Bury, LCL).

18. *Tim.* 92C (Bury, LCL, slightly revised).

19. So also van Kooten, *PA*, 94. In this connection, in terms of how this cosmology was later appropriated by different philosophers, I note Cox, *By the Same Word*, 29–30: "The intermediate reality is the most supple of the three in terms of how different philosophers present it. . . . What is clear is that this intermediate entity is that by which the transcendent first principle and the material principle are related."

20. However, on the influence of Eudorus in Alexandria in particular, cf. Dillon, *The Middle Platonists*, 114–38. On the influence of Middle Platonic intermediary doctrine on John 1.1–18 and Hebrews 1.1–4, a question which is far beyond our scope, cf. esp. Cox, *By the Same Word*, 193–276.

21. Winston, *Wisdom*, 180, notes the *Timaeus* in this connection.

22. For instance, why does Philo prefer πρωτόγονος, John μονογενής, and Paul (and Hebrews) πρωτότοκος? For this I have not been able to find a satisfactory answer. One *might* be able to explain Paul's (messianic) usage on the basis of LXX Ps. 89.27; however, this connection is uncertain.

23. Cox, *By the Same Word*, 193–276.

24. *Theaet.* 176B (R. G. Bury, LCL, slightly revised).

25. Dillon, *The Middle Platonists*, 43–44: "The first issue is . . . the purpose of life, or as it was termed 'the end of goods' (*telos agathōn*). This can also be taken as the definition of happiness [*eudaimonia*] . . . [the] formula of 'life in accordance with nature' . . . [came from] the Stoics. . . . When we turn to later Alexandrian Platonism . . . the Stoic-Antiochian definition has been abandoned in favour of a more spiritual, and perhaps more truly Platonic, ideal of 'Likeness to God' (*homoiōsis theōi*), derived from the famous passage of the *Theaetetus* (176B), and this formula remained the distinctive Platonic definition of the *telos* ever afterward."

26. *Themistocles* 27.1–3 (Bernadotte Perrin, LCL).

27. See *OGIS*, 1.142–43.

28. *Un. Rul.* 780E–F (H. N. Fowler, LCL, slightly revised).

29. As an aside, it is hard for the Pauline scholar not to be struck by the statement that "justice is the aim and end of the law" (cp. Rom. 10.4).

30. On these sculptors, see the entries in H. Cancik, H. Schneider, and M. Landfester, eds., Brill's New Pauly (http://referenceworks.brillonline.com/browse/brill-s-new-pauly).

31. *Essays in Portraiture Defended*, 28 (A. M. Harmon, LCL).

32. Classic studies of Philo include E. R. Goodenough, *By Light, Light* (New Haven: YUP, 1935); W. Völker, *Fortschritt und Vollendung bei Philo von Alexandrien: eine Studie zur Geschichte der Frömmigkeit*, TUGAL 49.1 (Leipzig: J. C. Hinrich, 1938); H. A. Wolfson, *Philo: Foundation of Religious Philosophy in Judaism, Christianity and Islam*, 2 vols. (Cambridge: HUP, 1947); Emile Bréhier, *Les ides philosophique et religieuses de Philon d'Alexandrie*, 3rd edn., EPM 8 (Paris: Vrin, 1950); J. Daniélou, *Philon d'Alexandrie* (Paris: Fayard, 1958); and the introduction of Samuel Sandmel, *Philo of Alexandria: An Introduction* (New York: Oxford University Press, 1979). More recently, see Kenneth Schenck, *A Brief Guide to Philo* (Louisville: Westminster John Knox, 2005); David Runia, *Philo of Alexandria and the Timaeus of Plato*, 2nd edn. (Leiden: Brill, 1986), 7–27; and Peder Borgen, "Philo of Alexandria: A Critical and Synthetical Survey of Research since World War II" ANRW 21.1 (1984): 98–154. For bibliography on the study of Philo, cf. esp. Roberto Radice and David T. Runia, *Philo of Alexandria: An Annotated Bibliography, 1937–1986*, VCSup 8 (Leiden: Brill, 1988); and Idem, *Philo of Alexandria: An Annotated Bibliography, 1987–1996, with Addenda for 1937–1986*, VCSup 57 (Leiden: Brill, 2000). On Philo's philosophical context in Alexandria, see esp. Dillon, *The Middle Platonists*, 114–38; and P. M. Fraser, *Ptolemaic Alexandria*, 3 vols. (Oxford: Clarendon Press, 1972), 1.485–94. On the *imago Dei* in Philo, see also van Kooten, *PA*, 48–68; and Lorenzen, *EK*, 69–138.

33. As we consider Philo, we do well to note the cautionary remarks of Cox, *By the Same Word*, 87–88, italics mine: "Philo's philosophical program . . . is pragmatic. That is, it centers on issues related to the advancement of the soul, or psychagogy. On occasion, he provides glimpses of the ontological and/or cosmological framework upon which his psychagogy rests. Such glimpses are not as frequent or as detailed as we might hope and Philo allows them only as they help illustrate his views on psychagogy. Hence, to inquire about Philo's views on a divine intermediary's role in cosmology and anthropological fulfillment is to inquire of material that is *infrequent in occurrence, illustrative in purpose, partial in extent, and unsystematic in presentation*." On the *logos* as God's "image" in Philo, cf. also van Kooten, *PA*, 48–91; and Cox, *By the Same Word*, 116–27.

34. Cf. esp. *Creation* 25; *All. Int.* 3.96; *Heir* 231; *Spec.* 1.81; 3.83, 207; *Questions* 2.62; *Tongues* 97; 147; *Flight* 101; and *Dreams* 1.239. On Platonism in Alexandria before and leading up to Philo, all of Dillon, *The Middle Platonists*, 52–183, is important. Regarding the relationship between Jewish *sophia* speculation and philosophical *logos* speculation in Philo, cf. the apposite comment of Cox, *By the Same Word*, 90: "Second, this study presumes that Philo honors previous exegetical traditions by preserving them even if he has moved beyond them. This is how we account for Philo's presentation of Sophia vis-à-vis the Logos. Philo will describe Sophia and the Logos in strikingly similar language at times and thus raises the question of their relationship. The answer is that Philo is aware of and preserves traditions that view Sophia as

occupying the same place as the Logos, i.e., that of divine intermediary (such traditions were likely responsible for Wisdom of Solomon)."

35. *All. Int.* 3.96 (Colson and Whitaker, LCL, slightly revised). On this text, cf. esp. Cox, *By the Same Word*, 103–111; and van Kooten, *PA*, 51.

36. *Questions* 2.62 (Marcus, LCL).

37. For a good discussion of the point, see esp. Dillon, *The Middle Platonists*, 366–72.

38. On this, cf. van Kooten, *PA*, 75–91, who also discusses several others texts, some of which are less relevant.

39. F. H. Colson, LCL, slightly revised.

40. Ibid.

41. Ibid.

42. This opening line almost certainly reflects an allusion to the crucial passage from Plato's *Timaeus* (28A) discussed above. Plato opened his discussion with this: "πᾶν δὲ αὖ τὸ γιγνόμενον ὑπ' αἰτίου τινὸς ἐξ ἀνάγκης γίγνεσθαι." Philo "parrots" some of his language with this: "γέγονέ τε γὰρ ὁ κόσμος καὶ πάντως ὑπ' αἰτίου τινὸς γέγονεν."

43. *Flight* 12 (Colson and Whitaker, LCL, slightly revised).

44. That the use of μεταμορφ- in this connection reflects a creative and soteriological Pauline adaptation would explain the total lack of ancient parallels: as an answer to van Kooten, *PA*, 84–5, 90–91.

45. As far as I have been able to tell, the phrase was coined by Willy Theiler, *Die Vorbereitung des Neuplatonismus* (Berlin: Weidmann, 1964), 17–34. On prepositional metaphysics in the New Testament more generally, see esp. Sterling, "Prepositional Metaphysics in Jewish Wisdom Speculation and Early Christian Liturgical Texts" *SPhiloA* 9 (1997): 219–38; and Cox, *By the Same Word*, 43–51, 103–11.

46. So esp. Sterling, "Prepositional Metaphysics," 235–36; and Idem, "Hellenistic Philosophy," 334–36.

47. I note that Fletcher-Louis, *JM*, 39–55, has recently made the case that "numerical criticism" of 1 Corinthians 8.6 unveils that the originator of the "confession" deliberately divided the twenty-six words of the confession exactly between the sections pertaining to "the one God" and "the one Lord," thereby creating a confession whose numerical value in Hebrew is equivalent to the numerical value of the divine name, YHWH (twenty-six). Herein, so Fletcher-Louis argues, Jesus was carefully and creatively included within the unique divine identity *via* the well-known ancient practice of gematria. I am inclined to think that this is correct.

48. On what follows, I have largely followed the discussion in Sterling, "Prepositional Metaphysics," 219–38.

49. See Aristotle, *Phys.* 2.3–9; *Metaph.* 1.3.1; and 5.2.1–3.

50. So Sterling, "Hellenistic Philosophy," 245–46; and Cox, *By the Same Word*, 44, n. 53.

51. *Ep.* 9.3. On Alcinous's revision of Arius's work, see John Dillon, *Alcinous: The Handbook of Platonism: Translated with an Introduction and Commentary*, repr. (Oxford: Clarendon Press, 2002 [1993]), xxvii–xxx. For the translation, see p. 16.

52. *Ep.* 65.2 (Gummere, LCL).

53. *Ep.* 65.8 (Gummere, LCL, slightly revised).
54. *Cherubim* 125 (Colson and Whitaker, LCL).
55. Sterling, "Prepositional Metaphysics," 233.
56. Ibid. 235–6.
57. We should note, however, that no New Testament text ever portrays Jesus as the one "from whom" (ἐξ αὐτοῦ) are all things, which would denote ultimate source. See the helpful chart in Sterling, "Prepositional Metaphysics," 232. I attempt to explain the unusual ἐν αὐτῷ below.
58. Ibid. 231.
59. Cf. Cox, *By the Same Word*, 2–3: "The relatively uniform manner with which these passages describe Jesus' divine nature and the cosmological activity it generates suggests a common tradition. The likelihood of such a common tradition is increased when one considers that these four texts are the sole New Testament evidence for early Christian claims about Jesus as divine agent of creation."
60. So van Kooten, *PA*, 53–54, citing Dillon, *The Middle Platonists*, 7.
61. So also Cox, *By the Same Word*, 11–12: "While we willingly accept some relationship between the biblical wisdom tradition and our four NT passages [John 1.1–18; 1 Cor. 8.6; Col. 1.15–20; and Heb. 1.1–4], that relationship does not adequately account for the ontologically-based cosmological agency the NT texts express. . . . The strongest arguments that 1 Cor 8:6, Col 1:15–20, Heb 1:1–4 and the Johannine prologue are related to Jewish sapientialism rest on how these texts describe the Son's relationship to God and his cosmological agency. Yet, while the biblical sapiential tradition seems to provide the NT texts the general framework of combined cosmic preexistence and soteriology, the specific parallels of ontology and cosmology we find in the NT occur only in a specific sub-set of that tradition, namely Wisdom of Solomon and Philo's writings."
62. *Dec.* 72–74 (Colson, LCL).
63. I also note 1 John 3.2, in which the writer states that, upon seeing the glorious Jesus at the *parousia*, believers "will be like him (ὅμοιοι αὐτῷ ἐσόμεθα)."
64. *Protrepticus* 12.122.4. The translation is taken from van Kooten, *PA*, 177. For discussion, cf. Ibid. 177–78.
65. *Theaet.* 176B (R. G. Bury, LCL, slightly revised).
66. So, e.g., Lossky, *In the Image and Likeness of God*.

Chapter 6

Paul and the Image of God

THE ORIGINS OF PAUL'S IMAGE CHRISTOLOGY

Before we turn to our key texts, we must ask the fundamental question: "whence, when, and why" came the *imago Dei* into Paul's christology?[1] Did Paul first conclude, on the basis that the resurrection had vindicated Jesus as the royal Messiah, that he must also be, on a parallel with or perhaps even upstaging pagan kings, the true "image of God"? This is the position taken by, for example, van Kooten, though it was anticipated by Bousset.[2] Moreover, as I indicated in an earlier section, the *religionsgeschichtliche Schule* maintained a Gnostic background for this christological conception. Others have postulated that Paul first associated Jesus with Adam and only then with the *imago Dei* language of Genesis 1.26–27.[3] On the other hand, some have seen the background in the Jewish wisdom traditions.[4] Furthermore, as I also indicated earlier, Seyoon Kim's 1981 dissertation, which was followed in this regard by Segal, Newman, and Vollenweider, argued that it was the "Damascus christophany" which suggested to Paul the connection between the now-exalted Jesus and the *imago Dei*.

Having indicated the weaknesses of some of these proposals already, and having indicated the strengths of my own, I simply recapitulate several points. That Paul's image christology reflects a creative christological appropriation of Jewish *sophia* speculation and particularly of Middle Platonic intermediary doctrine is evident from the following points: the formulaic and semi-technical collocation of (1) εἰκών and πρωτότοκος (Rom. 8.29; and Col. 1.15–16) and (2) μορφ- and εἰκών (2 Cor. 3.18; and Rom. 8.29), as well as (3) the use of prepositional metaphysics (1 Cor. 8.6; and Col. 1.15–16). Taken together, and when considered alongside the parallel christological traditions of John 1.1–18 and Hebrews 1.1–4, we are right to see these Pauline christological traditions as evidence of a deliberate christological adaptation of Middle Platonic intermediary doctrine in which Jesus is included within the unique divine identity as creator and yet distinguished from another figure (God "the father") within that identity. This evidence, moreover, allows us to pierce through the historical fog of earliest Christianity and to glimpse answers to the "whence, when, and why" questions. Whence: the origins of image christology ultimately lie in Middle Platonic intermediary doctrine, even if the relevant conceptions were mediated *via* Hellenistic Judaism. When: while the answer depends upon one's relative dating of Paul's letters and traditions found therein, the *terminus ante quem* of image christology is its earliest attestation in Paul (1 Cor. 15.49; or Col. 1.15–16). Why: image christology seems to be a part of a larger early Christian attempt—as can be seen from John 1.1–18 and Hebrew 1.1–4 as well—to appropriate elements of Middle Platonic intermediary doctrine so as to include Jesus within the one unique divine identity as Jewish monotheists and still to insist upon his distinction from another figure within that divine identity (the father).

THE *IMAGO DEI* AND BAPTISM

Before we turn to our key Pauline texts, I want to suggest the *possibility* that the *imago Dei* tradition had a liturgical status in the Pauline communities. Evidence for this might be found in the fact that *imago Dei* and Adam imagery cluster around passages about baptism. First, we note that in Galatians 3.27–28 Paul argues that the baptismal ritual creates a new situation in which there is now "no male and female" (οὐκ ἔνι ἄρσεν καὶ θῆλυ). Whatever the proper exegesis of this text, the allusion to Genesis 1.27 is clear.[5] Furthermore, in Colossians 3.9–11, Paul writes,

> (3.9) Do not lie to one another, because you have put off the old humanity with its practices (3.10) and put on the new humanity which is being renewed in knowledge according to the image of the creator (κατ' εἰκόνα τοῦ κτίσαντος αὐτόν), (3.11) where there is no Greek nor Jew, circumcised nor uncircumcised, Barbarian, Scythian, slave nor free, but the Messiah is everything and in everything.

Paul is obviously referring to baptism and speaks of a ritual "re-humanization" in which converts "are renewed in knowledge κατ' εἰκόνα τοῦ κτίσαντος αὐτόν."[6] However, we cannot be certain that these connections reflect the actual baptismal *practice* of Pauline communities and not simply the literary features of Paul's baptismal *theology*. In any case, the former is worth noting as a possibility.

PAULINE EXEGESIS: PRELIMINARY MATTERS

In what follows, I will treat 2 Corinthians 2.17–4.6; Romans 7–8; and Colossians 1.15–20; 3.10 in detail. Presently, I should say a few words about my treatment of these letters. According to the commonly accepted sequence, I will engage Romans after 2 Corinthians.[7] Because of the contested authorship (and, therefore, contested date) of Colossians, I will deal with this letter last of all.[8] In any case, for our purposes the sequence would only be of paramount importance if one could detect a development in Paul's *imago Dei* theology, evidence of which has not been forthcoming. As to the integrity of 2 Corinthians, I have found the recent treatment of Campbell to be particularly persuasive.[9] Even if, however, 2 Corinthians were composed of two or more letters, and if, therefore, the way in which I treat material from chapters 10–13 and from 2–4 as though it came from the same extant letter were historically and exegetically inappropriate, it would still be good historical and exegetical practice cautiously to read any one portion of our 2 Corinthians in light of the whole.

Regarding Colossians 1.15–20, which is routinely thought to predate the letter in which it is now found, I will argue that this "Christ-psalm" (so Stettler) was likely written at the same time as the letter *and in order to buttress its larger argument*.[10] Along with many others, I am unpersuaded by the claim that either the Christ-psalm or the larger letter betrays decidedly "unPauline vocabulary."[11] However, that the author of Colossians wrote 1.15–20 to be included within the letter does not mean that it might not also contain (and reflect) older, "traditional" material.[12]

NOTES

1. "Whence, when, and why" is an allusion to Andrews Chester's important article, "High Christology—Whence, When and Why?" *Early Christianity* 2 (2011): 22–50.

2. van Kooten, *PA*, 204–05; and Bousset, *Kyrios Christos*, 206.

3. So, e.g., Wright, *Climax*, 114, 116; Fee, *Christology*, 299; and Jipp, *Christ is King*, 103–07 (esp. 104). See also the discussion in Kim, *Paul's Gospel*, 162–93.

4. So, e.g., Hengel, *Son of God*, 48–56.

5. So, e.g., Richard B. Hays, "The Letter to the Galatians" in J. Paul Sampley, ed., *NIB XI* (Nashville: Abingdon, 2000), 181–348 (273); and J. L. Martyn, *Galatians: A New Translation with Introduction and Commentary*, AB33A (New Haven: YUP, 1993), 376–77.

6. On this as a baptismal passage, cp. esp. Rom. 6.6 within 6.1–11.

7. See esp. Douglas A. Campbell, *Framing Paul: An Epistolary Biography* (Grand Rapids: Eerdmans, 2014), 37–121.

8. However, regarding the authenticity of Colossians, I have found Campbell, *Framing*, 260–309, persuasive.

9. Ibid. 98–121.

10. Throughout and heuristically, I refer to Colossians 1.15–20 as a "Christ-psalm," here following Christian Stettler, *Der Kolosserhymnus: Untersuchungen zu Form, traditionsgesschichtlichem Hintergrund und Aussage von Col 1,15–20*, WUNT 2.31 (Tübingen: Mohr Siebeck, 2000), 79–86. Hurtado, *LJC*, 504–18 (esp. 507), rightly argues, "The principal stylistic feature of Colossians 1:15–20 is in fact the parallel structure that is also the primary poetic feature of the Psalms. The uneven length of lines does not conform to Greek poetic conventions of syllabic meter because this particular statement of hymnic praise was composed as what Stettler rightly characterizes as a 'Christ-psalm,' lauding Jesus in the cadences of the Psalter." See also Benjamin Edsall and Jennifer Strawbridge, "The Songs We Used to Sing? Hymn 'Traditions' and Reception in Pauline Letters" *JSNT* 37.3 (2015): 290–311. Matthew E. Gordley, *The Colossian Hymn in Context: An Exegesis in Light of Jewish and Greco-Roman Hymnic and Epistolary Conventions*, WUNT 2.228 (Tübingen: Mohr Siebeck, 2007), 3, has collected the following designations with which scholars have historically referred to Colossians 1.15–20: "a Christ-hymn, an encomium, a Christ-psalm, a Christological confession, a Christological midrash, a poetic passage, a redacted hymn to Sophia, epideictic rhetoric, or elevated prose." Moreover, I note that my position in which Colossians 1.15–20 was written for and in response to the situation in Colossae does not of itself necessitate that the author could not also have intended it to be used in the Colossian liturgy (e.g., as a hymn). The most recent and thorough attempt to argue that Colossians 1.15–20 predates the letter and represents traditional material is Matthew E. Gordley, *New Testament Christological Hymns: Exploring Texts, Contexts, and Significance* (Downers Grove: IVP, 2018), esp. ch. 1. Though his statement is careful and balanced, the nature of the evidence is such that even his case is unlikely to do more than to reassure the already convinced. See further my forthcoming review in *RBL*.

11. So, e.g., Edsall and Strawbridge, "The Songs," 294–95; Wright, *PFG*, 56–63 (esp. 60); Gordon Fee, "Philippians 2:5–11: Hymn or Exalted Pauline Prose" *BBR* 2 (1992): 29–46; Gordley, *The Colossian Hymn*, 5, n. 6. On the issue of unique vocabulary, see esp. Walter Bujard, *Stilanalytische Untersuchungen zum Kolosserbrief als Beitrag zur Methodik von Sprachvergleichen*, SUNT 11 (Göttingen: Vandenhoeck & Ruprecht, 1973); and Eduard Lohse, *Colossians and Philemon: A Commentary on the Epistles to the Colossians and to Philemon* (Philadelphia: Fortress, 1971), 85–89. On the question of whether or not the poetical piece (1.15–20) predates the letter, I am particularly unpersuaded by Cox's (representative) logic: "As we observed, Col 1:15–20 has several characteristics that lend to it an air of being an independent text, whether a hymn or similar kind of traditional material. . . . Part of the reason for asserting the independence of Col 1:15–20 is how phrases and concepts from the 'hymn' appear later in the letter" (Cox, *By the Same Word*, 169). But why would the possibility that 1.15–20 is hymnic and/or the fact that lexemes from 1.15–20 appear elsewhere in the letter betray two authors? This is simply a non sequitur.

12. However, on the unity and integrity of the psalm—i.e., that it does not represent a redaction(s) of an earlier psalm to *sophia* or some such—cf. esp. Stettler, *Der Kolosserhymnus*, 75–103.

Chapter 7

2 Corinthians 2.17–4.6

INTRODUCTION

In this section, I will argue the following case. (1) In 2.17–3.1, Paul echoes a tradition based upon a text from Plato's *Protagoras* in which Plato's Socrates offers a highly critical characterization of the sophists. Hereby, Paul intends to characterize his opponents as shallow sophists. (2) Furthermore, I will argue that these opponents are the same as those in view in the polemic of chapters 10–13. On this basis, I will argue that Paul casts *Jewish-Christian* opponents in philosophical dress, not least because this allowed him simultaneously to characterize his opponents as shallow sophists and himself and his sympathizers as true philosophers who attain to "the image of God" (3.18). (3) Moreover, especially in view of the intertext of Exodus 32–34, I will contend that the passage as a whole is a clear instance of "christological monotheism."

A BRIEF HISTORY OF RESEARCH

Because certain framing issues are so important for the larger construal of this passage, and because these issues are so contested, a brief history of research will prove helpful. We begin with the influential proposal of Hans Windisch, whose 1924 commentary argued two points in particular: (1) the passage reflects a *"Christian midrash on Ex 34:29–35"* and is, therefore, within the context of 2.17–4.6 as a whole, dispensable.[1] (2) Windisch further deduced the following conclusion: *"Der Abschnitt gibt sich als eine literarische Einlage* [The passage betrays itself as a literary insertion]."[2] He took this position, like so many after him, because the passage seemed (to him) so little connected to its current epistolary (i.e., argumentative) context.

In their different ways, Hans Lietzmann, Joseph Fitzmyer, and C. F. D. Moule all appropriated elements of Windisch's thesis. Paul had composed this "midrash" for another occasion and had inserted it, to somewhat awkward effect, at this point in the letter.[3] Also adapting Windisch's thesis, Siegfried Schulz proposed that in 2 Corinthians 3.7–18 Paul was alluding to an exegesis of Exodus 34 *produced by his missionary opponents in Corinth*.[4] Similarly, Dieter Georgi famously argued that Paul was extensively *quoting* these opponents.[5]

Richard Hays and N. T. Wright have expounded the passage in ways similar to one another, arguing both for its integrity and for the many ways in which it connects with the surrounding epistolary context.[6] Neither, however, has made the reconstruction of Paul's opponents or their teaching an integral part of their reading. Nevertheless, Hays admits that "although these rivals are nowhere directly mentioned in 2 Corinthians 3, the contrast that Paul develops in 3:7–18 between his own ministry and the ministry of Moses must play a role in his response to the awkward polemical situation that he is addressing."[7] In my view, in the particular case of 2 Corinthians 2.14–4.6, we cannot avoid the challenge of producing (at least) a general reconstruction of Paul's opponents. Not to do so is necessarily to treat the passage without attention to the argumentative *inclusio* of 2.17–3.1 and 4.1–3, an *inclusio* which, so most agree, alludes to Paul's opponents.

Recently, Paul B. Duff has produced the careful study *Moses in Corinth*, in which he argues the following case.[8] (1) After perhaps the most extended, recent *Forschungsgeschichte* on the integrity of 2 Corinthians, Duff concludes that canonical 2 Corinthians is composed of five separate letters— (1) 2.14–7.4; (2) chapters 10–13; (3) 1.1–2.13; 7.5–16; (4) chapter 8; and (5) chapter 9.[9] He suggests, furthermore, that 6.14–7.1 might represent a "curious fragment."[10] (2) As for the debate about Paul's opponents, having considered various proposals, Duff postulates that Paul's opposition came mainly from *within* the Corinthian community and consisted primarily of antagonism toward Paul's weak and unimpressive physical appearance and overall "worthiness" (cf. 2 Cor. 3.5–6) to be an apostle.[11] (3) Therefore, the argumentative rhetoric of 2 Corinthians 2.17–4.6 is not aimed at Jewish and/or Jewish-Christian opponents from *without* the community but at "gentile Christian" opponents *within* community.[12]

As for Duff's case concerning the composite nature of 2 Corinthians, I make the following points. (1) Many scholars still insist upon the letter's integrity, the most rigorous, recent contribution coming from Douglas Campbell.[13] It is unfortunate, in this regard, that Campbell's book (I assume) appeared too late for Duff to engage it, as the former treatment, at least to my mind, successfully responds to the major challenges. (2) In any case, even if 2 Corinthians were composed of five separate letters, it would *still* make good historical and exegetical sense to reconstruct the situation(s) at Corinth—allowing for the possibility of various chronological arrangements of the letters and for the probability that the local situation(s) changed over time—*in light of all of the evidence*. In other words, as is most pertinent to my case, even if chapters 10–13 represent a separate (and even later) letter than 2.14–7.4 (and 2.17–4.6 within that), it would still make good historical sense to assume that evidence from the former might shed light upon the latter.[14]

Furthermore, with respect to Duff's case concerning Paul's opponents, the following betrays an overly apologetic concern which seems to have influenced the reconstruction:

> As I will show, Paul's rhetoric in this section (2 Corinthians 3) does not disparage the Torah and, with the exception of 3:13, the apostle speaks only positively of Moses. Indeed, both Moses and the Torah function as positive examples in his argument. It should also be noted that Paul does not make the claim here (either implicitly or explicitly) that Israel has been replaced by the ἐκκλησία. Although Israel functions for Paul as a negative model in 2 Corinthians 3 (as she does in 1 Cor 10:1–11), the apostle in no way intended to demonstrate that the deity's "new covenant" with the gentiles was meant to take the place of God's original covenant with Israel.[15] *Ultimately, Paul's argument focuses on the gentile Corinthians, not on Israel.* Read from this perspective, the negative labels that the apostle applies to Moses' ministry ("the ministry of death" and "the ministry of condemnation") *are concerned not with Israel's condemnation but rather with the negative effects of Moses' ministry on the gentiles—specifically the Corinthian gentiles—prior to their conversion.*[16]

While I share Duff's concern to combat unnuanced articulations of the relationship between God's covenant with historical Israel and the Jew-plus-Gentile people of God which made up Paul's communities, I regard it as equally unnuanced implicitly to present only two dichotomous options: (1) a kind of "Two Ways" construal in which, for Paul, God's covenant with Israel is categorically distinct from his separate covenant with Gentile Christians; or (2) a straightforward "supersessionism" in which, from Paul's perspective, God had simply abandoned his former covenant with Israel and had established a "new covenant" with a new people, the Jew-plus-Gentile church. Though, to engage in detail on this point would take us too far afield.

For our purposes, we are concerned with the italicized portions of the quotation in which Duff offers a hypothesis concerning the rhetorical function of 2 Corinthians 3 vis-à-vis Paul's opponents. For Duff, Paul's appeal to Exodus 34 in 3.7–18—and within that section Paul's expressions "ministry of death" (3.7) and "ministry of condemnation" (3.9)—serve to indicate to Gentile

Christians in Corinth, inter alia, that when the Torah came to Israel they (the Gentiles) stood condemned by it. Therefore, importantly for Duff, nothing in 3.7–18 functions as a Pauline critique of historical Israel, of contemporary Jews, or of contemporary Jewish Christians.

To substantiate this point, Duff (rightly) insists that some second-temple Jewish texts (LAB 11.2; 4 Ezra 7.37–38, 72; 2 Bar. 82.2–9; and Sib. Or. 3.600–03) take the view that Gentiles are culpable for their ignorance of, and/or their disobedience to, Torah. However, crucially, Duff fails to demonstrate that this was *Paul's* view. His treatment of several texts from Galatians is unconvincing, and his omission of the supremely relevant Romans 2.12 is quite conspicuous. There Paul says, "As many as have sinned apart from Torah, they will also perish apart from Torah; and as many as have sinned with respect to Torah, they will be judged by [i.e., "according to"] Torah" (Ὅσοι γὰρ ἀνόμως ἥμαρτον, ἀνόμως καὶ ἀπολοῦνται, καὶ ὅσοι ἐν νόμῳ ἥμαρτον, διὰ νόμου κριθήσονται). Most commentators are agreed on Paul's meaning.[17] Gentiles sin "without [i.e., "not having"] Torah" (ἀνόμως ἥμαρτον), while Jews sin "with respect to Torah" (ἐν νόμῳ ἥμαρτον). The former will, therefore, "also perish apart from Torah" (ἀνόμως καὶ ἀπολοῦντ αι), while the latter will, in contradistinction, "be judged by [i.e., "according to"] Torah." The latter statement *must* mean, at least from Paul's present (i.e., "post-conversion") perspective, that those "apart from Torah" are precisely *not* judged "by/according to Torah." If we can assume, therefore, that Paul held this view only a short time earlier when he wrote 2 Corinthians 3—and we probably can—then this demonstrates the untenability of Duff's position.

Beyond this, it is very difficult to see how Duff's position accounts for 3.13–14, in which Paul explicitly refers to "the sons of Israel" (3.13) and to the hardening of their minds (3.14). Even if we were to conclude that this primarily serves as a rhetorical foil for Paul's argument against Gentile Christians at Corinth, we should remind ourselves that foils are only effective when the author and the readers largely agree to the terms of them. Finally, I note a few major bibliographical lacunae in the work of Duff: he nowhere engages the important and widely influential work of Winter, van Kooten, Litwa, or Blackwell, the first two of which we will come to presently.[18]

We now turn to Michael Cover's recent and rigorous treatment. Cover's thesis is extremely wide-ranging. He engages the question of Pauline hermeneutics,[19] of the *Forschungsgeschichte* of this passage,[20] of Paul's opponents,[21] of exegetical patterns in the Philonic *corpus*, several Greco-Roman commentaries, the Qumran *pesharim*,[22] several New Testament texts, and of course our own passage.[23] Nevertheless, as one of his main aims, Cover attempts "to address the question of the rhetorical 'fit' of Paul's exegesis of Exodus in its current location in the letter."[24] This is the question which governs his treatment of what he calls "hellenistic commentary traditions," by which he broadly refers to certain texts of the Hellenistic period which expound various precursor texts.

In light of his extensive and careful study, he concludes,

> [A] proper appreciation of Paul's employment of secondary-level exegesis reveals that 2 Cor 3:7–18, while certainly an excursus of sorts, fits well within the stylistic parameters expected for ancient literary unity and constitutes a completely licit digression.[25]

> The digressive character of Paul's exegesis of Exodus, moreover, was not out of place in his chosen genre, but conforms with conventional standards. All of the authors surveyed in this chapter also share with Paul not only a digressive compositional aesthetic, but also a desire to organically link their exegetical excursuses with the broader argument or narrative that they are constructing.[26]

Against such a long scholarly tradition and in view of the digressive poetical techniques of certain ancient commentary traditions, Cover rightly argues that we have no need of source-critical hypotheses to explain the rhetorical dynamics of 2 Corinthians 2.14–4.6. As to the question of Paul's opponents, Cover opts for what is in my view a very tempting but ultimately untenable solution: "Paul here is wrestling with a rival set of Christian ministers steeped in the philosophical and apologetic traditions of Hellenistic Judaism."[27] This broad position, Cover contends, captures the strengths of the other main views—that the opponents were (1) Galatian-style, Jewish-Christian "agitators";[28] (2) Gnostics;[29] or (3) Sophists[30]—without adopting their weaknesses.[31]

However, Cover adduces little evidence in favor of this position beyond the implicit argument throughout that Philo's exegesis significantly illuminates Paul's, an implicit argument with which, at least at this level of generality, I would not take issue. Cover goes on to hint, however, though one might have wished for a clearer statement of the case, that the figure of Apollos might be relevant to his construal.[32] After all, if Luke is to be trusted on these points, Acts 18.24–28 tells us that Apollos was a Jew from Alexandria who was ἀνήρ λόγιος ("an eloquent man") and who had "great capability in the scriptures (δυνατὸς ὢν ἐν ταῖς γραφαῖς)" (18.24) and who, moreover, had been sent to Achaia with letters of recommendation from Christians in Ephesus (18.27). After citing all of this evidence, however, Cover concludes, "It is unlikely that we will ever recover the exact teachings of Paul's opponents. One thing the foregoing study does suggest, however, is that their understanding of Moses and the Pentateuch posed problems for Paul."[33] Cover finally leaves us with "students of Platonizing Judaism, Christian ministers of this Hellenizing variety [who] may have been sowing exegetical seeds of dissension."[34]

For such a careful study, the vagueness and imprecision of the conclusion is disappointing. Despite the considerable care with which Cover has executed his case, and despite the many illuminating features of its constituent parts, his conclusion ultimately suffers from the same criticism which he leveled at van Kooten. Van Kooten postulates that the opponents in view in 2.17–4.6 are Jewish-Christian sophists who have been propagating a certain reading of Exodus 34 which takes Moses to be a paradigmatic example of sophistry. Cover rightly criticizes van Kooten's reconstruction—which we will come to presently—on the grounds that it does not "adequately address the Jewish, covenantal concerns" of the passage.[35] I quite agree, though it is difficult to see how Cover's proposal does any better on this count. If it were the case that Paul's opponents in 2.14–4.6 were "Christian ministers" and "students of Platonizing Judaism," how would this explain, on the one hand, Paul's apparent characterization of them as sophists (2.17), and, on the other hand, Paul's *a minore ad maius* argument about the old and new covenants? It seems to me that what mostly account for Cover's reconstruction are not so much the features of the Corinthian correspondence itself but the implicit argument throughout that several examples of Philonic exegesis significantly illuminate several instances of Pauline exegesis and that this Alexandrian-style exegesis might have been imported into Corinth by Apollos.[36] As tempting as it is to construe the Lukan data in this way, this does not get us very far in explaining the details of 3.7–18.

Van Kooten, following and supplementing the pioneering work of Bruce Winter, has convincingly shown that certain features of Paul's rhetoric in 1 and 2 Corinthians were designed to present himself and his sympathizers as true philosophers over against his opponents and their (actual or potential) sympathizers as shallow sophists.[37] We will come to some of this evidence below. In this connection, though scholars used to think that we could not date the "Second Sophistic" any earlier than ca. 68 CE, Winter demonstrates that "in the first half of the first century what came to be known in the next as the Second Sophistic was already flowering if not flourishing."[38] As to the sophists themselves, Taylor writes,

> Sophists [were] itinerant professors of higher education . . . who travelled widely through the Greek world. . . . They pioneered the systematic study of techniques of persuasion and argument. . . . He [Plato] believed, very probably truly, that the suspicion which certain sophists had attracted had contributed to the unpopularity and ultimately to the condemnation of Socrates, and therefore depicts the sophists predominantly as charlatans, in contrast to Socrates, the paradigm of the true philosopher.[39]

Nor should we restrict this movement to the major centers—such as Athens, Rome, Alexandria, Tarsus, and Corinth—as Philo suggests that it was widespread: "[M]ultitudes of those who are called sophists" win "the admiration of city after city."[40]

Van Kooten and Winter have further demonstrated that some of Philo's writings and the Corinthian correspondence reflect popular criticisms of sophistry. Philo, depending in particular upon Plato, regarded such rhetoric as deliberately deceptive. As Winter states, "ἀπάτη ("illusion" or "deception") was the goal of magic and, in Plato's estimation, also characterised rhetoric."[41] Philo also betrays the influence of Plato's (Socrates's) critique when he charges the sophists with the desire for personal gain:

> And the wisdom must not be that of the systems hatched by the word-catchers and sophists who sell their tenets and arguments like any bit of merchandise in the market (οἱ λογοθῆραι καὶ σοφισταὶ πιπράσκοντες ὡς ἄλλο τι τῶν ὠνίων ἐπ' ἀγορᾶς δόγματα καὶ λόγους).[42]

Plato's Socrates had said the following:

> And we must take care, my good friend, that the sophist, in commending his wares, does not deceive us (ὁ σοφιστής, ἐπαινῶν ἃ πωλεῖ, ἐξαπατήσῃ ἡμᾶς), as both merchant and peddler (ὁ ἔμπορός τε καὶ κάπηλος) do in the case of our bodily food.... And in the same way, those who take their doctrines the round of our cities, peddling them about to any odd purchaser who desires them, commend everything that they sell (οὕτω δὲ καὶ οἱ τὰ μαθήματα περιάγοντες κατὰ τὰς πόλεις καὶ πωλοῦντες καὶ καπηλεύοντες τῷ ἀεὶ ἐπιθυμοῦντι ἐπαινοῦσι μὲν πάντα ἃ πωλοῦσι).[43]

Paul echoes this critique of sophistry in 2 Corinthians 2.17:[44]

> (2.17) For, we are not like the many who peddle the word of God (καπηλεύοντες τὸν λόγον τοῦ θεοῦ), but from sincerity (εἰλικρινεία)—indeed, from God—we speak before God in the Messiah.
> (3.1) Are we beginning to commend ourselves (ἑαυτοὺς συνιστάνειν) again? Or, do we need, as some do, letters of recommendation (συστατικῶν ἐπιστολῶν) to you or from you?

Taken together with the reference to "peddling the word of God," the reference to letters of recommendation—though this could apply much more broadly—should probably be regarded as another allusion to the practice of the sophists. Near the end of the same argument, Paul picks up this characterization:

> (4.2) We have renounced shameful secrets (τὰ κρυπτὰ τῆς αἰσχύνης); we refuse to walk in cunning ways (ἐν πανουργίᾳ) and to tamper with the word of God (δολοῦντες τὸν λόγον τοῦ θεοῦ), but by the open manifestation of the truth we commend ourselves (συνιστάνοντες ἑαυτοὺς) to every human conscience before God.

Here Paul restates the themes of "sincerity," "truth," "the word of God," and not least the issue of commendation. In 2.17–3.1 and again in 4.2, therefore, Paul characterizes his opponents in specifically sophistic terms. This *inclusio*, I contend, should govern our reading of the whole passage.

It is precisely these features of this *inclusio*, however, which have caused scholars so many problems. If the *inclusio* of 2.17–3.1 and 4.2 reflects a critique of sophistry, how does this relate to the apparently Jewish and/or Jewish-Christian concerns of 3.7–18? This is the central question with which most studies (noted above) wrestle. Perhaps, some think, we should treat the Jewish and/or Jewish-Christian concerns of 3.7–18 without reference to the *inclusio*.[45] Or, perhaps we should treat the apparently Jewish and/or Jewish-Christian concerns of 3.7–18 as though they mask a more fundamental polemic, signaled more clearly by the *inclusio*, against "students of Platonizing Judaism" or "sophists."[46] Clearly, however, a proposal which gives due weight both to the nature of the *inclusio* and to the apparent concerns of 3.7–18 is to be preferred. It is just such a proposal which I will put forward presently.

First, I want to indicate that I am fully convinced by the *general* proposals of Winter and van Kooten: Paul deliberately polemicizes against sophistry in 1 and 2 Corinthians. However, I emphasize that this only proves (at least directly) that Paul criticized *the Corinthians* for valuing sophistry. It does not demonstrate that Paul's opponents in 2 Corinthians 2.17–4.6, *who were missionaries from without the Corinthian community*, were sophists. I will say more about this below.

Therefore, while I take some of the larger proposals of Winter and van Kooten into account, I suggest a different construal. I begin by noting the way in which the whole letter is tied together by the question of "commendation," precisely the theme out of which the whole of 2.17–4.6 grows.[47] The verb συνίστημι, connected with the question of commendation, occurs at 3.1; 4.2; 5.12; 6.4; 10.12, 18; and 12.11. In other words, the entire letter concerns the question of commendation, a theme which itself nests within and relates directly to Paul's defense of his apostleship. Crucially, as is demonstrated by the use of the verb in the *inclusio* of our passage at 3.1 and 4.2, taken together with the cognate adjective in the phrase συστατικαί ἐπιστολαί (3.1), we can see that our passage too is governed by the question of the "commendation" of Paul's apostolic ministry.

Furthermore, when Paul engages opponents in chapters 10–13, the question of "commendation" is central.

> (10.12) For we are not so bold as to classify or to compare ourselves with some of those who are commending themselves (τισιν τῶν ἑαυτοὺς συνιστανόντων).

(10.18) For it is not the one commending himself who is approved, but the one whom the Lord commends (οὐ γὰρ ὁ ἑαυτὸν συνιστάνων, ἐκεῖνός ἐστιν δόκιμος, ἀλλ' ὃν ὁ κύριος συνίστησιν).

(12.11) I have been a fool—you pushed me to it! Indeed, I should have been commended by you (ἐγὼ γὰρ ὤφειλον ὑφ' ὑμῶν συνίστασθαι). For I am in no way inferior to these "super-apostles," though I am nothing.

These three texts, and especially 12.11, which refers explicitly to "super-apostles," demonstrate that the question of "commendation" runs straight through the entire polemic of chapters 10–13. This evidence suggests that the polemic of chapters 10–13 might relate directly to the polemic of 2.17–4.6. If this is the case, then it is possible that the opponents in view in 10–13 are the same as those in view in 2.17–4.6.[48] But how does Paul depict the opponents of 10–13?

These are the relevant texts:

(11.5) I think that I am not in the least inferior to these "super-apostles" (τῶν ὑπερλίαν ἀποστόλων).[49] (11.6) I may be untrained in rhetoric (ἰδιώτης τῷ λόγῳ), but not in knowledge; certainly in every way and in all things we have made this evident to you. (11.7) Did I commit a sin by humbling myself so that you might be exalted, because I proclaimed God's good news to you free of charge? (11.8) I robbed other churches by accepting support from them in order to serve you. (11.9) And when I was with you and was in need, I did not burden anyone, for my needs were supplied by the friends who came from Macedonia. So I refrained and will continue to refrain from burdening you in any way (NRSV).

(11.22) Are they Hebrews? So am I. Are they Israelites? So am I. Are they Abraham's children? So am I. (11.23) Are they servants of the Messiah? I am speaking like a fool—I am a better one: with far greater labors, far more imprisonments, with countless floggings, and often near death.

The evidence of 11.22–23 is clear. Paul here refers to Jewish Christians.[50] Furthermore, 2 Corinthians 11.5–9 reveals two things. (1) These Jewish Christians apparently had a more impressive public *persona* than Paul, particularly in terms of their public address (speech).[51] In this regard, as Hans Dieter Betz argued several decades ago, when Paul contends that he is perhaps "untrained in rhetoric, but not in knowledge" (ἰδιώτης τῷ λόγῳ, ἀλλ' οὐ τῇ γνώσει/ 11.6), he picks up a contrastive characterization which ultimately derives from Plato's Socrates (so Plato, *Phaed.* 236D).[52] Hereby, exactly as in his echo of the tradition which ultimately derives from the *Protagoras* (313D-E) in 2.17, Paul implicitly contrasts himself as a true philosopher—who, therefore, concerns himself with "knowledge" rather than mere "rhetoric"—and his Jewish-Christian opponents who are like shallow, sophistic rhetoricians.

(2) For some reason, as a part of the polemic of 11.5–9, Paul defends his policy of *not* accepting financial assistance from the Corinthians.[53]

This is how I would coordinate this evidence with 2.17–4.6. (1) The consistent theme of "commendation" suggests that the opponents of chapters 10–13 are the same as those in view in 2.17–4.6, where the question of commendation is so central. The opponents in chapters 10–13, moreover, are Jewish Christians (so 11.22–23) whose public *persona* the Corinthians have favorably contrasted with Paul's (so 11.5–6). (2) Coordinating the reference to "peddling the word of God" (2.17) with Paul's defense that he had not accepted money (so 11.7–9), I suggest that these Jewish-Christian missionaries *had*, on the other hand, served among the Corinthians for pay.[54] These are the historical factors because of which Paul cleverly decided to depict these Jewish-Christian missionaries as sophists.

Stepping back, then, and taking Winter's case into account, this is my larger construal of the historical and argumentative context of Paul's polemic as it is reflected in 2 Corinthians 2.17–4.6 and 10–13. As Winter has shown, particularly with respect to 1 Corinthians 1–4 and 2 Corinthians 10–13 (esp. 10.10; 11.6; and 12.16), Paul characterizes himself, his associates, and his sympathizers as true philosophers, while he characterizes his opponents and their sympathizers as shallow sophists.[55] *However*, in distinguishing my view from the prevalent "true philosophy vs. sophistry" hypothesis, I contend that we have little direct evidence in either letter that this characterization is anything more than that: a polemical *characterization*.[56] At least as pertains to the case of 2 Corinthians 2.17–4.6 and 10–13, our *direct* evidence, which comes principally from 11.5–9, 22–23, suggests that Paul's opponents in 2 Corinthians are rival Jewish-Christian missionaries from *without* the community, missionaries who have likely come to Corinth with impressive letters of recommendation. On the other hand, with respect to 1 Corinthians 1–4 and 2 Corinthians 10–13 (esp. 10.10; 11.6; and 12.16), Winter has indeed demonstrated that *the Corinthians themselves* prized traits typical of the sophists. But, to restate the point, we have no evidence which directly suggests that *the missionary opponents themselves* were sophists. Rather, I suggest, having already characterized his polemic in 1 Corinthians as a kind of "true philosophy vs. sophistry," and having heard news of rival Jewish-Christian missionaries coming to Corinth with letters of recommendation and serving among the Corinthians for pay, Paul seized upon the rhetorical and argumentative opportunity of characterizing himself and his sympathizers as true philosophers and these rival missionaries—though they were actually Jewish Christians boasting in their distinctively *Jewish* pedigree (so 11.22–23)—as shallow sophists.

This explains the data of 2 Corinthians 2.17–4.6 and 10–13 in a way in which, I submit, no other construal currently does. Hereby, we are able to appreciate and not to downplay the clear characterization of "true philosophy vs. sophistry" but *also* to account for the fact that 3.6–18 and 11.22–23 reflect, exactly within the same context and as a part of the same polemic, substantially inner-Jewish and/or inner-Jewish-Christian concerns and not the concerns of "true philosophy vs. sophistry."

Before commencing the exegesis, I restate the main contours of my reconstruction. (1) In 2.17, where Paul introduces the argument of 2.17–4.6, he alludes to Plato's well-known characterization of the sophists when he refers to "peddlers of the word of God" (*Prot.* 313D–E). Hereby, Paul is implicitly introducing a contrast between himself, who has *not* accepted money from the Corinthians, and the rival Jewish-Christian missionaries who *have* accepted money (so 11.5–9, 22–23). (2) In light of this polemical characterization, Paul has in mind the crescendo of 3.18 all along, in which he presents himself and his sympathizers as attaining to the *telos* of true philosophy: "the image of God" (3.18). (3) However, despite this rhetorically charged double characterization, the substantive issues in 2.17–4.6 are inner-Jewish issues.

EXEGESIS

With my larger reconstruction in mind, we now work through the details of the text.

(2.17) οὐ γάρ ἐσμεν ὡς οἱ πολλοί[57] καπηλεύοντες τὸν λόγον τοῦ θεοῦ, ἀλλ' ὡς ἐξ εἰλικρινείας, ἀλλ' ὡς ἐκ θεοῦ κατέναντι θεοῦ ἐν Χριστῷ λαλοῦμεν.

(3.1) Ἀρχόμεθα πάλιν ἑαυτοὺς συνιστάνειν; ἢ μὴ χρῄζομεν ὥς τινες συστατικῶν ἐπιστολῶν πρὸς ὑμᾶς ἢ ἐξ ὑμῶν; (3.2) ἡ ἐπιστολὴ ἡμῶν ὑμεῖς ἐστε, ἐγγεγραμμένη ἐν ταῖς καρδίαις ἡμῶν,[58] γινωσκομένη καὶ ἀναγινωσκομένη ὑπὸ πάντων ἀνθρώπων, (3.3) φανερούμενοι ὅτι ἐστὲ ἐπιστολὴ Χριστοῦ διακονηθεῖσα ὑφ' ἡμῶν, ἐγγεγραμμένη οὐ μέλανι ἀλλὰ πνεύματι θεοῦ ζῶντος, οὐκ ἐν πλαξὶν λιθίναις ἀλλ' ἐν πλαξὶν καρδίαις σαρκίναις.

In 2.17, Paul implicitly contrasts himself and his associates with the Jewish-Christian missionaries who, according to his polemical characterization, "peddle the word of God." Then, in 3.1, with his first reference to "commendation," he contends that he and his associates have no need of the letters of recommendation with which the Jewish-Christian missionaries have come to Corinth.[59] Hereby, as I have already argued, Paul begins a subtle double characterization which will reach a crescendo in 3.18. The Jewish-Christian missionaries are like shallow sophists who come with letters of recommendation and offer services for a fee. Paul, his associates, and his sympathizers, on the other hand, are like true philosophers who are being "transformed to the same image [of the Messiah/God]" (3.18).

Picking up in 3.2, Paul argues that the Corinthian community itself (3.2a: ἡ ἐπιστολὴ ἡμῶν ὑμεῖς ἐστε) is the only necessary "letter" of recommendation, "inscribed on our hearts, known and read by all" (3.2). Paul hereby contrasts the missionaries' letter, presumably written with "ink" (3.3: μέλας), and the letter which commends him and his associates. This letter is inscribed on their very hearts. The very fact of the Corinthian community, in other words, attests to the validity of Paul's apostleship.[60] To undermine his apostleship, therefore, is de facto to undermine the foundations of the community.[61]

Indeed, Paul contends that the very existence and life of the Corinthian community demonstrates that they—the community-as-letter, written on Paul and his associates' hearts—are a letter authored by the Messiah himself (ἐστὲ ἐπιστολὴ Χριστοῦ/ 3.3).[62] The Messiah-as-author, then, "not with ink but with the Spirit of the living God," "authored" the existence of the Corinthian community. In this connection, as has been widely recognized, Paul's phrase ἐγγεγραμμένη ἐν ταῖς καρδίαις ἡμῶν ("written on our hearts") alludes to the new covenant passage of Jeremiah (MT Jer. 31.33/LXX Jer. 38.33), a passage to which he will allude even more clearly in 3.6 with the phrase καινὴ διαθήκη ("new covenant"), a *hapax legomenon* in LXX. Paul also alludes to another prophetic passage about the new covenant with his phrase οὐκ ἐν πλαξὶν λιθίναις ἀλλ' ἐν πλαξὶν καρδίαις σαρκίναις ("not on tablets of stone but on tablets of human hearts"), but this time to Ezekiel (cf. LXX Eze. 11.19 and 36.26).[63]

At this point, we should note what appears to be an exegetical feat of considerable cleverness on Paul's part. In the book of Exodus (31.18; 32.15; cp. Deut. 9.10), the finger of God inscribes the Torah on πλάκες λίθιναι ("stone tablets"). In the new covenant prophecies of Jeremiah, however, there is no mention of πλάκες λίθιναι; nevertheless, the prophet clearly states that God will one day "write them [νομοί] upon their hearts" (ἐπὶ καρδίας αὐτῶν γράψω αὐτούς/ LXX Jer. 38.33). However, Paul probably felt compelled somehow to conjoin this prophecy with the hope of (LXX) Ezekiel 36.26: "And I will give to you a new heart (καρδίαν καινὴν) and a new spirit (πνεῦμα καινὸν) and I will take away the heart of stone (τὴν καρδίαν τὴν λιθίνην) from your flesh and give to you a heart of flesh (καρδίαν σαρκίνην)." For Paul to conjoin these prophecies, however, he would need to take Ezekiel's new, "heart of flesh"—καρδία σάρκινη—rather than the old, "heart of stone"—καρδία λιθίνη—as the heart upon which God would internally inscribe the Torah.

If this were the case, on the basis of a combined reading of Jeremiah's and Ezekiel's prophecies, Paul had reasonable scriptural warrant to contrast a Torah written on something λιθίνη ("made of stone") with a Torah written on something σάρκινη ("made of flesh"). Moreover, because Exodus 31.18; 32.15; and Deuteronomy 9.10 state clearly that God had originally inscribed the Torah on πλάκες λίθιναι, the combined reading of Jeremiah's and Ezekiel's prophecies partly facilitated Paul's contrast between the two covenants. Or, to put this more accurately, this scriptural contrast partly facilitated Paul's contrast between the "heart conditions" of the people of the old and new covenants.[64]

In any case, these allusions amount to a subtle contrast between two covenants: (1) the Mosaic legislation on "tablets of stone," on the one hand, (2) and the Jeremianic and Ezekielian new covenant on "hearts of flesh," on the other. Not only are Paul's opponents shallow sophists, therefore, they are ministers of an old and now "invalidated" covenant arrangement (3.7, 11). Paul and his associates, on the other hand, are ministers of the new covenant. In this connection, it is crucial to bear in mind that it is precisely this double characterization—the opponents as ministers of the old covenant and Paul and his associates as ministers of the new—which organically develops into the full-blown *a minore ad maius* argument of 3.7–18. In other words, and although Paul here doubtless writes things of broader relevance to, for example, his theology of the new covenant, of Israel, of the Torah, and of (what we call) "hermeneutics," it is crucial to bear in mind that the subtle polemic of 2.17–4.6, and of 3.7–18 within it, fundamentally has in view *Paul's polemical double characterization of himself and his associates over against his Jewish-Christian missionary rivals*. In this regard, I will argue that Exodus 34 largely serves as a foil for Paul's polemic, though this does not mean that the details of the text do not also exercise influence on his exposition.[65]

We pick up in 3.4. Paul states, "We have such confidence (πεποίθης τοιαύτη) through the Messiah toward God." With the demonstrative pronoun "such" (τοιαύτη), Paul refers to the confidence—indeed, the audacity—which the exposition of 3.2–3 presupposes. In 3.5–6, Paul attempts to justify this bold position: "(3.5) Not that we are worthy of ourselves, as though we regard our worthiness as coming from ourselves. Rather, our worthiness comes from God, (3.6) who has made us worthy to be ministers of a new covenant, not of the letter but of the Spirit (οὐ γράμματος ἀλλὰ πνεύματος)."[66]

The phrase οὐ γράμματος ἀλλὰ πνεύματος (3.6) has been fiercely contested.[67] In this connection, we should note the striking similarity of this phrase to the contrastive phrase in 3.3:

2 Cor. 3.3: οὐ μέλανι   ἀλλὰ πνεύματι θεοῦ ζῶντος
2 Cor. 3.6: οὐ γράμματος   ἀλλὰ πνεύματος

The former phrase οὐ μέλανι ἀλλὰ πνεύματι θεοῦ ζῶντος is clearly a way of contrasting the old and new covenants and it seems best to take οὐ γράμματος ἀλλὰ πνεύματος similarly. "Letter" and "Spirit" are shorthands, therefore, for the old and new covenants (cp. Rom. 2.29; and 7.6), but here particularly (and in Rom. 7.6) for the way in which, at least as Paul sees it, the new covenant is characterized by the outpouring and operation of the Spirit in a way that the old covenant was not.[68]

We can now turn to the major section of 3.6b–11:

> (3.6b) For the letter kills (τὸ γὰρ γράμμα ἀποκτέννει), but the Spirit gives life. (3.7) Now if the ministry of death, chiseled in letters upon stone, came in glory, such that the sons of Israel could not gaze upon the face of Moses because of the glory of his face—a glory which has been set aside (τὴν καταργουμένην)—(3.8) how much more glory will the ministry of the Spirit have? (3.9) For if the ministry of condemnation had glory, how much more does the ministry of righteousness abound in glory? (3.10) Indeed, that which used to be glorious is no longer glorious for this very reason: because of the glory which surpasses it (καὶ γὰρ οὐ δεδόξασται τὸ δεδοξασμένον ἐν τούτῳ τῷ μέρει εἵνεκεν τῆς ὑπερβαλλούσης δόξης). (3.11) For if that which is set aside came through glory, how much more glorious will be that which remains (εἰ γὰρ τὸ καταργούμενον διὰ δόξης, πολλῷ μᾶλλον τὸ μένον ἐν δόξῃ)?

It is impossible to give a full account of this passage without an extended discussion of Paul's theology of Torah, a discussion which is out of place here.[69] We will, rather, content ourselves with a few basic points. First, we note the strikingly negative depiction of the old covenant: "the letter *kills*" (3.6b); "the ministry of *death*" (3.7); and "the ministry of *condemnation*" (3.9). Moreover, Paul speaks of the glory of Moses's face as a glory "which is set aside" (3.7: καταργέω).[70] How do we account for such an apparently negative depiction?

In this regard, I make two points in particular. (1) This strongly negative depiction of the old covenant depends in part upon Paul's desire *negatively to characterize his opponents whom he has already cast as ministers of that covenant* (so 2.17–3.3).[71] (2) However, we should not simply conclude that this negative depiction is wholly governed by Paul's argumentative needs and does not arise from a more coherent theology of Torah. Elsewhere Paul similarly characterizes the Torah (esp. 1 Cor. 15.56 and Rom. 7.11). In 1 Corinthians 15.56, he states, "The sting of Death is Sin, and the power of Sin is the Torah (τὸ δὲ κέντρον τοῦ θανάτου ἡ ἁμαρτία, ἡ δὲ δύναμις τῆς ἁμαρτίας ὁ νόμος)." Even though this statement is rhetorically jarring, its basic meaning is straightforward. Sin effects the "sting of Death" and Sin gets its power from the Torah.[72] Therefore, Sin, through the Torah, effects death, and this is a statement which the Corinthians have already heard from Paul prior to receiving 2 Corinthians. Romans 7.11 is even more illuminating: "For Sin, seizing an opportunity in the commandment, deceived me and through it [i.e., the commandment] killed me (ἡ γὰρ ἁμαρτία ἀφορμὴν λαβοῦσα διὰ τῆς ἐντολῆς ἐξηπάτησέν με καὶ δι' αὐτῆς ἀπέκτεινεν)." Again, whatever else Paul is saying, it is clear that Sin uses the commandment to bring about death.[73]

And, indeed, any second-temple Jew desiring to make the point that the Mosaic legislation simply dispensed "curse" and "death" to a historical Israel with "uncircumcised" (so Deut. 30.6) "hearts of stone" (so Eze. 36.26) upon which the Torah had never properly been inscribed (so Jer. 31.33) would have found plenty of prominent scriptural material on the basis of which to make the case (so, e.g., Deut. 30.1–20; Jer. 31.31–34; Ezek. 36.23–36; Isa. 40.1–2; Ps. 106; and cp. Bar.; and CD-A 1.1–12). When we add to this the startling and unprecedented notions that, on the one hand, Israel's Messiah had taken upon himself the "curse" and "death" incurred for a covenant breach (so Gal. 3.13) and, on the other hand, God's eschatological Spirit had been poured out upon Torah unobservant Gentiles (so esp. Gal. 2.16; 3.1–5; and Rom. 2.25–9 [esp. 2.29]), Paul's "negative" characterization of the Mosaic legislation becomes much more comprehensible. However, it must nevertheless be borne carefully in mind throughout that the entire exposition of the Mosaic legislation in 2 Corinthians 3 grows organically out of Paul's desire (so 2.17–3.3) to contrast himself and his associates as ministers of the new covenant with his missionary opponents as ministers of the old.

Now, before we can move through the details of 3.7–11, we must immediately grasp the nettle of the contested force of καταργέω. Initially, it is clear that there is no lexical basis for the translation "fade/fading."[74] With this translation in mind, many have imagined that Paul envisaged the glory of Moses's face gradually fading away in-between meetings with YHWH in the tabernacle.[75] This, in turn, has led some to seek an exegetical basis for this reading either in the text of Exodus and/or in its reception history.[76] Indeed, Philo (*Mos.* 2.70) and Pseudo-Jonathan both reflect exegetical traditions concerning the glorious countenance of Moses upon his descent from Mount Sinai; and it is not unlikely that Paul too was aware of such a tradition.[77] However, despite the (somewhat desperate) appeal to LAB 19.16, we have no evidence of ancient Jewish exegetical traditions which emphasized the *transience* of Moses's countenance in this connection.[78] Such a search for Jewish exegetical traditions, in any case, betrays a failure to appreciate the way in which this passage fundamentally serves as a polemical foil.[79] Rather than some putative Jewish exegetical tradition, it is Paul's desire negatively to depict the Jewish-Christian missionaries, whom he hopes negatively to depict through his (partly) negative characterization of the paradigmatic minister of the old covenant, which accounts for the otherwise inexplicable details of his construal.

Returning to the force of καταργέω, we see that in its usual Pauline usage (cf. Rom. 3.3, 31; 4.14; 6.6; 7.2, 6; 1 Cor. 1.28; 2.6; 6.13; 13.8, 10, 11; 15.24, 26; Gal. 3.17; 5.4, and 11), the verb means "to nullify," "to invalidate," "to set aside," "to bring to nothing," or some such.[80] It is, therefore, amply attested in Paul and nowhere means "to fade away." For Paul, therefore, the "glory" on Moses's face is not gradually "fading"; rather, it is simply "set aside . . . because of the glory which surpasses it (3.10: ἐν τούτῳ τῷ μέρει εἵνεκεν τῆς ὑπερβαλλούσης δόξης)." I note the logic of Paul's Greek: it is set aside precisely *because* (εἵνεκεν) the glory of the new covenant necessarily surpasses it.[81] Because, so Paul's argues, the new covenant has arrived, the old covenant is de facto nullified. This is the consistent meaning of καταργέω throughout the passage (3.7, 11, and 13).

Aside from this thorny issue, the passage is relatively straightforward. The "ministry of death," though it *was* a ministry of death, was itself so glorious that "the sons of Israel could not gaze upon the face of Moses because of the glory of his face—a glory which has been set aside" (3.7). This double characterization, both positive ("glorious") and negative ("ministry of death"), is followed by a clear statement of the wholly positive "ministry of the Spirit," which is more glorious (3.8). Second Corinthians 3.9–11 makes much the same point. However, it is important to bear in mind that Paul's double characterization of the old covenant is partly facilitated by his rhetorical needs. On the one hand, he wants negatively to depict the old covenant and its contemporary ministers (his Jewish-Christian opponents) while, on the other hand, his *a minore ad maius* argument demands that he also characterize the old covenant in glorious terms so as to argue for the even greater glory of the new covenant (and its ministers).[82]

We now move to 3.12–18. Paul writes, "(3.12) Therefore, because we have such a hope,"—that is, the hope of a more glorious covenant and a more glorious ministry—"we act with transparency. (3.13) And not like Moses." Here the contrast with Moses is pronounced. Paul contrasts his πολλή παρρησία with Moses, "(3.13) who placed a veil over his face πρὸς τὸ μὴ ἀτενίσαι τοὺς υἱοὺς Ἰσραὴλ εἰς τὸ τέλος τοῦ καταργουμένου."[83] Παρρησία can mean both "boldness" and "transparency."[84] In Paul, in 2 Corinthians 7.4, Philippians 1.20, and Philemon 8, it means "boldness." In Colossians 2.15, it means "openly" or "publicly." In this context, because Paul is contrasting himself and his associates with a *veiled* Moses, it is probably best to prefer something like "transparency," as opposed to "hiddenness" or "craftiness."[85] But what should we make of the striking infinitival phrase πρὸς τὸ μὴ ἀτενίσαι τοὺς υἱοὺς Ἰσραὴλ? Moses veiled himself *so that* the sons of Israel might not gaze upon τὸ τέλος τοῦ καταργουμένου?[86] We can only discern the meaning of this clause when we determine the meaning of τὸ τέλος τοῦ καταργουμένου.

Some take the phrase to mean "the end of what is fading," which might suggest that Paul is arguing that Moses veiled his face so that the Israelites might not see the glory of his face gradually fading away in-between tabernacle meetings.[87] However, we have already determined that "faded/fading" is an indefensible translation of καταργέω. It means, rather, "that which is set aside." Furthermore, this reading depends upon the assumption that Paul is performing an exegesis/exposition of Exodus 34 and/or that he depends upon some Jewish exegetical tradition. I have already argued that this is not the case. Exodus 34 continues to serve as a foil for Paul's polemic against his Jewish-Christian opponents.

If, however, καταργέω means "that which is set aside," then it likely refers to the old covenant. But if it refers to the old covenant, then how should we understand τέλος, which can mean "end," as in "termination point," or "end," as in "goal"?[88] Moreover, if καταργέω does not mean "fading," it is difficult to see what sense it would make for Paul to refer to "the *termination* of the old covenant."[89] If this were the case, then Paul would be saying that Moses veiled himself not because the glory on his face was "fading"—a reading without lexical justification—but because an unfading glory somehow demonstrated that the old covenant was coming to an "end." But this would make very little sense. It is far better, I suggest, to read τέλος as "goal" and to take the passage to mean: "Moses veiled his face so that the Israelites would not see the true goal of the old covenant."[90] In this case, τὸ τέλος τοῦ καταργουμένου would refer to the glory on Moses's face, a glory which is the reflection of the divine presence—a divine glory which, so Paul is about to argue, is none other than the Messiah's Glory (4.4). In this case, Moses veils himself to keep Israel from seeing that Jesus the Messiah is the true *telos* of the old covenant (cp. Rom. 10.4).[91]

Despite the close parallel in Romans 10.4, and despite the fact that—as Hays in particular has argued so strongly—καταργέω almost certainly means "set aside" (or some such) and *not* "faded/fading" (or some such) and that this renders the "teleological" construal of τέλος almost certain, most modern commentators have not read the text in this way. But this is due, I suggest, to the fact that most modern commentators have simply assumed that Paul is either performing a loose exegesis of Exodus 34 and/or is working with an established exegetical tradition. In light of this assumption, a construal in which Paul "reads" Exodus 34 to the effect that Moses had deliberately veiled the "sons of Israel" from seeing the glory on his face, a glory which was none other than the Messiah's (4.4), is so arbitrary as to be impossible. However, so I have argued, it seems as though, by the time they get to 3.7, most scholars have forgotten that Paul began this argument (2.17–3.1) with a polemical double characterization of himself and his associates, on the one hand, and their opponents, on the other. In my reading, therefore, Paul's otherwise arbitrary and almost inexplicable construal of Moses and his veil becomes much more intelligible. In Paul's use of Exodus 34 as a foil, Moses, the paradigmatic minister of the old covenant, stands in for Paul's Jewish-Christian opponents who, far from operating with Paul and his associates' "transparency" (3.12: παρρησία), behave deceptively (so the "veil"). Indeed, like Moses, they deliberately keep people from seeing the *telos* of the old covenant, the full Glory of the Messiah himself (4.4). In all likelihood, I suggest, these Jewish-Christian missionaries, perhaps not unlike those in Galatia, insisted that the Mosaic legislation was precisely not "set aside" (3.7, 11, 13: καταργέω) in the way that Paul imagined.

From here we move to 3.14–15:

> (3.14) But their minds were hardened. Indeed, to this very day, when they read the old covenant, the same veil remains. It is not lifted because it is set aside only in the Messiah (ἐν Χριστῷ). (3.15) But, to this very day, whenever Moses is read, a veil lies over their hearts.

At this point, Paul begins to explore the possible applications both of the figure of Moses and of the veil. On the one hand, Moses-as-person becomes Moses-as-text. Just as the face of Moses-as-person is veiled, so also is the surface of Moses-as-text.[92] "To this very day," Paul contends, "when they read the old covenant, the same veil remains. It is not lifted because it is set aside only in the Messiah." This appears to be a clear statement to the effect that one cannot properly understand the old covenant without being ἐν Χριστῷ. I will return to the force of this text below.

We now come to 3.16–17: "(3.16) But whenever a person turns to the Lord, the veil is lifted (ἡνίκα δὲ ἐὰν ἐπιστρέψῃ πρὸς κύριον, περιαιρεῖται τὸ κάλυμμα). (3.17) Now the Lord is the Spirit, and wherever the Spirit of the Lord is, there is freedom." As has long been recognized, 3.16 is nearly a direct quotation of LXX Exodus 34.34a: ἡνίκα δ' ἂν εἰσεπορεύετο Μωυσῆς ἔναντι κυρίου λαλεῖν αὐτῷ, περιῃρεῖτο τὸ κάλυμμα. However, Paul makes one crucial change.[93] The εἰσπορεύομαι of LXX Exodus 34.34a becomes ἐπιστρέφω. This likely reflects Paul's "conversion" language.[94] Then, as he continues to appropriate Exodus 34, he writes, "Now, the Lord is the Spirit." Hereby, Paul contends that, when a person—like the Moses of Exodus 34—turns to the true Lord ("for salvation," so ἐπιστρέφω), the veil which has kept such a person from properly seeing the *telos* of the old covenant is lifted. In this regard, moreover, it is best to take 3.17a as an explanatory gloss on 3.16, and, therefore, to take the κύριος of 3.16 (πρὸς κύριον) as a reference to the Spirit, which, in the context of this argument (so 3.3, 6, and 8), supremely characterizes the new covenant and its ministers.[95]

But, according to Paul's shifting use of the image of the veil, when the veil is lifted, such a person is not simply staring at Moses-as-person or even Moses-as-text; but such a person in fact assumes the position of Moses himself within the tabernacle and beholds the divine Glory: ἡμεῖς δὲ πάντες ἀνακεκαλυμμένῳ προσώπῳ τὴν δόξαν κυρίου κατοπτριζόμενοι τὴν αὐτὴν εἰκόνα μεταμορφούμεθα ἀπὸ δόξης εἰς δόξαν καθάπερ ἀπὸ κυρίου πνεύματος

(3.18).⁹⁶ While in 3.13 Paul had contrasted himself and his associates with Moses, he now takes Moses as the paradigmatic member of the new covenant.

But before we can turn our attention to 3.18, there are a few features of 3.14–17 and then of 4.1–6 which deserve comment. The "veil" is at once the veil over Moses-as-person, then the veil over Moses-as-text, and then the veil over the hearts' of non-Christian Jews. I take these to be the referent of the αὐτός in the phrase ἐπὶ τὴν καρδίαν αὐτῶν.⁹⁷ Any reading, therefore, which takes the passage to have in view *only* Paul's opponents—and not also non-Christian Jews more generally—fails sufficiently to account for this verse.⁹⁸ Nor is this a problem for my reading in which Paul's principal opponents are Jewish *Christians*. Beginning in 3.12 and reaching a crescendo in 4.3–4, Paul begins to provide an *apologia* for the very difficult and doubtless embarrassing fact that most of his own Jewish contemporaries had not accepted his message.⁹⁹ Particularly telling in this regard is the opening Greek of 4.3: "And *even if* (εἰ δὲ καὶ) our gospel is veiled, it is veiled among those who are perishing, among whom the god of this age (ὁ θεὸς τοῦ αἰῶνος τούτου) has blinded the minds of unbelievers so that they might not see the light of the gospel of the Glory of the Messiah, who is the image of God." The "even if" is doubtless a response to the implicit charge: "Even his own Jewish contemporaries have not accepted his gospel!."¹⁰⁰ The Jewish-Christian missionaries, I suggest, have leveled this criticism at Paul: "If Paul is an authorized minister of the gospel, why have more of his own people not believed his message?" With respect to this charge, Paul appeals to the workings of satan, whom I take to be the referent behind the phrase "the god of this age."¹⁰¹ The satan, so Paul argues, keeps his fellow Jews from seeing the Glory of the Messiah.

Before we can finally turn to 3.18, we must briefly consider a few features of 4.1–6:

(4.1) Therefore, since it is by God's mercy that we are engaged in this ministry, we do not lose heart. (4.2) We have renounced shameful secrets (τὰ κρυπτὰ τῆς αἰσχύνης), because we refuse to practice cunning or to falsify the word of God (δολοῦντες τὸν λόγον τοῦ θεοῦ), but by the open manifestation of the truth we commend (συνιστάνοντες) ourselves to every human conscience before God. (4.3) And even if our gospel is veiled, it is veiled among those who are perishing, (4.4) among whom the god of this age has blinded the minds of unbelievers so that they might not see the light of the gospel of the Glory of the Messiah (τὸν φωτισμὸν τοῦ εὐαγγελίου τῆς δόξης τοῦ Χριστοῦ), who is the image of God (ὅς ἐστιν εἰκὼν τοῦ θεοῦ). (4.5) For we do not proclaim ourselves but Jesus the Messiah as Lord and ourselves as your servants for Jesus's sake. (4.6) For it is the God who said, "Let light shine out of darkness," who has shone in our hearts to give the light of the knowledge of the Glory of God in the face of [Jesus] the Messiah (ὅτι ὁ θεὸς ὁ εἰπών· ἐκ σκότους φῶς λάμψει, ὃς ἔλαμψεν ἐν ταῖς καρδίαις ἡμῶν πρὸς φωτισμὸν τῆς γνώσεως τῆς δόξης τοῦ θεοῦ[102] ἐν προσώπῳ [Ἰησοῦ][103] Χριστοῦ).

I begin by noting that Paul picks up much of the same language which he earlier used to depict his opponents in 2.17–3.1. Paul refuses to act with deceit (τὰ κρυπτὰ τῆς αἰσχύνης/ cp. 2.17: εἰλικρίνεια) and he refers again to "the word of God" (cp. 2.17) and to the question of "commendation" (συνίστημι/ cp. 3.1).[104] Furthermore, as I noted a moment ago, he responds to the implicit charge that most of his fellow Jews have not believed his gospel (4.3). The satan has blinded their eyes "so that they might not see the light of the gospel of the Glory of the Messiah, who is the image of God" (4.4). Here, I contend, Paul clarifies what he had said compactly in 3.18. Precisely what did Moses see when he entered the tabernacle? He beheld, so Paul argues, "the Glory of the Lord," which I take, following Carey Newman's well known treatment of the Jewish "Glory tradition," to be a *terminus technicus* for the manifest presence of Israel's God. Furthermore, this phrase is nowhere more clearly a *terminus technicus* than in the book of Exodus itself (see Ex. 16.7, 10; 24.16, 17; 29.43; 33.18, 22; 40.34, 35), such that it is unsurprising to see Paul make use of it as a part of his larger use of Exodus 34.[105] What Paul has done, furthermore, is *christologically* to appropriate this Glory tradition, so that "the Glory of the Lord" is none other than "the Glory of the Messiah." The christological implications, moreover, are stunning. In 2 Corinthians 4.4, Paul takes the preexistent Jesus to be the theophany of the one God of Israel which appeared to Moses.[106] Jesus is not, however, the God of Israel without remainder; rather, he is "the image of God" (4.4), a point to which I will come presently.

But how does this relate to 3.18, in which Paul states, "But as we all, with unveiled faces, behold the Glory of the Lord, we are transformed into the same image, from one degree of glory to another"?[107] Here we meet two principle puzzles: the meaning of (1) τὴν δόξαν κυρίου κατοπτριζόμενοι and (2) τὴν αὐτὴν εἰκόνα.[108] With regard to (1), the lexical evidence concerning κατοπτρίζω strongly favors the translation "beholding" rather than "reflecting."[109] Moreover, we should take the reference to κύριος here, particularly in view of Paul's christological adaptation of the Jewish Glory tradition in 4.4, as a reference to Jesus.[110] My case concerning (2), however, will require a brief excursion.

At this point, the Jewish exegetical tradition does illuminate the text, and not least the logic of Paul's use of κατοπτρίζω and of the way in which this relates to his use of εἰκών. Here I largely follow the careful study of David Litwa.[111] The verb κατοπτρίζω is remarkably rare in ancient Greek. The online *Thesaurus Linguae Graecae* provides only five occurrences prior to the first century, two in the first century—one from Paul and Philo respectively—and then *one hundred and thirty* occurrences in the next three centuries, most of which come from early Christian theologians who are dependent upon 2 Corinthians 3.18. When we couple the paucity of this verb with the fact that Paul and Philo employ it *in the same connection*, and when we combine this with certain pieces of rabbinic evidence, we have good reason to conclude that Paul here presupposes a Jewish exegetical tradition.

The tradition seems to be based upon an ambiguity—indeed, a difficulty— in the Hebrew text of Numbers 12.6–8a.[112] Aaron and Miriam have spoken against Moses, who had married a Cushite woman (Num. 12.1). This situation generated the question: "Has the LORD spoken only through Moses? Has he not spoken through us also?" (12.2 NRSV). In response to this charge, the writer records these words of YHWH:

(12.6) And he said, "Hear my words:
    When there are prophets among you,
I the LORD make myself known to them in visions (במראה אליו אתודע);
    I speak to them in dreams.
    (12.7) Not so with my servant Moses;
    he is entrusted with all my house.
    (12.8a) With him I speak face to face—clearly, not in riddles;
    and he beholds the form of the Lord."
(NRSV /פה אל־פה אדבר־בו ומראה ולא בחידת ותמנת יהוה יביט)

From the rabbinic perspective, this text appears to have generated two problems.[113] (1) On the one hand, it seems clearly to contradict Exodus 33.20: "'But,' he said, 'you cannot see my face (פנה); for no one shall see me and live.'" However, our text states rather clearly: "With him I speak face to face (פה אל־פה /literally 'mouth to mouth')" (Num. 12.8a; cp. Exodus 33.11). Because, however, the Hebrew word used to describe this access to God is מראה, a word which regularly means "mirror" in rabbinic Hebrew—a meaning also attested in Ex. 38.26 (Heb. מראה/ Gr. κάτοπτρον)[114]—the rabbis were able to reconcile these texts.[115] Moses had had access to YHWH *via* a "mirror."

Moreover, this tradition of Mosaic vision is found in Leviticus Rabbah 1.14 and is there immediately expounded by this parable:

> R. Pinhas said in the name of R. Hosha'iah. [This may be compared] to a king who allowed himself to be seen by his intimate friend by means of his image (באיקונין).[116] Because in this world the Shekinah manifests itself to chosen individuals; but in the world to come what is written? "And the Glory of the LORD shall be revealed and they will see [it together]." (Isa. 40.5)

With respect to this text, I quote Litwa at length:

In context, this interpretation indicates that at Sinai Moses was looking at God's image.... Second, Moses looking at God's "image" is functionally equivalent to the "glory" seen by everyone in the world to come. The semantic associations of "glory" and "image" as well as "image" and "mirror" indicate that we are close to the kind of interpretation we see in 2 Cor. 3.18.

We will return to this point momentarily.

(2) However, the above rabbinic maneuver did not solve another problem. If the text intends to portray Moses as having *superior* access to God, why is מראה used both of ordinary prophetic vision and of apparently superior Mosaic vision? After all, according to the rabbinic construal, both Moses and the other prophets saw God *via* a mirror. In order to resolve this difficulty, Leviticus Rabbah 1.14 contends that, while other prophets saw God *via* nine mirrors, Moses only required one.[117]

In any case, for our purposes what matters is that the rabbis attest to an exegetical tradition in which Moses saw God reflected in a mirror/image. Indeed, 2 Corinthians 3.18 and the tradition preserved in Leviticus Rabbah 1.14 are so close and it is so unlikely that either depends upon the other that we should probably conclude that they both presuppose an independent exegetical tradition which predates 2 Corinthians 3.18. Philo too attests to this tradition in his *Allegorical Interpretation* (3.101):

> The mind of which I speak is Moses who said, "Manifest yourself to me, so that I might see you clearly [Ex. 33.13]. May you not be revealed to me through heaven or earth or water or air or any created thing at all, nor may I see your reflection (κατοπτρίζω) in anything but may I see your very Form (τὴν σὴν ἰδέαν)."[118]

In an exposition of Moses's request to see God, Philo utilizes his only instance of the rare verb κατοπτρίζω, a unique connection also attested in 2 Corinthians 3.18. Interestingly, however, Philo's Moses *rejects* the prospect of seeing God *via* a "reflection" or "mirror." This sort of vision, in Philo's Middle Platonic estimation, involves the undesirable situation in which knowledge of the uncreated, eternal "First Cause" is mediated *via* "created things" (*All. Int.* 3.100).[119] Rather, Philo's Moses wants a direct vision of God *via* God's *logos* (*All. Int.* 3.100). Following Litwa, it is best to take this Philonic text as an implicit polemic against the tradition now preserved in Leviticus Rabbah 1.14.

In any case, the above Philonic text is evidence of an early Jewish exegetical tradition which Paul is likely adapting in 2 Corinthians 3.18, a tradition in which Moses had a vision of God *via* a "mirror/image." This, furthermore, despite considerable debate, immediately clarifies the probable referent of the εἰκών to which believers are "transformed" in 3.18.[120]

What Paul has done, I suggest, is christologically to adapt this Jewish exegetical tradition concerning Moses's vision of God *via* a mirror/image, such that Moses—as a paradigmatic minister of the new covenant—actually saw the Glory of the LORD in and as his unique image, Jesus the Messiah (4.4).[121] This, furthermore, coordinates well with my reading of 3.13, in which Paul portrayed Moses as deliberately veiling the Israelites from seeing the Glory of the Messiah (3.18; 4.4) which was shining on his face. But this does not at all mean, as, for example, Litwa and Thrall seem to think, that Paul understands this vision of Jesus-as-God's-image as something *less* than coming "face-to-face" with the one God himself.[122] That is part of the point of 2 Corinthians 4.6. It is precisely the one God of creation (4.6: "It is the God who said, 'Let light shine out of darkness'") who has ἔλαμψεν ἐν ταῖς καρδίαις ἡμῶν πρὸς φωτισμὸν τῆς γνώσεως τῆς δόξης τοῦ θεοῦ ἐν προσώπῳ [Ἰησοῦ] Χριστοῦ.[123] While there is widespread agreement that Paul here alludes to Genesis 1.3–4, few readers have noticed in Paul's phrase ἐν προσώπῳ [Ἰησοῦ] Χριστοῦ a probable allusion to (LXX) Exodus 33.20, wherein YHWH clearly states, "Οὐ δυνήσῃ ἰδεῖν μου τὸ πρόσωπον, οὐ γὰρ μὴ ἴδῃ ἄνθρωπος τὸ πρόσωπόν μου καὶ ζήσεται" (You are not able to see my face, for no one shall see my face and live), a text with which he has been working since 3.7.[124]

This is, I propose, what has happened. In 3.12–15, Christians are contrasted with Moses; in 3.18, Moses serves as a kind of paradigm for Christian "transformation"; and finally, in 4.6, at least in terms of the text of LXX Exodus 33.20, Moses is transcended altogether. The face of the one God himself, the God who himself created the *kosmos—the face which, according to LXX Exodus 33.20, Moses was not allowed to see*—turns out to be the face of the Messiah himself, the Glory and image of God. In this connection, and in relation to what I have already argued, the point of the allusion to Genesis 1.3–4 is to present the one God in the very terms by which second-temple Jewish and early Christian thought most clearly demarcated the unique divine identity (cosmogonical activity).[125] Then, as a part of his overall use of Exodus 32–34 as foil for his polemic against his Jewish-Christian opponents, Paul alludes to Genesis 1.3–4 and then to (LXX) Exodus 33.20 to present Jesus as the embodiment of the one God of creation.[126]

The christological point of 3.18; 4.4; and 4.6, therefore, taken together, is that the one God of creation is himself revealed in and as his Glory and image, Jesus the Messiah, whose face Moses was not allowed to see (so LXX Ex. 33.20) but Christians are allowed to see (3.18). Moreover, returning to the force of 3.18 within my reconstruction, Paul contends that he and his sympathizers—all of those in Corinth (and implicitly elsewhere) who side with his gospel over against the Jewish-Christian missionaries—are progressively "transformed into the same image [of the Messiah/God]." As I argued earlier, the fact that the language of μορφ- and εἰκών occur together here, especially within a context in which the author refers to a paradigmatic "image" to which others are "(con/trans)formed," suggests that we are dealing with a christological adaptation of Middle Platonic intermediary doctrine. This further suggests, within a context in which Paul has portrayed his opponents and their sympathizers as shallow sophists (so esp. 2.17–3.1), that he intends to portray himself and his sympathizers as true philosophers who attain to Plato's *telos* of "the image of God."

Should the passage a whole, however, and particularly 3.18; 4.4, and 4.6 within it, be taken as an instance of "Adam christology"?[127] As I have argued throughout, several crucial features of Paul's image christology, and here not least the notion of a paradigmatic "image" to which believers are "transformed," suggests the influence of Middle Platonic intermediary doctrine. And this connection suggests, as I also argued above, that this image christology belongs with other christological traditions (esp. John 1.1–18; 1 Cor. 8.6; Col. 1.15–20; and Heb. 1.1–4) in which Jesus is deliberately included within the "unique divine identity" as creator. The christology of 2 Corinthians 3.18; 4.4; and 4.6, therefore, is best taken as an instance of what is often called "wisdom christology" rather than Adam christology, the latter of which has little explanatory force concerning the specific details of 3.18.[128] But this is not to deny that Paul's image christology depends in part upon his reading of Genesis 1 in general and Genesis 1.26 in particular. It is, rather, to insist that Paul took the preexistent Jesus to be the protological and cosmogonical image of God *according to which Adam himself was made and for which he was destined*. This formulation, it seems to me, is not captured by the label "Adam christology."

CONCLUSION

In this section, I have argued the following case. (1) In 2 Corinthians 2.17–4.6, Paul obliquely engages the very Jewish-Christian opponents he will go on more explicitly to polemicize against in chapters 10–13. (2) Because these opponents had apparently come to Corinth with letters of recommendation (2.17), had likely served among the Corinthians for pay (11.7–9), and had apparently made a more impressive public impression (11.5–6), Paul decided that it would be rhetorically advantageous to depict these opponents as shallow sophists and to characterize himself and his sympathizers as philosophers who attain to the *telos* of true philosophy: "the image of God" (3.18). (3) In 3.18, we see that Paul christologically adapts a Jewish exegetical tradition concerning Moses's vision of the one God and thereby expresses a divine christology. (4) Finally, I have argued that the christology of 3.18; 4.4; and 4.6 expresses a divine christology in which Jesus is included in the unique divine identity as God's Glory and image and that this is best taken as an instance of wisdom christology rather than Adam christology.

NOTES

1. On the question of how to describe Paul's treatment of Exodus 34—"midrash," "exegesis," "exposition," "appropriation," "foil"—see the discussion in Michael Cover, *Lifting the Veil: 2 Corinthians 3:7–18 in Light of Jewish Homiletic and Commentary Traditions*, BZNW 210 (Berlin: de Gruyter, 2015), 3–7, 18–29. See also Hays's critical comments on the ubiquitous and indiscriminate use of the term "midrash" in Hays, *Letters of Paul*, 10–14.

2. Hans Windisch, *Der zweite Korintherbrief* (Göttingen: Vandehoeck & Ruprecht, 1924), 112.

3. Hans Lietzmann, *An die Korinther I–II*, 4th edn., completed by W. G. Kümmel, HNT 9 (Tübingen: Mohr, 1949), 111; Joseph Fitzmyer, "Glory Reflected on the Face of Christ (2 Cor. 3.7–4.6) and a Palestinian Jewish Motif" *TS* 42 (1981): 630–44 (632); and C. F. D. Moule, *The Birth of the New Testament*, 3rd edn. (San Francisco: Harper and Row, 1982 [1962]), 54. Moule proposed that this passage reflects a Pauline synagogue sermon.

4. Siegfried Schulz, "Die Decke des Moses: Untersuchungen zu einer vorpaulinischen Überlieferung in 2 Kor. 3:17–18" *ZNTW* 49 (1958): 1–30 (27–30). Less influentially, Jerome Murphy-O'Connor, *Keys to Second Corinthians: Revisiting the Major Issues* (Oxford: OUP, 2010), 71, suggested that in 3.7–18 Paul was attempting to enter "into the thought world of the *pneumatikoi*."

5. Dieter Georgi, *The Opponents of Paul in Second Corinthians*, trans. by H. Attridge et al. (Philadelphia: Fortress, 1986 [1964]), e.g., 250, 261.

6. Hays, *Letters of Paul*, 122–53; and Wright, *Climax*, 175–92.

7. Hays, *Letters of Paul*, 126.

8. Paul B. Duff, *Moses in Corinth: The Apologetic Context of 2 Corinthians 3*, NovTestSup 159 (Leiden: Brill, 2015).

9. Duff, *Moses in Corinth*, 18–51 (51).

10. Ibid. 51.

11. Ibid. 52–92.

12. Ibid.

13. See the many scholars listed in Ibid. 46, n. 83; and Campbell, *Framing*, 98–121.

14. For those scholars who take chapters 10–13 to predate 2.14–7.4, see Duff, *Moses in Corinth*, 26–29, nn. 30, 33. For those who reverse the chronological sequence, see Ibid. 27, n. 34.

15. Here Duff, *Moses in Corinth*, 16, n. 18, provides the very telling footnote: "I infer from Rom 11 that Paul believed Israel's perceptual difficulties to be temporary."

16. Ibid. 16, italics added.

17. So, e.g., J. D. G. Dunn, *Romans 1–8*, WBC 38A (Dallas: Word, 1998), 95; Joseph A. Fitzmyer, *Romans: A New Translation with Introduction and Commentary*,

AB33 (New Haven: YUP, 1992), 307–08; and Thomas R. Schreiner, *Romans*, BECNT 6 (Grand Rapids: Baker, 1998), 118–19.

18. Bruce Winter, *Philo and Paul Among the Sophists* (Grand Rapids: Eerdmans, 2002 [1997]); van Kooten, *PA*, 245–68, 313–39; and Idem, "Why Did Paul Include an Exegesis of Moses' Shining Face (Exod 34) in 2 Cor 3?" in G. J. Brooke, H. Najman, and L. T. Stuckenbruck, eds., *The Significance of Sinai*, TBN 12 (Leiden: Brill, 2008), 149–81; David Litwa, "Transformation through a Mirror: Moses in 2 Cor. 3.18" *JSNT* 34.3 (2012): 286–97; and Blackwell, *Christosis*, 174–238.

19. Cover, *Lifting the Veil*, 3–105.
20. Ibid. 7–17.
21. Ibid. 251–56.
22. Ibid. 106–228.
23. Ibid. 160–295.
24. Ibid. 231, italics in original.
25. Ibid. 230.
26. Ibid. 249.
27. Ibid. 254, citing Georgi, *The Opponents*, 315–19; and Furnish, *II Corinthians*, 48–54, as taking a similar position.

28. Advocated by, e.g., Ralph P. Martin, *2 Corinthians*, WBC 40 (Waco: Word Books, 1986), lii–lxi; and Michael D. Goulder, "ΣΩΦΙΑ in 1 Corinthians" *NTS* 37 (1991): 516–34.

29. Advocated by, e.g., Walter Schmithals, *Gnosticism in Corinth: An Investigation of the Letters to the Corinthians*, trans. J. E. Steeley (Nashville: Abingdon, 1971); and Rudolf Bultmann, *The Second Letter to the Corinthians*, PNTC (Grand Rapids: Eerdmans, 1985 [1976]), *passim*.

30. Advocated esp. by van Kooten, *PA*, 245–68, 313–39; Idem, "Shining Face," 149–81; following Winter, *Philo and Paul*, 109–239.

31. Cover, *Lifting the Veil*, 254.
32. Ibid. 255–56.
33. Ibid. 256.
34. Ibid. 255.
35. Ibid. 254.
36. Ibid. 255–56.
37. van Kooten, *PA*, 245–68, 313–39; Idem, "Shining Face," 149–81; following Winter, *Philo and Paul*, 109–239.

38. Winter, *Philo and Paul*, 4. The whole of pp. 1–14 is relevant. On the Second Sophistic, see also Ewan Bowie in *OCD* 1337–38 (1337), whose dating of which, however, should be revised in light of Winter's work.

39. C. C. W. Taylor in *OCD* 1381.

40. *Agr.* 143. Strabo, *Geography* 14.673 (H. L. Jones, LCL), famously said: "The people at Tarsus have devoted themselves so eagerly, not only to philosophy, but also to the whole round of education in general, that they have surpassed Athens, Alexandria, or any other place that can be named where there have been schools and lectures of philosophers." All of Strabo, *Geography* 14.674–75, is relevant in this connection.

41. Winter, *Philo and Paul*, 88, citing Plato, *Helen* 10.

42. *Mos.* 2.212 (Colson, LCL).

43. *Prot.* 313D–E. (Lamb, LCL).

44. So also, e.g., van Kooten, "Shining Face," 154; Winter, *Philo and Paul*, 168; Thrall, *2 Corinthians*, 210–15; Martin, *2 Corinthians*, 50; Furnish, *II Corinthians*, 178; and Georgi, *The Opponents*, 234. In this connection, when I say that "Paul echoes this critique," I am deliberately not saying that Paul had actually *read* Plato's *Protagoras*. Rather, I am arguing that, in light both of this Pauline and of the above Philonic text (*Agr.* 143), we should likely identify Plato's *Protagoras* as the probable source of this standard characterization of sophistry.

45. This is, it seems to me, notwithstanding the considerable strengths of both analyses, the route taken by the influential studies of Hays, *Letters of Paul*, 122–53, and Wright, *Climax*, 175–92.

46. So Cover, *Lifting the Veil*, 254–56, on the one hand, and van Kooten, *PA*, 245–68, 313–39; Idem, "Shining Face," 149–81, on the other.

47. So esp. Scott J. Hafemann, "'Self-Commendation' and Apostolic Legitimacy in 2 Corinthians: A Pauline Dialectic?" *NTS* 36 (1990): 66–88 (70): "Given its pivotal role in Paul's two major apologetic arguments in 2 Corinthians (2.14–6.13 and chapters 10–13), it is not asserting too much to suggest that the issue of self-commendation stands squarely in the centre of the conflict between Paul and his opponents in Corinth"; and the discussion in George H. Guthrie, *2 Corinthians*, BECNT (Grand Rapids: Baker, 2015), 181–93. This had been noted already by Ernst Käsemann, "Die Legitimität des Apostels. Eine Untersuchung zu II Korinther 10–13" *ZNW* 41 (1942): 33–71.

48. As Thrall, *2 Corinthians*, 211–12, notes, those who argue either for the letter's integrity or for the priority of chapters 10–13 tend to see the opponents in view in 2.14–4.6 as the same as those in view in chapters 10–13. For a list of such scholars, cf. Duff, *Moses in Corinth*, 26–29, nn. 30, 33; 46, n. 83. For a critical discussion of the major hypotheses concerning Paul's opponents, cf. esp. Thrall, *2 Corinthians*, 926–45, who postulates three major views: (1) that the opponents are essentially "Judaizers" (928–32), insisting upon "the importance of the law" (928, 931–32: so Plummer and Barnett), their valid (as opposed to Paul's invalid) apostolic authority (928–30: so Käsemann), and/or the general "primacy of Israel" (930–31: so Oostendorp); (2) that they are and/or claim to be pneumatics and/or "divine men" (932–36: so esp. Georgi); or (3) that the opponents combine elements of "Judaizing" with pneumatic claims (936–8: so esp. Barrett and Murphy-O'Connor). I note that use of the term "Judaizing" in an attempt to refer to people who *are already practicing the Jewish way of life* and are trying to convince others to do the same is a misnomer.

49. On the "super-apostles," cf. esp. the critical discussion in Thrall, *2 Corinthians*, 671–76, who rightly concludes that the term refers to Paul's missionary rivals in Corinth rather than to Jerusalem apostles, with respect to the latter of whom Paul would hardly concede less "rhetorical" ability (so Ibid. 674; and Furnish, *II Corinthians*, 504).

50. For our purposes, we do not need to go into the details of the specific force of Ἑβραῖοί and Ἰσραηλῖται. On this, particularly with respect to the contested force of Ἑβραῖοί, Thrall, *2 Corinthians*, 723–30, notes four possibilities. Whether the force

is "ethnic" (Jews by birth and not proselytes), "linguistic" (a person who speaks Hebrew/Aramaic), "geographical" (a person with ties to Palestine), or "religio-cultural" (a person of the Jewish way of life) matters little to my proposal. In this regard, the summary comment of Thrall, *2 Corinthians*, 729, is to the point: "[W]hatever else may be implied, the three designations 'Hebrews,' 'Israelites,' and 'seed of Abraham' stress the Jewishness of Paul's rivals." Cf. also K. G. Kuhn and Gutbrod respectively, in *TDNT* 3.359–69, 369–91.

51. This is the point of Paul's concession that he, apparently unlike his missionary rivals, is ἰδιώτης τῷ λόγῳ. On taking ἰδιώτης τῷ λόγῳ to mean "untrained" (so ἰδιώτης) in "public rhetoric" (so τῷ λόγῳ), cf., e.g., Thrall, *2 Corinthians*, 676–81; Furnish, *II Corinthians*, 490; Harris, *2 Corinthians*, 748–50; Guthrie, *2 Corinthians*, 515–19; and Schlier in *TDNT* 3.215–17.

52. Cf. Hans Dieter Betz, *Der Apostel Paulus und die sokratische Tradition*, BHTh 45 (Tübingen: 1972), 60–63, 63, n. 128; and the whole discussion in Winter, *Philo and Paul*, 204–30. Plato's Socrates had said: "But, my dear Phaedrus, I shall make myself ridiculous if I, a mere amateur (ἰδιώτης), try without preparation to speak on the same subject in competition with a master of his art" (H. N. Fowler, LCL).

53. To be clear, I am not claiming that Paul refused support *because* the missionaries had accepted it. Rather, I am only claiming that, irrespective of why Paul had refused support, his refusal and their acceptance allowed him to portray the missionaries as sophists and himself as a true philosopher. On this whole question, see David E. Briones, *Paul's Financial Policy: A Socio-Theological Approach*, LNTS 494 (New York: Bloomsbury T & T Clark, 2013).

54. So, e.g., Thrall, *2 Corinthians*, 212–17; and *contra*, e.g., Harris, *2 Corinthians*, 254, who argues that Paul's use of καπηλεύω is "metaphorical," presumably because he does not countenance the possible connection with 11.5–9.

55. So Winter, *Philo and Paul*, 141–255.

56. On the influence of Winter's hypothesis, cf. esp. Timothy A. Brookins, *Corinthian Wisdom, Stoic Philosophy, and the Ancient Economy*, SNTS 159 (Cambridge: CUP, 2014), 8–61, from whom I borrow the label "true philosophy vs. sophistry hypothesis."

57. On the basis of its attestation in P[46], it is conceivable that the hyperbolic οἱ λοιποί ("the rest"; i.e., "everyone else") was later changed to the less hyperbolic οἱ πολλοί ("many"). See Bruce M. Metzger, *A Textual Commentary on the Greek New Testament*, 2nd edn. (London/New York: United Bible Societies, 1994), 508. After all, Paul was quite capable of such hyperbole: cf., e.g., Phil. 2.21.

58. I have followed the critical edition of NA[28], as well as the comments in Metzger, *Textual Commentary*, 509, in preferring ἡμῶν (so P[46] A B C D G K P Ψ 614 1739 *Byz Lect* it vg syr[p] cop[sa] goth arm) to ὑμῶν (so ℵ 33 88 436 1881 eth[ro]). However, I note that Thrall's case for ὑμῶν on internal grounds is not easily dismissable: so Thrall, *2 Corinthians*, 223–24; and also Bultmann, *2 Corinthians*, 74–75; Barrett, *2 Corinthians*, 96; and Martin, *2 Corinthians*, 51. My main proposals are little affected either way.

59. On the standard epistolary style of Greek letters of recommendation, cf. esp. C. W. Keyes, "The Greek Letter of Introduction" *AJP* 56 (1935): 28–44; and C. H.

Kim, *Form and Structure of the Familiar Greek Letter of Recommendation*, SBLDS 4 (Missoula: Scholars Press, 1972). For a critical discussion of the provenance of these letters of recommendation (e.g., Jerusalem or elsewhere), cf. Thrall, *2 Corinthians*, 217–22. On the use of letters of recommendation in early Christian missionary work, cf. esp. Acts 18.27.

60. Paul had already made the same point in 1 Corinthians 9.2.

61. On this, cf. esp. Hays, *Letters of Paul*, 127.

62. *Contra*, e.g., Karl Prümm, *Diakonia Pneumatos. Theologie des Zweiten Korintherbriefes. Bd. I–II*, (Freiburg: Herder, 1962) 1.102–03, ἐπιστολὴ Χριστοῦ should be taken as a "genitive of origin/authorship."

63. On these allusions, cf., e.g., Thrall, *2 Corinthians*, 226–28; Guthrie, *2 Corinthians*, 188–93; Harris, *2 Corinthians*, 263–66; but esp. Hays, *Letters of Paul*, 125–35; and *contra*, e.g., Scott J. Hafemann, *Suffering and Ministry in the Spirit: Paul's Defense of His Ministry in 2 Corinthians 2:14–3:3* (Grand Rapids: Eerdmans, 1990), 193–94, 205–07, who argues against any such allusion to Jeremiah in 3.3.

64. Wright, *Climax*, 175–92, rightly emphasizes this contrast, though without noticing its implicit scriptural basis.

65. So also Hays, *Letters of Paul*, 132: "Because Paul does not give this text close exegetical scrutiny, it appears to serve merely as a foil for his own reflections."

66. Duff, *Moses in Corinth*, 14, suggests the fascinating possibility that Paul's discussion of his "worthiness" (ἱκανός, ἱκανότης) reflects a deliberate contrast with the Moses of LXX Exodus 4.10, who claims that he is not "worthy" (ἱκανός) of his divine commission.

67. Thrall, *2 Corinthians*, 234–35, lists three major views: "(i) Paul has in mind two ways of understanding Scripture, the literal and the spiritual.... Hence, in the present verse the γράμμα is the law of Moses in its literal sense whilst the πνεῦμα is the spirit of the law, its inward meaning.... (ii) The term γράμμα connotes the law, written on stone tablets, as something which exerts an external and tyrannical control over those under its sway, evoking fear and a sense of slavery. The new order of things, by contrast, is characterised by the power of the Spirit of God operating within the heart of the believer. The law was powerless to produce the behaviour it enjoined; it is far otherwise with the covenant of the Spirit (cf. Rom 8:2–4).... (iii) The antithesis is to be seen as the contrast between human activity and divine activity, and γράμμα will signify the law interpreted and used in a legalistic sense so as to promote purely human achievement." For (i), cf., e.g., B. Cohen, "Note on Letter and Spirit in the New Testament" *HTR* 47 (1954): 197–203. For (ii), cf., e.g., Harris, *2 Corinthians*, 271–75; Thrall, *2 Corinthians*, 234–35; and Furnish, *II Corinthians*, 199–201. For (iii), cf., e.g., Ernst Käsemann, *Perspectives on Paul*, repr. (Philadelphia: Fortress, 1971), 146–47; Barrett, *2 Corinthians*, 112–13; and Prümm, *Diakonia Pneumatos*, 1.118.

68. So Harris, *2 Corinthians*, 271–75; Thrall, *2 Corinthians*, 234–35; and Furnish, *II Corinthians*, 199–201.

69. On Paul's theology of Torah in general, cf. esp. Wright, *PFG*, 495–537.

70. I discuss the force of καταργέω presently.

71. Though the point is widely noted in the commentaries, it rarely receives sufficient emphasis.

72. So, e.g., Gordon D. Fee, *The First Epistle to the Corinthians*, NICNT (Grand Rapids: Eerdmans, 1987), 805–07; and Ben Witherington III, *Conflict and Community in Corinth: A Socio-Rhetorical Commentary on 1 and 2 Corinthians* (Grand Rapids: Eerdmans, 1995), 311.

73. So, e.g., Fitzmyer, *Romans*, 468–69; and Dunn, *Romans*, 384–85.

74. So *BAGD*, 525–26; Delling in *TDNT*, 1.452–54; Scott Hafemann, *Paul, Moses, and the History of Israel: The Letter/Spirit Contrast and the Argument from Scripture in 2 Corinthians 3* (Peabody: Hendrickson, 1996), 301–09; and Hays, *Letters of Paul*, 133–40.

75. So, e.g., the list of scholars and translation in Harris, *2 Corinthians*, 284, n. 44.

76. So, e.g., Martin J. McNamara, *The New Testament and the Palestinian Targums to the Pentateuch* (Rome: Pontifical Biblical Institute, 1966), 171–74; and Linda L. Belleville, *Reflections of Glory: Paul's Polemical Use of the Moses-Doxa Tradition in 2 Corinthians 3.1–18*, JSNTSup 52 (Sheffield: SAP, 1992), 41–42, 67.

77. Cf. esp. McNamara, *Palestinian Targums*, 171–74; and Belleville, *Reflections of Glory*, esp. 26–79.

78. So both of the writers in the note above.

79. Similarly, Hays, *Letters of Paul*, 134, writes, "Paul's *katargoumenēn* is not a narrative description but a retrospective theological judgement."

80. Cf. also Hafemann, *Paul, Moses*, 301–09.

81. On the force of ἕνεκεν, cf. *BAGD*, 334.

82. My reading of 3.7–11 as a whole is quite close to Hays, *Letters of Paul*, 133–40, though Hays's reading is strengthened in my view when one sees that Paul offers this "reading" of Exodus 34 *not for its own sake* but as a polemic against—as Paul sees it—Jewish-Christian missionaries of this old Mosaic legislation.

83. Cover, *Lifting the Veil*, 273–77, provides a helpful discussion of παρρησία in this connection.

84. Cf. *BAGD*, 781–82.

85. So also Harris, *2 Corinthians*, 295; Thrall, *2 Corinthians*, 255–6; Furnish, *II Corinthians*, 206–07; and Belleville, *Reflections of Glory*, 197–98.

86. On infinitival constructions with πρὸς as instances of "purposive (rather than 'resultative') infinitives," cf. esp. Harris, *2 Corinthians*, 297, with the grammars listed in n. 15.

87. So, e.g., though not without minor distinctions, Thrall, *2 Corinthians*, 258; Martin, *2 Corinthians*, 68, 73; Barrett, *2 Corinthians*, 119; Windisch, *Korintherbrief*, 120; and J. F. Collange, *Énigmes de la deuxième épître de Paul aux Corinthiens: Étude exégétique de 2 Cor. 2:14–7:4*, SNTSM 18 (Cambridge: CUP, 1972), 96–97. On the major options, cf. Thrall, *2 Corinthians*, 259–61, with others listed in nn. 488–98; and Harris, *2 Corinthians*, 296–300. The construal of Hafemann, *Paul, Moses*, 310–13, 354, is extremely clever, though successfully critiqued by Harris, *2 Corinthians*, 298, n. 23.

88. *BAGD*, 998–99, confidently prefers "termination" for 2 Corinthians 3.13 but "goal" for the closely parallel instance of Romans 10.4. For the commentators on both sides, cf. esp. Thrall, *2 Corinthians*, 256, nn. 457 and 468; and Harris, *2 Corinthians*, 299, nn. 25–26.

89. On this difficulty, cf. esp. Hays, *Letters of Paul*, 136–37.

90. So also Hays, *Letters of Paul*, with those in nn. 47–49. Ibid. also notes that this was the view of "patristic interpreters such as Augustine and Theodoret."

91. Here I am quite close to Hays, *Letters of Paul*, 136–40.

92. Cf. esp. Hays, *Letters of Paul*, 140–45.

93. N.b. that I say "crucial." For all of the "changes," cf. Thrall, *2 Corinthians*, 268, n. 549.

94. So, e.g., Hays, *Letters of Paul*, 146; and Harris, *2 Corinthians*, 307.

95. *Contra* Thrall, *2 Corinthians*, 271–73, who does not even list this is as a possibility; Harris, *2 Corinthians*, 308; and Furnish, *II Corinthians*, 211–12. Cf. Hays, *Letters of Paul*, 143; and J. D. G. Dunn, "2 Corinthians III. 17—'The Lord is the Spirit'" *JTS* 21 (1970): 309–20. Hays, *Letters of Paul*, 143, rightly notes, "The abrupt identification of *kyrios* and *pneuma* . . . is to be explained as Paul's exegetical gloss on the text he has just quoted."

96. The closing genitival phrase of 3.18 is difficult: καθάπερ ἀπὸ κυρίου πνεύματος. I take πνεύματος as an "appositional genitive": that is, it defines who the κύριος is. On the "appositional" use of the genitive, cf., e.g., Stanley E. Porter, *Idioms of the Greek New Testament*, 2nd edn., repr. (Sheffield: SAP, 2005 [1992]), 94. Hays, *Letters of Paul*, 144, compellingly proposes, "Paul's strangely compressed formulation (*kathaper apo kyriou pneumatos*) should be read as a contrapuntal echo answer to his earlier *ou kathaper Mōysēs* . . . and *ouch hoti aph' heautōn hikanoi esmen*." For the major grammatical options, cf. Furnish, *II Corinthians*, 216. Though my argument will shortly focus upon the christological implications of the passage, one should not overlook the striking use of κύριος in relation to the Spirit and not least in view of the intertext of Exodus 34.

97. So also, e.g., Thrall, *2 Corinthians*, 266–67; Harris, *2 Corinthians*, 300–01; and Furnish, *II Corinthians*, 207, 233–34.

98. *Pace*, e.g., Collange, *Énigmes*, 88–100; and W. J. Dalton, "Is the Old Covenant Abrogated (2 Cor 3.14)?" *ABR* 35 (1987): 88–94.

99. In this connection, I cite the apposite construal of Thrall, *2 Corinthians*, 261, at length: "Paul turns here to the phenomenon of unbelief, on the part of the Israelites in the past and of his Jewish contemporaries in the present. This is still related to the defense of his own διακονία, however. Jewish failure to respond to the Christian gospel, and particularly, in Corinth, to Paul's preaching of it, may have begun to worry some of the Corinthian Christians. . . . Perhaps, after all, his own claim to be διάκονος of this new covenant was invalid, and his ministry unauthentic. He explains that this unbelief was foreshadowed in Scripture, in the obduracy of the Israelites in the days of Moses, but that the Moses-story also foreshadows conversion to belief." Cf. also Harris, *2 Corinthians*, 300–01.

100. So also, e.g., Thrall, *2 Corinthians*, 303: "Having spoken of his preaching as a revelation of the truth, Paul now has to admit that to some it is not a revelation at all. He is responding, in all probability, to some kind of criticism"; Harris, *2 Corinthians*, 327; and Furnish, *2 Corinthians*, 247.

101. See, e.g., Thrall, *2 Corinthians*, 305–08, with critical discussion of other views; Harris, *2 Corinthians*, 327; and Furnish, *II Corinthians*, 247.

102. αυτου receives a reasonably strong external attestation, appearing in P[46] C* and D*.

103. With Metzger, *Textual Commentary*, 510, I regard Ιησου as secondary: "The reading that best explains the origin of the others is [the simple] Χριστου."

104. All of this is well noted in two charts in Harris, *2 Corinthians*, 320. Cf. also the comments in Furnish, *II Corinthians*, 246. Thrall, *2 Corinthians*, 300–03, does not appear to notice the strong connection.

105. On all of this, see Newman, *Glory Christology*, 17–156, 229–34.

106. So Ibid. 229–34; and Wright, *PFG*, 677–80.

107. E.g., Kim, *Paul's Gospel*, 235, wrongly restricts the reference of the "we all" to Paul himself, largely because he assumes that the whole passage concerns Paul's Damascus Road christophany. Thrall, *2 Corinthians*, 282–83; Harris, *2 Corinthians*, 313; and Blackwell, *Christosis*, 183–84, rightly infer a reference to all believers. However, we should bear in mind that, within this polemical context, Paul particularly has in mind his sympathizers over against the Jewish-Christian missionaries and their sympathizers.

108. On the major options, see esp. Blackwell, *Christosis*, 183–91.

109. With, e.g., Wright, *Climax*, 185: "There is general agreement that linguistic evidence favours the meaning 'behold as in a mirror'"; Thrall, *2 Corinthians*, 290–92; Harris, *2 Corinthians*, 313–14; Collange, *Énigmes*, 116–18; and Norbert Hugedé, *La métophore du miroir dans les Epîtres de saint Paul aux Corinthiens* (Neuchatel: Delachaux et Niestlé, 1957); and *contra*, e.g., Blackwell, *Christosis*, 187–88. A. Feuillet, *Le Christ Sagesse de Dieu d'après les épîtres pauliniennes*, (Paris, 1966), 143, makes a strong case, largely on the basis of the combination of the words ἀτενίζω (2 Cor. 3.7, 13) and the unusual ἐνοπτρίζω (2 Cor. 3.18), that 1 Clement 36.2 reflects a very early reading of 2 Corinthians 3.18 in which Jesus is taken as the "mirror-image" in which one "beholds" a vision of God.

110. *Contra* Thrall, *2 Corinthians*, 283, who thinks 4.6 tells against this reading; and Harris, *2 Corinthians*, 314–16, both of whom think the Exodus Glory tradition— *which Paul clearly christologically adapts in 4.4*—tells against a christological reading. For a helpful chart of the scholars who take various views, cf. Blackwell, *Christosis*, 186.

111. Cf. David Litwa, "Transformation through a Mirror: Moses in 2 Cor. 3.18" *JSNT* 34.3 (2012): 286–97. Litwa provides a succinct summary of the major options on pp. 286–90.

112. For this point, see Litwa, "Transformation through a Mirror," 290–95, who admits, "I claim absolutely no originality in pointing out these traditions, which have often been used to interpret 1 Cor. 13.12 . . . [but] the traditions have not gained sufficient recognition among interpreters of 2 Cor. 3.18" (290).

113. Ibid. 290–93.

114. Surprisingly, Litwa, "Transformation through a Mirror," appears to have been unaware of this text.

115. On מראה as "mirror" in rabbinic Hebrew, cf. esp. M. Jastrow, *Dictionary of Targumim, the Talmud Babli and Yerushalmi, and the Midrashic Literature*, 2 vols. (New York: Pardes), 1.835.

116. איקונין is simply a transliteration of the Greek εἰκών. Litwa, "Transformation through a Mirror," 292, n. 23, notes that some other manuscripts read באותנין ("signs") instead of איקונין.

117. So Ibid. 291 and esp. n. 19, depending upon M. Margulies, *Midrash Wayyikra Rabbah: A Critical Edition Based on Manuscripts and Genizah Fragments with Variants and Notes*, 2 vols. (New York: Jewish Theological Seminary, 1993), 1.30–32. Another solution appears in the same context: namely that, while Moses looked through a polished mirror, other prophets looked through dirty mirrors (so Litwa, "Transformation through a Mirror," 291).

118. (Colson and Whitaker, LCL, slightly revised). Indeed, Philo will soon quote Numbers 12.6–8 (*All. Int.* 3.103) in this connection. On Philo's request for *unmediated* vision, cf. the discussion in Cover, *Lifting the Veil*, 288–89 and n. 73.

119. Of course, Paul too can use the trope of "seeing through a mirror" to denote imperfect vision: 1 Cor. 13.12.

120. For charts of the various views, listing numerous scholars, cf. esp. Blackwell, *Christosis*, 186–87. For a critique of other explanations of the *religionsgeschichtliche* background of 3.18, cf. Litwa, "Transformation through a Mirror," 286–90. Thrall, *2 Corinthians*, 285, is quite right to emphasize: "The participle κατοπτριζόμενοι contains within itself the idea of 'mirror,' which will at the same time suggest 'mirror-image.'" Cf. also Furnish, *2 Corinthians*, 215.

121. Cf. again the helpful chart of Blackwell, *Christosis*, 186, for the scholars who take various views. Cf. esp. Thrall, *2 Corinthians*, 284–85; Harris, *2 Corinthians*, 315; and Hafemann, *Paul, Moses*, 411, n. 239.

122. *Contra*, e.g., Litwa, "Transformation through a Mirror," 294; and Thrall, *2 Corinthians*, 284.

123. On the allusion to Genesis 1.3–4 here, perhaps also influenced by the wording of Isaiah 9.1, cf. esp. Thrall, *2 Corinthians*, 314–15 and those listed in n. 863; and Harris, *2 Corinthians*, 334–35 and n. 96, who mentions other passages which might have influenced Paul.

124. Fee, *Christology*, 182, however, gets the point exactly: "The first significant christological point in v. 18, therefore, is the identification of Christ with 'the glory of the LORD,' an identification that turns out to be full of words and images from portions surrounding Exod 34. Paul thus continues to keep alive the contrast with Moses. In the immediately preceding narrative (Exod 33:18–23), Moses has specifically requested of Yahweh, 'Show me your glory.' The divine response is, 'You cannot see my face, for no one may see me and live . . .' By way of obvious contrast, God's new covenant people, when they turn to the Lord, are enabled by the Spirit to behold, as though looking into a mirror, 'the glory of the Lord.' So the glory that Moses was not allowed to see 'we all' behold in Christ, where 'the glory of the Lord' . . . is fully revealed *in the face of the Son*, the perfect bearer of the divine image" (italics mine).

125. This is an answer to, for example, Thrall, *2 Corinthians*, 315: "Why, then, is God so described?"

126. *Contra*, e.g., Thrall, *2 Corinthians*, 316 and all those listed in n. 878; and Harris, *2 Corinthians*, 336–37; and with, to an extent, Furnish, *II Corinthians*, 225, I reject the common construal in which, with his reference to "the face of [Jesus] the Messiah," Paul subtly alludes to his own conversion experience. Rather, the phrase ἐν προσώπῳ [Ἰησοῦ] Χριστοῦ is better taken, within a context in which Paul has been making extensive use of this narrative (Ex. 32–34), as an allusion to LXX Exodus 33.20.

127. The Gnostic hypothesis of esp. Jervell, *Imago Dei*, 136–40, 174–75, 215, is, as I have already indicated, untenable.

128. With, e.g., Wright, *PFG*, 677–80; and, to an extent, Thrall, *2 Corinthians*, 310; Furnish, *II Corinthians*, 215, 222; and Eltester, *Eikon*, 133–36; and *contra*, e.g., Dunn, *Christology*, 106, 145, 189, 196; Idem, *Paul*, 289–90; and Fee, *Christology*, 184–87, who largely rejects "wisdom christology" in this and other instances because Paul does not display extensive linguistic dependence upon any one Jewish wisdom text. This is, however, as I argued above, somewhat beside the point. Cf. also Scroggs, *The Last Adam*, 96–102.

Chapter 8

Romans 7–8

EXTENDED INTRODUCTION

We now come to what is widely regarded as the most integrated and carefully crafted Pauline writing we possess.[1] This, however, creates a particular problem for the exegete who is attempting only to expound one smaller section of the letter, not least because this section is likely to be inextricably integrated into the rest of the letter in a way which is not as characteristic of Paul's other writings. In this vein, while there is of course no question of engaging all of the historical, exegetical, and theological features of Romans, it will prove necessary to provide an extended introduction and summary of certain features of the argument of 1–8 as a whole in order historically and argumentatively to locate my treatment of chapters 7–8 and of the *imago Dei* theology therein.

These are the larger factors which must be borne in mind. Paul has already written 2 Corinthians and writes this letter from that locale (Rom. 16.23).[2] Moreover, throughout the letter he seems particularly concerned to argue that God has been faithful to his covenant with Israel. Even on a cautious mirror reading, the "Jew first" construction (1.16; 2.9–10), the sequence running from 3.1 to 3.8, the whole of Romans 9–11, and the tell-tale *inclusio* of 15.8a ("For I tell you that the Messiah became a servant of the circumcised on behalf of God's truthfulness . . .") suggest that Paul at least thought that the Roman Christians were in danger of thinking that God had—and/or perhaps that Paul had—"written off" his faithfulness to the covenant with Israel.[3]

In view of my treatment of chapters 7–8, I now work through certain feature of chapters 1–6. Many scholars rightly note that 1.17 appears to be the "thesis statement": "For the covenant faithfulness of God (δικαιοσύνη θεοῦ) is unveiled in it [the gospel] by faithfulness for those who are [also] faithful"

(1.17).⁴ In this connection, I follow several others in taking δικαιοσύνη θεοῦ broadly to denote "God's faithfulness to his covenant with Israel," a meaning which resonates strongly with the overall argument of the letter.⁵ Therefore, Paul sets out to demonstrate, inter alia, that God has indeed been faithful to his covenant with (and, as I will argue, *through*) Israel.

I now briefly consider the force of two "framing" texts for the argument of the whole letter. In 1.28, Paul offers a summary statement of the dehumanization described in 1.21–27: "And just as they did not determine (οὐκ ἐδοκίμασαν) to acknowledge God, God delivered them up to a debased mind (ἀδόκιμον νοῦν), so that they did what should not be done (ποιεῖν τὰ μὴ καθήκοντα)." We should note the logic of the Greek: a failure to δοκιμάζειν results in ἀδόκιμον νοῦν, which itself predisposes humans ποιεῖν τὰ μὴ καθήκοντα.⁶ This is the scenario which God will ultimately remedy: "but be transformed by the renewal of your mind *in order that you might be able to determine* (εἰς τὸ δοκιμάζειν ὑμᾶς) the will of God" (12.2).⁷

As several scholars have noted, in 1.28 Paul employs technical Stoic terminology: τὰ μὴ καθήκοντα.⁸ Herein we see another connection between 1.28 and 12.1–2. In the latter, along with the renewal of the mind, Paul speaks of those in the Messiah offering "rational worship" (λογικὴ λατρεία).⁹ Though similar language can be found elsewhere in the ancient world, Epictetus provides the most striking parallel:

> Why, if we had sense (εἰ γὰρ νοῦν εἴχομεν), ought we to be doing anything else . . . than sing to the Deity (ἄλλο τι ἔδει ἡμᾶς ποιεῖν . . . ἢ ὑμνεῖν τὸ θεῖον). . . . If, indeed, I were a nightingale, I should be singing as a nightingale; if a swan, as a swan. But as it is, I am a rational being (νῦν δὲ λογικός εἰμι), therefore I must be singing hymns of praise to God.¹⁰

Therefore, at two crucial "framing" points in the letter (1.28 and 12.2), Paul employs language which resonates with popular philosophical discourse. This will prove important in the argument which follows.

We now turn to 2.17–24:¹¹

> (2.17) If you call yourself a Jew and you rely upon Torah and boast in God, and (2.18) you know his will and you can determine what is excellent because you are instructed by Torah (γινώσκεις τὸ θέλημα καὶ δοκιμάζεις τὰ διαφέροντα κατηχούμενος ἐκ τοῦ νόμου), (2.19) being confident that you are a guide to the blind, a light to those in darkness, (2.20) a corrector of the foolish, a teacher of children, because you have the form of knowledge and truth in the Torah (ἔχοντα τὴν μόρφωσιν τῆς γνώσεως καὶ τῆς ἀληθείας ἐν τῷ νόμῳ)—(2.21) The one, therefore, who teaches another, do you teach yourself? . . . (2.23) Whoever boasts in Torah, through the transgression of Torah, you dishonor God. (2.24) For, as it is written, "The name of God is blasphemed among the Gentiles because of you." (Isa. 52.5)

Whatever else should be said of Romans 1.1–2.16, verse 2.11 serves as a summary of at least one central point Paul wants to make: "For there is no favoritism with God." Jews and Gentiles alike, so Paul has argued, are on the same footing.[12] Both have, to use the language of 3.23, "sinned and fallen short of the glory of God." This was, however, an extremely daring position for a Jew to take, and, so Paul knew, would naturally have elicited the Jewish response: "But what about the election? What about the gift of Torah?" (cf. Rom. 9.4–5). This is precisely the implicit response which Paul engages in 2.17–24.

Bearing in mind 1.28 and 12.1–2, I contend that the imaginary Jewish interlocutor makes three specific claims. (1) God gave Israel the Torah, the very "form of knowledge and truth." (2) The Torah's instruction allows Israel both "to know God's will" and to δοκιμάζειν "what is excellent." The gift of Torah, therefore, either exempts or rescues Israel from the human plight described in summary fashion in 1.28, looking ahead to the renewal of 12.1–2.[13] (3) The Jewish interlocutor portrays Israel's election *in missiological terms*: "a guide to the blind, a light to those in darkness, a corrector of the foolish, a teacher of children."[14] Israel, so the interlocutor claims, is the solution to the problems outlined in 1.18–32, and this is a point with which Paul would have emphatically agreed. Indeed, as I argued above, although certain Jewish texts and traditions provide a partial parallel to Paul's language, his thoroughly missiological construal of Israel's election owes to his own unique mission *as an apostle to the Gentiles*. In any case, though Israel was called to be the solution, she has indeed failed (in Paul's eyes) in that missiological task: "The name of God is [rather] blasphemed among the Gentiles because of you" (2.24). I repeat: as I argued above, I am not arguing that this missiological construal of Israel's purpose, in relation to which Paul argues that she has failed, was a common construal of Israel's purpose either in second-temple texts or in second-temple practice. Rather, this is likely *Paul's own construal* of Israel's purpose and her consequent failure *in the light of his own missionary efforts among Gentiles*. I note, furthermore, that this Pauline criticism concerns far more than Israel simply not "obeying" or "keeping" the Mosaic legislation.[15] The point here and for Paul, in other words, is not simply about the covenantal relationship *between* God and Israel but about the covenantal purpose *from* God, *through* Israel, and *for* the broken humanity described in 1.18–32.

In connection to my construal of the thrust of 2.17–24, I briefly consider a recent, revisionist reading(s) of the passage. Apparently, Runar Thorsteinsson and Rafael Rodríguez independently came to a similar reading, which was itself anticipated and paralleled in a few other studies, in which the imaginary interlocutor of Romans 2.17–24 is actually a Gentile who has, so to speak, "Judaized."[16] This reading, furthermore, is self-confessedly designed further to buttress the increasingly influential "Paul-within-Judaism Perspective."[17]

Disappointingly, however, rather than making separate and rigorous cases of their own, Rodríguez and, for example, Zetterholm appear simply to endorse Thorsteinnson's study, which itself is not very strong in this regard.[18] Other than the growing energy surrounding the "Paul-within-Judaism Perspective," Thorsteinnson's main piece of evidence, picked up by, for example, Rodríguez, Zetterholm, and Novenson, is that the verb ἐπονομάζω in 2.17 *can* refer to the ascription or assumption of a name/designation/label which is *not* proper (i.e., ethnic) to the thing/person in question, such that one can imagine a "Gentile" in Rome assuming the label Ἰουδαῖος.[19] As Novenson's cautious and exploratory essay notes, however, the lexical evidence is "not decisive."[20] Novenson also notes, as well as Thorsteinsson before him, that the force of Romans 3.9 appears to devastate this reading, a text in which Paul apparently claims that earlier in the letter he has "already charged (προητιασάμεθα) that all, both *Jews* and Greeks, are under Sin."[21] This at least appears to be a huge problem for readings like Thorsteinsson's and Novenson's, in relation to which the latter writes, "On my reading, however, Paul has not in fact indicted the Jews in Romans 2."[22]

The solution of both of the latter scholars is to postulate that the aorist verb προητιασάμεθα actually refers to the catena of scriptural passages which *follows* (3.11–20) rather than to anything which precedes.[23] This, however, especially in view of the prepositional πρό (here denoting temporal anteriority), makes this reading very unlikely. Rather, therefore, and with several other commentators, it is best to take the aorist verb προητιασάμεθα as a reference to an anterior act of "charging" both Jews and Gentiles as under Sin, a charge which is implicit at least in 2.17–24 if not elsewhere in 1.18–3.9.[24]

We now move quickly through a few other sections of the letter. If Israel has, at least in Paul's eyes, failed in her commission, what will become of the covenant, especially if God seems to be including Gentiles into the people of God irrespective of Torah observance (2.25–29)?[25] Indeed:

> (3.1) What, then, is the advantage of the Jew? Or what is the value of circumcision? (3.2) Much in every way. Principally (πρῶτον), they were entrusted (ἐπιστεύθησαν) with the oracles of God. (3.3) So what, then? If some were faithless (ἠπίστησάν), will not their faithlessness nullify the faithfulness of God (μὴ ἡ ἀπιστία αὐτῶν τὴν πίστιν τοῦ θεοῦ καταργήσει)? (3.4) By no means!

It is precisely Paul's critique of boasting in one's ethnic Jewishness—especially in the election and in the gift of Torah (so 2.17–24)—which precipitates this line of questioning.[26] If, so this line of questioning presumes, Paul has so thoroughly divested the historical people of Israel of any divine privileges, he has surely also divested both the covenant and the very fact of being Jewish of any theological significance.

To this, Paul answers emphatically in the negative (3.4: μὴ γένοιτο). Indeed, the Jew is advantaged πολὺ κατὰ πάντα τρόπον (3.2). The "principal" advantage, so Paul argues, is that they were "entrusted" with the oracles of God. I note that, in this regard, as in the cases of 1 Timothy 1.16 and 1.17, it is best to take πρῶτος to mean "foremost" rather than "the first of a sequence."[27] Paul has not lost his train of thought; nor is he enumerating several advantages of ethnic Israel.[28] Rather, *and particularly in light of his mission to Gentiles*, he is audaciously arguing that ethnic Israel had (and still has) one principal "privilege": they were "entrusted" with the oracles of God (implicitly) *for the nations*. The force of this point, however, as N. T. Wright in particular has argued, has rarely been noticed.[29] The passive form of πιστεύω in this instance does not refer, as Dunn argues, generally to "Jewish responsibility within the covenant";[30] nor, as Schreiner argues, simply to the fact that "[Israel] had promises from God ensuring them of future salvation";[31] nor, as Fitzmyer states, simply to Israel's "possession of such oracles."[32] Rather, this section flows logically from 2.17–24, in which Paul had construed Israel's election in fundamentally missiological terms. Israel has failed, so Paul has argued, at her missiological task.

When Paul goes on, therefore, to ask, "If some were faithless, will not their faithlessness nullify the faithfulness of God?" (3.4), he has in mind by his use of the root πιστ—both God's and "their [i.e., the Israelites']"—not only faithfulness to the covenant *between* God and Israel but faithfulness to the covenant plan *from* God, *through* Israel, and *to* the nations among whom Paul is presently preaching the gospel.[33] If God's covenant with Israel ultimately fails, so Paul reasons according to his missiological construal of Israel's election, the human race will remain in the problems outlined in 1.18–32. God will, however, remain faithful.

This is where the logic of Romans 3.21–24 comes in:

(3.21) But now, apart from the Torah, the covenant faithfulness of God has been unveiled—though it was attested to by the Torah and the Prophets—(3.22) indeed, the covenant faithfulness of God [has been unveiled] through the faithfulness of Jesus the Messiah for the benefit of all those who are faithful (διὰ πίστεως Ἰησοῦ Χριστοῦ εἰς πάντας τοὺς πιστεύοντας). For there is no distinction, (3.23) because all sinned and have fallen short of (ὑστεροῦνται) the glory of God, (3.24) being justified as a gift by his grace through the redemption which is in the Messiah Jesus.

The goal of the covenant, jeopardized by Israel's ἀπιστία ("faithlessness") but ensured by God's πίστις ("faithfulness"), is finally effected διὰ πίστεως Ἰησοῦ Χριστοῦ. The faithfulness of Jesus the Messiah stands in for Israel's faithlessness.[34] And this faithfulness, moreover, is that because of which

"(3.23) there is [now] no distinction, (3.23) because all sinned and have fallen short of the glory of God" (3.23). Here we see the universal affects of God's covenant with Israel. In this connection and with several others, I take all of 3.23 as an allusion to Adam and Eve's original sin and to our participation in such.[35] In this regard, even if we should not take the reference to "the glory of God" as an allusion to the tradition of Adam and Eve's original "glory" before their fall (cp. esp. Greek LAE 21.6 and, on the phrase "all the glory of Adam" in the Scrolls, above), this reading of 3.23–24 is confirmed by the allusion back to 3.24 in Paul's explicit discussion of Adam in 5.12–17.

In 5.12, Paul states that, through "the one man [Adam]," "Sin entered the world and through Sin Death" (5.12). This allowed, furthermore, "Death to reign (ἐβασίλευσεν ὁ θάνατος)" (5.14). In Paul's logic, therefore, the sovereignty which God originally intended for Adam *was forfeited to something else:* namely, Death. (2) However, it is precisely this "Adamic sovereignty" which is reclaimed by those "justified as a gift" in 3.24:

> If, by the trespass of the one man, Death reigned through that one man (ὁ θάνατος ἐβασίλευσεν διὰ τοῦ ἑνός), how much more shall those who have received the abundance of the gracious gift of righteousness reign in life through the one man Jesus the Messiah (πολλῷ μᾶλλον οἱ τὴν περισσείαν τῆς χάριτος καὶ τῆς δωρεᾶς τῆς δικαιοσύνης λαμβάνοντες ἐν ζωῇ βασιλεύσουσιν διὰ τοῦ ἑνός Ἰησοῦ Χριστοῦ/ 5.17).

In 3.24, Paul spoke of those δικαιούμενοι δωρεὰν τῇ αὐτοῦ χάριτι, whereas here he speaks of οἱ τὴν περισσείαν τῆς χάριτος καὶ τῆς δωρεᾶς τῆς δικαιοσύνης λαμβάνοντες. The language is unmistakably parallel and, in this latter text, the theme of Adamic sovereignty is unambiguous. Here, as in 3.23–24, therefore, those "justified" are ensured of the sovereignty which Adam originally forfeited, a sovereignty ultimately reclaimed in resurrection life (ἐν ζωῇ/ cp. 1 Cor. 15.50–55).[36]

In between the dense statement of 3.21–26 (esp. 3.23–24) and the explication of 5.12–21 (esp. 5.12–17), however, Paul radically redefines that which constitutes a person as a "justified child of Abraham" (Rom. 4).[37] Having "already charged that all, both Jews and Greeks, are under Sin" (3.9) and having argued that, therefore, all are "justified" διὰ πίστεως Ἰησοῦ Χριστοῦ without "distinction" (3.22), he then turns emphatically to affirm God's covenant with Abraham *but to redefine* that which constitutes a person as one of its members (Rom. 4). For our purposes, however, I simply note one crucial feature of chapter 4 and of the way in which it relates to 5.12–17. In Romans 4.13, in a larger exposition of what Paul takes to be the proper reading and appropriation of the promises God made to Abraham in Genesis 12; 15; 17; and 22 (esp. 15.6), he states what he—somewhat to the reader's surprise—takes to be one of the fundamental features of those promises: "For the promise that Abraham and his seed would inherit the *kosmos* (τὸ κληρονόμον αὐτὸν εἶναι κόσμου) was not through the Torah but through the righteousness which is dependent upon faithfulness (ἀλλὰ διὰ δικαιοσύνης πίστεως)" (4.13). With respect to this text, I make two points. (1) The phrase διὰ δικαιοσύνης πίστεως, while alluding back *intertextually* to (LXX) Genesis 15.6, alludes back *intratextually* to the language in 3.24 which Paul had used to describe the reversal of Adam and Eve's sin and its affects.[38] (2) Hereby, by taking the content of the Abrahamic promise to consist of the gift of the whole *kosmos*, and on the basis of the relationship between 3.23–24; 4.13; and 5.12–17, we see that Paul presents the family of Abraham, characterized by πίστις, as the people who assume the sovereignty over the whole *kosmos* which Adam had forfeited to Death (5.14).[39]

We are now nearly ready to turn our full attention to Romans 7–8. However, first, I should make one uncontroversial point about the way in which Romans 6 leads into the argument of chapter 7. In Paul's discussion of baptism in Romans 6, he portrays the forces of Sin and Death as slavemasters (esp. 6.6–10, 12–23). It is quite shocking, then, within the same context, that Paul should portray the Torah similarly: "But now, we are free from the Torah because we have died to that which held us captive (ἀποθανόντες ἐν ᾧ κατειχόμεθα), such that we are 'enslaved' in the newness of the Spirit and not the oldness of the letter" (7.6). This jarring statement immediately prompts the reflections of 7.7–25.[40] Has Paul essentially equated the Torah and Sin?[41] We now turn to Romans 7.7–8.30.

EXEGESIS: ROMANS 7.7–8.30

Because Romans 7.7–25 is so dense and so contested, a brief delineation of the major options and their respective supporters will prove helpful. Fitzmyer's list of five major readings, to which I will add a sixth, is useful in this regard.[42] (1) Some take the passage as an autobiographical account of Paul's pre-Christian life.[43] (2) As a kind of subdivision within the former reading, some take the passage to represent Paul's psychological reflections on the particular struggles of adolescence under the Torah.[44] (3) On the other hand, certain others, not least patristic writers, have taken the text as a Pauline "impersonation" (i.e., as *prosōpopoiia*) of Adam.[45] (4) Some scholars contend that the passage concerns Paul's and/or the normal Christian's struggle with sin and the Torah.[46] (5) Still others suggest that the text generally concerns life under the Torah for those apart from the Messiah.[47] (6) A few scholars have argued that the Pauline "I" dramatically impersonates (i.e., as *prosōpopoiia*) the whole of historical Israel as she struggled and, indeed (from the perspective of the "I"), failed to keep the Torah.[48]

With respect to these major positions, before providing my own analysis, I make the following points. Position (1) fundamentally fails to account for the purpose of the passage at this point in the letter. Why, in other words, *at this point in the argument*, would Paul provide an autobiographical account of his pre-Christian life, especially if this account is not designed to be representative of a larger situation. Position (2), I suggest, suffers from the same criticism. Why would Paul provide extensive and possibly unrepresentative psychological reflections about his pre-Christian life, particularly if his audience could respond: "That's interesting, but it doesn't resonate with *my* experience." Proposal (3)—that the Pauline "I" represents Adam—fails to account for the fact that Paul is concerned with the Torah throughout, a Torah which, as he says earlier in the same letter (Rom. 5.12–14), came long after Adam. This does not, of course, rule out the possibility, which I will put forward below, that Paul *evokes* Genesis 3 as he tells the story of Israel under the Torah.

Proposal (4), in which the undesirable moral situation of 7.7–25 is characteristic of life in the Messiah, cannot sufficiently explain the explosion of praise in 7.25. In other words, why would Paul conclude the passage with a thanksgiving, as well as go on to speak of the great rescue effected by the Messiah in 8.1–11, if the state of his and other Christians' lives was characterized by the moral paralysis of 7.14–24? As I argued in a previous section, position (5) assumes that Paul regarded Gentiles as "under the Torah," a position which, according to Romans 2.12, he did not hold. Below, therefore, I will build on the superior strengths of position (6).

Separate mention, however, should be made of the very influential analysis of Stanley K. Stowers.[49] Stowers is quite concerned, inter alia, to controvert traditional readings in which Romans 7.7–25 offers the "supposed analysis of the human predicament to which Christ was the solution."[50] Indeed, "Interpreters in this tradition have placed much weight on Romans 7 as they make Pauline Christianity the antithesis of an imagined Jewish religiosity." Instead, Stowers contends, we must reject this "Augustinian tradition of reading Romans 7.7–25 and especially 14–25."[51]

Following his statement of these concerns, Stowers begins his positive analysis with a crucial observation. Paul alludes to the popular philosophical trope of the Medea paradox in Romans 7.15, 17, a point to which I will come below.[52] On this basis and in part following Kümmel's influential analysis, Stowers proposes that 7.7–25 should be treated as an instance of "*prosōpopoiia*, speech-in-character."[53] In this vein, Stowers follows Kümmel's definition of this phenomenon: "He defined *prosōpopoiia* as follows: 'where the speaker places a speech in the mouth of another person or where inanimate things can speak.'"⁵⁴ Further to buttress his case, Stowers appeals to Origin's rhetorical expertise and to the fact that the latter famously regarded Romans 7.7–25 as an instance of *prosōpopoiia*.⁵⁵

While Stowers's careful case concerning Paul's rhetorical use of *prosōpopoiia* in 7.7–25 is convincing, his specific interpretation of the text is not. For example, I do not follow the apparently (to his mind) necessary logic of this statement: "If we understand the anachronism of introducing a third term, 'Christian,' then the persona of Romans 7 can only be a gentile."⁵⁶ For Stowers, therefore, Paul assumes the character of a "godfearer."⁵⁷ More specifically, Paul assumes the *persona* of a "godfearing" Gentile who is neither "fully Jew nor fully Greek . . . [but] torn between the passions of an idolator and the law of the one true God."⁵⁸

In response to Stowers, I make three points. (1) While Stowers's concern to ward off historical anachronism is commendable, I submit that there is nothing particularly anachronistic or straightforwardly implausible about supposing that Paul the Jewish Christian here offers a retrospective analysis of Israel's life under the Torah. (2) Moreover, while the sin of idolatry features prominently in Romans 1.18–32, very little in the rest of the letter suggests that Paul was very concerned about the idolatrous behavior of his audience; nor is this reconstruction of the Roman Christians common in the commentators.⁵⁹ (3) Furthermore, Romans, unlike Galatians, does not feature the kind of rhetoric in which Paul sternly warns Gentile Christians not "to Judaize." In sum, therefore, while Stowers is quite right to stress the device of *prosōpopoiia* and Paul's evocation of the Medea paradox in 7.15, 19, his interpretation of the passage is unconvincing.

As I stated above, my reading is a variation on (6).⁶⁰ The Pauline "I" represents an instance of *prosōpopoiia* in which Paul impersonates, from 7.7 to 7.13, the experience of historical Israel when she received the Torah at Mount Sinai. This past reference explains Paul's consistent use of past-tense verbs throughout 7.7–13, in contradistinction to his consistent use of present-tense verbs throughout 7.14–25.⁶¹ In 7.14–21, the Pauline "I" still represents an "Israelite under Torah" but "an Israelite under Torah *at the time of Paul's writing*." Finally, signaled not least by the conclusion formula in 7.21a, εὑρίσκω ἄρα τὸν νόμον ("I, therefore, *conclude* about the Torah"), the Pauline "I" ceases to be *only* an Israelite apart from the Messiah.⁶² In other words, in 7.22–25, the Pauline "I" represents in one "person" what happens when, on the one hand, one keeps "the Torah of God" (7.22) or "the Torah of the mind" (7.23) and, on the other hand, "another Torah" or "the Torah of Sin" (7.23). The latter Torah, as happened with historical Israel, will take one into captivity (exile), while the former Torah will set one free (so 8.2).

In my reading, therefore, Paul is not simply offering an abstract theology of, and/or an apology for, Torah.⁶³ Rather, he hopes to accomplish the following: (1) to defend himself against the charge that he has either "nullified Torah" (so 3.31) in his missionary work and/or implicitly treated the Torah as Sin (so 5.20; and 7.7); (2) to argue that, though he regards the Torah as "holy and righteous and good" (7.12), Sin has, nonetheless, found a good base of operations in the Torah (7.8, 11); (3) and that, therefore, anyone who attempts to keep the Torah "according to the oldness of the letter" (7.6) will end up in a state no better than the current (theological) state of "exiled Israel" (7.23).[64]

We now commence the exegesis. Throughout the section, Paul is particularly concerned to argue that the Torah itself is not Sin. Rather, the Torah is "holy and righteous and good" (7.12). The problem is not, therefore, strictly to do with Torah but with Sin which takes an "opportunity through the commandment" (7.8). Indeed, the commandment which was "unto life" produced death (7.10). However, historical Israel—represented by the Pauline "I" from 7.7–13—was actually alive until Sin was raised to fresh life (ἡ ἁμαρτία ἀνέζησεν/ 7.9). This looks back, I suggest, to the equally cryptic 5.13: "For before the Torah, Sin was indeed in the world, but Sin is not reckoned when there is no Torah." Israel, so Paul argues, was in some sense "alive" from Abraham to Moses, but when the commandment came—that is, the gift of Torah—Sin found fresh life (7.9).[65] Or, to use Paul's language in 7.8 and 7.11, Sin found a good base of operations (ἀφορμὴν δὲ λαβοῦσα ἡ ἁμαρτία).[66] Indeed, Sin uses this new base of operations to deceive Israel and to kill her (ἐξηπάτησέν με καὶ δι' αὐτῆς ἀπέκτεινεν/ 7.11). As several scholars have argued, this is an allusion to LXX Genesis 3.13, a text to which Paul unambiguously alludes later in Romans 16.20.[67] Sin, like the serpent in the garden, commits a deceit which leads to death. In this regard, Moo is wrong, however, to play off a reference to Adam and to Israel, preferring only to see a reference to the latter.[68] Two features of the passage suggest that it is precisely Paul's (audacious) point that, when Israel received the Torah at Sinai, she recapitulated the sin of Adam and Eve; or, to state it differently, following Paul's discussion of Sin in chapter 6, part of his point in 7.7–25 is to argue that Sin has used the Torah to place Israel in exactly the same position as Adam/humanity.[69]

(1) Paul's use of the word ἐντολή (simply "commandment") throughout, even though he is actually discussing the whole νόμος, might suggest that he has the archetypal sin of Adam and Eve in mind (cp. Apoc. Sed. 4.5; GLAE 10; 23; 24 [2x]; 25; 39; and Josephus, *Ant.* 1.43).[70] (2) ἐξαπατάω is likely an allusion Genesis 3.13.[71] The verb occurs in the undisputed Pauline letters at Romans 7.11; 16.18; 1 Corinthians 3.18; and 2 Corinthians 11.3. It appears in the disputed letters at 2 Thessalonians 2.3 and 1 Timothy 2.14. Of these six instances, in 2 Corinthians 11.3 and 1 Timothy 2.14 the verb describes the way in which Eve was "deceived" in the garden of Eden. Moreover, the

instance of Romans 16.18, in which Paul warns of "those who deceive the hearts of the simple-minded," is followed two verses later by a clear allusion to Genesis 3.15: "And the God of peace will soon crush the satan under your feet" (Rom. 16.20). Therefore, leaving aside the case of Romans 7.11, three of the six instances in the thirteen letters attributed to Paul involve allusions to Genesis 3. The verb is attested nowhere else in the New Testament and appears only once in LXX (Ex. 8.25) in a different connection (LXX Gen. 3.13 has the simple, though related, ἀπατάω). Most relevant, however, is the fact that the verb occurs precisely in this connection in Josephus's *Antiquities* 1.49; Greek LAE 16; and Sibylline Oracles 1.40.

Before moving on, however, I repeat a point that I have tried to stress. However much continuity might exist between Saul of Tarsus and Paul the Apostle on the question of the nature and function of the Torah and of the status of Israel (apart from the Messiah), the argument of Romans reflects retrospective theological judgments informed not least by the following: (1) the crucifixion and resurrection of Jesus *as* Israel's Messiah; (2) the confirmation of point (1) by Paul's Damascus christophany; and (3) the outpouring of the eschatological Spirit upon Pauline communities partly composed of Torah-unobservant Gentiles. Note well, therefore, that I am *not* arguing that Paul's construal of Israel or of the purpose and function of Torah would have found wide and uncritical assent among his Jewish contemporaries.

We pick up in Romans 7.14. I recall my hypothesis concerning Paul's shift from the consistent use of past-tense verbs (7.7–13) to the consistent use of present-tense verbs (7.14–25). Though we will come to 7.22–25 below, I have argued that, in 7.7–13, the Pauline "I" represents historical Israel when she received the Torah and recapitulated the sin of Adam and Eve. In 7.14–21, however, the Pauline "I" represents Paul's Jewish *contemporaries*. Beginning in 7.14, Paul clearly states, the problem does not lie with Torah, which is "spiritual," but with Israel (the Pauline "I"), which "is fleshly, having been sold as a slave under Sin" (7.14).[72] Paul then expounds the problem precipitated by the gift of the good Torah to "fleshly Israel":

> (7.15) For I do not understand what I am doing. Because I do not do what I want to do, but, rather, I do what I hate. (7.16) Now, if I do what I do not want to do, I agree with the Torah, that it is good. (7.17) But now, I am no longer the one doing it but Sin dwelling in me. (7.18) For I know that nothing good dwells in my flesh. Although I have the desire to do good, I do not have the ability to bring it about. (7.19) For I do not do the good which I want to do, but rather the evil which I do not want to do. (7.20) But if I do that which I do not want to do, I am no longer the one doing it but Sin dwelling in me. (7.21) I, therefore, conclude about the Torah (εὑρίσκω ἄρα τὸν νόμον): when I want to do good, evil is close at hand.

As Gerd Theissen demonstrated over three decades ago, Paul here alludes to the popular philosophical trope of the Medea paradox.[73] Euripides (ca. 480–406 BCE) provides our earliest attestation to this tradition, but it is also attested in Plato, Ovid, Seneca, Galen, and others.[74] Epictetus, however, provides the most striking parallel:

> Every error (Πᾶν ἁμάρτημα) involves a contradiction. For since he who is in error does not wish to err (ἐπεὶ γὰρ ὁ ἁμαρτάνων οὐ θέλει ἁμαρτάνειν), but to be right, it is clear that he is not doing what he wishes (δῆλον ὅτι ὃ μὲν θέλει οὐ ποιεῖ). . . . He, then, who can show to each man the contradiction which causes him to err, and can clearly bring home to him how he is not doing what he wishes, and is doing what he does not wish (πῶς ὃ θέλει οὐ ποιεῖ καὶ ὃ μὴ θέλει ποιεῖ).[75]

But why would Paul depict the contemporary Jewish attempt to keep the Torah with the Medea paradox? Moreover, as several scholars have noted, why does Paul's apparent characterization of ἀκρασία (i.e., "weakness of the will") not correspond to the major construals of the philosophical traditions?[76] For instance, "the Stoic tradition claimed that the person does evil because he or she lacks knowledge of what is right," while the "Platonic tradition maintained that the problem results from a conflict between the rational and irrational parts of a human."[77] Paul, however, emphasizes the deadly power of Sin, the vivifying power of the Spirit, and his anthropological analysis of the human state in which people must be freshly reconstituted through death and resurrection with Jesus *via* baptism (so 6.1–11). This, of course, is totally without parallel in any of the *akrasia* traditions.[78]

Why, then, would Paul evoke this philosophical tradition *at this point in the letter*, and why, in particular, does his use of it not correspond to the use of the same tradition by *any* of the philosophers? As to the latter question, I contend, as with Paul's inner-Jewish polemic in 2 Corinthians 2.17–3.1, the philosophical characterization in 7.15–19 largely serves *rhetorical purposes*. As is evident, inter alia, from Paul's notion of "indwelling Sin" in 7.17, 20, Paul does not intend to map onto either the Platonic or the Stoic position. The point is, rather, rhetorical. Therefore, picking up the first question of this paragraph, I contend that Paul intends rhetorically to characterize life under the Torah as no better than the moral paralysis reflected in the philosophical *akrasia* traditions. Indeed, Paul will soon imply, both with his language of "inner humanity" (ὁ ἔσω ἄνθρωπος) in 7.22 and with his language of the *imago Dei* in 8.29, that those in the Messiah, far from being morally paralyzed by the problem of *akrasia*, attain to the *telos* of true philosophy: the image of God. Again, therefore, Paul has cast essentially inner-Jewish issues in philosophical dress, hoping hereby to achieve a strong rhetorical and argumentative affect. This hypothesis, I submit, allows us to explain *all* of the data—that the topic of 7.7–25 is the Jewish Torah but that Paul makes use of the philosophical trope of the Medea paradox in 7.15–19—rather than half of it, as do hypotheses which either suppose that Paul is fundamentally concerned with philosophical anthropology (and not the Torah) or that Paul does not, in fact, allude to the Medea paradox.

We pick up in 7.21. Signaled not least by the conclusion formula εὑρίσκω ἄρα τὸν νόμον ("I, therefore, *conclude* about the Torah"), Paul properly concludes his reflections upon the historic and contemporary Jewish failure to keep the Torah.[79] In 7.22–25, the Pauline "I" begins to bifurcate. The one "person" of the Pauline "I" is divided between one who keeps "the Torah of God" (7.22) or "the Torah of the [my] mind" (7.23), on the one hand, and the one who keeps "another Torah" or "the Torah of Sin" (7.23), on the other. In 7.22–25, therefore, the one Pauline "I" ceases *only* to be a Jew apart from the Messiah. Now, in 7.22–25, the one person of the Pauline "I" represents *a divided Israel*, an Israel apart from the Messiah that keeps, on the one hand, "another Torah" or "the Torah of Sin" (7.23), and an Israel in the Messiah that keeps "the Torah of God" (7.22) or "the Torah of the [my] mind" (7.23), on the other.

> (7.22) For I rejoice in the Torah of God in my inner humanity (κατὰ τὸν ἔσω ἄνθρωπον). (7.23) But I see another Torah in my members, waging war against the Torah of my mind and attempting to take me into the captivity of the Torah of Sin (αἰχμαλωτίζοντά με) which is in my members.[80] (7.24) Wretched person that I am! Who will rescue me from this body of death? (7.25) But thanks be to God through Jesus the Messiah our Lord! Therefore, on the one hand, I am enslaved with my mind to the Torah of God, but, on the other hand, with my flesh to the Torah of Sin.

There are two Torahs, so Paul argues, "another Torah" or the "Torah of Sin," on the one hand, and the "Torah of God" or the "Torah of my mind," on the other. These are shorthands, I suggest, respectively, for the Torah according to "the oldness of the letter" and the Torah according to "the newness of the Spirit" (7.6); or, to state it differently, these are shorthands for the old and new covenants *as Paul construes them*.[81] In his view, he and other Jewish (and Gentile) Christians genuinely rejoice in (and keep) the Torah of God—that is, the Torah according to "the newness of the Spirit." But Paul sees "another Torah," according to the "oldness of the letter," in his members. With this dramatic language of two Torahs and the one Pauline "I," Paul depicts himself as a paradigmatic Israelite who has the choice of keeping only *one Torah*. The "other Torah," the "Torah of Sin," wants to take Paul-the-paradigmatic-Jew into captivity. In this connection, the lexical choice of αἰχμ αλωτίζω ("to take into captivity") is hardly coincidental.⁸² Paul alludes here, I suggest, to Israel's exile, to which the LXX ubiquitously refers with this verb and its cognates ([αἰχμαλωτίζω] 3 Kgs. 8.46; 4 Kgs. 24.14; 2 Chr. 30.9; [αἰχμαλωτεύω] Esth. 1.1; 2.6; 1 Macc. 9.72; Am. 1.5, 6; 5.5 [2x]; Mic. 1.16; Oba. 11; Isa. 14.2; 49.24, 25; Jer. 27.33; Ezek. 6.9; 12.3; 39.23; the nouns αἰχμαλωσία and αἰχμάλωτος are ubiquitous in this connection).⁸³ This reading, moreover, coalesces extremely well with the theme of the return from exile which permeates Romans 8.

In any case, with the juxtaposition of two Torahs—one "of Sin" and one "of God"—Paul contrasts his construal of Torah keeping with another, obviously common construal in which the covenant markers of circumcision, sabbath, and the food laws are *precisely* the ways in which one expresses Torah faithfulness.⁸⁴ In this connection, even if the issues discussed in Romans 14 were more potential than actual, it is clear that Paul is concerned to place "not keeping kosher" and "not keeping sabbath" on the same theological footing as keeping kosher and keeping sabbath (14.1–6). In fact, he implicitly regards the former as the "strong position" (so 14.1).⁸⁵ Furthermore, what Paul says cryptically in 2.14–16, 25–29; 3.31; 7.22; 8.2–4; and 9.30–10.13 he states clearly and in different words in 13.8: "For the one who loves another has fulfilled Torah." This is part of the point of the two Torahs in 7.22–25. Paul insists, no doubt scandalously to most contemporary Jews and to many contemporary Jewish Christians, that *his* kind of Torah keeping is inspired by God's eschatological Spirit and shorn of the classic Jewish markers of Torah faithfulness. This reading, furthermore, in which the one Pauline "I" in 7.22–25 represents a divided Israel, is able sufficiently to account for the explosion of praise in 7.25. Paul can depict the Pauline "I" in desperate terms in 7.7–21, and then in liberated terms in 7.25, *because the struggles outlined in 7.7–21 are not characteristic of Paul's liberated Christian life.*⁸⁶

Before moving to Romans 8, however, I make one further point about 7.22–25. When Paul says, "For I rejoice in the Torah of God *in my inner humanity* (κατὰ τὸν ἔσω ἄνθρωπον)" (7.22), he impersonates a Jewish *Christian* and uses language characteristic of Middle Platonism (cp. 2 Cor. 4.16 and Eph. 3.16).⁸⁷ However, in this regard, for example, Jewett is quite right to insist that "although Paul uses a Platonic concept here, his anthropology is not dualistic."⁸⁸ Indeed, as with Paul's use of the Medea paradox, his principal purpose is *rhetorical*. Jews who keep "another Torah," "the Torah of Sin" (7.23), "according to the oldness of the letter" (7.6), are plagued by *akrasia*, while those in the Messiah, who keep "the Torah of God" or "the Torah of the mind" (7.22)—the new covenant "according to the newness of the Spirit" (7.6)—are like true philosophers who are not plagued by *akrasia* but "rejoice in the Torah of God κατὰ τὸν ἔσω ἄνθρωπον" (7.22). Indeed, the former Jews are still in a theological state of "exile" (7.23) while Jews (and Gentiles) in the Messiah, who keep the Torah of God, are the people of Abraham (Rom. 4) who are liberated from exile and assume the sovereignty over the (renewed) *kosmos* (8.19–21) which Adam had forfeited to the forces of Sin and Death (5.12–14).

I now step back to summarize my case regarding Romans 7.7-25. (1) In 7.7–13, indicated not least by the consistent use of past-tense verbs, the Pauline "I" represents historical Israel when she received the Torah at Mount Sinai. (2) From 7.14 to 7.21, Paul switches to the consistent use of present-tense verbs because he is impersonating an Israelite apart from the Messiah and under the Torah *at the time of writing*. (3) In Romans 7.21a, signaled not least by the conclusion formula εὑρίσκω ἄρα τὸν νόμον, Paul properly concludes his reflections upon historic and contemporary Israel's failure to keep the Torah. (4) From 7.22 to 7.25, the Pauline "I" bifurcates and represents in one "person" a divided Israel, an Israel whom "the Torah of Sin" has taken into exile, on the one hand, and an Israel in the Messiah who genuinely rejoices in the Torah of God in her inner being (7.22), on the other. (5) By Paul's use of the Medea paradox in 7.15, 19 to characterize Jewish life apart from the Messiah and under the Torah, and by his use of the Platonic expression "inner humanity" in 7.22, Paul contrasts Jews apart from the Messiah and under the Torah with Jews (and Gentiles) in the Messiah and under his construal of Torah keeping. The former are paralyzed moralists while the latter are true philosophers.

We now come to Romans 8. Only certain features of this chapter are relevant to my overall hypothesis. We begin with 8.1–3:

> (8.1) There is, therefore, now no condemnation for those in the Messiah Jesus, (8.2) because the Torah of the Spirit of life has set you free (ἠλευθέρωσέν) in the Messiah Jesus from the Torah of Sin and Death. (8.3) For what the Torah could not do, because of the weakness of the flesh, God has done, having sent his own son (ὁ θεὸς τὸν ἑαυτοῦ υἱὸν πέμψας) in the likeness of sinful flesh and as a sin offering, he [God] condemned Sin in the flesh [of Jesus].

Paul has had to walk a tightrope. On the one hand, he clearly relativizes circumcision (esp. Rom. 4.9–12; 1 Cor. 7.19; Gal. 2.3; 5.1–6; and 6.11–16), the food laws (esp. Gal. 2.11–14; and Rom. 14), and sabbath observance (esp. Rom. 14). On the other hand, he insists that he and his converts keep the Torah of God. He now makes the most dramatic statement of all: "*the Torah of the Spirit of life has set you free.*"[89] In other words, turning from the "Torah of Sin and Death" and toward the "Torah of the Spirit of life" ("in the Messiah Jesus") has finally liberated God's people from the exile alluded to in 7.23.[90]

This liberation was effected, moreover, when God "sent" his own son (8.3). I take this formulation, along with several others, as an instance of wisdom christology in which Paul simply presupposes the doctrine of Jesus's preexistence and that *this doctrine will be uncontroversial to a church he did not plant.*[91] A widely noted parallel is found in Wisdom 9.10: "Send her [*sophia*] from the holy heavens and from the throne of your Glory send her (ἐξαπόστειλον αὐτὴν ἐξ ἁγίων οὐρανῶν καὶ ἀπὸ θρόνου δόξης σου πέμψον αὐτήν)." To be sure, the use of ἐξαποστέλλω provides a much stronger parallel to Galatians 4.4, but, as this passage is thematically and structurally (Gal. 4.4: ἐξαπέστειλεν ὁ θεὸς τὸν υἱὸν αὐτοῦ/ Rom. 8.3: ὁ θεὸς τὸν ἑαυτοῦ υἱὸν πέμψας) so close to Romans 8.3, it makes sense to take them both as instances of wisdom christology.

What should we make, however, of Dunn's rejection of wisdom christology here (and in Gal. 4.4) and, by implication, his rejection of any notion of Jesus's preexistence in Romans 8.3 or elsewhere in Paul?[92] In this regard, his construal of 1 Corinthians 8.6b, in which Paul states that "the one Lord Jesus the Messiah" was the one "δι' οὗ τὰ πάντα," is very unconvincing. Despite the clear cosmogonical formula, Dunn insists that the text refers to Jesus's "*present* Lordship" and *not* to his preexistent cosmogonical activity.[93] This is, however, a false antithesis. As to his account of Romans 8.3 (and, by implication, of Gal. 4.4), while Dunn is certainly correct to insist that "sending language when used of God does not tell us anything about the origin or point of departure of the one sent," he fails both (1) to note the contextual function, and (2) properly to understanding the meaning, of the image christology of Romans 8.29.[94] (1) As is routinely recognized, Romans 8.28–30 functions as a macro-summary of Paul's theological vision—at least as he expresses it in Romans—and as a sort of climax to the argument of chapters 5–8 in general and of 8.1–30 in particular.[95] As such, we ought to interpret the *Sendungsformel* of 8.3 in relation to the image christology of 8.29. (2) As I have already argued in detail, the image christology of Romans 8.29 is an instance of wisdom christology in which Jesus serves as the preexistent, cosmogonical, and paradigmatic "image" whose "form" believers will ultimately share.[96] As such, insofar as the christology of 8.29 should inform our reading of 8.3, it is best, with the majority of interpreters, to take 8.3 as in instance of wisdom christology in which Jesus's personal preexistence is simply presupposed.

Dunn, however, protests against this reading:

> The Adam Christology involved is clear: Christ is the image of God which Adam was intended to be.... Others argue that εἰκών has in view the other side of the act of creation, the Son as mediator of creation, where it is Wisdom rather than Adam to whom Paul alludes.... But while the overlap of usage of εἰκών

(Wisdom/Adam) has important implications for a theology of creation, it is the *outcome* (the *eschatological* outcome) of God's creative purpose which seems to be in view here rather than that of Wisdom's agency in creation.[97]

Here Dunn fails to appreciate the way in which, as I argued above, Paul's image christology reflects the appropriation of Middle Platonic intermediary doctrine and thereby expounds a particular teleology. In other words, in the dense statement of Romans 8.29, Paul contends that *in the beginning*, "those whom he [God] foreknew, he also predestined [*ultimately*] to share the same form as the image of his son." This is a teleological vision in which Jesus serves as the protological and *paradigmatic* image, a vision for which Adam traditions provide no convincing parallel. Furthermore, as I also argued above, Paul's immediate use of πρωτότοκος ("firstborn"), in such close conjunction to his use of εἰκών ("image"), points in the direction of wisdom christology. Dunn's rejection of this connection and his insistence that we look to the parallels of Colossians 1.18 and Revelation 1.5 *instead of* the closest and most obvious parallel of Colossians 1.15—in which, according to most interpreters, Jesus is conceived of as God's cosmogonical image—is quite unpersuasive.[98]

We now turn to consider a few features of 8.14–21 and of the way in which these relate to Paul's allusion to Israel's exile in 7.23. In 8.14–21, I suggest, following several other scholars, Paul evokes the theme of a "return from exile" or what is often called a "new exodus" (principally on the basis of the Exodus imagery of Isa. 43.1–2).[99] I note the following features in particular. (1) In 8.14–15, those "led by the Spirit of God are sons of God" (8.14), who "did not receive the spirit of slavery to go back again into fear but the Spirit of adoption" (8.15). (2) These same "sons of God," moreover, look forward to their "inheritance": "And, if children, then heirs; heirs of God and fellow-heirs with the Messiah (εἰ δὲ τέκνα, καὶ κληρονόμοι· κληρονόμοι μὲν θεοῦ, συγκληρονόμοι δὲ Χριστοῦ), if we suffer with him in order that we might also be glorified with him (ἵνα καὶ συνδοξασθῶμεν)" (8.17). (3) And the "inheritance" turns out to be, unsurprisingly in view of Romans 4.13 (ἡ ἐπαγγελία τῷ Ἀβραὰμ ἢ τῷ σπέρματι αὐτοῦ, τὸ κληρονόμον αὐτὸν εἶναι κόσμου), the whole, liberated *kosmos*, a *kosmos* which is, at present, "futile" (8.20) and eagerly awaiting "the revelations [these same] sons of God" (8.19).

With respect to (1), as has often been recognized, the designation "son of God" for Israel is intimately associated with the exodus both in the book of Exodus itself (Ex. 4.23) and in other Jewish literature (Hos. 11.1; Wis. 18.13; and 4Q504, frag. 1–2, col. 3.5–6).[100] When we combine this observation with the fact that Paul immediately refers to (the spirit of) slavery, we are right to prepare our ears for other possible echoes of the (new) exodus. (2) The language of "inheritance" (κληρονομία) is not only abundantly attested for the "promised land" in LXX (cf. e.g., Deut. 2.12; 12.9; Josh. 11.23; 12.6; Judg. 2.6; 20.6; 21.24; 3 Kgs. 8.36; 1 Chr. 16.18; 2 Chr. 6.27; Jud. 4.12; 8.22; 1 Macc. 15.33–34 [2x]; Ps. 104.11; 134.12; Sir. 44.23; and 46.8), but it is also associated with God's original promise to Abraham *in Romans itself* (4.13: κληρονόμος). (3) The theme of personified Jerusalem/creation (8.19–21) eagerly awaiting the return of God's people from exile (in the new exodus) is a prominent theme in Isaiah 40–55, a text to which Paul frequently alludes in Romans:[101]

For you shall go out in joy,
and be led back in peace;
the mountains and the hills before you shall burst into song,
and all the trees of the field shall clap their hands
 (Isa. 55.12 NRSV, emphasis added).

Taken *independently*, points (1) to (3) are not strong enough to make the case. Taken *together*, I contend, points (1) to (3) strongly suggest that Paul is evoking the theme of the new-exodus return from exile. In this way, therefore, whatever else should be said of Romans 8.1–21, Paul presents those in the Messiah as the people who have come out of the exile alluded to in 7.23.

When the people of God are liberated from exile, moreover, they are eagerly awaited by the "futile creation":

> (8.19) For the creation eagerly awaits the revelation of the sons of God—(8.20) because the creation was subjected to futility, not of its own will but rather because of the one who subjected it (τῇ γὰρ ματαιότητι ἡ κτίσις ὑπετάγη, οὐχ ἑκοῦσα ἀλλὰ διὰ τὸν ὑποτάξαντα)—in the hope (8.21) that the creation itself will be set free from its bondage to decay into the freedom brought about by the glorious children of God.[102]

Syntactically, I take 8.20, from τῇ γὰρ ματαιότητι to διὰ τὸν ὑποτάξαντα, as a parenthetical clarification. Within this parenthesis, Paul simply intends to indicate that the creation's futility is no fault of its own but rather the fault of τὸν ὑποτάξαντα ("the one who subjected it"). This latter phrase, moreover, refers to Adam, hereby reflecting a sequence of thought very close to 5.12–14.[103] I do not, therefore, take διὰ τὸν ὑποτάξαντα to run directly into ἐφ' ἐλπίδι. Many commentators, supposing this to be the case, have been forced to read the text to mean that "*God* subjected the creation to futility *in the hope* that the creation itself will be set free*.*"[104] It is very difficult, however, to see the sense that this would make. It is far better, therefore, to take the clause beginning with τῇ γὰρ ματαιότητι and ending with διὰ τὸν ὑποτάξαντα as a parenthetical reference to Adam's forfeiture of world sovereignty to the decaying forces of Sin and Death (cp. 5.12–14).

This reading suggests the following as the main clause: "(8.19) For the creation eagerly awaits the revelation of the sons of God . . . in the hope (8.21) that the creation itself will be set free from its bondage to decay into the freedom brought about by the glorious children of God." In this case, Paul would be saying that the (presently) futile creation eagerly awaits the returned-from-exile "sons of God" to assume the sovereignty over the *kosmos* which Adam forfeited to the decaying forces of Sin and Death, hereby providing something of an *inclusio* with 5.12–14.

I have gone into this detailed exegesis of Romans 7–8 for the following two reasons. (1) I have attempted to demonstrate that, not unlike the case of 2 Corinthians 2.17–4.6, though Paul's concerns are actually "inner-Jewish" concerns (e.g., the purpose and function of Torah), for rhetorical and argumentative purposes he also cast these inner-Jewish concerns in philosophical dress. Those who attempt to keep Torah according to "the oldness of the letter" (7.6) will be plagued by the *akrasia* to which the Medea paradox refers; however, those in the Messiah who keep the Torah according to "the newness of the Spirit" are like true philosophers who will eventually "share the same form as the image of [God] his son" (8.29). (2) I have also attempted to show that, though Paul's image christology certainly bears the influence of Middle Platonic intermediary doctrine, and though he puts this Middle Platonic association to rhetorical and argumentative effect in Romans 7–8, the argument through and through operates with the *fundamentally Jewish narrative worldview* which I briefly highlighted in an earlier section. (a) God had intended to steward the *kosmos* through Adam and Eve, though they forfeited this world sovereignty to the decaying forces of Sin and Death (esp. 5.12–14); (b) God, therefore, transferred this vocation of world sovereignty to Abraham's family *via* the covenant (esp. 4.13); (c) though Abraham's family, Israel—at least according to Paul's construal—failed in her vocation (esp. 2.17–24) and, having broken the Torah which was given precisely to enable that vocation (2.18), went into exile (esp. 7.23), God sent his own son to accomplish what the Torah—rendered ineffective because of human sinfulness—could not (8.3): namely, to bring God's people out of exile (8.3, 14–21) and thereby to produce renewed human beings in the form of the image of his son (8.29) through whom, as was his original intention (8.28–29), he could steward his (now broken) *kosmos* (8.19–21). This is Paul's great reworking of the Jewish narrative.

CONCLUSION

I now summarize my case concerning Paul's *imago Dei* theology in Romans 7–8. (1) At the rhetorical level, exactly as he had done in 2 Corinthians

2.17–4.6, Paul casts essentially inner-Jewish issues in philosophical dress, presenting life apart from the Messiah and under the Torah as a life plagued by *akrasia* (so the Medea paradox; 7.15, 19), while he presents life in the Messiah as the life of a true philosopher (so rejoicing "in the Torah of God in *my inner being*" [7.22] and ultimately "sharing the same form" as the *imago Dei* [8.29]). (2) Though Paul is certainly indebted to certain features of Middle Platonic intermediary doctrine, the philosophical contrasts in chapters 7–8 largely serve rhetorical purposes and the expression of his *imago Dei* theology reflects a large-scale adaptation of a characteristically *Jewish* narrative. (3) Finally, Romans 8.29, within 8.28–30, represents one of the densest statements of Paul's macro-theological vision: the preexistent son, as God's protological, paradigmatic, and cosmogonical image, serves as the teleological pattern to which believers will ultimately be conformed.

NOTES

1. On the structure of Romans, cf. esp. N. T. Wright, "The Letter to the Romans" in *NIB X* (Nashville: Abingdon, 2000), 393–770 (395–406); Dunn, *Romans*, lviii–lxiii; and Fitzmyer, *Romans*, 96–102, who provides a helpful list of the main views and their supporters.

2. So esp. Campbell, *Framing*, 37–121, who has also, over against attempts to argue that Rom. 16 did not originally belong with the rest of the letter, made a strong case for the integrity of the whole of chapters 1–16 (41–52). In a now classic work, Harry Y. Gamble, *Books and Readers in the Early Church: A History of Early Christian Texts* (New Haven: YUP, 1995), esp. 98, has argued that Rom. 16 was deliberately omitted in the early transmission of Romans so as to present a Pauline letter bereft of "local addresses . . . and other particulars . . . in favor of broad designations of . . . recipients."

3. So esp. Wright, "Romans," 397–406; Dunn, *Romans*, liv–ll, who, after discussing three major views of Paul's purpose in writing Romans and their proponents—(1) a "missionary purpose"; (2) an "apologetic purpose"; and (3) a "pastoral purpose"—emphasizes this point (lxiii); and, to a lesser extent, Schreiner, *Romans*, 10–23. E.g., C. E. B. Cranfield, *Romans*, 2 vols., ICC (Edinburgh: T & T Clark, 1975), 22–24; and Robert Jewett, *Romans*, Hermeneia (Minneapolis: Fortress, 2007), 80–91, insufficiently emphasize the point.

4. So, e.g., Longenecker, *Romans*, NIGTC (Grand Rapids: Eerdmans, 2016), 154–67; Wright, "Romans," 397–406, 423–26; Jewett, *Romans*, 135–47; Dunn, *Romans*, 37; Schreiner, *Romans*, 58–76; Douglas Moo, *Romans*, NICNT (Grand Rapids: Eerdmans, 1996), 63–79; Fitzmyer, *Romans*, 253–68; and Cranfield, *Romans*, 1.87.

5. See esp. Wright, "Romans," 397–403; Dunn, *Romans*, 40–42; Hays, *Letters of Paul*, 53–54; J. Ross Wagner, *Heralds of the Good News: Isaiah and Paul in Concert in the Letter to the Romans*, NovTSup 51 (Boston: Brill, 2002), 44 n. 5, 68–71;

and the comment in Schreiner, *Romans*, 68: "Many scholars today suggest that the emphasis in the term δικαιοσύνη θεοῦ is his covenantal faithfulness." Cf. also Richard B. Hays, "Justification" in *ABD* 3.1131–32.

6. On the wordplay on the δοκιμ- root, cf., e.g., Jewett, *Romans*, 181–82; Dunn, *Romans*, 66; Schreiner, *Romans*, 93; Fitzmyer, *Romans*, 288–89; and Cranfield, *Romans*, 128.

7. On this connection, cf. esp. Jewett, *Romans*, 733; Dunn, *Romans*, 714–15; and the discussion in van Kooten, *PA*, 340–92.

8. So, e.g., Jewett, *Romans*, 181–83; Schreiner, *Romans*, 97; Dunn, *Romans*, 66–67, who cites Philo, *All. Int.* 1.56 and 2.32 (66); Fitzmyer, *Romans*, 289; and Cranfield, *Romans*, 128–29, who cites *Diog. Laert.* 7.92, 107–09; Cicero, *Att.* 16.11.4; and Adrian, *Epict.* 2.17.31 (p. 129 n. 2).

9. On this, cf. esp. Jewett, *Romans*, 729–31; Dunn, *Romans*, 711–12; and Cranfield, *Romans*, 601–4.

10. Epictetus, *Disc.* 1.16.15–20 (W. A. Oldfather, LCL). See also Idem, *Disc.* 2.9.2.

11. On the entire construal of 2.17–24, I follow N. T. Wright, *Perspectives*, 489–509.

12. So also, e.g., Jewett, *Romans*, 209–10; Schreiner, *Romans*, 114–15; and Cranfield, *Romans*, 152–53.

13. Despite the helpful discussion, Jewett, *Romans*, 223–24, does not notice this point; nor does, e.g., Schreiner, *Romans*, 130; Cranfield, *Romans*, 165–66; or Fitzmyer, *Romans*, 641. Dunn, *Romans*, 715, however, rightly observes in relation to 12:2: "It must be judged highly probable that in this opening basic statement of the foundation for Christian ethics Paul intends to pose a contrast with the equivalent claim of his fellow Jewish religionists as characterized in 2:18."

14. On the most likely scriptural intertexts for this language, cf. esp. Dunn, *Romans*, 111–13; and Schreiner, *Romans*, 130–32.

15. *Contra* Longenecker, *Romans*, 292, 317, who reads the passage as Paul's "denunciation of Jews and Jewish legalism"; and Schreiner, *Romans*, 128–35.

16. Cf. Runar Thorsteinsson, *Paul's Interlocutor in Romans 2: Function and Identity in the Context of Ancient Epistolography*, ConBNT 40 (Stockholm: Almqvist & Wiksell, 2003); Rafael Rodríguez, *If You Call Yourself a Jew: Reappraising Paul's Letter to the Romans* (Eugene: Wipf & Stock, 2014); but also the collection of essays in Rafael Rodríguez and Matthew Thiessen, eds., *The So-Called Jew in Paul's Letter to the Romans* (Minneapolis: Fortress, 2016); esp. Magnus Zetterholm, "The Non-Jewish Interlocutor in Romans 2:17 and the Salvation of the Nations: Contextualizing Romans 1:18–32" in Rodríguez and Thiessen, eds., *The So-Called Jew*, 39–58; and Matthew V. Novenson, "The Self-Styled Jew of Romans 2 and the Actual Jews of Romans 9–11" in Rodríguez and Thiessen, eds., *The So-Called Jew*, 133–62. It is clear from Thorsteinsson's brief history of scholarship on Romans 2.17–24 (pp. 1–4), as well as from Rodríguez's (pp. 47–50), that their reading is very revisionist.

17. Cf. esp. the overtly apologetic remarks of Magnus Zetterholm, "The Non-Jewish Interlocutor," 39–43; but also all of those cited in the above note. For Zetterholm, this reading is at least partly substantiated by the fact that, after all, "Paul's

'religion' should be considered one of many manifestations of Second-Temple Judaism, that his main interest was the Gentile nations, not the Jewish people, and that he consequently addressed predominantly non-Jews." This is, however, a patent non sequitur, however much force it might have for those who subscribe to the "Paul-within-Judaism Perspective." For instance, no specialist in second-temple Judaism would want to say that—of, e.g., the Pharisees, the Sadducees, or the Qumran sectarians—because they represent "manifestations of Second-Temple Judaism" and their primary "audiences" were composed of other Jews, these groups simply cannot have polemicized against each other and/or have been interested in saying anything about people outside of their immediate audience (non-Jews).

18. So Rodríguez, *If You Call Yourself a Jew*, 48–61; Zetterholm, "The Non-Jewish Interlocutor," 39–53 (53): "Assuming that Thorsteinsson's suggestion is correct . . ."

19. Thorsteinsson, *Paul's Interlocutor*, 196–203.

20. Novenson, "The Self-Styled Jew," 141.

21. Stanley K. Stowers, *A Rereading of Romans: Justice, Jews and Gentiles* (New Haven/London: YUP, 1994), 180, is right to regard the plural προῃτιασάμεθα as an instance of what he calls "a dialogical 'we,' that is, 'I, Paul, and you, the interlocutor, in our discussion have already concluded' . . ." On the meaning of προαιτιάομαι, cf. *BAGD*, 865 (italics mine): "to reach a charge of guilt *prior to an implied time*, accuse *beforehand*."

22. Novenson, "The Self-Styled Jew," 152; and also Thorsteinsson, *Paul's Interlocutor*, 235–36.

23. Ibidem.

24. So, e.g., Jewett, *Romans*, 258; Dunn, *Romans*, 148; Schreiner, *Romans*, 164; and Cranfield, *Romans*, 191. Novenson, "The Self-Styled Jew," 152, notes that this is the "conventional reading."

25. The identification of those described cryptically in 2.26–29 is, of course, contested. The clear allusion to the new covenant passage of Deuteronomy 30 (2.29: "circumcision of the heart, by the Spirit"; cp. Deut. 30.6), however, suggests that these people are Christians: so, e.g., Wright, "Romans," 448–50; Dunn, *Romans*, 122–28; Cranfield, *Romans*, 172–76. On the passage as a whole, cf. esp. John M. G. Barclay, *Pauline Churches and Diaspora Jews* (Grand Rapids: Eerdmans, 2011), 61–79.

26. Cf. esp. Barclay, *Pauline Churches*, 68–70: "(p. 68) [In Romans 2] Paul is out to destabilise a Jewish sense of confidence that Jews were in a different category from Gentiles. . . . In a series of rhetorical moves, Paul pulls this rug from under the feet of his Jewish dialogue partner stage by stage. . . . (p. 70) It is because Paul has finally [by 2.29] removed *all* the supports on which his Jewish interlocutor can stand that the questions of 3.1 arise."

27. For the adverb πρῶτος with the meaning "foremost" or "most importantly" rather than "the first of a *sequence*," cf. *BAGD*, 893, (2), which actually (and wrongly) adopts meaning (1) in this regard. *Contra*, e.g., Dunn, *Romans*, 130; Fitzmyer, *Romans*, 326; Cranfield, *Romans*, 178, all of whom claim that Paul simply lost his train of thought. Cf., rather, Jewett, *Romans*, 243.

28. *Contra*, e.g., the scholars in the above note.

29. Cf. esp. Wright, *Perspectives*, 489–509 (esp. 491). However, cf. also Stowers, *Rereading*, 166–67; and Jewett, Romans, 243.
30. Dunn, *Romans*, 131.
31. Schreiner, *Romans*, 149.
32. Fitzmyer, *Romans*, 326; and similarly Cranfield, *Romans*, 179.
33. *Contra*, e.g., Jewett, *Romans*, 244–45; Schreiner, *Romans*, 150–1; Dunn, *Romans*, 132; and Fitzmyer, *Romans*, 179–81. Moo, *Romans*, 185, is representative when he argues that "God's faithfulness" here refers simply to "God's continuing care for and commitment to his people."
34. See esp. Wright, "Romans," 469–70; Idem, *Perspectives*, 503–04; and Idem, *PFG*, 836–51. We do not have space to consider the debates surrounding the proper reading of *pistis Christou*. Cf. my "ΠΙΣΤΙΣ ΧΡΙΣΤΟΥ: The Current State of Play and the Key Arguments" *CBR* 14.2 (2016): 244–55. *Contra* Barclay's claim that "Israel's ἀπιστία (Rom 3:3) is never brought in contrast with Jesus's πίστις" (*Paul and the Gift* [Grand Rapids: Eerdmans, 2015], 477, n. 68). What degree of syntactical proximity is required for a "contrast"? On the likelihood that διὰ πίστεως Ἰησοῦ Χριστοῦ should especially be taken as an instance of the subjective genitive here, cf. Kugler, "ΠΙΣΤΙΣ ΧΡΙΣΤΟΥ," 249–51.
35. *Contra*, e.g., Longenecker, *Romans*, 416; and Fitzmyer, *Romans*, 347, the former commending the latter's statement: "A reference to Adam is here eisexegetical [*sic*; Fitzmyer wrote 'eisegetical']"; and with, e.g., Dunn, *Romans*, 167–68; Schreiner, *Romans*, 187, who states, "Most [scholars] understand it [3.23] in terms of the glory Adam lost when he fell into sin"; and Cranfield, *Romans*, 204, the latter two of whom rightly note Greek LAE 21.6; and Gen. Rab. 12.5.
36. Surprisingly, the strong parallel between 3.24 and 5.17 is not noted by, e.g., Jewett, *Romans*, 283–85; Schreiner, *Romans*, 286; Dunn, *Romans*, 281–82; Fitzmyer, *Romans*, 420; Cranfield, *Romans*, 284–86.
37. So, e.g., Jewett, *Romans*, 305, who rightly argues that Romans 4 offers "a distinctively Pauline answer to the questions of the nature of Abraham's righteousness and the identity of his true descendants"; and Dunn, *Romans*, 196–97.
38. This intratextual connection with 3.23–24 and, indeed, with 5.17, is not noted by, e.g., Jewett, *Romans*, 324–26; Schreiner, *Romans*, 227–29; Dunn, *Romans*, 213; Fitzmyer, *Romans*, 384; Cranfield, *Romans*, 238–40.
39. On the promise involving the whole *kosmos* and not simply the promised land in 4.13, cf., e.g., Wright, "Romans," 495–96; Cranfield, *Romans*, 239–40; and Fitzmyer, *Romans*, 384. Particularly illuminating is Sir. 44.21, which states that God would give Abraham "an inheritance from sea to sea and from the Euphrates to the ends of the earth." This text, as Wright, "Romans," 495, suggests, is a reading of the Abrahamic promise *through* the messianic hope of Psalm 72.8. *Contra* Longenecker, *Romans*, 510, who vaguely states that Paul understood the promise of 4.13 to involve "(1) the new status and life credited to him by God *and* (2) the widespread and significant presence of Abraham and his progeny in the then-known world" (italics original).
40. So also, e.g., Wright, "Romans," 560–61; Dunn, *Romans*, 366–67; and Cranfield, *Romans*, 339–40.

41. So, e.g., Dunn, *Romans*, 376: "With v 7 the crucial issue is posed: has Paul's treatment of the law . . . consigned the law to sin, as a power to be redeemed from, and so without positive reference for the believer?"

42. Cf. also the discussion in Jewett, *Romans*, 441–45.

43. Fitzmyer, *Romans*, 463–64, notes the following supporters: "So Bruce, Deissmann, Dodd, Gundry, Jeremias, Kühl, Packer, Weinel, Zahn, and seemingly Moo," to which I would add Jewett, *Romans*, 441–45 (443), who oddly cites Troels Engberg-Pedersen's even odder statement to the affect that this reading has nearly attained a consensus status: so Troels Engberg-Pedersen, "The Reception of Graeco-Roman Culture in the New Testament: The Case of Romans 7:7–25" in M. Müller and H. Tronier, eds., *The New Testament as Reception*, JSNTSup 230, CIS 11 (Sheffield: SAP, 2002), 32–57 (37); and Jan Lambrecht, *The Wretched "I" and Its Liberation: Paul in Romans 7 and 8*, LTPM 14 (Grand Rapids: Eerdmans, 1992). The famous essay of Krister Stendahl, "The Apostle Paul and the Introspective Conscience of the West" *HTR* 56.3 (1963): 199–215, in which the latter argued that this construal of Paul's pre-Christian "conscience" did not square with texts like Philippians 3.5–6, successfully refuted this and similar readings.

44. Fitzmyer, *Romans*, 464, notes the following supporters: "So Bardenhewer, Billerbeck, Bläser, Comely, Davies, Franzmann, and Knox . . ."

45. Fitzmyer, *Romans*, 464, notes the following supporters: "So Methodius of Olympia, Theodore of Mopsuestia, Cajetan, Dibelius, Feuillet, Leenhardt, Lietzmann, Lyonnet, Michel, and Pesch."

46. Fitzmyer, *Romans*, 464, notes the following supporters: "So Augustine, Thomas Aquinas, Luther, Calvin, Althaus, Barth, Giese, Nygren, to an extent Cranfield, Packer, and seemingly Dunn," to which I would add Longenecker, *Romans*, 651–60; Schnelle, *Paul*, 335; Reinhard Weber, "Die Geschichte des Gesetzes und des Ich in Römer 7,7–8,4" *NZST* 29 (1987): 147–79 (157); and Otfried Hofius, *Paulusstudien* II, WUNT 1.143 (Tübingen: Mohr Siebeck, 2002), 110–21.

47. Fitzmyer, *Romans*, 464–65, notes the following supporters: "So many of the Greek Fathers, especially Diodore of Tarsus (Staab, *Pauluskatenen*, 47), John Chrysostom (In *Ep. ad Romanos*, Hom. 12.5 [PG 60.501]), and Cyril of Alexandria (*In Ep. ad Romanos* 7.7 [PG 74.801]); also Ambrosiaster, *In Ep. ad Romanos* 7.7: '*sub sua quasi persona generalem agit causam*' (under his own quasi-person he treats of the general issue [CSEL 81.223]); among modern commentators Stauffer (*TDNT* 2.358–59), Schrenk (*TDNT* 2.551), Achtemeier, Benoit ('The Law'), Black, Bornkamm ('Law and Death,' 93–94), Bover, Huby (*Romains*, 239), Käsemann (*Commentary*, 192), Kümmel, and seemingly Schlier (*Römerbrief*, 232)," to which I would add Jason Maston, *Divine and Human Agency in Second Temple Judaism and Paul*, WUNT 2.297 (Tübingen: Mohr Siebeck, 2010). This is also the position that Fitzmyer, *Romans*, 465, takes.

48. So Wright, "Romans," 549–57; and, to a lesser extent, Moo, *Romans*, 409–10, 423–31; Schreiner, *Romans*, 343–44, 356–71; and Ulrich Wilckens, *Der Brief an die Römer*, 3 vols., EKK 6 (Neukirchener-Vluyn: Neukirchener Verlag, 1978–1982), 2.75.

49. Stowers, *A Rereading of Romans*. I also note the study of Emma Wasserman, *The Death of the Soul in Romans 7*, WUNT 2.256 (Tübingen: Mohr Siebeck, 2008),

in which she argues the following case: "I contend that Rom 7:7–25 depicts the plight of reason or mind imprisoned by the passions and appetites. In fact, the monologue can be read more coherently by understanding the speaker as reason or mind and sin as a personified representation of the passions" (8). But this does not get us very far in explaining the sense this would make in the argument *at this point in the letter*. Indeed, Wasserman, *Romans 7*, 114, concedes this (major) weakness: "Yet, this does not explain why Paul develops this argument in the literary and argumentative context of Romans."

50. Stowers, *Rereading*, 258.

51. Ibid. 259. This was, of course, the major burden of Stendahl, "Introspective Conscience."

52. Ibid. 260–64.

53. Ibid. 264.

54. Ibid. citing Kümmel, *Römer und das Bild*, 132.

55. Ibid. 266–69.

56. Ibid. 277.

57. Ibid.

58. Ibid. 278.

59. So, e.g., the comments of the following commentators on Romans 1.23: Jewett, *Romans*, 160–62; Schreiner, *Romans*, 87–89; Dunn, *Romans*, 61–62; Fitzmyer, *Romans*, 283–84; Cranfield, *Romans*, 119–20, none of whom base a reconstruction of the Roman Christians upon this text.

60. I note at this point that, because the (at least) six different approaches radically effect the interpretation of each individual verse, it goes without saying that throughout I de facto disagree with the interpretation of every single verse—to one degree or another—of those who take the positions of 1–5.

61. *Contra*, e.g., Fitzmyer, *Romans*, 463, "The description in the present tense in vv 14–25 is undoubtedly so composed for the sake of vividness; past events are vividly recalled." For a recent and nuanced statement of the way in which Greek indicative verbs grammaticalize not only "aspect" and "space" but *also* "time," cf. Timothy Brookins, "A Tense Discussion: Rethinking the Grammaticalization of Time in Greek Indicative Verbs" *JBL* 137.1 (2018): 147–68.

62. On εὑρίσκω ἄρα τὸν νόμον as a "conclusion formula," cf., e.g., Wright, *Climax*, 198; Idem, *PFG*, 1017–18; Schreiner, *Romans*, 371; and *BAGD*, 412.

63. *Contra*, e.g., Schreiner, *Romans*, 358; Dunn, *Romans*, 377; Fitzmyer, *Romans*, 463; J. C. Beker, *Paul the Apostle: The Triumph of God in Life and Thought* (Philadelphia: Fortress, 1980), 105; Kümmel, *Römer*, 7; and Stendahl, "Introspective Conscience," 92–3.

64. Though I do not agree with Jewett's construal (*Romans*, 440), therefore, he is right to contend that "Paul's concern is not to develop an abstract doctrine of the law but rather to clarify its bearing on the situation of the Roman church."

65. So Wright, "Romans," 563; and *contra*, e.g., Jewett, *Romans*, 450; Schreiner, *Romans*, 364–65; and Fitzmyer, *Romans*, 467, all of whom take the verse as a reference to Paul's prepubescent life; and *contra* Dunn, *Romans*, 381; and Cranfield, *Romans*, 351, both of whom take it principally as a reference to Adam before his fall. It is difficult to see what sense it would make, if Paul were referring either to

prepubescent life and/or to Adam's fall, to use the word ἀναζάω, which means "to come to life *again*" (so *BAGD*, 62). However, this would make excellent sense on a reading in which the original sin of Adam and its affects—ineffectual from the election of Abraham until the time of Moses, principally because "Sin is not reckoned where there is no Torah" (so esp. 5.13b)—found a fresh base of operations in the gift of Torah to Israel.

66. On ἀφορμή, *BAGD*, 158, provides "a base or circumstance from which other action becomes possible, such as the starting-point or base of operations for an expedition."

67. So, e.g., Wright, "Romans," 563–64; Dunn, *Romans*, 384–85; Cranfield, *Romans*, 352–53; and Fitzmyer, *Romans*, 468.

68. Moo, *Romans*, 439–40. I note the important essay, Nicholas Elder, "'Wretch I Am!' Eve's Tragic Speech-in-Character in Romans 7:7–25" *JBL* 137.3 (2018): 743–63, which appeared too late for me to engage with it.

69. So esp. Wright, "Romans," 563–64.

70. Neither e.g. Wright, "Romans," 563–64; nor Moo, *Romans*, 439–40, considers this possibility.

71. So, e.g., Jewett, *Romans*, 452, with other scholars cited in n. 116; Dunn, *Romans*, 384–5; Fitzmyer, *Romans*, 468; and Cranfield, *Romans*, 352–53.

72. See also Wright, "Romans," 566; and Moo, *Romans*, 453–54.

73. So Gerd Theissen, *Psychological Aspects of Pauline Theology*, trans. J. P. Galvin (Philadelphia: Fortress, 1987 [1983]), 211–21. Cf. also, in their different ways, Stowers, *Rereading*, 260–64, 279–81; A. van den Beld, "Romans 7:14–25 and the Problem of *Akrasia*" *RS* 21.4 (1985): 495–515; Thomas H. Tobin, *Paul's Rhetoric in Its Contexts: The Argument of Romans* (Peabody: Hendrickson, 2004), 332–36, 242; Engberg-Pedersen, "Reception," 47, 54–56; Hermann Lichtenberger, *Das Ich Adams und das Ich der Menschheit: Studien zum Menschenbild in Römer 7*, WUNT 164 (Tübingen: Mohr Siebeck, 2004), 176–86.

74. Cf. Euripides, *Hippolytus* 373–81; Plato, *Protagoras* 352D; Ovid, *Metamorphoses* 7.17–21; Seneca, *Medea* 938–44; and Galen, *On the Doctrines of Hippocrates and Plato* 4.2.27, 4.6.20–22; with the discussion in Theissen, *Psychological Aspects*, 211–21.

75. *Disc.* 2.26.1–2, 4–5 (Oldfather, LCL). Cf. also *Disc.* 1.28.6–8.

76. So, e.g., Jewett, *Romans*, 463; R. V. Huggins, "Alleged Classical Parallels to Paul's 'What I Want to Do I Do Not Do, but What I Hate, That I do' (Rom 7:15)" *WTJ* 54 (1992): 158–61; Tobin, *Paul's Rhetoric*, 235; and esp. Maston, *Divine and Human Agency*, 148–52 (149): "Paul's view does not square with either of the standard positions." Stowers, *Reading Romans*, 279; and Wasserman, *Romans 7*, argue that Paul essentially adopts a Platonic position; while, e.g., Engberg-Pedersen, *Paul and the Stoics*, 239–46; Idem, "Reception," 55–6, places him within the Stoic tradition.

77. Maston, *Divine and Human Agency*, 149.

78. So, e.g., Maston, *Divine and Human Agency*, 148–52; Jewett, *Romans*, 464; and Theissen, *Psychological Aspects*, 216.

79. On εὑρίσκω ἄρα τὸν νόμον as a "conclusion formula," cf., e.g., Wright, *Climax*, 198; Idem, *PFG*, 1017–18; Schreiner, *Romans*, 371; and *BAGD*, 412.

80. I take the participle αἰχμαλωτίζοντά as an ingressive present.

81. This possibility is not noticed by, e.g., Jewett, *Romans*, 469–70; Schreiner, *Romans*, 377–94; Dunn, *Romans*, 393–6; Fitzmyer, *Romans*, 467; Cranfield, *Romans*, 362–5.

82. *Contra*, e.g., Jewett, *Romans*, 470–01, who takes the verb as a general allusion to "being taken captive after a defeat in war" (470); Dunn, *Romans*, 395–96; and Cranfield, *Romans*, 364–5.

83. On the lexeme αἰχμαλωτίζω and its cognates in LXX as a term used to refer to the Babylonian exile, see esp. Robert J. V. Hiebert, "Exile and Restoration Terminology in the Septuagint and the New Testament" in Scott, ed., *Exile*, 93–117. It was not until I had already constructed this argument independently that I noticed the very important, and very congenial, article of John K. Goodrich, "Sold under Sin: Echoes of Exile in Romans 7.14–25" *NTS* 59.4 (2013): 476–95, who argues, inter alia, the following: (1) in 7.14, πεπραμένος ὑπὸ τὴν ἁμαρτίαν is an allusion to LXX Isa. 50.1; and that (2) 7.7–13 concerns Israel's "*early* history" and 7.14–25 concerns "her *later* history" and not least the exile itself (447, italics original).

84. It is not *entirely* correct, therefore, simply to take νόμος throughout 7.22–25 as a reference to the Mosaic law, as do, e.g., Jewett, *Romans*, 469–73; Schreiner, *Romans*, 375–77; Wilckens, *Römer*, 89–92; Dunn, *Romans*, 392–95; Cranfield, *Romans*, 361–70; P. von der Osten-Sacken, *Römer 8 als Beispiel paulinischer Soteriologie*, FRLANT 112 (Göttingen: Vandenhoeck & Ruprecht, 1975), 209–12; Eduard Lohse, *Neues Testament und christliche Existenz* (Tübingen: Mohr Siebeck, 1973), 279–87 (285–6). Nor is it correct, however, to take νόμος throughout 7.22–25 as a reference to a general "principle," as do, e.g., Moo, *Romans*, 487–88, 490–92; Heikki Räisänen, *Jesus, Paul, and Torah: Collected Essays*, trans. by D. E. Orton, JSNTSup 43 (Sheffield: JSOT Press, 1992), 48–94; Cranfield, *Romans*, 361–62; Ernst Käsemann, *Commentary on Romans*, trans. and ed. by G. W. Bromiley (Grand Rapids: Eerdmans, 1980), 205; A. van Dülmen, *Die Theologie des Gesetzes bei Paulus*, Stuttgarter biblische Monographien 5 (Stuttgart: Katholisches Bibelwerk, 1968), 115–16. Rather, from 7.7 to 7.21, νόμος refers to the Mosaic legislation—in Paul's language, the Torah according to "the oldness of the letter" (7.6). But, in 7.22–25, while "another νομός" and "the νομός of Sin" indeed refer to the Mosaic legislation with its prescriptions for circumcision, sabbath, and the food laws, the "Torah of God" and "the Torah of my mind" refer to the new covenant *as Paul controversially construes it.*

85. On Romans 14, I here follow particularly the careful treatment of Barclay, *Pauline Churches*, 37–60.

86. It is unnecessary, therefore, to postulate that 7.25a is an interpolation which actually belongs after 7.25b and immediately before 8.1: *contra* Jewett, *Romans*, 456–8, and those listed in n. 11. As I argued above, those who take 7.7–25 as generally characteristic of the Christian life struggle mightily with this explosion of praise.

87. So van Kooten, *PA*, 358–70; and W. Burkert, "Towards Plato and Paul: The 'Inner' Human Being" in Adela Y. Collins, ed., *Ancient and Modern Perspectives on the Bible and Culture: Essays in Honor of Hans Dieter Betz* (Atlanta: Scholars Press, 1998), 59–82; and *contra* esp. C. Markschies, "Die platonische Metapher vom 'inneren Menschen': Eine Brücke zwischen antiker Philosophie und altchristlicher

Theologie" *ZK* 105 (1994): 1–17. However, cf. the nuanced studies of Hans Dieter Betz, "The Concept of the 'Inner Human Being' (ὁ ἔσω ἄνθρωπος) in the Anthropology of Paul" *NTS* 46.3 (2000): 315–41; and Theo K. Heckel *Der innere Mensch: Die Paulinische Verarbeitung eines Platonischen Motivs*, WUNT 2.53 (Tübingen: Mohr Siebeck, 1993). Cf. esp. Plato's *Protagoras*, 589A–B.

88. Jewett, *Romans*, 470.

89. There has been, it seems to me, unnecessary confusion and debate as to why and how Paul could refer to the νομός as an agent of liberation here: cf. esp. Jewett, *Romans*, 481–82, and nn. 42–59. Fitzmyer, *Romans*, 482–83, is correct to note this formulation's largely *rhetorical* purpose; Dunn, *Romans*, 416–18, essentially argues rightly that "the Torah of the Spirit of Life" is *Paul's* new-covenant construal of Torah. E.g., Schreiner, *Romans*, 400 and those in n. 3, are not correct, therefore, simply to take νομός here as a reference to the Mosaic law which is no longer under "the powers of sin and death" but "in the realm. . .of the Holy Spirit." E.g., Cranfield, *Romans*, 373–78 and those in 375 n. 2, are also wrong to take νομός here as a reference to the Holy Spirit. Rather, the point is rhetorical: "Not only [, says Paul,] will the Torah 'according to the oldness of the letter' [Rom. 7.6] only take you into exile, but the Torah as *we uphold it* [Rom. 3.31] will liberate you from exile."

90. Many have struggled both to see the relationship between chapters 7 and 8 and to explain how Romans 7.7–8.13 fits within the overall argument of the letter. It seems to me that my argument goes some way toward an answer to both of these questions. See, e.g., Maston, *Divine and Human Agency*, 127: "Romans 7.7–8.13 is typically recognised as two parts of an argument, although there is little agreement over the precise connection."

91. Hurtado, *LJC*, 118–26 (119), notes that this is among the passages regularly taken as a reference to Jesus's preexistence. On this as an instance of wisdom christology, see the classic study of Eduard Schweizer, "Zum religionsgeschichtlichen Hintergrund der 'Sendungsformel' Gal. 4.4f., Röm. 8.3f., John 3.16f., 1 John 4.9" *ZNW* 57 (1966): 199–210. Cf. also Wright, *PFG*, 659–61; Kramer, *Christ*, 111–15; Lichtenberger, *Ich Adams*, 192–3; Leander E. Keck, "The Law and 'The Law of Sin and Death' (Rom 8:1–4): Reflections on the Spirit and Ethics in Paul" in Crenshaw and Sandmel, eds., *The Divine Helmsman: Studies on God's Control of Human Events, Presented to Lou H. Silberman* (New York: Ktav, 1980), 43–4. Dunn, *Romans*, 420, notes that this reading is virtually "unanimous."

92. Dunn, *Christology*, 44–46, 111–12; and Idem, *Paul*, 277–9. Since Dunn gives such a prominent place to wisdom traditions in Paul's christology more generally, it is somewhat ironic that he rejects it precisely where most scholars most clearly detect it (so Gal. 4.4; and Rom. 8.3).

93. Dunn, *Christology*, 179–83 (181). Cf. also Idem, *Paul*, 252–55; and Idem, *Did the First Christian Worship Jesus*, 108–09.

94. For instance, Dunn, *Christology*, 38–39; Idem, *Paul*, 278, draws particular attention to the "sending" of "human messengers" (esp. prophets) in LXX and suggests that it was Jesus's own practice of referring to himself as "sent" by God which serves as the principal background of the *Sendungsformeln* (so, e.g., "(Mark 9.37 pars.; 12.6 pars.; Matt. 15.24; Luke 4.18; 10.16) . . . [and in] particular the parable of the dishonest tenants" [*Christology*, 40])).

95. So, e.g., the relevant sections of Wright, "Romans"; Jewett, *Romans*, 526–30; and Dunn, *Romans*, 466–67.

96. So also, to an extent, e.g., Jewett, *Romans*, 529; and Cranfield, *Romans*, 432.

97. Dunn, *Romans*, 483–84, italics original.

98. *Contra* Dunn, *Romans*, 484–85; and Schreiner, *Romans*, 453–54.

99. Cf. esp. Wright, "Romans," 590–04; Sylvia Keesmaat, *Paul and His Story: (Re)Interpreting the Exodus Tradition*, JSNTSup 181 (Sheffield: Sheffield Academic Press, 1999), esp. 54–96; James Scott, *Adoption as Sons of God*, WUNT 2.48 (Tübingen: Mohr Siebeck, 1992), 244–66; and the discussion in Daniel L. Smith, "The Uses of 'New Exodus' in New Testament Scholarship: Preparing a Way Through the Wilderness" *CBR* 14 (2016): 207–43 (esp. 217–19).

100. So, e.g., Jewett, *Romans*, 497; Schreiner, *Romans*, 423; and Dunn, *Romans*, 451.

101. See esp. Hays, *Letters of Paul*, 63: "The letter to the Romans is salted with numerous quotations of and allusions to Isaiah 40–55"; and J. Ross Wagner, *Heralds of the Good News*, who, however, states that Paul's extensive use of the rest of Isaiah "should caution us against asserting that Paul shows a special interest in Isaiah 40–55 in distinction from the rest of the book" (344). It is surprising how few commentators draw specific attention to this text.

102. With respect to the final, extended phrase in 8.21, εἰς τὴν ἐλευθερίαν τῆς δόξης τῶν τέκνων τοῦ θεοῦ, I take τῆς δόξης adjectivally to modify τῶν τέκνων τοῦ θεοῦ (the "glorious children of God") and the whole genitive expression τῆς δόξης τῶν τέκνων τοῦ θεοῦ to be a subjective genitive in which the "freedom" is brought about precisely by the "glorious children of God." *Contra* Jewett, *Romans*, 515, who argues that, though creation's liberation "clearly correlates with the 'revelation of the sons of God' . . . the inference is rarely drawn concerning the means by which God intends to restore the nature world"; and Schreiner, *Romans*, 437, who loosely states, "The return of nature to its purpose *will coincide* with the freedom of the children of God" (italics mine); and much closer to, e.g., Cranfield, *Romans*, 415–16.

103. So also, e.g., B. Byrne, *Romans*, SP (Collegeville: Glazier, Liturgical Press, 1996), 258, 260–61; and G. W. H. Lampe, "The New Testament Doctrine of *Ktisis*" *SJT* 17 (1964): 449–62 (458).

104. So, e.g., Jewett, *Romans*, 513; Schreiner, *Romans*, 436: "God subjected the created world to frustration on account of the sin of Adam. The words ἐφ' ἐλπίδι (*eph' helpidi*, in hope) are somewhat awkward to interpret, and it is difficult to identify what they modify. . . . Paul has overloaded the sentence, so it is difficult to follow the train of thought"; Dunn, *Romans*, 470: "The phrasing is awkward and suggests a dictation where Paul's thought became slightly tangled but where he decided to press on"; Cranfield, *Romans*, 413–14. Fitzmyer, *Romans*, 507–09, notes well the difficulties.

Chapter 9

Colossians 1.15–20; 3.10

EXTENDED INTRODUCTION

Having already indicated that I regard Colossians as an authentically Pauline composition, and because below I will argue that Paul himself likely crafted the poetical piece of 1.15–20 precisely in order to buttress the larger argument of the letter, we begin with the contested question of Paul's opponents. There have been myriad proposals and, in the words of Andrew Lincoln, the discussion shows "no signs of abating."[1] Was Paul combating some kind of early Gnosticism,[2] the influence of the mystery cults,[3] Cynics,[4] a local Jewish influence,[5] or perhaps some combination of these?[6] Richard DeMaris, on the other hand, rightly noting the resonances of Middle Platonic thought in 1.15–20, argues that Paul might have been combating what he perceived to be the negative influences of certain philosophical traditions.[7]

In this regard, there are three principal pieces of data in the letter itself which any account of the "Colossian heresy" must explain:[8] (1) the meaning of "θρησκεία τῶν ἀγγέλων, ἃ ἑόρακεν ἐμβατεύων" in 2.18; (2) the meaning of "ὁ συλαγωγῶν διὰ τῆς φιλοσοφίας καὶ κενῆς ἀπάτης" in 2.8; and (3) the fact that in 2.8–23 the issues are *Jewish* issues, and not least the ones which introduce the contested passage which features "θρησκεία τῶν ἀγγέλων, ἃ ἑόρακεν ἐμβατεύων" (e.g., 2.11: circumcision; 2.16: food laws, festal days, new moons, and sabbaths).

We will consider first (1) the meaning of θρησκεία τῶν ἀγγέλων, ἃ ἑόρακεν ἐμβατεύων. Despite Fred O. Francis's very influential analysis, Clinton Arnold insists that the genitive phrase θρησκεία τῶν ἀγγέλων should be construed objectively rather than subjectively, a construal which would make the angels the *objects* rather than the *subjects* of worship.[9] Having demonstrated generally that genitive constructions involving θρησκεία can be either objective or subjective,[10] he takes the following as decisive evidence in favor of the objective-genitive construal: when θρησκεία occurs in Jewish sources within genitive constructions *involving a "divine being,"* the genitive is objective in every single case.[11] This is, however, largely beside the point. After all, as I argued above, Arnold has not successfully demonstrated that Jews regarded angels as "divine beings." We are left, then, with three simple observations: (a) we do not have evidence that Jews worshipped angels and/or regarded them as divine; (b) θρησκεία within a genitive construction can be either objective or subjective; and (c) we do not have evidence of Jews referring, with an objective-genitive construction, to the θρησκεία of beings other than the one God. This evidence, therefore, points in the opposite direction, the direction of the subjective-genitive reading. Paul refers, in this case, to the angelic liturgy, a point to which I will return below.[12]

But before turning to consider the force of ἃ ἑόρακεν ἐμβατεύων, I note one further possibility. It is possible, not least in view of the way in which I will construe 2.8 and 2.18, that Paul here polemically (mis)characterizes a local Jewish interest in the angelic liturgy and, therefore, *does* intend θρησκείᾳ τῶν ἀγγέλων to be understood as a reference to the idolatrous (from the Jewish and Jewish-Christian perspective) human worship of the angels (so objectively).[13] However, if this were the case, it would still coordinate well with a reconstruction in which Paul's opponents were local Jews boasting in their access to the heavenly liturgy and it would *not* be direct evidence that these same Jews actually worshipped angels.

We now turn to consider the force of ἃ ἑόρακεν ἐμβατεύων. Arnold, who has proposed that the "Colossian heresy" consisted of a syncretistic teaching in which elements of Jewish mysticism were combined with elements of the pagan mysteries, takes ἃ ἑόρακεν ἐμβατεύων as a reference to the "second stage" of "initiation" in which initiates could expect an ecstatic visionary experience.[14] On this basis, Arnold infers that certain mystery initiates had been tempting and troubling the Colossian Christians with their tales of ecstatic visionary experiences.[15] However, even if Arnold is correct to take ἐμβατεύω as a technical term *when it is explicitly used in connection with the pagan mysteries*, he has not demonstrated that it is a technical term when it is *not* explicitly used in this connection. In this regard, Arnold (and Ramsay and Dibelius before him) has clearly demonstrated from the inscriptional evidence that ἐμβατεύω occurs in connection with pagan mystery initiation. What he has *not* demonstrated, however, is that ἐμβατεύω *by itself* is a technical term which necessarily evokes the rite of mystery initiation.[16] Absent such evidence, several commentators are right to construe ἃ ἑόρακεν ἐμβατεύων simply to mean something like "which things he had seen upon entering."[17]

Indeed, Dunn's construal of ἃ ἑόρακεν ἐμβατεύων makes much more sense within the overall *Jewish* concerns of 2.8–23 and in relation to our construal of θρησκείᾳ τῶν ἀγγέλων:

In fact, however, it is dubious whether ἐμβατεύω was, strictly speaking, a technical term.... Its basic meaning is simply "enter."... So in the two Old Testament (LXX) occurrences (Josh. 19:49, 51), where the thought is of entering into possession of the promised land.... Moreover, when we set the usage here against the background already sketched out above, we cannot but be aware that the revelations described usually involved a visionary or mystical ascent to (entry into) or through the heavens (e.g., *1 Enoch* 14:8–13; *2 Enoch* 3; *3 Baruch* 2:2; 3:1–2; *Testament of Levi* 2:5–7; Rev. 4:1–2).... Most interesting of all are the clear indications in the *Songs of the Sabbath Sacrifice* that heaven was seen as a temple where the angelic worship took place and the prominence given to doorways of the temple ... and to the theme of entering in 4Q405 14–15i:3–4 ... and 4Q405 23i:8–10.... [T]here was [, therefore,] a prominent strand among the Colossian Jews who thought of heaven either (or both) as a promised land into which they should aspire even now to enter, or particularly as the temple of God into which they could now enter by means of appropriate spiritual disciplines in order to share the worship of the angels in heaven.[18]

(2) Coming to our second crucial piece of data, what sense should we make of Paul's warning in 2.8: "See that no one takes you captive through an empty and deceitful philosophy ... ! (Βλέπετε μή τις ὑμᾶς ἔσται ὁ συλαγωγῶν διὰ τῆς φιλοσοφίας καὶ κενῆς ἀπάτης ...)"?[19] According to a search in the *Thesaurus Linguae Graecae*, this text is our first attestation to the word συλαγωγέω, a verb which occurs nowhere else in the LXX or in the New Testament. What, then, might explain Paul's use of such a rare verb? N. T. Wright's suggestion is particularly compelling: the word is a deliberate and "contemptuous pun with the word *synagogue*": ΣΥΝΑΓΩΓ-/ΣΥΛΑΓΩΓ-.[20] In this case, Paul would be warning the Colossians against what he sees as the dangerous influence of the local synagogue; or, because we cannot be sure that there even was a synagogue in the immediate environs of Colossae, he would be warning the Colossians against what he sees as a dangerous local Jewish influence, an influence which, if this reading is on target, he depicts as a "deceitful *philosophy*."

Why, however, if Paul is essentially referring to a local *Jewish* influence, does he refer to it as a "philosophy"? The appeal to the same convention in several Jewish texts from the diaspora does not resolve the issue (e.g., 4 Macc. 5.22; 7.9; Josephus, *Ant.* 18.9–23 [4x]; Idem, *Apion* 1.54; 2.47; Philo, *Creation* 8 [and *passim*]). After all, the authors of 4 Maccabees, Josephus, and Philo were attempting to present the Jewish way of life as a proper—and, indeed, as the *best* kind of—philosophy. But this would hardly account for Paul's usage in Colossians 2.8.[21] Or, perhaps, with a few scholars, should we take this as an indication that Paul's polemic has at least partly in view what he sees as the negative influences of certain philosophical traditions? I think this is unlikely. Rather, as in the cases of 2 Corinthians 2.17–4.6 and Romans 7–8, I suggest, Paul is casting essentially *Jewish* issues in philosophical dress, hoping hereby to achieve a rhetorical and argumentative effect. The local Jews who boast in traditional Torah observance (2.11, 16, 20–23) and not least in their access to the heavenly liturgy are adherents of "an empty and deceitful philosophy," while Paul, his associates, and the Colossian Christians are true philosophers who are "being renewed in knowledge according to the image of [God] the creator" (3.10; who, in Colossians 1.15–20, is Jesus himself).

(3) The third crucial piece of data which any account of the *Sitz im Leben* of Colossians must explain is the fact that the concerns of 2.8–23 appear to be Jewish concerns. In this regard, I have already made the case that, following Wright in particular, συλαγωγέω is a deliberate pun on the word συναγωγή. Moreover, in Paul's language of a "circumcision without hands" (περιτομή ἀχειροποίητα), which is a "circumcision of the Messiah" (ἡ περιτομὴ τοῦ Χριστοῦ), many commentators have rightly detected an implicit contrast with the Jewish practice of physical circumcision.[22] The references to "food . . . drink . . . observing festivals, new moons, or sabbaths" are also all regularly and rightly taken as references to common Jewish observances.[23]

We should also inquire as to what kind of opposition Paul has in view in 2.20–23. He appears to refer to things which some of the Colossian Christians refuse to "handle," "taste," or "touch" (2.21), things which, in Paul's view, pertain to "[merely] human commandments and teachings" (2.22) and, though they "indeed [have] an appearance of wisdom in promoting self-imposed piety, humility, and severe treatment of the body (ἐθελοθρησκίᾳ καὶ ταπεινοφροσύνῃ καὶ ἀφειδίᾳ σώματος), . . . are of no value in checking self-indulgence" (2.23 NRSV). First, I note that the phrase ἐθελοθρησκίᾳ καὶ ταπεινοφροσύνῃ καὶ ἀφειδίᾳ σώματος clearly alludes back to the very similar expression in 2.18 (θέλων ἐν ταπεινοφροσύνῃ καὶ θρησκείᾳ τῶν ἀγγέλων) a mere five verses earlier.[24] On this basis, therefore, it is reasonable to interpret the force of 2.20–23 in relation to 2.16–18. I contend, then, with several other commentators, that here as in 2.8–18 Paul polemicizes against a local Jewish influence which insists upon the characteristically Jewish practices of circumcision (2.11), holy days (2.16), and food laws (2.16, 21) and boasts in its access to the heavenly liturgy (2.18).[25] However, and although my reading is not very much effected either way, it is possible that 2.21 ("Neither handle nor taste nor touch!") and 2.23 ("severe treatment of the body") presuppose ascetical practices which were *not* generally characteristic of first-century Jews. On the other hand, it is also possible that Paul here deliberately (mis)characterizes standard Jewish practices so as to cast them in an unfavorable light.[26] Either way, for our purposes, it is sufficient to say that the opponents which Paul has in view are local Jews who insist upon the characteristically Jewish practices of circumcision (2.11), holy days (2.16), and food laws (2.16, 21) and boast in their access to the heavenly liturgy (2.18).

This reconstruction of the *Sitz im Leben* of Colossians, moreover, provides a plausible and satisfying context for the "Christ-Psalm" of Colossians 1.15–20, the main thrust of which is the supremacy of Jesus and not least over the very "thrones," "dominions," "rulers," and "powers" (1.16: i.e., angelic beings) in which the Colossian Jews were so interested.[27]

EXEGESIS

(1.15) ὅς ἐστιν εἰκὼν τοῦ θεοῦ τοῦ ἀοράτου,[28]
πρωτότοκος πάσης κτίσεως,
(1.16) ὅτι ἐν αὐτῷ ἐκτίσθη τὰ πάντα
ἐν τοῖς οὐρανοῖς καὶ ἐπὶ τῆς γῆς,
τὰ ὁρατὰ καὶ τὰ ἀόρατα,
εἴτε θρόνοι εἴτε κυριότητες
εἴτε ἀρχαὶ εἴτε ἐξουσίαι·
τὰ πάντα δι' αὐτοῦ καὶ εἰς αὐτὸν ἔκτισται·
(1.17) καὶ αὐτός ἐστιν πρὸ πάντων
καὶ τὰ πάντα ἐν αὐτῷ συνέστηκεν,
(1.18) καὶ αὐτός ἐστιν ἡ κεφαλὴ τοῦ σώματος τῆς ἐκκλησίας·
ὅς ἐστιν ἀρχή,
πρωτότοκος ἐκ τῶν νεκρῶν,
ἵνα γένηται ἐν πᾶσιν αὐτὸς πρωτεύων . . .[29]

For two reasons, I provide no structural analysis of the passage. (1) On the one hand, recent and extensive analyses of this sort are available.[30] (2) On the other hand, it is not clear that such an analysis has or would materially contribute to my particular considerations. I begin, therefore, with a consideration of N. T. Wright's reworking of C. F. Burney's original hypothesis, in which the psalm embodies the author's reflection upon, and creative christological appropriation of, the first word unit (preposition + noun) of the Hebrew scriptures: בראשית.[31] Wright argues that the author (for him, Paul) made christological use of Jewish wisdom speculation in which the *sophia* of Proverbs 8.22, there referred to as ראשית דרכו ("the beginning of his [God's] ways"), was taken by some Jews as the allusive referent behind the ראשית of Genesis 1.1: "By/In/Through ראשית [i.e. *sophia*], God created the heavens and the earth."[32] Furthermore, still largely following Burney, Wright contends that the psalm's key christological descriptors reflect Paul's exploitation of possible translations of ראשית: εἰκών ("image"; 1.15), πρωτότοκος ("firstborn"; 1.15), πρὸ πάντων ("before all things"; 1.17), κεφαλή ("head"; 1.18) and ἀρχή ("beginning"; 1.18).[33] Likewise, Wright follows (and slightly adapts) Burney's suggestion that the psalm's various prepositional phrases—ἐν αὐτῷ ("in/by whom"), δι' αὐτοῦ ("through whom"), εἰς αὐτόν ("for whom")—are best explained on the hypothesis that Paul exploited the possible renderings of the Hebrew ב of Genesis 1.1.

This proposal, however, does not appear to have convinced many. For instance, in Christopher A. Beetham's careful study, he mentions in a footnote: "I am less confident of Burney's hypothesis, however ... since the data can be explained better in light of the overall Jewish Wisdom tradition."[34] This is, however, an odd objection as both Burney and Wright propose that Paul reflected upon Genesis 1.1 precisely *through* the lens of the Jewish wisdom tradition:

> He [Burney] is not vulnerable to the criticism of Schweizer, who seems to think that he was suggesting a rabbinic background as opposed to a Hellenistic-Jewish one. ... Burney makes it quite clear that he is talking about Hellenistic-Jewish ideas, though it is true that his theory is then used by W. D. Davies ... as part of his case for finding "rabbinic" material in Paul. In fact ... such exposition [Burney's proposal] is equally at home in much older Jewish wisdom-traditions.[35]

Therefore, to propose that Paul exploited the בראשית of Genesis 1.1 is not at all incompatible with the view that he did so in light of the Jewish wisdom tradition. Nor is this position incompatible with Beetham's own stated case: "Paul has not alluded to Prov 8:22–31 in a strict sense, but rather to it *in its first century C.E. interpretive development*, which was 'in the air' of his day."[36] On this point, I quite agree. The psalm reflects neither a strict "exegesis" of Genesis 1.1, nor of Proverbs 8.22, but rather a creative christological appropriation of contemporary Jewish *sophia* speculation and of Middle Platonic intermediary doctrine.

I now make the point in more detail. As I have already argued, the Pauline collocation of εἰκών ("image") and πρωτότοκος ("firstborn"; cp. Rom. 8.29) reflects the influence of Middle Platonic intermediary doctrine, a contention which is immediately confirmed by the explanatory clause: "*because* by him all things were created" (1.16a).[37] In other words, it is appropriate to refer to Jesus as the "firstborn image of God" precisely because he created the *kosmos*.[38] Furthermore, the Burney-Wright thesis—in which Paul has creatively appropriated the בראשית of Genesis 1.1—explains one particularly puzzling feature of Paul's use of prepositional metaphysics in this passage. While John, Paul, and the author of Hebrews provide instances of the christological use of the preposition δι' αὐτοῦ/δι' οὗ in "cosmological" contexts (John 1.3, 10; 1 Cor. 8.6b; Col. 1.16; and Heb. 1.2), the prepositional phrase ἐν αὐτῷ is exceptional in this connection.[39] This usage, however, would be elegantly explained if it arose from one of Paul's translations of the ב of Genesis 1.1. After all, as is clear from LXX Genesis 1.1, ἐν was a natural rendering of the ב. I now cite the relevant portions of LXX Genesis 1.1 and of Colossians 1.16 to demonstrate how closely the latter parallels the former.

LXX Genesis 1.1: Ἐν ἀρχῇ ἐποίησεν ὁ θεὸς   τὸν οὐρανὸν καὶ τὴν γῆν.
Colossians 1.16: ἐν αὐτῷ ἐκτίσθη τὰ πάντα ἐν τοῖς οὐρανοῖς καὶ ἐπὶ τῆς γῆς

Colossians 1.16a–b almost looks like a gloss of LXX Genesis 1.1, in which case Paul would be glossing the בראשית/ἀρχή with αὐτός [Jesus/*sophia*].[40] In any case, the Burney-Wright thesis would well explain (1) why all of the christological descriptors of 1.15–20 appear together and (2) why Paul has included a prepositional phrase (ἐν αὐτῷ) otherwise unattested in this connection.

The main objection to this proposal is represented by Gordley's contention that the Colossian audience would not have been able to discern this creative appropriation of the בראשית of Genesis 1.1.[41] However, as I argued in an earlier section, the criterion of "audience competency" is of especially little value in such cases. For example, on the one hand, the main points of the Christ-psalm are quite understandable apart from any knowledge of the author's possible appropriation of בראשית. On the other hand, how do we know that Paul, like many authors ancient and modern, was not happy to write things which were not immediately, easily, or fully intelligible to his audiences?

Following this argument, I also want to mention a more speculative proposal. I put the question this way: If another thoughtful first-century Jew were to compose the same psalm about someone or something else, what might this something else be? Of course, as we see in the book of Wisdom (esp. Wis. 7), it might concern *sophia* herself. However, on the basis of Sirach 24.23–34 and the tradition preserved in Genesis Rabbah 1.1, we can well imagine a first-century Jew composing such a psalm about the Torah.[42] *Perhaps* it is the case, therefore—though one can only say *perhaps*—that Paul has deliberately ascribed to Jesus things which contemporary Jews would have naturally ascribed to Torah.[43]

We now return to the question of the christology of 1.15–16. In this regard, I make two points. (1) This is a case of wisdom *and not* Adam (or "royal") christology;[44] and (2) Paul deliberately presents Jesus as far superior to the very angelic powers in which the Colossian Jews were interested.

Taking point (1) first, I contend that neither royal nor Adam traditions get us very far in explaining the cosmogonical and cosmological dimensions of the passage. Indeed, that Jesus's role as God's "firstborn image" (1.15–16) is *explained* by his cosmogonical activity effectively rules out royal or Adam traditions as a sufficient explanation of the passage.[45] When Jesus's role as God's firstborn, cosmogonical image is articulated *via* prepositional metaphysics, and when the passage as a whole likely reflects a creative christological appropriation of the בראשית of Genesis 1.1 *via* the בראשית of Proverbs 8.22, we are right to see the whole passage as a statement of wisdom christology.[46]

Indeed, as I have argued throughout, Paul's image christology does not present Jesus on a direct parallel with the Adam of Genesis 1.26. Rather, dependent upon a christological appropriation of the Jewish wisdom tradition and of Middle Platonic intermediary doctrine, Paul presents Jesus as the protological and cosmogonical image of God *according to which Adam himself was made and toward which he was destined.*

This christology is well demonstrated in Colossians 3.9–10:

(3.9) Do not lie to one another, having put off the old humanity with its practices (3.10) and having put on the new humanity which is being renewed in knowledge according to the image of the creator (τὸν νέον τὸν ἀνακαινούμενον εἰς ἐπίγνωσιν κατ' εἰκόνα τοῦ κτίσαντος αὐτόν).

With respect to this text, I make the following points. (a) In the context of Colossians, it is the preexistent Jesus himself, as the "firstborn image of God" (1.15–16), who is the "creator" "according" to whose "image" believers are "being renewed in knowledge."[47] As in the cases of 2 Corinthians 3.18 and Romans 8.29, therefore, Jesus is presented as the cosmogonical and paradigmatic image of God according to which humanity was made and toward which it was destined. (b) Also as in the cases of 2 Corinthians 2.17–4.6 and Romans 7–8, I suggest, Paul has cast inner-Jewish issues in philosophical dress and thereby presented his opponents as adherents of an "empty and deceitful philosophy" (2.8) and himself, his associates, and the Colossian Christians as true philosophers "being renewed in knowledge according to the image of [God] the creator."

Before concluding, I pick up point (2) from above concerning the import of Paul saying in 1.16 that Jesus created "all things in heaven and on earth..., visible and invisible, whether thrones or dominions or rulers or powers (εἴτε θρόνοι εἴτε κυριότητες εἴτε ἀρχαὶ εἴτε ἐξουσίαι)."[48] Though there is no consensus on the precise referent of each of the words θρόνοι, κυριότητες, ἀρχαὶ, and ἐξουσίαι, there can be little doubt that Paul's reference to "all things in heaven" at least *includes* the angelic host; and, indeed, it is possible that *all* of the words should be taken in this way. In any case, I submit, part of the point is that Paul wants to emphasize Jesus's total supremacy over any and all angelic beings in which the Colossian Jews might be interested.

CONCLUSION

To summarize my case, I make the following points. (1) Colossians was written to combat a local Jewish influence in which certain Jews boasted in their Torah observance (2.11, 16–18, 20–23) and in their access to the angelic liturgy (2.16–18). (2) In response to this situation, Paul carefully crafted the whole letter, and particularly the Christ-psalm of 1.15–20, inter alia, to present Jesus as totally superior to all angelic beings (1.16) and, indeed, to the whole universe (1.16a–b: "all things in heaven and upon the earth"). (3) As he had done in 2 Corinthians 2.17–4.6 and Romans 7–8, Paul cast essentially inner-Jewish issues in philosophical dress, thereby presenting his opponents as adherents of an "empty and deceitful philosophy" (2.8) and himself, his associates, and the Colossian Christians as true philosophers who are "being renewed in knowledge according to the image of [God] the creator" (3.10). (4) Finally, I have argued that Colossians 1.15–16 is best characterized as an instance of wisdom christology—rather than Adam and/or "royal" christology—in which Paul has reworked Jewish wisdom speculation and Middle Platonic intermediary doctrine so as to include Jesus within the most exclusive conceptual category of "the unique divine identity": the doctrine of creation.

NOTES

1. Andrew Lincoln, "Colossians," *NIB XI* (Nashville: Abingdon, 2000), 531–85 (560). On the whole question, cf. now Adam K. Copenhaver, *Reconstructing the Historical Background of Paul's Rhetoric in the Letter to the Colossians*, LNTS (New York/London: Bloomsbury T & T Clark, 2018), 1–39.

2. So esp. Günther Bornkamm, "The Heresy of Colossians" in F. Francis and W. Meeks, eds., *Conflict at Colossae*, SBLSBS 4 (Missoula: Scholars, 1973), 123–46; and E. Lohse, *Colossians and Philemon*, Hermeneia (Philadelphia: Fortress, 1971), *passim*; with the discussion in Dunn, *Colossians and Philemon*, 27–28 (and see those listed in 27, n. 22). For a recent review and critique of this position, cf. esp. Copenhaver, *Reconstructing*, 2–12.

3. So esp. Arnold, *Syncretism, passim*; and before him esp. Martin Dibelius, "The Isis Initiation in Apuleius and Related Initiatory Rites" in Francis and Meeks, eds., *Conflict*, 61–126. Cf. also T. J. Sappington, *Revelation and Redemption at Colossae*, JSNTSup 53 (Sheffield: JSOT, 1991). For a review and critique of this thesis, cf. Kopenhaver, *Reconstructing*, 13–18.

4. So Troy Martin, *By Philosophy and Empty Deceit*, JSNTSSup 118 (Sheffield: SAP, 1996), *passim*, who is critiqued by Kopenhaver, *Reconstructing*, 20–22.

5. So esp. the careful discussion in Scot McKnight, *The Letter to the Colossians*, NICNT (Grand Rapids: Eerdmans, 2018), 18–34; and also Dunn, *Colossians and Philemon*, 23–35 (esp. 29–35); N. T. Wright, *The Epistles of Paul to the Colossians and to Philemon*, TNTC (Downers Grove: IVP, 1986), 25–33; Christopher Rowland, "Apocalyptic Visions and the Exaltation of Christ in the Letter to the Colossians" *JSNT* 19 (1983): 73–83; Craig A. Evans, "The Colossian Mystics" *Biblica* 63 (1982): 188–205; and the very influential analyses of Fred O. Francis, "Humility and Angelic Worship in Col 2:18" *ST* 16 (1963): 109–34, now found in and cited from Francis

and Meeks, eds., *Conflict*, 163–95; and Idem, "The Background of Εμβατευων (Col 2:18) in Legal Papyri and Oracle Inscriptions" in Francis and Meeks, eds., *Conflict*, 197–207.

6. Esp. Lohse, *Colossians and Philemon, passim*, who postulates a general Gnosticism but also detects Jewish and mystery-cult influence; Bornkamm, "The Heresy of Colossians," 123–46, who refers to a highly syncretistic Jewish Gnosticism; Dibelius, "The Isis Initiation," 61–126, who postulates a combination of Gnostic and mystery-cult influence; and J. B. Lightfoot, *St. Paul's Epistles to the Colossians and to Philemon* (Lynn: Hendrickson, 1980), *passim*, who refers to Jewish Gnosticism. For a review and critique of this position, cf. Kopenhaver, *Reconstructing*, 2–12.

7. See Richard E. DeMaris, *The Colossian Controversy*, WUNT 2.77 (Tübingen: J. C. B. Mohr, 1995), and esp. the summary on pp. 16–17. Eduard Schweizer, *The Letter to the Colossians: A Commentary*, trans. by Andrew Chester (Minneapolis: Fortress, 1982 [1976]), had postulated a Pythagorean background.

8. Of course, one must also reconstruct, insofar as the evidence allows, the ancient environment of Colossae. This is complicated, however, by two factors: (1) it was destroyed by an earthquake in ca. 61 CE (so Tacitus, *Annals*, 14.27) and (2) the cite has never properly been excavated, though excavations are forthcoming: cf. Michael Trainor, "Colossae: The State of Forthcoming Excavations" *JSPL* 1 (2011): 133–35. On Colossae in general, cf., e.g., H. Cadwallader and Michael Trainor, eds., *Colossae in Space and Time: Linking to an Ancient City*, NTOA 94 (Göttingen: Vandenhoeck & Ruprecht, 2011); and the recent and apposite summary of McKnight, *Colossians*, 20 (italics mine): "The city of Colossae was *predominantly* Gentile, *though there is solid evidence for the presence of Jews*, the first hints of which we get from Josephus, who said that two thousand families were settled in Colossae (*Jewish Antiquities* 12.3–4). Cicero, too, witnesses to sizable taxes for Jerusalem's temple being collected in Colossae (*For Flaccus* 28). *We infer, then, that Paul's audience was predominantly Gentile* (see Col 1:12, 21, 27; 2:13; 3:5–7 as Gentile vices), *even if the so-called opponents were Jewish*. There is also solid evidence that Colossae was active with religious cults." On the Jewish presence in Asia Minor, cf. esp. Paul Trebilco, *Jewish Communities in Asia Minor* (Cambridge: CUP, 1991). On the presence and influence of the mystery cults, cf. esp. Arnold, *Syncretism*, 103–57. In other words, appeals to the historical environment of Colossae will not and cannot solve the problem of the "Colossian heresy."

9. Arnold, *Syncretism*, 90–95, who states that, prior to the work of Francis: "The angels have almost universally been regarded as the object of the veneration throughout the history of the interpretation of the passage" (90, citing scholars on 91, n. 2). Cf. Fred O. Francis, "Humility and Angelic Worship in Col 2:18" *ST* 16 (1963): 109–34, now found in and cited from Francis and Meeks, eds., *Conflict*, 163–95; followed by, e.g., Hurtado, *OGOL*, 33–34, and those listed on 203–04, n. 58; Dunn, *Colossians and Philemon*, 179–82, and those listed on 29, n. 27; and those listed in R. M. Wilson, *A Critical and Exegetical Commentary on Colossians and Philemon*, ICC (London/New York: T&T Clark International, 2005), 51, n. 103; and Markus Barth and H. Blanke, *Colossians: A New Translation with Introduction and Commentary*, AB 34B, trans. by A. B. Beck (New York: Doubleday, 1994), 345.

10. Arnold, *Syncretism*, 90–95 (92): "The noun θρησκεία is not very common in the Greco-Roman secular writers. In Jewish writings it only appears four times in the LXX and five times in Philo. The term is very common in Josephus, however, occurring a total of 91 times."

11. Arnold, *Syncretism*, 91, italics mine.

12. McKnight, *Colossians*, 274, however, mentions the very interesting possibility of something like a "descriptive genitive," in which τῶν ἀγγέλων would adjectivally modify θρησκείᾳ, with the result that Paul would be referring to "angel-like worship." Not only would this coordinate well with certain evidence in the Scrolls and in Jewish apocalyptic literature more generally—in which humans were sometimes thought to have been "patterned" after the angels (so 4Q417, frag. 2, col. 1.15–18) and in which they also hoped to become more like them—it might also go some way toward explaining the asceticism referred to in 2.16–18, 20–23: so esp. McKnight, *Colossians*, 273–76.

13. So Wright, *Colossians and Philemon*, 126–27.

14. Arnold, *Syncretism*, 103–57 (esp. 109–20). Arnold was here also influenced by Sir William M. Ramsay, *The Teaching of Paul in Terms of the Present Day*, 2nd edn. (London: Hodder & Stoughton, 1914), 283–305; and Dibelius, "The Isis Initiation."

15. Ibid. 155–58.

16. *Contra* also, e.g., Wilson, *Colossians and Philemon*, 35–58, 220–24, who is heavily influenced by Arnold.

17. So Dunn, *Colossians and Philemon*, 171; and, e.g., McKnight, *Colossians*, 262, "Such a person also goes into great detail about what they have seen"; and Wilson, *Colossians and Philemon*, 215: "entering into what he has seen."

18. Dunn, *Colossians and Philemon*, 183–84; and also Idem, "The Colossian Philosophy: A Confident Jewish Apologia" *Biblica* 76 (1995): 153–81; McKnight, *Colossians*, 271–79 (277): "[T]he halakic mystics are Jewish, given to traditional observance of the food laws and calendrical matters, and they are also convinced that ascetic rigor can lead to exalted angel-like worship experiences that are quasi entrances into heaven, where they perhaps discover revelation"; Wright, *Colossians and Philemon*, 24–27; and Barth and Blanke, *Colossians*, 345; and *contra*, e.g., Wilson, *Colossians and Philemon*, 220–24; and Lohse, *Colossians and Philemon*, 114–21, both of whom are heavenly influenced by the Ramsay/Dibelius/Arnold reading.

19. In order to draw out the meaning of διὰ τῆς φιλοσοφίας καὶ κενῆς ἀπάτης, which is likely an instance of hendiadys, I have taken κενῆς ἀπάτης as the adjectival modifier of τῆς φιλοσοφίας, with the resultant rendering: "an empty and deceitful philosophy." So also, e.g., Jerry Sumney, *Colossians*, NTL (Louisville: Westminster John Knox, 2008), 130, who, instead of speaking of hendiadys, argues that "'and' (*kai*) is epexegetical, so that 'empty deceit' describes the 'philosophy'"; David Pao, *Colossians & Philemon*, ECNT (Grand Rapids: Zondervan, 2012), 159; and Barth and Blanke, *Colossians*, 310.

20. So Wright, *Colossians and Philemon*, 105. See also Idem, *Fresh Perspective*, 117, in which Wright notes a similar phenomenon at Philippians 3.2–3, where Paul undoubtedly puns on the word "circumcision": ΠΕΡΙΤΟΜΗ/ΚΑΤΑΤΟΜΗ.

McKnight, *Colossians*, 224, n. 35, cites Wright favorably in this regard. I further note that, as a part of his polemic in Colossians (2.23), Paul appears also to have coined the word ἐθελοθρησκία: so *BAGD*, 276; and, e.g., Wilson, *Colossians and Philemon*, 230; and Dunn, *Colossians and Philemon*, 195.

21. Nor should we say, with, e.g., Barth and Blanke, *Colossians*, 308, that by "philosophy" Paul simply means "religion."

22. So McKnight, *Colossians*, 234: "[I]t is reasonable to think the Colossians were being pressed to be circumcised to complete their conversion"; Dunn, *Colossians and Philemon*, 153–58 (155): "[C]ircumcision was indeed a factor in the threatening situation in Colossae"; Wright, *Colossians and Philemon*, 109–12; and Barth and Blanke, *Colossians*, 317–20; and *contra*, e.g., Wilson, *Colossians and Philemon*, 201–04, who, being so influenced here as elsewhere by the Ramsay/Dibelius/Arnold thesis, tries to read Paul's reworked theology of circumcision as an implicit polemic against mystery-cult initiation.

23. So McKnight, *Colossians*, 263–68. Wilson, *Colossians and Philemon*, 216–19 (216), who elsewhere prefers the Ramsay/Dibelius/Arnold thesis, admits, "This verse, particularly in its reference to the Sabbath, provides a clear indication that the 'false teaching' at least included a Jewish element." Cf. also Dunn, *Colossians and Philemon*, 171–75; Wright, *Colossians and Philemon*, 123–26; and Barth and Blanke, *Colossians*, 337–39.

24. Cf., e.g., McKnight, *Colossians*, 286, n. 277; Wilson, *Colossians and Philemon*, 230; Dunn, *Colossians and Philemon*, 195; Barth and Blanke, *Colossians*, 361; and Lohse, *Colossians*, 126.

25. With, e.g., McKnight, *Colossians*, 281–87; Wilson, *Colossians and Philemon*, 226–33; and Dunn, *Colossians and Philemon*, 188–98.

26. E.g., McKnight, *Colossians*, 286, assumes that Paul accurately refers to local Jews who are uncharacteristically ascetical. E.g., Wilson, *Colossians and Philemon*, 229–33, while ably and carefully considering several possibilities, assumes that Paul accurately reports his opponents' asceticism; as does Lohse, *Colossians*, 124–31. However, e.g., Barth and Blanke, *Colossians*, 361, are right, I think, to take "severe treatment of the body" (2.23) as a (polemically and rhetorically charged) reference to the (as Paul well knew) characteristically Jewish practices of circumcision (so 2.11) and a kosher diet (so 2.16, 21).

27. This is a partial response to, e.g., Pao, *Colossians and Philemon*, 85: "It is unclear exactly how Paul intends to use this hymn to respond directly to the false teachers"; Dunn, *Colossians and Philemon*, 86: "It remains unclear what light the passage sheds on the situation at Colossae"; Lohse, *Colossians and Philemon*, 41: "By inserting the hymn into the letter's train of thought a certain tension arises regarding its present context."

28. In this connection, I note a text from Philo, *Creation* (Colson and Whitaker, LCL, slightly revised), 146: "Every man, in respect of his mind, is allied to the divine *logos*, having come into being as a copy or fragment or ray of that blessed nature, but in the structure of his body he is allied to all the world, for he is compounded of the same things, earth, water, air, and fire, each of the elements having contributed the share that falls to each, to complete a material absolutely sufficient in itself for the Creator to take in order to fashion this visible image (τὴν ὁρατὴν ταύτην εἰκόνα)."

In Philo's view, humanity serves as the *visible* image of the *logos*, which itself is the *invisible* image of God. In the view of Colossians 1.15, the exalted human being Jesus now is and (in some sense) always has been the *visible* image of God.

29. As printed in NA[28].

30. Cf. esp. Gordley, *Colossian Hymn*, 5–16; Stettler, *Der Kolosserhymnus*, 86–94; and the helpful chart in Cox, *By the Same Word*, 163–69 (166).

31. See Wright, *Climax*, 99–119 (esp. 110–3); and C. F. Burney, "Christ as the APXH of Creation" *JTS* 27 (1925): 160–77. This hypothesis is mentioned favorably by, e.g., McKnight, *Colossians*, 138, n. 280; Moo, *Colossians and Philemon*, 113–14 (esp. n. 21); and Barth and Blanke, *Colossians*, 238–39. I note that Burney, "APXH," 160–69, was at great pains to make a case for the proper historical-exegetical construal of Proverbs 8.22. However, the question of how we ought historically and exegetically to construe Proverbs 8.22 and of how a first-century Jew might construe that text are quite separate questions.

32. Genesis Rabbah 1.1 is the earliest evidence we have of a text which explicitly takes the ראשית of Genesis 1.1 as the ראשית of Proverbs 8.22. However, within a larger celebration of God as creator, LXX Psalm 103.24b states, "[Y]ou have made all things by your wisdom (πάντα ἐν σοφίᾳ ἐποίησας)."

33. Wright, *Climax*, 110–13, however, slightly differs from Burney on this point.

34. Christopher A. Beetham, *Echoes of Scripture in the Letter of Paul to the Colossians* (Leiden: Brill, 2008), 134 n. 95. Cf. also Cox, *By the Same Word*, 170, n. 77: "A consensus now exists which takes Col 1:15–20 as most closely related to Hellenistic Jewish Wisdom texts, though how this relationship is understood varies from scholar to scholar ... C. F. Burney argued that Col 1:15–20 represents Paul's reflection on the first words of the Bible (בראשית). Burney's reconstruction presumes the use of the Hebrew version of Genesis as the primary impetus for the Col passage, a notion that seems unlikely in light of the passage's allusion to Greek-speaking Jewish texts ... as well as non-Jewish Hellenistic parallels"; and Lohse, *Colossians and Philemon*, 47, n. 101, "This thesis would presuppose that the passage was an exegesis of the Hebrew text." For the Burney-Wright hypothesis to work, however, only one of the following needs to be true: (1) the author had a basic facility with Hebrew and Greek and was aware of traditions of reading Genesis 1 *via* wisdom speculation in general and Proverbs 8 in particular; and/or (2) the author had close access to a person who had a basic facility with Hebrew and Greek and was aware of traditions of reading Genesis 1 *via* wisdom speculation in general and Proverbs 8 in particular. In this regard, I note that Beetham himself, who has provided one of the most recent and careful treatments of "echoes" of scripture in Colossians, has argued that the author of Colossians (whom Beetham takes throughout to be Paul) knew *both* Greek and Hebrew and sometimes preferred proto-MT to proto-LXX: so Beetham, *Echoes*, 36–38, 258–60.

35. Wright, *Climax*, 110–11, citing W. D. Davies, *Paul and Rabbinic Judaism*, 4th edn. (Philadelphia: Fortress, 1980 [1948]), 150–52.

36. Beetham, *Echoes*, 113, italics original.

37. Neither Burney nor Wright was aware of the resonances of Middle Platonic intermediary doctrine. On this, cf. esp. Cox, *By the Same Word*, 161–92.

38. This also rather clearly indicates that, as I will argue below, an "Adam" and/or generally "royal/imperial" background cannot sufficiently account for the passage.

39. Cox, *By the Same Word*, 175–80, it seems to me, who rejects the Burney-Wright thesis (cf. Idem, 170, n. 77), struggles to explain this usage.

40. Cf. also Wilson, *Colossians and Philemon*, 139: "The reference to heaven and earth recalls the opening words of Genesis."

41. Gordley, *Colossian Hymn*, 20.

42. So, e.g., Beetham, *Echoes*, 130: "Wisdom was often identified with Torah in early Judaism, and this became the fixed interpretation in the later rabbinic writings."

43. Cf. the suggestive remark of McKnight, *Colossians*, 148: "That is to say, this hymn is adopting and adapting the Jewish wisdom tradition, *as understood in part in the Torah-revelation tradition*, to God's manifestation in Christ."

44. As I mentioned in an earlier note, Gordley, *New Testament Christological Hymns*, appeared too late to feature in the body of the argument, though I note here that his treatment of the poem as a thoroughgoing instance of wisdom christology is not dissimilar to my own: pp. 124–32.

45. *Contra*, e.g., Joshua Jipp, *Christ is King* (Minneapolis: Fortress, 2015), 104; Fee, *Christology*, 299; and Wright, *Climax*, 114, 116; G. Kittel, "εἰκών" in *TDNT*, 2.381-97 (395-96): "If he [Paul] here refers it [the *imago Dei*] to Christ instead of Adam, it is because he equates Christ with the Adam intended in Gn. 1:27"; and Adolf Schlatter, *Die Theologie der Apostel* (Stuttgart: Calwar, 1922), 299. Stettler, *Der Kolosserhymnus*, 33 (italics mine), is right to say: "Im Einzelnen bedarf an Wrights Entwurf einiges auch der Präzisierung oder der Korrektur. Sein Gliederungsvorschlag wird sich so nicht halten lassen, *das Verständnis von V. 15 von der Adam Christologie her wird der Eikon Christologie nicht gerecht . . .*"

46. So esp. Beetham, *Echoes*, 130–34, 242 with nn. 62–64; Gordley, *Colossian Hymn*, 206–18; Cox, *By the Same Word*, 172–80; Stettler, *Der Kolosserhymnus*, 104–65, who also soundly critiques Käsemann's famous (and untenable) Gnostic Erlösermythus hypothesis (so Ibid. 3–26, 39–43); McKnight, *Colossians*, 138–50; Dunn, *Colossians and Philemon*, 83–90 (86, n. 8): "The Wisdom character of the hymn is a matter of broad consensus."; Lohse, *Colossians and Philemon*, 86; Eduard Schweizer, *Der Brief an die Kolosse*, EKK 12 (Zürich-Einsiedeln-Köln: Benzinger and Neukirchen-Vluyn: Neukirchener, 1976), 57; Eltester, *Eikon*, 76. McKnight, *Colossians*, 138–50 (146–47), rightly argues that this is a case of wisdom christology and of christological monotheism and that Adam christology does not sufficiently explain the passage, but he then goes on wrongly to expound Colossians 1.15 as an instance of royal (messianic) christology: "This, then, is not so much Adamic Christology, as if Jesus is merely Adam Version 2.0. . . . To call Jesus the *eikōn* of the invisible God is to say that Jesus is the one who rules over all as the Davidic king (Ps 89:27)."

47. So also, e.g., McKnight, *Colossians*, 311: "[E]ach person . . . is being renewed into the image of God, which is Christ himself"; Wilson, *Colossians and Philemon*, 252: "This new man is being renewed according to the image of his creator (κατ' εἰκόνα τοῦ κτίσαντος αὐτόν), which of course recalls 1:15 with its description of Christ as εἰκὼν τοῦ θεοῦ τοῦ ἀορατου . . ."; and Dunn, *Colossians and Philemon*, 220–23.

48. So, e.g., McKnight, *Colossians*, 151–52 (152): "It seems 'thrones' (Dan 7:9) and 'powers' (Eph 1:20–21) are heavenly, invisible potentates, while 'rulers' and 'authorities' are more likely their earthly, visible servants (cf. 1 Cor 15:24; Eph 1:21)"; Wilson, *Colossians and Philemon*, 139–42 (142), who considers several possibilities and judiciously states, "The essential point of this passage is that all things in heaven and on earth owe their existence to the firstborn of creation"; Dunn, *Colossians and Philemon*, 92–93 (92): "[W]e should suppose a hierarchy of heavenly powers—'thrones' superior to 'lordships,' and so on"; Wright, *Colossians and Philemon*, 76, who also judiciously states, "Paul has here chosen to mention especially what we today call the power structures of the universe. . . . Paul, however, is not concerned so much with listing them in a particular order, or with distinguishing carefully between them, as with asserting Christ's supremacy over them"; and Barth and Blanke, *Colossians*, 202: "Any attempt to limit the scope of the titles will not do justice to the intention of the hymn in Col 1, where the first strophe emphasizes the universality of the dominion of the Messiah."

Chapter 10

Paul and the Image of God

Conclusion

In this book, I have made the following case. (1) While instances of the *imago Dei* in biblical and second-temple Jewish sources are diverse and pluriform, they are nonetheless illuminating for Paul's *imago Dei* theology. (2) However, this theology is best explained on the hypothesis that Paul, like Philo and the author of Wisdom, made use of "intermediary speculation" in which the *kosmos* came into being *via* an intermediary "figure": in the latter's case *sophia* and/or the *logos* and in Paul's case the preexistent Jesus. (3) In this connection, while the resources of the Jewish wisdom tradition (e.g., Prov. 8; Sir. 1; 24; 1 En. 42; Wis. 7; and Bar. 3–4) did not provide Paul with the precision afforded by the "prepositional metaphysics" of the philosophical tradition (cf. 1 Cor. 8.6; and Col. 1.15–20; cp. John 1.3, 10; and Heb. 1.2), the general contours of that tradition—in which *sophia* attended to the creation, maintenance, and salvation of the *kosmos*—were appreciated and appropriated in Paul's *imago Dei* theology (esp. Col. 1.15–20). (4) Beyond this, a few features of Paul's *imago Dei* theology—especially his collocations of εἰκών ("image") and πρωτότοκος ("firstborn") (cf. Rom. 8.29; and Col. 1.15) and εἰκών and μορφ- language (cf. 2 Cor. 3.18; and Rom. 8.29), as well as his "teleological" construal of the *imago Dei* conception in which Jesus serves as the archetypal "image" to which believers will ultimately be conformed (2 Cor. 3.18; Rom. 8.29; cp. Phil. 3.21)—strongly suggest that Paul was here influenced (directly or indirectly) by Middle Platonic intermediary doctrine.

(5) On the basis of points (2) through (4), therefore, it is wisdom christology, rather than Adam (and/or "royal") christology, which serves as the principal background of Paul's "image christology." This "image christology," furthermore, in which Jesus serves as the protological and cosmogonical image of God, is an instance of "christological monotheism." In this regard, especially in the case of Colossians 1.15–20, Jesus is included in the one

activity (creation) which most clearly demarcates the "unique divine identity" in second-temple Jewish thought. (6) Finally, my argument concerning the way in which Paul adapts certain features of the philosophical *imago Dei* tradition has allowed for a fresh reading of three major Pauline texts: 2 Corinthians 2.17–4.6; Romans 7–8, and Colossians 1.15–20; 3.10. In these texts, I have argued, Paul casts essentially inner-Jewish debates in philosophical dress. While the substantive issues are "inner-Jewish" issues, Paul presents his opponents and/or opposing views as bound up with a futile and/or deceitful philosophy, while he presents himself and his sympathizers as people who attain to the *telos* of true philosophy: the image of God (2 Cor. 3.18; Rom. 8.29; and Col. 3.10).

More generally, this study has made the case that, although Paul's *imago Dei* theology certainly bears the influence of Middle Platonic intermediary doctrine, it is also fundamentally grounded in the Jewish tradition. Indeed, as our study of Romans in particular has shown, Paul's narrative worldview—within which and in relation to which he expresses his *imago Dei* theology—is still recognizably a christological and pneumatological variation on the characteristically, though variously expressed, Jewish narrative worldview. In this regard, for example, van Kooten's study failed to note the crucial ways in which Paul's *imago Dei* theology radically differs from the philosophical *imago Dei* traditions. For instance, in Plato's famous, original statement of what would later become associated in Philo and Plutarch with the *imago Dei* doctrine, he explicitly states,

> Therefore, we ought *to try to escape from earth to the dwelling of the gods* as quickly as we can; *and to escape is to become like god*, so far as this is possible (φυγὴ δὲ ὁμοίωσις θεῷ κατὰ τὸ δυνατόν).[1]

This represents a crucial distinction from Paul's *imago Dei* theology, in which, at least in the case of Romans 8, attaining to the image of God involves bodily resurrection (8.23) and the reassumption of sovereignty over God's physically renewed *kosmos* (8.19–21).

In this connection, this study shines a light on a few perennial questions of earliest Christianity. (1) What kind of Jew was Paul, and how influenced was he by "Hellenistic thought"? (2) At what point in the history of christological reflection were philosophical categories put to use? What were the use of such categories and how do they relate to the categories and conceptions of Jewish monotheism?

With respect to (1), this study has shown that, at least in relation to the *imago Dei* conception, Paul participates—though to a lesser extent than Philo and even the author of Wisdom—in Jewish wisdom and philosophical intermediary speculation. However, as I argued above, Paul, not unlike the authors of John (John 1.3, 10) and Hebrews (1.2), seems principally to have been interested in the way in which wisdom speculation and Middle Platonic intermediary doctrine allowed him to include Jesus within the "unique divine identity" as creator while also allowing him to express a distinction within that unique divine identity. Furthermore, with his conception of Jesus as the cosmogonical and *paradigmatic* image of God, an image to which believers will ultimately be "conformed" (2 Cor. 3.18; and Rom. 8.29; cp. Phil. 3.21), Paul seems to have been interested in the way in which the Middle Platonic intermediary served as an archetype. Beyond this, however, as our study of Romans in particular has shown, Paul remained committed to the (christologically reworked) creational monotheism of Genesis 1, a monotheism in which the one God intended to steward the world in and through his images.

As to point (2), this study has shown that, at least as early as 1 Corinthians 8.6, philosophical intermediary speculation was used in the service of a Jewish creational monotheism in which an executed-and-then-exalted human being was now included within the most exclusive conceptual category of that monotheism, and yet he was also distinguished from God "the father."

I close with a final thought. Even though I have emphasized throughout that Paul's image christology represents something closer to what is often called "wisdom christology" than what is called "Adam christology," this requires clarification. I have made this distinction so as to emphasize the fact that, in Romans 8.29; 2 Corinthians 3.18; 4.4; and Colossians 1.15–20, 3.10, Jesus is the protological and cosmogonical image of God *according to which Adam himself was made and toward which he was destined*; as such, Jesus is deliberately included within the unique divine identity as *creator* (rather than creature). Nevertheless, the reason why Paul thinks it *still* appropriate to refer to the now-human—bodily crucified, bodily resurrected, and bodily enthroned—Jesus as the paradigmatic *imago Dei* is because, in his reading of Genesis 1.26, the creative *imago Dei* made the created *imago Dei* not least in view of the day when it would be appropriate fully to bring the two together. In other words, and this is also the basis of Paul's vision of *theōsis*, the creative *imago Dei* made the created *imago Dei* with *capax Dei*.[2]

NOTES

1. *Theaet.* 176B (R. G. Bury, LCL, slightly revised).
2. On *theōsis* in Paul, see, e.g., Michael Gorman, *Inhabiting the Cruciform God: Kenosis, Justification, and Theosis in Paul's Narrative Soteriology* (Grand Rapids: Eerdmans, 2009), esp. 1–8 with literature cited therein; and Ben Blackwell, *Christosis: Engaging Paul's Soteriology with his Patristic Interpreters* (Grand Rapids: Eerdmans, 2016 [2011]).

Bibliography

COMMENTARIES, LEXICA, AND REFERENCE WORKS

Adams, Sean A. *Baruch and the Epistle of Jeremiah: A Commentary Based on the Texts in Codex Vaticanus*. SCS. Leiden: Brill, 2014.
Alexander, T. Desmond, and David W. Baker, eds. *Dictionary of the Old Testament Pentateuch*. Downers Grove: IVP, 2003.
Anderson, Gary A., and Michael E. Stone, eds. *A Synopsis of the Books of Adam and Eve*. EJL 17. Atlanta: Scholars, 1999.
Balz, Horst, and Gerhard Schneider, eds. *Exegetical Dictionary of the New Testament*. 3 vols. Grand Rapids: Eerdmans, 1990 (1978–80).
Barnett, Paul. *The Second Epistle to the Corinthians*. NICNT. Grand Rapids: Eerdmans, 1997.
Barth, Markus, and Helmut Blanke. *Colossians: A New Translation with Introduction and Commentary*. Trans. Astrid B. Beck. AB 34B. New York: Doubleday, 1994.
Bauckham, Richard, James R. Davila and Alexander Panayotov. *Old Testament Pseudepigrapha: More Noncanonical Scriptures*. Grand Rapids: Eerdmans, 2013.
Bauer, W., W. Arndt, F. W. Gingrich and F. W. Danker, eds. *A Greek-English Lexicon of the New Testament and Other Early Christian Literature*. 3rd edn. Chicago: UCP, 2001.
Bensly, R. L. *The Fourth Book of Ezra, the Latin Version Edited from the MSS*. T&S 3.2. Cambridge: 1895.
Bentzen, A. *Daniel*. HAT 19. Tübingen: J. C. B. Mohr, 1937.
Bergsma, John S. "The Persian Period as Penitential Era: The 'Exegetical Logic' of Daniel 9.1–27." Pages 50–64 in *Exile and Restoration Revisited: Essays on the Babylonian and Persian Periods in Memory of Peter R. Ackroyd*. Edited by Knoppers, Grabbe, and Fulton. LSTS. London: T & T Clark, 2009.
Black, Matthew. *The Book of Enoch or 1 Enoch. A New English Edition*. SVTP 7. Leiden: Brill, 1985.

Black, Matthew, and Albert Marie Denis. *Apocalypsis Henochi Graece: fragmenta pseudepigraphorum quae supersunt graeca.* Vol. 3 of *Pseudepigrapha veteris testamenti graece.* Leiden: Brill, 1970.

Bultmann, Rudolf. *The Second Letter to the Corinthians.* PNTC. Grand Rapids: Eerdmans, 1985 (1976).

Byrne, B. *Romans.* Sacra Pagina. Collegeville: Glazier, Liturgical Press, 1996.

Charles, R. H. *The Greek Versions of the Testaments of the Twelve Patriarchs.* Oxford: Clarendon Press, 1908.

Charlesworth, James H., ed. *The Old Testament Pseudepigrapha.* 2 vols. Peabody: Hendrickson, 1983.

Collins, John J. *Daniel: A Commentary on the Book of Daniel.* Hermeneia. Minneapolis: Fortress Press, 1993.

Conzelmann, Hans. *1 Corinthians: A Commentary on the First Epistle to the Corinthians.* Trans. James W. Leitch. Hermeneia. Philadelphia: Fortress, 1975.

Cranfield, C. E. B. *A Critical and Exegetical Commentary on the Epistle to the Romans.* 2 vols. ICC. Edinburgh: T & T Clark, 1975, 1979.

Dittenberger, Wilhelm. *Orientis graeci inscriptiones selectae: supplementum sylloges inscriptionum graecarum.* 2 vols. Leipzig: Hirzel, 1903.

Dochhorn, Jan. *Die Apokalypse des Mose: Text, Übersetzung, Kommentar.* TSAJ 106. Tübingen: Mohr Siebeck, 2005.

Dunn, James D. G. *Romans.* 2 vols. WBC 38A–B. Dallas: Word Books, 1988.

———. *The Epistles to the Colossians and to Philemon: A Commentary on the Greek Text.* NIGTC. Grand Rapids: Eerdmans, 1996.

Eshel, Esther, Hanan Eshel, Carol Newsom, Bilhah Nitzan, Eileen Schuller and Ada Yardeni, eds. *Qumran Cave 4: VI: Poetical and Liturgical Texts: Part 1. Discoveries in the Judaean Desert.* XI. Oxford: Clarendon Press, 1998.

Fee, Gordon D. *The First Epistle to the Corinthians.* NICNT. Grand Rapids: Eerdmans, 1987.

Fitzmyer, Joseph A. *Romans: A New Translation with Introduction and Commentary.* AB33. New York: Doubleday, 1993.

Fox, Michael V. *Proverbs 1–9: A New Translation with Introduction and Commentary.* AB18A. New Haven: YUP, 2000.

Freedman, David Noel, ed. *The Anchor Bible Dictionary.* 6 vols. Yale: YUP, 1992.

Furnish, Victor P. *II Corinthians: Translated with Introduction, Notes, and Commentary.* AB32A. New York: Doubleday, 1984.

Geffcken, J. *Die Oracula Sibyllina.* GCS 8. Leipzig: 1902.

Gnilka, J. *Der Kolosserbrief.* HKNT. Freiburg/Basel/Wien: Herder, 1980.

Goldingay, John E. *Daniel.* WBC 30. Dallas: Word Books, 1989.

Guthrie, George H. *2 Corinthians*, BECNT. Grand Rapids: Baker, 2015.

Hammer, R. *The Book of Daniel.* CBC. Cambridge: CUP, 1976.

Harris, Murray J. *The Second Epistle to the Corinthians: A Commentary on the Greek Text.* NIGTC. Grand Rapids: Eerdmans, 2005.

Hartman, Louis F., and Alexander A. Di Lella. *The Book of Daniel: A New Translation with Notes and Commentary on Chapters 1–9 by Louis F. Hartman; Introduction and Commentary on Chapters 10–12 by Alexander A. Di Lella.* AB 23. New York: Doubleday, 2005 (1978).

Hawthorne, Gerald F., and Ralph P. Martin. *Dictionary of Paul and His Letters*. Downers Grove: IVP, 1993.
Hayes, John H. *Dictionary of Biblical Interpretation*. 2 vols. Nashville: Abingdon, 1999.
Hays, Richard B. "The Letter to the Galatians." Pages 181–348 in *NIB IX*. Nashville: Abingdon, 2000.
Hornblower, Simon, Antony Spawforth and Esther Eidenow, eds. *The Oxford Classical Dictionary*. 4th edn. Oxford: OUP, 2012 (1968).
Jastrow, M. *Dictionary of Targumim, the Talmud Babli and Yerushalmi, and the Midrashic Literature*. 2 vols. New York: Pardes, 1903.
Jewett, Robert. *Romans*. Hermeneia. Minneapolis: Fortress, 2007.
Joüon, P., and T. Muraoka. *A Grammar of Biblical Hebrew*. 2 vols. Roma: Pontificio Istituto Biblico, 2003.
Käsemann, Ernst. *Commentary on Romans*. Trans. and ed. G. W. Bromiley. Grand Rapids: Eerdmans, 1980.
Kittel, G., G. W. Bromiley, and G. Friedrich, eds. *Theological Dictionary of the New Testament*. 10 vols. Grand Rapids: Eerdmans, 1976.
Kuss, Otto. *Der Römerbrief*. 3 vols. Regensburg: F. Pustet, 1963–1978.
Lacocque, André. *The Book of Daniel*. Trans. David Pellauer. London: SPCK, 1979 [1976].
Lietzmann, Hans. *An die Korinther I–II*. 4th edn. Completed by W. G. Kümmel. HNT 9. Tübingen: Mohr, 1949.
Lightfoot, J. B. *St. Paul's Epistles to the Colossians and to Philemon*. Lynn: Hendrickson, 1980.
Lincoln, Andrew T. "The Letter to the Colossians." Pages 531–85 in *NIB XI*. Nashville: Abingdon, 2000.
Lohse, Eduard. *Colossians and Philemon: A Commentary on the Epistles to the Colossians and to Philemon*. Trans. Poehlmann and Karris. Hermeneia. Philadelphia: Fortress, 1971 (1968).
Longenecker, Richard. *Romans*. NIGTC. Grand Rapids: Eerdmans, 2016.
Margulies, M. *Midrash Wayyikra Rabbah: A Critical Edition Based on Manuscripts and Genizah Fragments with Variants and Notes*. 2 vols. New York: Jewish Theological Seminary, 1993.
Martin, Ralph P. *2 Corinthians*. WBC 40. Waco: Word Books, 1986.
Martínez, F. García, and E. J. C. Tigchelaar, eds. *The Dead Sea Scrolls Study Edition*. 2 vols. New York: Brill, 1997—98.
Martyn, J. L. *Galatians: A New Translation with Introduction and Commentary*. AB33A. New Haven: YUP, 1993.
Matera, Frank J. *II Corinthians*. NTL. Louisville: Westminster John Knox, 2003.
McKnight, Scot. *The Letter to the Colossians*. NICNT. Grand Rapids: Eerdmans, 2018.
Meyer, W. "Vita Adae et Evae" in *Abhandlungen der königlich bayerischen Akademie der Wissenschaften, Philosophische-philologische Klasse*, vol. 14. Munich: 1878.
Milik, Józef. *The Books of Enoch*. Oxford: OUP, 1976.
Montgomery, James A. *Daniel: A Critical and Exegetical Commentary on the Book of Daniel*. ICC. Edinburgh: T & T Clark, 1979.

Moo, Douglas. *Romans*. NICNT. Grand Rapids: Eerdmans, 1996.
Muraoka, T. *A Greek-English Lexicon of the Septuagint*. Leuven: Peeters, 2009.
Neusner, Jacob. *The Mishnah: A New Translation*. New Haven: YUP, 1988.
Newsom, Carol. *Songs of the Sabbath Sacrifice: A Critical Edition*. HSS 27. Atlanta: Scholars Press, 1985.
Nickelsburg, George W. E. *1 Enoch 1: A Commentary on the Book of 1 Enoch Chapters 1–36, 81–108*. Hermenia. Minneapolis: Fortress, 2001.
Nickelsburg, George W. E., and James C. VanderKam. *1 Enoch 2: A Commentary on the Book of 1 Enoch Chapters 37–82*. Minneapolis: Fortress, 2012.
Odeberg, Hugo. *3 Enoch or the Hebrew Book of Enoch*. New York: Ktav, 1973.
Pao, David. *Colossians & Philemon*. ECNT. Grand Rapids: Zondervan, 2012.
Pietersma, Albert, and Benjamin G. Wright. *A New English Translation of the Septuagint and the other Greek Translations Traditionally Included under That Title*. Oxford: OUP, 2007.
Sailhamer, John H. *The Pentateuch as Narrative: A Biblical-Theological Commentary*. Grand Rapids: Zondervan, 1992.
Sampley, J. Paul, "The First Letter to the Corinthians." Pages 771–1003 in *NIB X*. Nashville: Abingdon, 2002.
Schreiner, Thomas. *Romans*. BECNT. Grand Rapids: Baker Academic, 1998.
Schweizer, Eduard. *The Letter to the Colossians: A Commentary*. Trans. Andrew Chester. Minneapolis: Fortress, 1982 (1976).
Sharpe, J. L. *Prolegomena to the Establishment of the Critical Text of the Greek Apocalypse of Moses*. Diss. Duke University, 1969.
Silva, Moises. *Philippians*. BECNT. 2nd edn. Grand Rapids: Baker, 2005 (1992).
Skehan, Patrick W., and Alexander A. Di Lella. *The Wisdom of Ben Sira: A New Translation with Notes by Patrick W. Skehan; Introduction and Commentary by Alexander A. Di Lella*. AB 39. New York: Doubleday, 1987.
Speiser, E. A. *Genesis: A New Translation with Introduction and Commentary*. AB. New York: Doubleday, 2007.
Stone, Michael E., and Matthias Henze. *4 Ezra and 2 Baruch: Translations, Introductions, and Notes*. Minneapolis: Fortress, 2013.
Stuckenbruck, Loren. *1 Enoch 91—108*. CEJL. New York/Berlin: de Gruyter, 2007.
Sumney, Jerry. *Colossians*. NTL. Louisville: Westminster John Knox, 2008.
Taylor, A. E. *A Commentary on Plato's Timaeus*. New York: Garland, 1987.
Thrall, Margaret. *The Second Epistle to the Corinthians*. ICC. 2 vols. Edinburgh: T & T Clark, 1994.
Tov, Emanuel, ed. *Discoveries in the Judaean Desert: The Texts from the Judaean Desert*, 39 vols. Oxford: Clarendon, 1951–2002.
VanderKam, James C. *The Book of Jubilees: Text and Translation*. 2 vols. CSCO 510–11. Scriptores Aethiopici 87–88. Leuven: Peeters, 1989.
von Rad, Gerhard. *Genesis*. OTL. rev. edn. Philadelphia: Westminster John Knox, 1973 (1972).
Walton, John H. *Genesis*. NIVAC. Grand Rapids: Zondervan, 2001.
Wenham, Gordon J. *Genesis 1—15*. WBC 1. Grand Rapids: Zondervan, 1987.

Westermann, Claus. *Genesis 1–11: A Commentary.* Trans. John J. Scullion. London: SPCK, 1984 (1974).
Wilckens, Ulrich. *Der Brief an die Römer.* 3 vols. EKK 6. Neukirchener-Vluyn: Neukirchener Verlag, 1978–82.
Wilson, R. M. *A Critical and Exegetical Commentary on Colossians and Philemon.* ICC. London/New York: T&T Clark International, 2005.
Windisch, Hans. *Der zweite Korintherbrief.* Göttingen: Vandehoeck & Ruprecht, 1924.
Winston, David. *The Wisdom of Solomon: A New Translation with Introduction and Commentary.* AB 43. New York: Doubleday, 1979.
Witherington III, Ben. *Conflict and Community in Corinth: A Socio-Rhetorical Commentary on 1 and 2 Corinthians.* Grand Rapids: Eerdmans, 1995.
Wolfe, C. *Der zweite Brief des Paulus an die Korinther.* Berlin: Evangelische Verlagsanstalt, 1989.
Wright, N. T. *The Epistles of Paul to the Colossians and to Philemon.* TNTC. Grand Rapids: Eerdmans, 1986.
———. "The Letter to the Romans." Pages 393–770 in *NIB X.* Nashville: Abingdon, 2000.
Young, D. *Theognis, Ps-Pythagoras, Ps.-Phocylides, Chares, Anonymi aulodia, fragmentum teleiambicum.* Leipzig, 1971.
Zeller, Dieter. *Der Brief an die Römer.* RNT. Regensburg: Verlag Friedrich Pustet, 1985.
Ziegler, Joseph. *Sapientia Salomonis.* Septuaginta: Vetus Testamentum Graecum, Band 12.1. Göttingen: Vandenhoeck & Ruprecht, 1981.

GENERAL BIBLIOGRAPHY

Aejmelaeus, L. *Schwachheit als Waffe: die Argumentation des Paulus im Tränenbrief (2. Kor. 10 –13).* Göttingen: Vandenhoeck & Ruprecht, 2000.
Agourides, S. "Apocalypse of Sedrach" in *The Old Testament Pseudepigrapha.* Edited by James H. Charlesworth. 2 vols. Peabody: Hendrickson, 1983.
Aitken, James K. "The Semantics of 'Glory' in Ben Sira—Traces of a Development in Post- Biblical Hebrew." Pages 1–24 in *Sirach, Scrolls, and Sages: Proceedings of the Second International Symposium on the Hebrew of the Dead Sea Scrolls, Ben Sira, and the Mishnah, held at Leiden University, 15–17 December 1997.* Edited by T. Muraoka and J. F. Elwolde. STDJ 33. Leiden: Brill, 1999.
Aletti, J.-N. *Colossiens 1,15–20: Genre et Exégèse Du Texte; Fonction de la Thématique Sapientielle.* Analecta Biblical. Rome: Pontifical Biblical Institute Press, 1981.
Alexander, Philip. "'The Agent of the King is Treated as the King Himself': Does the Worship of Jesus Imply His Divinity?." Pages 97–114 in *In the Fullness of Time: Essays on Christology, Creation, and Eschatology in Honor of Richard Bauckham.* Edited by Gurtner, Macaskill and Pennington. Grand Rapids: Eerdmans, 2016.

Allison, Dale C. "Acts 9:1–9, 22:6–11, 26:12–18: Paul and Ezekiel" *JBL* 135.4 (2016): 807–26.

Amir, Yehoshua. "Die Begegnung des biblischen und des philosophischen Monotheismus als Grundthema des jüdischen Hellenismus" *EvT* 38 (1978): 2–19.

Andersen, F. I. "2 (Slavonic Apocalypse of) Enoch" in *The Old Testament Pseudepigrapha*. Edited by James H. Charlesworth. 2 vols. Peabody: Hendrickson, 1983.

Anderson, Gary A. "The Exaltation of Adam and the Fall of Satan." Pages 83–110 in *Literature on Adam and Eve: Collected Essays*. Edited by Gary A. Anderson, Michael E. Stone and Johannes Tromp. SVTP 15. Leiden: Brill, 2000.

———. "The Penitence Narrative in the Life of Adam and Eve." Pages 1–42 in *Literature on Adam and Eve: Collected Essays*. Edited by Gary Anderson, Michael Stone and Johannes Tromp. Leiden: Brill, 2000.

———. *The Genesis of Perfection: Adam and Eve in Jewish and Christian Imagination*. Louisville: Westminster John Knox, 2001.

———. "Adam and Eve in the 'Life of Adam and Eve'." Pages 7–32 in *Biblical Figures Outside the Bible*. Edited by Michael E. Stone and Theodore A. Bergren. Harrisburg: Trinity, 2002.

Arnold, Clinton E. *The Colossian Syncretism: The Interface between Christianity and Folk Belief at Colossae*. Grand Rapids: Baker, 1996.

Athanassiadi, Polymnia, and Michael Frede, eds. *Pagan Monotheism in Late Antiquity*, repr. Oxford: OUP, 2008 (1999).

Avemarie, Friedrich. "Image of God and Image of Christ: Developments in Pauline and Ancient Jewish Anthropology." Pages 209–36 in *The Dead Sea Scrolls and Pauline Literature*. Edited by Jean-Sébastien Rey. Leiden: Brill, 2013.

Back, Frances. *Verwandlung durch Offenbarung bei Paulus: eine religionsgeschichtlich- exegetische Untersuchung zu 2 Kor 2,14–4,6*. Tübingen: Mohr Siebeck, 2002.

Bakon, Shimon. "Creation, Tabernacle and Sabbath" *JBQ* 25 (1997): 79–85.

Balz, Horst R. *Heilsvertrauen und Welterfahrung: Strukturen der paulinischen Eschatologie nach Römer 8,18–39*. München: Chr. Kaiser, 1971.

Barclay, John M. G. *Jews in the Mediterranean Diaspora: From Alexander to Trajan (323 BCE–117 CE)*. Edinburgh: T & T Clark, 1996.

———. *Pauline Churches and Diaspora Jews*. Grand Rapids: Eerdmans, 2011.

———. "Paul and the Faithfulness of God" *SJT* 68.2 (2015): 235–43.

———. *Paul and the Gift*. Grand Rapids: Eerdmans, 2015.

Barker, Margaret. *The Great Angel: A Study of Israel's Second God*. London: SPCK, 1992.

———. *The Risen Lord: The Jesus of History as the Christ of Faith*. Edinburgh: T & T Clark, 1996.

———. "The High Priest and the Worship of Jesus." Chapter 5 in *The Jewish Roots of Christological Monotheism*. Edited by Carey C. Newman, James R. Davila and Gladys S. Lewis. LEC. Waco: Baylor University Press, 2017 (1999).

———. *The Great High Priest: The Temple Roots of Christian Liturgy*. London: T & T Clark, 2003.

Bauckham, Richard. "The Worship of Jesus in Apocalyptic Christianity" *NTS* 27.3 (1981): 322–41.

———. *Jesus and the God of Israel: "God Crucified" and Other Studies on the New Testament's Christology of Divine Identity*. Milton Keynes, UK: Paternoster, 2008.

———. "Devotion to Jesus Christ in Earliest Christianity: An Appraisal and Discussion of the Work of Larry Hurtado." Pages 176–200 in *Mark, Manuscripts, and Monotheism: Essays in Honor of Larry W. Hurtado*. Edited by Chris Keith and Dieter T. Roth. London: Bloomsbury, 2014.

Beard, M., J. North and S. Price. *Religions of Rome*. 2 vols. Cambridge: CUP, 1998.

Beker, J. C. *Paul the Apostle: The Triumph of God in Life and Thought*. Philadelphia: Fortress, 1980.

Becking, Bob, Meindert Dijkstra, Marjo C. A. Korpel and Karel J. H. Vriezen, eds. *Only One God? Monotheism in Ancient Israel and the Veneration of the Goddess Asherath*. New York: Sheffield Academic Press, 2001.

Beetham, Christopher A. *Echoes of Scripture in the Letter of Paul to the Colossians*. Leiden: Brill, 2008.

Belleville, Linda L. *Reflections of Glory: Paul's Polemical Use of the Moses-Doxa Tradition in 2 Corinthians 3.1–18*. JSNTSup 52. Sheffield: SAP, 1992.

Benoit, P. "L'hymne christologique de Col i,15–20. Jugement critique sue l'état des recherches." Pages 226–63 in *Judaism, Christianity and Other Greco-Roman Cults: Studies for Morton Smith at Sixty*. Edited by J. Neusner. Vol. 1. Leiden: E. J. Brill, 1975.

Berger, Peter, and Thomas Luckmann. *The Social Construction of Reality: A Treatise in the Sociology of Knowledge*. Garden City: Doubleday, 1966.

Bernett, Monika. *Der Kaiserkult in Judäa unter den Herodiern und Römern: Untersuchungen zur politischen und religiösen Geschichte Judäas von 30 v. bis 66 n. Chr*. Tübingen: Mohr Siebeck, 2007.

Betz, Hans Dieter. "The Concept of the 'Inner Human Being' (ὁ ἔσω ἄνθρωπος) in the Anthropology of Paul" *NTS* 46.3 (2000): 315–41.

Bindemann, Walther. *Die Hoffnung der Schöpfung: Römer 8,18–27 und die Frage einer Theologie der Befreiung von Mensch und Natur*. Neukirchen-Vluyn: Neukirchener, 1983.

Blackwell, Ben C. "Immortal Glory and the Problem of Death in Romans 3.23" *JSNT* 32.3 (2010): 285–308.

———. *Christosis: Engaging Paul's Soteriology with his Patristic Interpreters*. Grand Rapids: Eerdmans, 2016 (2011).

Boccaccini, Gabriele. *Enoch and the Messiah Son of Man: Revisiting the Book of Parables*. Grand Rapids: Eerdmans, 2007.

Bohak, G. *Ancient Jewish Magic: A History*. Cambridge: CUP, 2008.

Borgen, Peder. "Philo of Alexandria: A Critical and Synthetical Survey of Research Since World War II" *ANRW* 21.1 (1984): 98–154.

Bornkamm, Günther. "The Heresy of Colossians." Pages 123–47 in *Conflict at Colossae*. Edited by F. Francis and W. Meeks. SBLSBS 4. Missoula: Scholars, 1973.

Bousset, Wilhelm. *Kyrios Christos: A History of the Belief in Christ from the Beginnings of Christianity to Irenaeus*. A new introduction by Larry W. Hurtado. Trans. J. E. Steely. Waco: Baylor University Press, 2013 (1913).

Bowie, Ewan. "Second Sophistic." Pages 1337–8 in *The Oxford Classical Dictionary*. Edited by Simon Hornblower, Antony Spawforth and Esther Eidenow. 4th edn. Oxford: OUP, 2012 (1968).

Boyarin, Daniel. *Border Lines: The Partition of Judaeo-Christianity*. DRLAR. Philadelphia: University of Pennsylvania Press, 2004.

———. "Two Powers in Heaven; or, the Making of a Heresy." Pages 331–70 in *The Idea of Biblical Interpretation: Essays in Honor of James L. Kugel*. Edited by H. Najman and J. Newman. JSJSup 83. Leiden: Brill, 2004.

———. "Beyond Judaisms: Metatron and the Divine Polymorphy of Ancient Judaism" *JSJ* 41 (2010): 323–65.

Bréhier, Emile. *Les ides philosophique et religieuses de Philon d'Alexandrie*. 3rd edn. EPM 8. Paris: Vrin, 1950.

Briones, David E. *Paul's Financial Policy: A Socio-Theological Approach*. LNTS 494. New York: Bloomsbury T & T Clark, 2013.

Brooke, George J. "Biblical Interpretation in the Wisdom Texts from Qumran." Pages 201–20 in *The Wisdom Texts from Qumran and the Development of Sapiential Thought: Studies in the Wisdom at Qumran and Its Relationship to Sapiential Thought in the Ancient Near East, the Hebrew Bible, Ancient Judaism and the New Testament*. Edited by Hempel, Lange & Lichtenberger. BETL 159. Louvain: Peeters, 2001.

Brookins, Timothy A. *Corinthian Wisdom, Stoic Philosophy, and the Ancient Economy*, SNTS 159. Cambridge: CUP, 2014.

———. "A Tense Discussion: Rethinking the Grammaticalization of Time in Greek Indicative Verbs" *JBL* 137.1 (2018): 147–68.

Bryan, Steven M. "The End of Exile: The Reception of Jeremiah's Prediction of a Seventy-Year Exile" *JBL* 137.1 (2018): 107–26.

Bujard, Walter. *Stilanalytische Untersuchungen zum Kolosserbrief als Beitrag zur Methodik von Sprachvergleichen*, SUNT 11. Göttingen: Vandenhoeck & Ruprecht, 1973.

Bultmann, Rudolf. *Theology of the New Testament*. Trans. K. Grobel. 2 vols. Waco: Baylor University Press, 2007 (1951, 1955).

Burkert, W. "Towards Plato and Paul: The 'Inner' Human Being." Pages 59–82 in *Ancient and Modern Perspectives on the Bible and Culture: Essays in Honor of Hans Dieter Betz*. Edited by Adela Y. Collins. Atlanta: Scholars Press, 1998.

Burney, C. F. "Christ as the APXH of Creation" *JTS* 27 (1925): 160–77.

Byrne, B. *"Sons of God"—"Seed of Abraham": A Study of the Idea of the Sonship of God of All Christians in Paul against the Jewish Background*. Analecta Biblica 83. Rome: Pontifical Biblical Institute Press, 1979.

Cadwallader, H., and Michael Trainor, eds. *Colossae in Space and Time: Linking to an Ancient City*. NTOA 94. Göttingen: Vandenhoeck & Ruprecht, 2011.

Campbell, Douglas. *Framing Paul: An Epistolary Biography*. Grand Rapids: Eerdmans, 2014.

Capes, David B. *Old Testament Yahweh Texts in Paul's Christology*, LEC. Waco: Baylor University Press, 2017 (1992).

Capes, David B., April D. DeConick, Helen K. Bond and Troy Miller, eds. *Israel's God and Rebecca's Children: Christology and Community in Early Judaism and*

Christianity: Essays in Honor of Larry W. Hurtado and Alan F. Segal. Waco: Baylor University Press, 2007.

Carrez, Maurice. *De la Souffrance à la Gloire: De la Δοξα dans la Pensée paulienne.* Neuchâtel: Delachaux & Niestlé, 1964.

Casey, P. M. "Monotheism, Worship and Christological Development in the Pauline Churches." Chapter 12 in *The Jewish Roots of Christological Monotheism.* Edited by Carey C. Newman, James R. Davila and Gladys Lewis. LEC. Waco: Baylor University Press, 2017 (1999).

⸻. "Method in our Madness, and Madness in their Methods: Some Approaches to the Son of Man in Recent Scholarship." Pages 97–116 in *The Son of Man Problem: Critical Readings.* Edited by Benjamin E. Reynolds. CRBS. London/New York: Bloomsbury T & T Clark, 2018.

Charlesworth, James H. "Prayer of Jacob." Pages 2.715–23 in *The Old Testament Pseudepigrapha.* Edited by James H. Charlesworth. 2 vols. Peabody: Hendrickson, 1983.

⸻. "From Messianology to Christology: Problems and Prospects." Pages 3–35 in *The Messiah: Developments in Earliest Judaism and Christianity.* Edited by James H. Charlesworth. Minneapolis: Fortress, 1992.

⸻. "Wright's Paradigm of Early Jewish Thought: Avoidance of Anachronisms?." Pages 207–34 in *God and the Faithfulness of Paul: A Critical Examination of the Pauline Theology of N. T. Wright.* Edited by Christoph Heilig, J. Thomas Hewitt and Michael F. Bird. WUNT 2.413. Tübingen: Mohr Siebeck, 2016.

Chazon, E. G. "Hymns and Prayers in the Dead Sea Scrolls." Pages 244–70 in *The Dead Sea Scrolls After Fifty Years: A Comprehensive Assessment.* Edited by Peter W. Flint and James C. VanderKam. Leiden: Brill, 1998.

Chester, Andrew. *Messiah and Exaltation: Jewish Messianic and Visionary Traditions and New Testament Christology.* WUNT 207. Tübingen: Mohr Siebeck, 2007.

⸻. "High Christology—Whence, When and Why?" *Early Christianity* 2 (2011): 22–50.

Christiansen, Ellen Juhl. *The Covenant in Judaism and Paul: A Study of Ritual Boundaries as Identity Markers.* AGJU 27. Leiden: Brill, 1995.

Clifford, Richard. *Creation Accounts in the Ancient Near East and in the Bible.* CBQMS. Washington, DC: The Catholic Biblical Association of America, 1994.

Clines, D. J. A. "The Image of God in Man" *TB* 19 (1968): 53–103.

Cohen, B. "Note on Letter and Spirit in the New Testament" *HTR* 47 (1954): 197–203.

Cohen, Samuel S. "The Unity of God: A Study in Hellenistic and Rabbinic Theology" *HUCA* 26 (1955): 425–79.

Collange, J. F. *Énigmes de la deuxième épître de Paul aux Corinthiens: Etude exégétique de 2 Cor. 2.14–7:4.* SNTSMS 18. Cambridge: CUP, 1972.

Collins, Adela Yarbro. "The Worship of Jesus and the Imperial Cult." Chapter 13 in *The Jewish Roots of Christological Monotheism.* Edited by Carey C. Newman, James R. Davila and Gladys S. Lewis. LEC. Waco: Baylor University Press, 2017 (1999).

Collins, Adela Yarbro, and John J. Collins. *King and Messiah as Son of God: Divine, Human, and Angelic Messianic Figures in Biblical and Related Literature.* Grand Rapids: Eerdmans, 2008.

Collins, John J. *The Apocalyptic Vision of the Book of Daniel*. Missoula: Scholars, 1977.

———. "Sibylline Oracles" in *The Old Testament Pseudepigrapha*. Edited by James H. Charlesworth. 2 vols. Peabody: Hendrickson, 1983.

———. *The Scepter and the Star: The Messiahs of the Dead Sea Scrolls and Other Ancient Literature*. New York: Doubleday, 1995.

———. *Jewish Wisdom in the Hellenistic Age*. OTL. Louisville, KY: Westminster John Knox Press, 1997.

———. "In the Likeness of the Holy Ones: The Creation of Humankind in a Wisdom Text from Qumran." Pages 609–18 in *The Provo International Conference on the Dead Sea Scrolls: Technological Innovations, New Texts, and Reformulated Issues*. Edited by D. W. Parry and E. C. Ulrich. STDJ 30. Leiden: Brill, 1999.

———. *Beyond the Qumran Community: The Sectarian Movement of the Dead Sea Scrolls*. Grand Rapids: Eerdmans, 2010.

Colpe, C. *The religionsgeschichtliche Schule*. FRLANT 87. Göttingen: 1961.

Copenhaver, Adam K. *Reconstructing the Historical Background of Paul's Rhetoric in the Letter to the Colossians*. LNTS. New York/London: Bloomsbury T & T Clark, 2018.

Cover, Michael. *Lifting the Veil: 2 Corinthians 3:7–18 in Light of Jewish Homiletic and Commentary Traditions*. BZNW 210. Berlin: de Gruyter, 2015.

Cox, Ronald. *By the Same Word: Creation and Salvation in Hellenistic Judaism and Early Christianity*. BZNW 145. Berlin: de Gruyter, 2007.

Cremer, A. Hermann. *Die Paulinische Rechtfertigungslehre*. Gütersloh: Bertelsmann, 1900.

Crenshaw, J. L. *Old Testament Wisdom: An Introduction*. Atlanta: John Knox Press, 1981.

Curtis, Edward M. *Man as the Image of God in Genesis in the Light of Ancient Near Eastern Parallels*. Ann Arbor: University of Michigan Microfilms International, 1984.

———. "Image of God" in *The Anchor Bible Dictionary*. Edited by David Noel Freedman. 6 vols. Yale: YUP, 1992.

Dalton, W. J. "Is the Old Covenant Abrogated (2 Cor 3.14)?" *ABR* 35 (1987): 88–94.

Daniélou, J. *Philon d'Alexandrie*. Paris: Fayard, 1958.

Davidson, Maxwell J. *Angels at Qumran: A Comparative Study of 1 Enoch 1–36, 72–108 and Sectarian Writings from Qumran*, JSPSup 11. Sheffield: JSOT, 1992.

Davies, W. D. *Paul and Rabbinic Judaism*. 4th edn. Philadelphia: Fortress, 1980 (1948).

Davila, James D. *The Provenance of the Pseudepigrapha: Jewish, Christian, or Other?* JSJSup 105. Leiden: Brill, 2005.

Day, John, ed. *King and Messiah in Israel and the Ancient Near East: Proceedings of the Oxford Old Testament Seminar*. JSOTSup 270. Sheffield: SAP, 1998.

Day, John. *Yahweh and the Gods and Goddesses of Canaan*. JSOTSup 265. Sheffield: SAP, 2000.

———. *From Creation to Babel: Studies in Genesis 1—11*. New York: Bloomsbury, 2013.

Deissmann, Gustav Adolf. *Light from the Ancient East: The New Testament Illustrated by Recently Discovered Texts of the Graeco-Roman World.* London: Hodder & Stoughton, 1927.
DeMaris, R. E. *The Colossian Controversy.* WUNT 2.77. Tübingen: J. C. B. Mohr, 1995.
Dibelius, Martin. "The Isis Initiation in Apuleius and Related Initiatory Rites." Pages 61–126 in *Conflict at Colossae*. Edited by F. Francis and W. Meeks. SBLSBS 4. Missoula: Scholars, 1973.
Dick, Michael B., ed. *Born in Heaven, Made on Earth: The Making of the Cultic Image in the Ancient Near East.* Winona Lake: Eisenbrauns, 1999.
Dietzfelbinger, Christian. *Die Berufung des Paulus als Ursprung seiner Theologie.* WMANT 58. Neukirchen-Vluyn: Neukirchener Verlag, 1985.
Dijkstra, Meindert. "I Have Blessed you by YHWH of Samaria and his Asherah: Texts with Religious Elements from the Soil Archive of Ancient Israel." Pages 17–44 in *Only One God? Monotheism in Ancient Israel and the Veneration of the Goddess Asherath*. Edited by Bob Becking, Meindert Dijkstra, Marjo C. A. Korpel and Karel J. H. Vriezen. New York: Sheffield Academic Press, 2001.
Dillon, John. *The Middle Platonists: 80 B.C. to A.D. 220.* Rev. edn. Ithaca, NY: Cornell University Press, 1996 (1977).
———. *Alcinous: The Handbook of Platonism: Translated with an Introduction and Commentary.* Repr. Oxford: Clarendon Press, 2002 (1993).
Dimant, Devorah. "Men as Angels: The Self-Image of the Qumran Community." Pages 93–103 in *Religion and Politics in the Ancient Near East*. Edited by A. Berlin. STJHC. Potomac: University Press of Maryland, 1996.
Donaldson, Terence L. *Judaism and the Gentiles: Jewish Patterns of Universalism (to 135 CE).* Waco: Baylor University Press, 2008.
Dozeman, Thomas B., Konrad Schmid and Baruch J. Schwartz, eds. *The Pentateuch: International Perspectives on Current Research.* FAT 78. Tübingen: Mohr Siebeck, 2011.
Duff, Paul B. *Moses in Corinth: The Apologetic Context of 2 Corinthians 3.* NovTestSup 159. Leiden: Brill, 2015.
Dülmen, A. van. *Die Theologie des Gesetzes bei Paulus.* Stuttgarter biblische Monographien 5. Stuttgart: Katholisches Bibelwerk, 1968.Dunn, J. D. G. "2 Corinthians III. 17—'The Lord is the Spirit'" *JTS* 21 (1970): 309–20.
———. *Christology in the Making: A New Testament Inquiry into the Origins of the Doctrine of the Incarnation*, 2nd edn. Grand Rapids: Eerdmans, 1996 (1980).
———. *The Parting of the Ways between Christianity and Judaism and their Significance for the Character of Christianity*, 2nd edn. London: SCM, 2006 (1991).
———. "The Colossian Philosophy: A Confident Jewish Apologia" *Biblica* 76 (1995): 153–81.
———. *The Theology of Paul the Apostle.* Edinburgh: T & T Clark, 1998.
———. *Did the First Christians Worship Jesus? The New Testament Evidence.* London: SPCK, 2010.
Dupont, Jacques. "Le Chrétien, Miroir de la Gloire divine d'après II Cor. III, 18" *RB* 56 (1949): 392–411.

Eco, Umberto. *A Theory of Semiotics*. Indiana: IUP, 1976.

Edsall, Benjamin, and Jennifer Strawbridge, "The Songs We Used to Sing? Hymn 'Traditions' and Reception in Pauline Letters" *JSNT* 37.3 (2015): 290–311.

Ehrman, Bart D. *How Jesus Became God*. New York: HarperCollins, 2014.

Elder, Nicholas. "'Wretch I Am!' Eve's Tragic Speech-in-Character in Romans 7:7–25" *JBL* 137.3 (2018): 743–63.

Eldridge, Michael D. *Dying Adam with His Multiethnic Family: Understanding the Greek Life of Adam and Eve*. SVTP 16. Leiden: Brill, 2001.

Elgvin, T. "The Mystery to Come: Early Essene Theology of Revelation." Pages 113–50 in *Qumran between the Old and New Testaments*. Edited by Cryer & Thompson. JSOTSup 290. Sheffield: SAP, 1998.

Ellis, E. E. *The Old Testament in Early Christianity*. Grand Rapids: Baker, 1992.

Elnes, Eric E. "Creation and Tabernacle: The Priestly Writer's 'Environmentalism'" *HBT* 16 (1994): 144–55.

Eltester, Friedrich-Wilhelm. *Eikon im Neuen Testament*. BZNW 23. Berlin: 1958.

Enermalm-Ogawa, A. *Un langage de prière juif en grec: Le témoignage des deux premiers livres des Maccabées*. ConBNT 17. Uppsala: Almquist & Wiksell, 1987.

Engberg-Pedersen, Troels, ed. *Paul Beyond the Judaism/Hellenism Divide*. Louisville: Westminster John Knox Press, 2001.

———. *From Stoicism to Platonism: The Development of Philosophy 100 BCE—100 CE*. Cambridge: CUP, 2017.

Engberg-Pedersen, Troels. *Paul and the Stoics*. Edinburgh: T & T Clark, 2000.

———. "The Reception of Graeco-Roman Culture in the New Testament: The Case of Romans 7:7–25." Pages 32–57 in *The New Testament as Reception*. Edited by M. Müller and H. Tronier. JSNTSup 230. CIS 11. Sheffield: SAP, 2002.

———.*Cosmology and Self in the Apostle Paul: The Material Spirit*. Oxford: OUP, 2010.

———. "Setting the Scene: Stoicism and Platonism in the Transitional Period in Ancient Philosophy." Pages 1–15 in *Stoicism in Early Christianity*. Edited by Tuomas Rasimus, Troels Engberg-Pedersen, and Ismo Dunderberg. Grand Rapids: Baker, 2010.

Eskola, Timo. *Messiah and the Throne: Jewish Merkabah Mysticism and Early Christian Exaltation Discourse*. WUNT 2.142. Tübingen: Mohr Siebeck, 2001.

Esler, Philip F. "Giving the Kingdom to an *Ethnos* That Will Bear Its Fruit: Ethnic and Christ-Movement Identities in Matthew." Pages 177–96 in *In the Fullness of Time: Essays on Christology, Creation, and Eschatology in Honor of Richard Bauckham*. Edited by Gurtner, Macaskill and Pennington. Grand Rapids: Eerdmans, 2016.

Evans, Craig A. "The Colossian Mystics" *Biblica* 63 (1982): 188–205.

———. "Listening for Echoes of Interpreted Scripture." Pages 47–51 in *Paul and the Scriptures of Israel*. Edited by Craig A. Evans and James A. Sanders. BSEC. New York/ London: Bloomsbury, 2015 (1993).

Evans, Craig A., and James A. Sanders, eds. *Paul and the Scriptures of Israel*. BSEC. New York/ London: Bloomsbury, 2015 (1993).

Falk, D. K. *Daily, Sabbath, and Festival Prayers in the Dead Sea Scrolls*. Leiden: Brill, 1998.

Fantin, Joseph. *The Lord of the Entire World*. NT 31. Sheffield: Sheffield Phoenix Press, 2011.

Fee, Gordon D. "Philippians 2:5–11: Hymn or Exalted Pauline Prose" *BBR* 2 (1992): 29–46.

———. *Pauline Christology: An Exegetical-Theological Study*. Peabody: Hendrickson, 2007.

Feullet, A. "La Création de L'Univers 'dans le Christ' D'après L'Epître Aux Colossiens (i.16a)" *NTS* 12 (1965): 1–9.

———. "L'Hymne Christologique de l'épître aux Philippiens (ii:6–11)" *RB* 72 (1965): 352–80, 481–507.

———. *Le Christ Sagesse de Dieu d'après les épîtres pauliniennes*. Paris, 1966.

———. *Christologie Paulinienne et Tradition Biblique*. Paris: Desclee de Brouwer, 1972.

Fiensy, D. A. "Hellenistic Synagogal Prayers" in *The Old Testament Pseudepigrapha*. Edited by James H. Charlesworth. 2 vols. Peabody: Hendrickson, 1983.

Firmage, E. B. "Genesis 1 and the Priestly Agenda" *JSOT* 82 (1999): 97–114.

Fitzmyer, Joseph A. "Glory Reflected on the Face of Christ (2 Cor. 3.7–4.6) and a Palestinian Jewish Motif" *TS* 42 (1981): 630–44.

Fletcher-Louis, Crispin H. T. *Luke-Acts: Angels, Christology and Soteriology*. WUNT 2.94. Tübingen: Mohr Siebeck, 1997.

———. "The High Priest as Divine Mediator in the Hebrew Bible: Daniel 7:13 as a Test Case" *SBLSP* (1997): 161–93.

———. "The Worship of Divine Humanity and the Worship of Jesus." Chapter 6 in *The Jewish Roots of Christological Monotheism*. Edited by Carey C. Newman, James R. Davila and Gladys Lewis. LEC. Waco: Baylor University Press, 2017 (1999).

———. *All the Glory of Adam: Liturgical Anthropology in the Dead Sea Scrolls*. STDJ 42. Leiden: Brill, 2002.

———. "The Temple Cosmology of P and Theological Anthropology in the Wisdom of Jesus ben Sira." Pages 69–113 in *Of Scribes and Sages: Early Jewish Interpretation and Transmission of Scripture*. Edited by Craig A. Evans. LSTS 50. SSEJC 9. Sheffield, UK: Sheffield Academic Press, 2004.

———. "The Worship of the Jewish High Priest by Alexander the Great." Pages 71–102 in *Early Christian and Jewish Monotheism*. Edited by Loren T. Stuckenbruck and Wendy E. S. North. JSNTSup 263. London: Continuum, 2004.

———. "Jesus as the High Priestly Messiah: Part 1" *JSHJ* 4 (2006): 155–175.

———. "Jesus as the High Priestly Messiah: Part 2" *JSHJ* 5 (2007): 57–79.

———. "Jewish Apocalyptic and Apocalypticism." Pages 1569–607 in *Handbook for the Study of the Historical Jesus*. Edited by Tom Holmén and Stanley E. Porter. Leiden: Brill, 2011.

———. "The Similitudes of Enoch (1 Enoch 37–71): The Son of Man, Apocalyptic Messianism & Political Theology." Pages 58–79 in *The Open Mind: Essays in Honour of Christopher Rowland*. Edited by Jonathan Knight and Kevin Sullivan. London: T & T Clark, 2014.

———. *Jesus Monotheism: Volume I—Christological Origins: The Emerging Consensus and Beyond*. Eugene: Cascade Books, 2015.

Fossum, Jarl E. *The Name of God and the Angel of the Lord: Samaritan and Jewish Concepts of Intermediation and the Origin of Gnosticism.* LEC. Waco: Baylor University Press, 2017 (1985).

———. "The New *Religionsgeschichtliche Schule*: The Quest for Jewish Christology." Pages 638–46 in *SBLSP* 1991. Edited by E. Lovering. Atlanta: Scholars, 1991.

———. *The Image of the Invisible God: Essays on the Influence of Jewish Mysticism on Early Christology.* NTOA 30. Göttingen: Vandenhoeck & Ruprecht, 1995.

Foster, Paul. "Echoes without Resonance: Critiquing Certain Aspects of Recent Scholarly Trends in the Study of the Jewish Scriptures in the New Testament" *JSNT* 38.1 (2015): 96–111.

Francis, Fred O. "Humility and Angelic Worship in Col 2:18" *ST* 16 (1963): 109–34.

———. "The Background of Εμβατευων (Col 2:18) in Legal Papyri and Oracle Inscriptions." Pages 197–207 in *Conflict at Colossae.* Edited by F. Francis and W. Meeks. SBLSBS 4. Missoula: Scholars, 1973.

Fraser, P. M. *Ptolemaic Alexandria.* 3 vols. Oxford: Clarendon Press, 1972.

Frede, Michael. "Epilogue." Pages 771–97 in *The Cambridge History of Hellenistic Philosophy.* Edited by Keimpe Algra, Jonathan Barnes, Jaap Mansfeld and Malcolm Schofield. Cambridge: CUP, 2005.

Fredriksen, Paula. "Mandatory Retirement: Ideas in the Study of Christian Origins Whose Time Has Come to Go." Pages 25–38 in *Israel's God and Rebecca's Children: Christology and Community in Early Judaism and Christianity.* Edited by David B. Capes, April D. DeConick, Helen K. Bond and Troy Miller. Waco: Baylor University Press, 2007.

———.. "Judaizing the Nations: The Ritual Demands of Paul's Gospel" *NTS* 56 (2010): 232–52.

Frey, Jörg. "Eine neue religionsgeschichtliche Perspektive: Larry W. Hurtados *Lord Jesus Christ* und die Herausbildung der frühen Christologie." Pages 117–69 in *Reflections on the Early Christian History of Religion. Erwägungen zur frühchristlichen Religionsgeschichte.* Edited by Cilliers Breytenbach and Jörg Frey. AJEC 81. Leiden: Brill, 2013.

Gamble, Harry Y. *Books and Readers in the Early Church: A History of Early Christian Texts.* New Haven: YUP, 1995.

Garr, W. Randall. *In His Own Image and Likeness: Humanity, Divinity, and Monotheism.* CHANE 15. Leiden: Brill, 2003.

Geertz, Clifford. *The Interpretation of Cultures.* New York: Basic Books, 2000 (1973).

Geffcken, J. *Komposition und Entstehungszeit der Oracula Sibyllina.* repr. TU 23. NF 8.1. Leipzig: 1967 (1902).

Georgi, Dieter. *The Opponents of Paul in Second Corinthians.* Trans. H. Attridge et al. Philadelphia: Fortress, 1986 (1964).

Gertz, Jan Christian. "The Partial Compositions." Trans. P. Altmann. Pages 293–382 in *T & T Clark Handbook of the Old Testament: An Introduction to the Literature, Religion and History of the Old Testament.* Edited by Jan Christian Gertz, Angelika Berlejung, Konrad Schmid and Markus Witte. New York: T & T Clark, 2012 (2008).

Gieschen, Charles A. *Angelmorphic Christology: Antecedents and Early Evidence*. LEC. Waco: Baylor University Press, 2017 (1995).

Gnuse, Robert K. *No Other Gods: Emergent Monotheism in Israel*. JSOTSup 241. Sheffield: SAP, 1997.

Goff, M. J. *The Worldly and Heavenly Wisdom of 4QInstruction*. STDJ 50. Leiden: Brill, 2003.

Goodenough, E. R. *By Light, Light*. New Haven: YUP, 1935.

Gooder, Paula. *Only the Third Heaven? 2 Corinthians 12:1–10 and Heavenly Ascent*. LNTS 313. London: T & T Clark, 2006.

Goodrich, John K. "Sold under Sin: Echoes of Exile in Romans 7.14–25" *NTS* 59.4 (2013): 476–95.

Gordley, Matthew E. *The Colossian Hymn in Context: An Exegesis in Light of Jewish and Greco-Roman Hymnic and Epistolary Conventions*. WUNT 2.228. Tübingen: Mohr Siebeck, 2007.

———. *New Testament Christological Hymns: Exploring Texts, Contexts, and Significance*. Downers Grove: IVP, 2018.

Gorman, Michael J. *Cruciformity: Paul's Narrative Spirituality of the Cross*. Grand Rapids: Eerdmans, 2001.

———. *Inhabiting the Cruciform God: Kenosis, Justification, and Theosis in Paul's Narrative Soteriology*. Grand Rapids: Eerdmans, 2009.

Goulder, Michael D. "ΣΟΦΙΑ in 1 Corinthians" *NTS* 37.4 (1991): 516–34.

Grabbe, Lester L. *An Introduction to First Century Judaism: Jewish Religion and History in the Second Temple Period*. Edinburgh: T & T Clark, 1996.

———. *Judaic Religion in the Second Temple Period: Belief and Practice from the Exile to Yavneh*. London: Routledge, 2000.

———. *A History of the Jews and Judaism in the Second Temple Period (vol. 1): Yehud: A History of the Persian Province of Judah*. LSTS 47. London: T & T Clark, 2004.

Green, Joel B. "Paul's Anthropology in Context: the Image of God, Assimilation to God and Tripartite Man in Ancient Judaism, Ancient Philosophy and Early Christianity" *RBL* 1 (2011).

———. "Why the *Imago Dei* Should Not Be Identified with the Soul." Pages 179–90 in *Theological Anthropology*. Edited by Joshua R. Farris and Charles Taliaferro. ARCTA. Surrey: Ashgate Publishing, 2015.

Green, Thomas. *The Light in Troy: Imitation and Discovery in Renaissance Poetry*. New Haven: YUP, 1982.

Green, William Scott. "Introduction: Messiah in Judaism: Rethinking the Question." Pages 1–13 in *Judaisms and Their Messiahs at the Turn of the Christian Era*. Edited by Jacob Neusner, William Scott Green and Ernest Frerichs. Cambridge: CUP, 1987.

Grindheim, Sigurd. *The Crux of Election: Paul's Critique of the Jewish Confidence in the Election of Israel*. WUNT 2.202. Tübingen: Mohr Siebeck, 2005.

———. "Election and the Role of Israel." Pages 329–46 in *God and the Faithfulness of Paul: A Critical Examination of the Pauline Theology of N. T. Wright*. Edited by Christoph Heilig, J. Thomas Hewitt and Michael F. Bird. WUNT 2.413. Tübingen: Mohr Siebeck, 2016.

Gross, W. "Gottebenbildlichkeit des Menschen im Kontext der Priesterschrift" *ThQ* 161 (1981): 244–64.

———. "Die Gottebenbildlichkeit des Menschen nach Gen 1,26.27 in der Diskussion des letzten Jahrzehnts" *BN* 68 (1993): 35–48.

Gruber, M. M. *Herrlichkeit im Schwachheit: Eine Auslegung der Apologie des Zweiten Korintherbriefs: 2 Kor 2,14–6,13*. FB. Würzburg: Echter, 1998.

Gurtner, Daniel M., Grant Macaskill and Jonathan T. Pennington, eds. *In the Fullness of Time: Essays on Christology, Creation, and Eschatology in Honor of Richard Bauckham*. Grand Rapids: Eerdmans, 2016.

Habermann, Jürgen. *Präexistenzsaussagen im Neuen Testament*. Frankfurt am Main: Lang, 1990.

Hafemann, Scott J. *Suffering and Ministry in the Spirit: Paul's Defense of His Ministry in 2 Corinthians 2:14—3:3*. Grand Rapids: Eerdmans, 1990.

———. "'Self-Commendation' and Apostolic Legitimacy in 2 Corinthians: A Pauline Dialectic?" *NTS* 36 (1990): 66–88.

———. *Paul, Moses, and the History of Israel: The Letter/Spirit Contrast and the Argument from Scripture in 2 Corinthians 3*. Peabody: Hendrickson, 1996.

Hahne, Harry. *The Corruption and Redemption of Creation*. LNTS 336. New York: T & T Clark, 2006.

Halvorson, Martien A. *Enduring Exile: The Metaphorization of Exile in the Hebrew Bible*. VTSup 141. Leiden: Brill, 2011.

Hannah, Darrell D. *Michael and Christ: Michael Traditions and Angel Christology in Early Christianity*. WUNT 2.109. Tübingen: Mohr Siebeck, 1999.

Harrington, D. J. "Pseudo-Philo" in *The Old Testament Pseudepigrapha*. Edited by James H. Charlesworth. 2 vols. Peabody: Hendrickson, 1983.

Hartman, Lars. *"Into the Name of the Lord Jesus": Baptism in the Early Church*. SNTW. Edinburgh: T & T Clark, 1997.

Hay, David M. *Glory at the Right Hand: Psalm 110 in Early Christianity*. SBLMS. Atlanta: Scholars Press, 1973.

Hayman, Peter, "Monotheism—A Misused Word in Jewish Studies?" *JJS* 42 (1991): 1–15.

Hays, Richard B. *The Faith of Jesus Christ: The Narrative Substructure of Galatians 3.1–4.11*. 2nd edn. Grand Rapids: Eerdmans, 2002 (1983).

———. *Echoes of Scripture in the Letters of Paul*. New Haven: YUP, 1989.

———. *Echoes of Scripture in the Gospels*. Waco: Baylor University Press, 2016.

Hayward, C. T. R. *The Jewish Temple: A Non-Biblical Sourcebook*. London: Routledge, 1996.

Heckel, Theo K. *Der innere Mensch: Die Paulinische Verarbeitung eines Platonischen Motivs*. WUNT 2.53. Tübingen: Mohr Siebeck, 1993.

Hegermann, H. *Die Vorstellung vom Schöpfungsmittler im hellenistischen Judentum und Urchristentum*. TU 82. Berlin: Akademie-Verlag, 1961.

Heilig, Christoph, J. Thomas Hewitt and Michael F. Bird, eds. *God and the Faithfulness of Paul: A Critical Examination of the Pauline Theology of N. T. Wright*. WUNT 2.413. Tübingen: Mohr Siebeck, 2016.

Heiser, Michael S. "The Divine Council in Late Canonical and Non-Canonical Second Temple Jewish Literature." PhD Diss., University of Wisconsin-Madison, 2004.

———. "Monotheism, Polytheism, Monolatry, or Henotheism? Toward an Assessment of Divine Plurality in the Hebrew Bible" *BBR* 18 (2008): 1–30.

Hengel, Martin. *Judaism and Hellenism: Studies in their Encounter in Palestine during the Early Hellenistic* Period. 2 vols. London: SCM, 1974.

———. *The Son of God: The Origin of Christology and the History of Jewish Hellenistic Religion*. Philadelphia: Fortress, 1976 (1975).

———. *Between Jesus and Paul*. London: SCM Press, 1983.

———. *Studies in Early Christology*. Edinburgh: T & T Clark, 1995.

Hengel, Martin, and Roland Deines, eds. *The Pre-Christian Paul*. Trans. John Bowden. Philadelphia: Trinity Press International, 1991.

Henze, Matthias. *Jewish Apocalypticism in Late First Century Israel: Reading Second Baruch in Context*. TSAJ 142. Tübingen: Mohr Siebeck, 2011.

Herring, Stephen L. "A 'Transubstantiated' Humanity: The Relationship between the Divine Image and the Presence of God in Genesis i 26f" *VT* 58 (2008): 480–94.

———. *Divine Substitution: Humanity as the Manifestation of Deity in the Hebrew Bible and the Ancient Near East*. FRLANT 247. Göttingen: Vandenhoeck & Ruprecht, 2013.

Heschel, Susannah. *The Aryan Jesus: Christian Theologians and the Bible in Nazi Germany*. Princeton: PUP, 2008.

Hess, R. S. "Yahweh and his Asherah? Epigraphic Evidence for Religious Pluralism in Old Testament Times." Pages 5–33 in *One God, One Lord in a World of Religious Pluralism*. Edited by Andrew D. Clarke and Bruce W. Winter. Cambridge: Tyndale House, 1991.

Hiebert, Robert J. V. "Exile and Restoration Terminology in the Septuagint and the New Testament." Pages 93–117 in in *Exile: A Conversation with N. T. Wright*. Edited by James M. Scott. London: IVP, 2017.

Hill, Wesley. *Paul and the Trinity: Persons, Relations and the Pauline Letters*. Grand Rapids: Eerdmans, 2015.

Hinschberger, R. "Image et ressemblance dans la tradition sacerdotale: Gen 1:26–8; 5:1–3; 9:6b" *RSR* 59 (1985): 185–99.

Hofius, Otfried. *Der Christushymnus Philipper 2,6–11: Untersuchungen Zu Gestalt und Aussage Eines Urchristlichen Psalms*. WUNT. Tübingen: Mohr Siebeck, 1976.

———. *Paulusstudien* II. WUNT 1/143. Tübingen: Mohr Siebeck, 2002.

Holladay, Carl R. *Theios Aner in Hellenistic Judaism: A Critique of the Use of is Category in New Testament Christology*. SBLDS 40. Missoula: Scholars, 1977.

Hommel, Hildebrecht. *Sebasmata: Studien zur antiken Religionsgeschichte und zum frühen Christentum*. 2 vols. WUNT 31–32. Tübingen: Mohr Siebeck, 1983.

Horbury, William. *Jewish Messianism and the Cult of Christ*. London: SCM, 1998.

———. *Messianism among Jews and Christians: Twelve Biblical and Historical Studies*. London: T & T Clark, 2003.

———. "Jewish and Christian Monotheism in the Herodian Age." Pages 15–44 in *Early Jewish and Christian Monotheism*. Edited by Loren T. Stuckenbruck and Wendy E. S. North. JSNTSup 263. London: Continuum, 2004.

Hugedé, Norbert. *La métophore du miroir dans les Epîtres de saint Paul aux Corinthiens*. Neuchatel: Delachaux et Niestlé, 1957.

Huggins, R. V. "Alleged Classical Parallels to Paul's 'What I Want to Do I Do Not Do, but What I Hate, That I do' (Rom 7:15)" *WTJ* 54 (1992): 158–61.

Hurtado, Larry W. "New Testament Christology: A Critique of Bousset's Influence" *TS* 40.2 (1979): 306–17.

———. "First-Century Jewish Monotheism" *JSNT* 71 (1998): 3–26.

———. *One God, One Lord: Early Christian Devotion and Ancient Jewish Monotheism*. 3rd edn. New York: Bloomsbury T & T Clark, 2015 (1988).

———.. "Pre-70 C.E. Jewish Opposition to Christ-Devotion" *JTS* 50 (1999): 35–58.

———.. "Religious Experience and Religious Innovation in the New Testament" *JR* 80.3 (2000): 183–205.

———. *Lord Jesus Christ: Devotion to Jesus in Earliest Christianity*. Grand Rapids: Eerdmans, 2003.

———. *How on Earth Did Jesus Become a God? Historical Questions about Earliest Devotion to Jesus*. Grand Rapids: Eerdmans, 2005.

———. "'Ancient Jewish Monotheism' in the Hellenistic and Roman Periods" *JAJ* 4 (2013): 379–400.

———. "Jesus Monotheism Volume 1: Christological Origins: The Emerging Consensus and Beyond" *RBL* 8 (2016).

———. *Ancient Jewish Monotheism and Early Christian Jesus Devotion: The Context and Character of Christological Faith*. LEC. Waco: Baylor University Press, 2017.

Hurtado, Larry W., and Paul L. Owen, eds. *Who Is this Son of Man? The Latest Scholarship on a Puzzling Expression of the Historical Jesus*. LNTS 208. New York/London: Bloomsbury T & T Clark, 2011.

Isaac, E. "1 (Ethiopic Apocalypse of) Enoch" in *The Old Testament Pseudepigrapha*. Edited by James H. Charlesworth. 2 vols. Peabody: Hendrickson, 1983.

Jacob, Haley Goranson. *Conformed to the Image of His Son: Reconsidering Paul's Theology of Glory in Romans*. Downers Grove: IVP, 2018.

Janowski, B. "Tempel und Schöpfung: Schöpfungstheologische Aspekte der priesterschriftlichen Heiligtumskonzeption" *JBT* (1990): 37–69.

———."Die lebendige Statue Gottes: zur Anthropologie der priesterlichen Urgeschichte." Pages 183–214 in *Gott und Mensch im Dialog: Festschrift für Otto Kaiser zum 80, Geburstag*. Edited by M. Witte. BZAW 345.1. vol. 1. New York: de Gruyter, 2004.

Jervell, Jacob. *Imago Dei: Gen 1:26f. im Spätjudentum, in der Gnosis und in den paulinischen Briefen*. Göttingen: Vandenhoeck & Ruprecht, 1960.

Jipp, Joshua. *Christ is King: Paul's Royal Ideology*. Minneapolis, Fortress, 2015.

Johnson, M. D. "Life of Adam and Eve" in *The Old Testament Pseudepigrapha*. Edited by James H. Charlesworth. 2 vols. Peabody: Hendrickson, 1983.

Johnson, N. B. *Prayer in the Apocrypha and Pseudepigrapha: A Study of the Jewish Concept of God*. SBLMS 2. Philadelphia: Society of Biblical Literature, 1948.

Jonge, M. de. "The Christian Origin of the *Greek Life of Adam and Eve*." Pages 347–64 in *Literature on Adam and Eve: Collected Essays*. Edited by Gary A. Anderson and Michael E. Stone. SVTP 15. Leiden: Brill, 2000.

Jonge, M. de, and J. Tromp. *The Life of Adam and Eve and Related Literature*. GAP. Sheffield: SAP, 1997.

Jónsson, G. A. *The Image of God: Genesis 1:26–28 in a Century of Old Testament Research*. CBOTS 26. Almqvist & Wiksell International, 1988.

Jonquiere, T. M. *Prayer in Josephus*. Leiden: Brill, 2007.

Kaminsky, Joel. *Yet I Loved Jacob: Reclaiming the Biblical Concept of Election*. Nashville: Abingdon, 2007.

Käsemann, Ernst. *Leib und Leib Christi: eine Untersuchung zur paulinischen Begrifflichkeit*, BHTh 9. Tübingen: 1933.

———. "Die Legitimität des Apostels. Eine Untersuchung zu II Korinther 10–13", *ZNW* 41 (1942): 33–71.

———. *Perspectives on Paul*, repr. Philadelphia: Fortress, 1971.

Kearney, P. J. "Creation and Liturgy: The P Redaction of Exodus 25–40" *ZAW* 89 (1977): 375–87.

Kearns, R. *Vorfragen zur Christologie. III: Religionsgeschichtliche und Traditionsgeschichtliche Studie zur Vorgeschichte eines christologischen Hoheitstitels*. Tübingen: J. C. B. Mohr, 1982.

Keck, Leander E. "The Law and 'The Law of Sin and Death' (Rom 8:1–4): Reflections on the Spirit and Ethics in Paul" in *The Divine Helmsman: Studies on God's Control of Human Events, Presented to Lou H. Silberman*. Edited by Crenshaw and Sandmel. New York: Ktav, 1980.

Keesmaat, Sylvia. *Paul and His Story: (Re)Interpreting the Exodus Tradition*. JSNTSup 181. Sheffield: SAP, 1999.

Keith, Chris, and Dieter T. Roth, eds. *Mark, Manuscripts, and Monotheism: Essays in Honor of Larry W. Hurtado*. London: Bloomsbury, 2014.

Kenney, John P. "Monotheistic and Polytheistic Elements in Classical Mediterranean Spirituality." Pages 269–92 in *Classical Mediterranean Spirituality*. Edited by A. H. Armstrong. New York: Crossroad, 1986.

Kee, H. C. "Testaments of the Twelve Patriarchs" in *The Old Testament Pseudepigrapha*. Edited by James H. Charlesworth. 2 vols. Peabody, MA: Hendrickson, 1983.

Keyes, C. W. "The Greek Letter of Introduction", *AJP* 56 (1935): 28–44.

Kiefer, Jörn. "Not All Gloom and Doom: Positive Interpretations of Exile and Diaspora in the Hebrew Bible and Early Judaism." Pages 119–34 in *Exile: A Conversation with N. T. Wright*. Edited by James M. Scott. London: IVP, 2017.

Kim, Byung-mo. *Die paulinische Kollekte*. Tübingen: Francke, 2002.

Kim, C. H. *Form and Structure of the Familiar Greek Letter of Recommendation*. SBLDS 4. Missoula: Scholars Press, 1972.

Kim, Seyoon. *The Origin of Paul's Gospel*. Eugene: Wifp and Stock, 2007 (1981).

Klausner, Joseph. *The Messianic Idea in Israel: From Its Beginning to the Completion of the Mishnah*. Trans. W. F. Stinespring. New York: Macmillan, 1955.

Klein, Ralph. "Back to the Future: The Tabernacle in the Book of Exodus" *Int* 50.3 (1996): 264–76.

Koortbojian, Michael. *The Divinization of Caesar and Augustus: Precedents, Consequences, Implications*. New York: Cambridge University Press, 2013.

Kratz, R. G., and H. Spieckermann, eds. *Götterbilder, Gottesbilder, Weltbilder: Polytheismus und Monotheismus in der Welt der Antike*. 2 vols. FAT 2.17, 18. Tübingen: Mohr Siebeck, 2006.

Kugler, Chris. "ΠΙΣΤΙΣ ΧΡΙΣΤΟΥ: The Current State of Play and the Key Arguments" *CBR* 14.2 (2016): 244–55.

Kugler, Robert. "Continuing Exile Among the People of the Dead Sea Scrolls." Pages 163–82 in *Exile: A Conversation with N. T. Wright*. Edited by James M. Scott. London: IVP, 2017.

Kuhli, H. "εἰκών, όνος, ἡ." Pages 1.388–91 in *Exegetical Dictionary of the New Testament*. Edited by Balz, Horst, and Schneider. 3 vols. Grand Rapids: Eerdmans, 1990 (1978–80).

Kuschnerus, B. *Die Gemeinde als Brief Christi: die kommunikative Funktion der Metapher bei Paulus am Beispiel von 2 Kor 2–5*. Göttingen: Vandenhoeck & Ruprecht, 2002.

Kutsko, John. *Between Heaven and Earth: Divine Presence and Absence in the Book of Ezekiel*. BJSUCSD 7. Winona Lake: Eisenbrauns, 2000.

———. "Ezekiel's Anthropology and Its Ethical Implications." Pages 119–41 in *The Book of Ezekiel: Theological and Anthropological Perspectives*. Edited by M. S. Odell & J. T. Strong. SSSBL 9. Atlanta: Society of Biblical Literature, 2000.

Kvanvig, Helge S. "The Son of Man and the Parables of Enoch." Pages 179–215 in *Enoch and the Messiah Son of Man: Revisiting the Parables of Enoch*. Edited by Gabriele Boccaccini. Grand Rapids: Eerdmans, 2007.

Lambrecht, Jan. *The Wretched "I" and Its Liberation: Paul in Romans 7 and 8*. LTPM 14. Grand Rapids: Eerdmans, 1992.

Lampe, G. W. H. "The New Testament Doctrine of *Ktisis*" *SJT* 17 (1964): 449–62.

Lange, A. *Weisheit und Prädestination: Weisheitliche Urordnung und Prädestination in den Textfunden von Qumran*. STDJ 18. Leiden: Brill, 1995.

Larsson, Edvin. *Christus als Vorbild: Eine Untersuchung zu den paulinischen Tauf- und Eikontexten*, ASNU 23.19. Uppsala: 1962.

Lehmkühler, Karsten. *Kultus und Theologie: Dogmatik und Exegese in der religionsgeschichtliche Schule*. Göttingen: Vandenhoeck & Ruprecht, 1996.

Lendon, John. *Empire of Honor*. Oxford: Clarendon Press, 1997.

Lenglet, A. "La structure litteraire de Daniel 2–7" *Bib* 53 (1972): 169–90.

Lenz, John R. "Deification of the Philosopher in Classical Greece." Pages 47–67 in *Partakers of the Divine Nature: The History and Development of Deification in the Christian Traditions*. Edited by Michael J. Christensen and Jeffery A. Wittung. Madison: Fairleigh Dickinson University Press, 2007.

Levenson, Jon D. "The Temple and the World" *JR* 64.3 (1984): 275–98.

———. *Creation and the Persistence of Evil: The Jewish Drama of Divine Omnipotence*. San Francisco: Harper & Row, 1988.

Levison, John R. *Portraits of Adam in Early Judaism: From Sirach to 2 Baruch*. New York: Bloomsbury, 2015 (1988).

———. "Adam and Eve in Romans 1:18–25 and the Greek Life of Adam and Eve" *NTS* 50 (2004): 519–34.

Lichtenberger, Hermann. *Das Ich Adams und das Ich der Menschheit: Studien zum Menschenbild in Römer 7*. WUNT 164. Tübingen: Mohr Siebeck, 2004.

Lim, Timothy H., and John J. Collins. eds. *The Oxford Handbook of the Dead Sea Scrolls*. Oxford: OUP, 2010.

Lincicum, David. *Paul and the Early Jewish Encounter with Deuteronomy*. Grand Rapids: Baker, 2013 (2010).

Litwa, David. "2 Corinthians 3:18 and Its Implications for *Theosis*" *JTI* 2 (2008): 117–33.

———. "Transformation through a Mirror: Moses in 2 Cor. 3.18" *JSNT* 34.3 (2012): 286–97.

———. *We Are Being Transformed: Deification in Paul's Soteriology*. Berlin: de Gruyter, 2012.

———. *Iesus Deus: The Early Christian Depiction of Jesus as a Mediterranean God*. Minneapolis: Fortress, 2014.

Lohfink, Norbert. *Theology of the Pentateuch: Themes of the Priestly Narrative and Deuteronomy*. Trans. Linda M. Maloney. Edinburgh: T & T Clark, 1994.

Lohse, Eduard. *Neues Testament und christliche Existenz*. Tübingen: Mohr Siebeck, 1973.

Lorenzen, Stefanie. *Das paulinische Eikon-Konzept: Semantische Analysen zur Sapientia Salomonis, zu Philo und den Paulusbriefen*. WUNT 2.250. Tübingen: Mohr Siebeck, 2008.

Lossky, Vladimir. *In the Image and Likeness of God*. New edn. Trans. Thomas E. Bird. Eds. Thomas E. Bird and John H. Erickson. New York: St Vladimir's Seminary Press, 2001 (1974).

Lust, J. "Daniel 7,13 and the Septuagint" *ETL* (1978): 68–9.

Macaskill, Grant. *Union with Christ in the New Testament*. Oxford: OUP, 2013.

MacDonald, Nathan. *Deuteronomy and the Meaning of "Monotheism"*. 2nd corrected edn. Tübingen: Mohr Siebeck, 2012 (2003).

———. "The Origin of 'Monotheism'." Pages 204–15 in *Early Jewish and Christian Monotheism*. Edited by Loren T. Stuckenbruck and Wendy North. JSNTSup 263. London: Continuum, 2004.

Mach, Michael. *Entwicklungsstadien des judischen Engelglaubens in vorrabinischer Zeit*. TSAJ 34. Tübingen: Mohr Siebeck, 1992.

Mack, B. L. *Logos und Sophia: Untersuchungen zur Weisheitstheologie im hellenistischen Judentum*. Göttingen: Vandenhoeck & Ruprecht, 1973.

———. *Wisdom and the Hebrew Epic: Ben Sira's Hymn in Praise of the Fathers*. Chicago: UCP, 1985.

MacRae, George W. "Heavenly Temple and Eschatology in the Letter to the Hebrews" *Semeia* 12 (1978): 179–99.

Malherbe, Abraham. *Paul and the Popular Philosophers*. Minneapolis: Fortress, 1989.

Manns, F. "Col. 1,15–20: Midrash Chrétien de Gen. 1,1" *RSR* 53 (1979): 100–110.

Marchand, Suzanne L. *German Orientalism in the Age of Empire: Religion, Race, and Scholarship*. Cambridge: CUP, 2009.

Marcus, Joel. "Son of Man as Son of Adam" *RB* 110–11 (2003): 38–61, 370–86.

Marcus, Ralph. "Divine Names and Attributes in Hellenistic Jewish Literature" *PAAJR* (1931–1932): 43–120.

Markschies, C. "Die platonische Metapher vom 'inneren Menschen': Eine Brücke zwischen antiker Philosophie und altchristlicher Theologie" *ZK* 105 (1994): 1–17.

Marques, Valdir. *"Eikón" em Paulo. Investigação teológica e bíblica à la luz da LXX.* Rome: Pontificia Università Gregoriana, 1986.

Marshall, Paul, Sander Griffioen, and Richard Moew, eds. *Stained Glass: Worldviews and Social Science.* Lanham: University Press of America, 1989.

Martin, Dale B. "Paul and the Judaism/Hellenism Dichotomy: Toward a Social History of the Question." Pages 29–62 in *Paul Beyond the Judaism/Hellenism Divide.* Edited by Troels Engberg-Pedersen. Louisville: John Knox Press, 2001.

Martin, Troy. *By Philosophy and Empty Deceit.* JSNTSSup 118. Sheffield: SAP, 1996.

Martin-Achard, Robert. *A Light to the Nations: A Study of the Old Testament Conception of Israel's Mission to the World.* Trans. J. P. Smith. Edinburgh: Oliver and Boyd, 1962.

Maston, Jason. *Divine and Human Agency in Second Temple Judaism and Paul.* WUNT 2.297. Tübingen: Mohr Siebeck, 2010.

McDonough, Sean M. *Christ as Creator: Origins of a New Testament Doctrine.* Oxford: OUP, 2009.

McGrath, James. *The Only True God: Early Christian Monotheism in Its Jewish Context.* Urbana: University of Illinois Press, 2009.

McLay, Tim. *The OG and Th Versions of Daniel.* SBLSCS 43. Atlanta: Scholars Press, 1996.

McNamara, Martin J. *The New Testament and the Palestinian Targums to the Pentateuch.* Rome: Pontifical Biblical Institute, 1966.

Meeks, Wayne A. "Judaism, Hellenism, and the Birth of Christianity." Pages 17–28 in *Paul Beyond the Judaism/Hellenism Divide.* Edited by Troels Engberg-Pedersen. Louisville: John Knox Press, 2001.

Merrill, E. H. "Image of God." Pages 441–5 in *Dictionary of the Old Testament Pentateuch.* Edited by T. Desmond Alexander and David W. Baker. Downers Grove: IVP, 2003.

Metzger, Bruce M. "The Fourth Book of Ezra" in *The Old Testament Pseudepigrapha.* Edited by James H. Charlesworth. 2 vols. Peabody: Hendrickson, 1983.

Middleton, J. Richard. *The Liberating Image: The Imago Dei in Genesis 1.* Grand Rapids: Brazos, 2005.

Milgrom, Jacob. "Priestly ('P') Source." Pages 5.454–61 in *The Anchor Bible Dictionary.* Edited by David Noel Freedman. 6 vols. Yale: YUP, 1992.

Mitchell, S., and P. van Nuffelen, eds. *One God: Pagan Monotheism in the Roman Empire.* Cambridge: CUP, 2010.

Moffitt, David M. *Atonement and the Logic of Resurrection in the Epistle to the Hebrews.* NovTSup 141. Leiden: Brill, 2011.

———. "Serving in the Tabernacle in Heaven: Sacred Space, Jesus's High-Priestly Sacrifice, and Hebrews' Analogical Theology." Pages 259–79 in *Hebrews in Contexts.* Edited by Gabrielle Gelardini and Harold W. Attridge. AJEC. Leiden: Brill, 2016.

Mohr, Richard D. *The Platonic Cosmology*. Leiden: Brill, 1985.
Moor, Johannes C. de. *The Rise of Yahwism: The Roots of Israelite Monotheism*. BETL 91. Leuven: University Press/Peeters, 1997.
Moule, C. F. D. *The Birth of the New Testament*. 3rd edn. San Francisco: Harper and Row, 1982 (1962).
———. *The Origin of Christology*. Cambridge: CUP, 1977.
Moyise, Steve. "Wright's Understanding of Paul's Use of Scripture." Pages 165–80 in *God and the Faithfulness of Paul: A Critical Examination of the Pauline Theology of N. T. Wright*. Edited by Christoph Heilig, J. Thomas Hewitt, and Michael F. Bird. WUNT 2.413. Tübingen: Mohr Siebeck, 2016.
Mulder, Otto. *Simon the High Priest in Sirach 50: An Exegetical Study of the Significance of Simon the High Priest as Climax to the Praise of the Fathers in Ben Sira's Concept of the History of Israel*. JSJSupp 78. Leiden: Brill, 2003.
Murphy-O'Connor, Jerome. *Keys to Second Corinthians: Revisiting the Major Issues*. Oxford: OUP, 2010.
Naugle, David. *Worldview: The History of a Concept*. Grand Rapids: Eerdmans, 2002.
Newman, Carey C. *Paul's Glory Christology: Tradition and Rhetoric*. NovTSup 69. Leiden: Brill, 1992.
Newman, Carey C., James R. Davila, and Gladys S. Lewis, eds. *The Jewish Roots of Christological Monotheism*. LEC. Waco: Baylor University Press, 2017 (1999).
Newsom, Carol. "'He Has Established for Himself Priests': Human and Angelic Priesthood in the Qumran Sabbath Shirot." Pages 101–20 in *Archaeology and History in the Dead Sea Scrolls: The New York University Conference in Memory of Yigael Yadin*. Edited by L. Schiffman. JSPSup 8. Sheffield: JSOT Press, 1990.
Niehoff, Maren R. *Philo of Alexandria: An Intellectual Biography*. New Haven: YUP, 2018.
Novenson, Matthew V. *Christ Among the Messiahs: Christ Language in Paul and Messiah Language in Ancient Judaism*. New York: Oxford University Press, 2012.
———. "The Self-Styled Jew of Romans 2 and the Actual Jews of Romans 9–11." Pages 133–62 in *The So-Called Jew in Paul's Letter to the Romans*. Edited by Rafael Rodríguez and Matthew Thiessen. Minneapolis: Fortress, 2016.
———. *The Grammar of Messianism: An Ancient Jewish Political Idiom and Its Users*. Oxford: OUP, 2017.
Oeming, M., and K. Schmid, eds. *Der eine Gott und die Götter: Polytheismus und Monotheismus im antiken Israel*. Zurich: Theologischer Verlag Zürich, 2003.
Olyan, Saul. *A Thousand Thousands Served Him: Exegesis and the Naming of Angels in Ancient Judaism*. TSAT 36. Tübingen: Mohr Siebeck, 1993.
Osten-Sacken, P. von der. *Römer 8 als Beispiel paulinischer Soteriologie*. FRLANT 112. Göttingen: Vandenhoeck & Ruprecht, 1975.
Pearson, B. A. "Hellenistic-Jewish Wisdom Speculation and Paul." Pages 43–66 in *Aspects of Wisdom in Judaism and Early Christianity*. Edited by R. L. Wilken. Notre Dame: UNDP, 1975.
Peppard, Michael. *The Son of God in the Roman World: Divine Sonship in its Social and Political Context*. Oxford: OUP, 2012.

Petry, Sven. *Die Entgrezung JHWHs: Monolatrie, Bilderverbot, und Monotheismus im Deuteronomium, in Deuterojesaja und im Ezechielbuch*. Tübingen: Mohr Siebeck, 2007.

Peuch, E. *La croyance des Esséniens en la vie future: immortalité, résurrection, vie éternelle? Histoire d'une croyance dans le Judaisme ancien*, 2 vols. Paris: Cerf, 1993.

Philonenko, Marc. "Sur l'expression 'vendu au péché' dans l' 'Epître aux Romains'" *Revue de l'histoire des religions* 103 (1986): 41–52.

Piotrowski, Nicholas G. "The Concept of Exile in Late Second Temple Judaism: A Review of Recent Scholarship" *CBR* 15.2 (2017): 214–47.

Pöhlmann, W. "Die hymnischen All-Prädikationen in Col 1 15–20" *ZNW* 64 (1973): 53–74.

Pomykala, Kenneth. *The Davidic Dynasty Tradition in Early Judaism*. Atlanta: Scholars, 1995.

Popovic, M. *Reading the Human Body: Physiognomics and Astrology in the Dei Sea Scrolls and Hellenistic-Early Roman Period Judaism*. STDJ 67. Leiden: Brill, 2007.

Porter, Stanley, and Christopher Stanley, eds. *As It Is Written: Studying Paul's Use of Scripture*. Atlanta: SBL Press, 2008.

Porter, Stanley E. *Verbal Aspect in the Greek of the New Testament with Reference to Tense and Mood*. SBG 1. New York: Lang, 1989.

Price, S. R. F. *Rituals and Power: The Roman Imperial Cult in Asia Minor*. Repr. Cambridge: CUP, 1998 (1984).

Prümm, Karl. *Diakonia Pneumatos. Theologie des Zweiten Korintherbriefes. Bd. I–II*. Freiburg: Herder, 1962.

Radice, Roberto, and David T. Runia. *Philo of Alexandria: An Annotated Bibliography, 1937–1986*. VCSup 8. Leiden: Brill, 1988.

———. *Philo of Alexandria: An Annotated Bibliography, 1987–1996, with Addenda for 1937–1986*. VCSup 57. Leiden: Brill, 2000.

Rainbow, Paul A. "Monotheism and Christology in 1 Corinthians 8:4–6." PhD Diss., Oxford University, 1987.

Räisänen, Heikki. *Jesus, Paul, and Torah: Collected Essays*. Trans. D. E. Orton. JSNTSup 43. Sheffield: JSOT Press, 1992.

Ramsay, Sir William M. *The Teaching of Paul in Terms of the Present Day*. 2nd edn. London: Hodder & Stoughton, 1914.

Rasimus, Tuomas, Troels Engberg-Pedersen, and Ismo Dunderberg, eds. *Stoicism in Early Christianity*. Grand Rapids: Baker, 2010.

Reiterer, Friedrich V. "Das Verhältnis der המכח zur הרות im Buch Ben Sira. Kriterien zur gegenseitigen Bestimmung." Pages 97–134 in *Studies in the Book of Ben Sira*. Edited by Géza Xeravits and Jóseph Zsengellér. JSJSup 127. Leiden: Brill, 2008.

Reitzenstein, Richard. *Die Hellenistischen Mysterienreligionen: nach ihren Grundgedanken und Wirkungen*. mit 2 Bildtafeln. Gebundene Ausgabe. Darmstadt: Miss. Buchgesellschaft, 1956.

Reydams-Schils, Gretchen J. *Demiurge and Providence: Stoic and Platonist Readings of Plato's Timaeus*. Turnhout: Brepols, 1999.

Reynolds, Benjamin E. "The 'One Like a Son of Man' According to the Old Greek of Daniel 7, 13–14" *Biblica* 89 (2008): 70–80.

Rodríguez, Rafael, and Matthew Thiessen, eds. *The So-Called Jew in Paul's Letter to the Romans*. Minneapolis: Fortress, 2016.

Rodríguez, Rafael. *If You Call Yourself a Jew: Reappraising Paul's Letter to the Romans*. Eugene: Wipf & Stock, 2014.

Rösel, Martin. *Übersetzung als Vollendung der Auslegung: Studien zur Genesis-Septuaginta*. BZAW 223. Berlin: de Gruyter, 1994.

Rowe, C. Kavin. "Romans 10:13: What is the Name of the Lord?" *HBT* 22 (2000): 135–73.

———. *Early Narrative Christology: The Lord in the Gospel of Luke*. Grand Rapids: Baker, 2009.

———. *One True Life: The Stoics and Early Christians as Rival Traditions*. New Haven: YUP, 2016.

Rowley, Harold H. *The Biblical Doctrine of Election*. London: Lutterworth, 1950.

Rowland, Christopher. "The Vision of the Risen Christ in Rev. i. 13 ff.: The Debt of an Early Christology to an Aspect of Jewish Angelology" *JTS* 39.1 (1980): 1–11.

———. *The Open Heaven: A Study of Apocalyptic in Judaism and Early Christianity*. Eugene: Wipf & Stock, 2002 (1982).

Runia, David. *Philo of Alexandria and the Timaeus of Plato*. 2nd edn. Leiden: Brill, 1986.

Sanders, E. P. *Paul and Palestinian Judaism: A Comparison of Patterns of Religion*. Minneapolis: Fortress, 1977.

———. *Judaism: Practice and Belief 63 BCE–66 CE*. Minneapolis: Fortress, 2016 (1992).

———. *Paul: The Apostle's Life, Letters and Thought*. Minneapolis: Fortress, 2016.

Sandmel, Samuel. *Philo of Alexandria: An Introduction*. New York: Oxford University Press, 1979.

Sappington. T. J. *Revelation and Redemption at Colossae*. JSNTSup 53. Sheffield: JSOT, 1991.

Schade, H. H. *Apokalyptische Christologie bei Paulus: Studien zum Zusammenhang von Christologie und Eschatologie in den Paulusbriefen*. Göttingen: Vandenhoeck & Ruprecht, 1984.

Schäfer, Peter. *Rivalität zwischen Engeln und Menschen: Untersuchungen zur rabbinischen Engelvorstellung*, Studia Judaica. FWJ 8. Berlin: de Gruyter, 1975.

Schenck, Kenneth. *A Brief Guide to Philo*. Louisville: Westminster John Knox, 2005.

Schenk, W. *Der Segen im Neuen Testament*. Berlin, 1967.

Schlatter, Adolf. *Wie sprach Josephus von Gott?* BFCT 1.14. Gütersloh: Bertelsmann, 1910.

———. *Die Theologie der Apostel*. Stuttgart: Calwar, 1922.

———. *Die Theologie des Judentums nach dem Bericht des Josephus*. BFCT 2.26. Gütersloh: Bertelsmann, 1932.

Schmidt, Werner H. *The Faith of the Old Testament*. Trans. John Sturdy. Oxford: Blackwell, 1983.

Schmithals, Walter. *Gnosticism in Corinth: An Investigation of the Letters to the Corinthians*. Trans. J. E. Steeley. Nashville: Abingdon, 1971.

Schnelle, Udo. *The Human Condition: Anthropology in the Teachings of Jesus, Paul, and John*. Trans. O. C. Dean. Minneapolis: Fortress, 1996 (1991).

———. "Heilsgegenwart. Christologische Hoheitstitel bei Paulus." Pages 178–93 in *Paulinische Christologie*. Edited by U. Schnelle, T. Söding and M. Labahn. Göttingen: Vandenhoeck & Ruprecht, 2000.

———. *Apostle Paul: His Life and Theology*. Grand Rapids: Baker, 2005 (2003).

Schrage, W. *Unterwegs zur Einzigkeit und Einheit Gottes: zum "Monotheismus" des Paulus und seiner alttestamentlich-frühjüdischen Tradition*. Neukirchen-Vluyn: Neukirchener Verlag, 2002.

Schüle, Andreas. "Made in the Image of God: The concepts of Divine Images in Gen 1–3" *ZAW* 117.1 (2005): 1–20.

Schulz, Siegfried. "Die Decke des Moses: Untersuchungen zu einer vorpaulinischen Überlieferung in 2 Kor. 3:17–18" *ZNTW* 49 (1958): 1–30.

Schwanz, Peter *Imago Dei als christologisch-anthropologisches Problem in der Geschichte der Alten Kirche von Paulus bis Clemens von Alexandria*. AGR 2. Halle: 1970.

Schweitzer, Albert. *The Mysticism of Paul the Apostle*. Trans. William Montgomery. Baltimore: Johns Hopkins University Press, 1998 (1931).

Schweizer, Eduard. "Zum religionsgeschichtlichen Hintergrund der 'Sendungsformel' Gal. 4.4f., Röm. 8.3f., John 3.16f., 1 John 4.9" *ZNW* 57 (1966): 199–210.

Scott, James M. *Adoption as Sons of God*. WUNT 2.48. Tübingen: Mohr Siebeck, 1992.

———. "'For as Many as Are of Works of the Law Are under a Curse' (Gal 3:10)." Pages 187–221 in *Paul and the Scriptures of Israel*. Edited by Craig A. Evans and J. A. Sanders. Sheffield: JSOT Press, 1993.

———. *Exile: Old Testament, Jewish & Christian Conceptions*. Leiden: Brill, 1997.

———, ed. *Exile: A Conversation with N. T. Wright*. London: IVP, 2017.

Scroggs, Robin. *The Last Adam: A Study in Pauline Anthropology*. Philadelphia: Fortress, 1966.

Scullion, J. J. "Righteousness." Pages 729–36 in *The Anchor Bible Dictionary*. Edited by David Noel Freedman. 6 vols. Yale: YUP, 1992.

Segal, Alan F. *Two Powers in Heaven: Early Rabbinic Reports about Christianity and Gnosticism*. LEC. Waco: Baylor, 2017 (1977).

———. *Paul the Convert: The Apostolate and Apostasy of Saul the Pharisee*. New Haven: YUP, 1990.

Shanks, Hershel, and Jack Meinhardt, eds. *Aspects of Monotheism: How God Is One*. Symposium at the Smithsonian Institution. Washington: Biblical Archaeology Society, 1997.

Sim, David C., and James S. McLaren, eds. *Attitudes to Gentiles in Ancient Judaism and Early Christianity*. LNTS. London: T & T Clark, 2015.

Sire, J. W. *Naming the Elephant: Worldview as a Concept*. Downers Grove: IVP, 2004.

Smith, Daniel L. "The Uses of 'New Exodus' in New Testament Scholarship: Preparing a Way Through the Wilderness" *CBR* 14 (2016): 207–43.

Smith, Mark. *The Early History of God: Yahweh and the Other Deities in Ancient Israel*. 2nd edn. Grand Rapids: Eerdmans, 2002 (1990).

———. *The Origins of Biblical Monotheism: Israel's Polytheistic Background and the Ugaritic Texts*. Oxford: OUP, 2001.

———. *God in Translation: Deities in Cross-Cultural Discourse in the Biblical World*. Grand Rapids: Eerdmans 2010 (2008).

Sohn, Seock-Tae. *The Divine Election of Israel*. Grand Rapids: Eerdmans, 1991.

Sommer, Benjamin D. "Conflicting Constructions of Divine Presence in the Priestly Tabernacle" *BibInt* 9.1 (2001): 41–63.

Stanley, Christopher, ed. *Paul and Scripture: Extending the Conversation*. Atlanta: SBL Press, 2012.

Staudt, Darina. *Monotheistische Formeln im Urchristentum und ihre Vorgeschichte bei Griechen und Juden*, NTOA 80. Göttingen: Vandenhoeck & Ruprecht, 2012.

Steck, O. H. *Israel und das gewaltsame Geschick der Propheten: Untersuchungen zur Überlieferung des deuteronomistischen Geschichtbildes im Alten Testament, Spätjudentum und Urchristentum*. Neukirchen-Vluyn: Neukirchener Verlag, 1967.

———. "Das Problem theologischer Strömungen in nachexilischer Zeit" *ET* 28 (1968): 445–58.

———. *Apokryphe Baruchbuch: Studien zu Rezeption und Konzentration 'kanonischer' Überlieferung*. FRLANT 160. Göttingen: Vandenhoeck & Ruprecht, 1993.

Steenburg, D. "The Case against the Synonymity of *Morphē* and *Eikōn*" *JSNT* 34 (1988): 77–86.

———. "The Worship of Adam and Christ as the Image of God" *JSNT* 39 (1990): 95–109.

Stendahl, Krister. "The Apostle Paul and the Introspective Conscience of the West" *HTR* 56.3 (1963): 199–215.

Sterling, Gregory. "Hellenistic Philosophy and the New Testament." Pages 313–58 in *Handbook to Exegesis of the New Testament*. Edited by Stanley Porter. NTTS 25. Leiden: Brill, 1997.

———. "Prepositional Metaphysics in Jewish Wisdom Speculation and Early Christian Liturgical Texts" *SPhiloA* 9 (1997): 219–38.

———. "'The Jewish Philosophy': The Presence of Hellenistic Philosophy in Jewish Exegesis in the Second Temple Period." Pages 131–53 in *Ancient Judaism in its Hellenistic Context*. Edited by Carol Bakhos. JSJSS 95. Leiden: Brill, 2005.

———. "Philosophy as the Handmaid of Wisdom: Philosophy in the Exegetical Tradition of Alexandrian Jews." Pages 67–98 in *Religiöse Philosophie und philosophische Religion der frühen Kaiserzeit*. Edited by Rainer Hirsch-Luipold, Herwig Görgemanns, Michael von Albrecht and Mitra v. Tobias Thum. SAC 51. Tübingen: Mohr Siebeck, 2009.

———. "'The Image of God': Becoming Like God in Philo, Paul, and Early Christianity." Pages 157–73 in *Portraits of Jesus: Studies in Christology*. Edited by Susan Myers. WUNT 2.321. Tübingen: Mohr Siebeck, 2012.

———. "The Role of Philosophy in the Thought of Paul." Pages 235–53 in *God and the Faithfulness of Paul: A Critical Examination of the Pauline Theology of N. T. Wright*. Edited by Christoph Heilig, J. Thomas Hewitt, and Michael F. Bird. WUNT 2.413. Tübingen: Mohr Siebeck, 2016.

———. "The Love of Wisdom: Middle Platonism and Stoicism in the Wisdom of Solomon." Pages 198–213 in *From Stoicism to Platonism: The Development of Philosophy 100 BCE—100 CE*. Edited by Troels Engberg-Pedersen. Cambridge: CUP, 2017.

Stern, Ephraim. "From Many gods to the One God: The Archaeological Evidence." Pages 395–403 in *One God, One Cult, One Nation: Archaeological and Biblical Perspectives*. Edited by Reinhard G. Kratz and Hermann Spieckermann. BZAW 405. New York: de Gruyter, 2010.

Stettler, Christian. *Der Kolosserhymnus: Untersuchungen zu Form, traditionsgesschichtlichem Hintergrund und Aussage von Col 1,15–20*. WUNT 2.31. Tübingen: Mohr Siebeck, 2000.

Stone, Michael E. *A History of the Literature of Adam and Eve*. Early Judaism and its Literature 3. Atlanta: Scholars, 1992.

———. "The Fall of Satan and Adam's Penance: Three Notes on *The Books of Adam and Eve*" *JTS* 44 (1993): 143–56.

Stowers, Stanley K. *A Rereading of Romans: Justice, Jews and Gentiles*. New Haven/London: YUP, 1994.

Stuckenbruck, Loren T. *Angel Veneration and Christology: A Study in Early Judaism and in the Christology of the Apocalypse of John*. LEC. Waco: Baylor University Press, 2017 (1995).

———. "'One like a Son of Man as the Ancient of Days' in the Old Greek Recension of Daniel 7,13: Scribal Error or Theological Translation" *ZNW* 86 (1995): 268–76.

———. "'Angels' and 'God': Exploring the Limits of Early Jewish Monotheism." Pages 45–70 in *In Early Jewish and Christian Monotheism*. Edited by Loren T. Stuckenbruck and Wendy North. JSNTSup 263. London: Continuum, 2004.

———. *The Myth of Rebellious Angels: Studies in Second Temple Judaism and New Testament Texts*. Grand Rapids: Eerdmans, 2017 (2014).

Stuckenbruck, Loren T., and Wendy E. S. North, eds. *Early Jewish and Christian Monotheism*. JSNTSup 263. London: Continuum, 2004.

Sullivan, Kevin P. *Wrestling with Angels: A Study of the Relationship between Angels and Humans in Ancient Jewish Literature and the New Testament*. AGJU 55. Leiden: Brill, 2004.

Sumney, Jerry L. *Identifying Paul's Opponents: The Question of Method in 2 Corinthians*. JSNTSup 40. Sheffield: JSOT Press, 1990.

Taylor, C. C. W. "Sophists." Page 1381 in *The Oxford Classical Dictionary*. Edited by Simon Hornblower, Antony Spawforth and Esther Eidenow. 4th edn. Oxford: OUP, 2012 (1968).

Teixidor, J. *The Pagan God: Popular Religion in the Graeco-Roman Near East*. Princeton: PUP, 1977.

Theiller, Willy. *Die Vorbereitung des Neuplatonismus*. Berlin: Weidmann, 1964.

Theissen, Gerd. *Psychological Aspects of Pauline Theology*. Trans. J. P. Galvin. Philadelphia: Fortress, 1987 (1983).

Thom, Johan C. "Paul and Popular Philosophy." Pages 47–74 in *Paul's Greco-Roman Context*. Edited by Cilliers Breytenbach. BETL 277. Leuven: Peeters, 2015.

Thorsteinsson, Runar. *Paul's Interlocutor in Romans 2: Function and Identity in the Context of Ancient Epistolography*. ConBNT 40. Stockholm: Almqvist & Wiksell, 2003.

Tilling, Chris. *Paul's Divine Christology*. Grand Rapids: Eerdmans, 2015 (2012).

Tobin, Thomas. "Logos." Pages 4.348–56 in *The Anchor Bible Dictionary*. Edited by David Noel Freedman. 6 vols. Yale: YUP, 1992.

———. *Paul's Rhetoric in Its Contexts: The Argument of Romans*. Peabody: Hendrickson, 2004.

Tooman, William. *Gog of Magog: Reuse of Scripture and Compositional Technique in Ezekiel 38–39*. 2.52. Tübingen: Mohr Siebeck, 2011.

Tov, Emmanuel. *The Greek and Hebrew Bible: Collected Essays on the Septuagint*, VTSup 72. Leiden: Brill, 1999.

———. *Textual Criticism of the Hebrew Bible*. 3rd edn., rev. and exp. Minneapolis: Fortress, 2012.

Trainor, Michael. "Colossae: The State of Forthcoming Excavations" *JSPL* 1 (2011): 133–35.

Trebilco, Paul. *Jewish Communities in Asia Minor*. Cambridge: CUP, 1991.

VanderKam, James C. "Exile in Apocalyptic Jewish Literature." Pages 89–109 in *Exile: A Conversation with N. T. Wright*. Edited by James M. Scott. London: IVP, 2017.

van den Beld, A. "Romans 7:14–25 and the Problem of *Akrasia*" *RS* 21.4 (1985): 495–515.

van der Horst, P. W. "Pseudo-Phocylides" in *The Old Testament Pseudepigrapha*. Edited by James H. Charlesworth. 2 vols. Peabody: Hendrickson, 1983.

van Dülmen, A. *Die Theologie des Gesetzes bei Paulus*, Stuttgarter biblische Monographien 5. Stuttgart: Katholisches Bibelwerk, 1968.

van Kooten, George H. *Paul's Anthropology in Context: The Image of God, Assimilation to God, and Tripartite Man in Ancient Judaism, Ancient Philosophy and Early Christianity*. WUNT 232. Tübingen: Mohr Siebeck, 2008.

———. "Why Did Paul Include an Exegesis of Moses' Shining Face (Exod 34) in 2 Cor 3?." Pages 149–81 in *The Significance of Sinai*. Edited by G. J. Brooke, H. Najman and L. T. Stuckenbruck. TBN 12. Leiden: Brill, 2008.

Vermeylen, Jacques. "Le Récit du Paradis et la Question des Origines du Pentateuque" *Bijdragen* 41 (1980): 230–50.

Völker, W. *Fortschritt und Vollendung bei Philo von Alexandrien: eine Studie zur Geschichte der Frömmigkeit*, TUGAL 49.1. Leipzig: J. C. Hinrich, 1938.

Vollenweider, Samuel. *Horizonte neutestamentlicher Christologie: Studien zu Paulus und zur frühchristlichen Theologie*. WUNT 144. Tübingen: Mohr Siebeck, 2002.

———. "Zwischen Monotheismus und Engelchristologie: Überlegungen zur Frühgeschichte des Christusglaubens" *ZThK* 99 (2002): 21–44.

———. "Christozentrisch oder theozentrisch? Christologie im Neuen Testament." Pages 19–40 in *Christologie*. Edited by E. Gräb-Schmidt and R. Preul. Leipzig, 2011.

von Rad, Gerhard. *Wisdom in Israel*. Nashville: Abingdon, 1972.

Vriezen, Theodorus C. *Die Erwählung Israels nach den Alten Testament.* ATANT 24. Zürich: Zwingli, 1953.
Waaler, Erik. *The Shema and the First Commandment in First Corinthians: An Intertextual Approach to Paul's Re-reading of Deuteronomy.* WUNT 2.253. Tübingen: Mohr Siebeck, 2008.
Waddell, James Alan. *The Messiah: A Comparative Study of the Enochic Son of Man and the Pauline Kyrios.* London: T & T Clark, 2011.
Wagner, J. Ross. *Heralds of the Good News: Isaiah and Paul in Concert in the Letter to the Romans.* NovTSup 51. Boston: Brill, 2002.
Walck, Leslie W. "The Social Setting of the Parables of Enoch." Pages 669–86 in *A Teacher for All Generations. Essays in Honor of James C. VanderKam.* Edited by Eric F. Mason, Kelley Coblentz Bautch, Angela Kim Harkins, and Daniel A Machiela. Leiden: Brill, 2012.
Walton, John H. *Genesis 1 as Ancient Cosmology.* Winona Lake: Eisenbrauns, 2011.
Wassen, Cecilia. "Angels and Humans: Boundaries and Synergies." Pages 523–39 in *Celebrating the Dead Sea Scrolls: A Canadian Contribution.* Edited by Flint, Duhaime, and Baek. EJL 30. Atlanta: SBL, 2011.
Wasserman, Emma. *The Death of the Soul in Romans 7.* WUNT 2.256. Tübingen: Mohr Siebeck, 2008.
Weber, Reinhard. "Die Geschichte des Gesetzes und des Ich in Römer 7,7–8,4" *NZST* 29 (1987): 147–79.
Weinfeld, Moshe. "Sabbath, Temple and the Enthronement of the Lord—The Problem of the *Sitz im Leben* of Genesis 1:1–2:3." Pages 501–12 in *Mélanges bibliques el orientaux en l'honneur de M. Henri Cazelles.* Edited by André Caquot and Mathias Delcor. Neukirchen-Vluyn: Neukirchener Verlag, 1982.
Weiss, H. F. *Untersuchungen zur Kosmologie des hellenistischen und palästinischen Judentum.* TU 97. Berlin: Akademie-Verlag, 1966.
Wevers, John William. *Notes on the Greek Text of Genesis.* SCS 35. Atlanta: Scholars, 1993.
White, Joel R. "N. T. Wright's Narrative Approach." Pages 181–204 in *God and the Faithfulness of Paul: A Critical Examination of the Pauline Theology of N. T. Wright.* Edited by Christoph Heilig, J. Thomas Hewitt, and Michael F. Bird. WUNT 2.413. Tübingen: Mohr Siebeck, 2016.
Wilkens, U. *Weisheit und Torheit.* BHT 26. Tübingen: J. C. B. Mohr, 1959.
Winter, Bruce. *Philo and Paul among the Sophists.* Grand Rapids: Eerdmans, 2002 (1997).
Winter, I. "Idols of the King: Royal Images as Recipients of Ritual Action in Ancient Mesopotamia" *Journal of Ritual Studies* 6 (1992): 13–42.
Wittenberg, G. "The Image of God: Demythologization and Democratization in the Old Testament" *JTSA* 13 (1975): 12–23.
Wold, B. G. *Women, Men, and Angels: The Qumran Wisdom Document Musar leMevin and its Allusions to Genesis Creation Traditions.* WUNT 2.201. Tübingen: Mohr Siebeck, 2005.
Wolfson, H. A. *Philo: Foundation of Religious Philosophy in Judaism, Christianity and Islam,* 2 vols. Cambridge: Harvard University Press, 1947.

Wolter, Michael. *Paul: An Outline of His Theology*. Trans. Robert L. Brawley. Waco: Baylor University Press, 2015 (2011).
Woyke, Johannes. *Götter, "Götzen", Götterbilder: Aspekte einer paulinischen "Theologie der Religionen"*. Berlin: de Gruyter, 2005.
Wright, Benjamin G. *No Small Difference: Sirach's Relationship to Its Hebrew Parent Text*. Atlanta: Scholars Press, 1989.
Wright, N. T. *The Climax of the Covenant: Christ and the Law in Pauline Theology*. Edinburgh: T & T Clark, 1991.
———. *The New Testament and the People of God*. Vol. 1 of *Christian Origins and the Question of God*. Minneapolis: Fortress, 1992.
———. *Jesus and the Victory of God*. Vol. 2 of *Christian Origins and the Question of God*. Minneapolis: Fortress, 1996.
———. *The Resurrection of the Son of God*. Vol. 3 of *Christian Origins and the Question of God*. Minneapolis: Fortress, 2003.
———. *Paul: In Fresh Perspectives*. Minneapolis: Fortress, 2009 (2005).
———. *Paul and the Faithfulness of God*. 2 vols. Vol. 4 of *Christian Origins and the Question of God*. Minneapolis: Fortress, 2013.
———. *Pauline Perspectives: Essays on Paul 1978–2013*. Minneapolis: Fortress, 2013.
———. *Paul and His Recent Interpreters*. Minneapolis: Fortress, 2015.
———. "The Challenge of Dialogue: A Partial and Preliminary Response." Pages 711–67 in *God and the Faithfulness of Paul: A Critical Examination of the Pauline Theology of N. T. Wright*. Edited by Christoph Heilig, Christoph, J. Thomas Hewitt, and Michael F. Bird. WUNT 2.413. Tübingen: Mohr Siebeck, 2016.
Xeravitis, Géza G. *Dualism in Qumran*. LSTS 208. New York/London: T & T Clark, 2010.
Zetterholm, Magnus. "The Non-Jewish Interlocutor in Romans 2:17 and the Salvation of the Nations: Contextualizing Romans 1:18–32." Pages 39–58 in *The So-Called Jew in Paul's Letter to the Romans*. Edited by Rafael Rodríguez and Matthew Thiessen. Minneapolis: Fortress, 2016.

Author Index

Adams, Sean A., 14nn20–23
Agourides, S., 82n20
Alexander, Philip, 54n37; 55n42
Alison, Dale, 28n24
Amir, Yehoshua, 52n18
Andersen, F. I., 82n23; 85nn63–66
Anderson, Gary A., 58n76; 82n27
Arnold, Clinton, 34–35, 53nn24, 30;
    54nn32–33; 179–80, 187n3; 188nn8–9; 189nn10–11, 14–16
Athanassiadi, Polymnia, 17n56; 59n94

Barclay, J. M. G., 12n9; 13n13;
    170nn25–26; 171n34; 175n85
Barker, Margaret, 55n44
Barnett, Paul, 28n26
Barrett, C. K., 142n58; 143n67; 144n87
Barth, Markus, 188n9; 189nn18–19;
    190nn21–24, 26; 191n31; 193n48
Bauckham, Richard, 10, 11, 12n6;
    17n64; 29n43; 29–30n46; 37–39,
    48–49, 50nn1, 3; 54n35; 55nn41,
    47–48; 55–56n49; 56n50, 52–55
Becking, Bob, 50n4
Beetham, Christopher A., 184; 191nn34,
    36; 192nn42, 46
Beker, J. C., 173n63
Belleville, Linda L., 144nn76–78, 85
Bensly, R. L., 84n45

Berger, Peter, 11n4
Bergsma, John S., 14n19
Betz, Hans Dieter, 123, 142n52; 176n87
Black, Matthew, 66, 83nn31–32
Blackwell, Ben C., 86n71; 118, 140n18;
    146nn107–9; 147nn120–21; 197n2
Blanke, H., 188n9; 189nn18–19;
    190nn21–24, 26; 191n31; 193n48
Bohak, G., 53n30
Borgen, Peder, 107n32
Bornkamm, Günther, 187n2; 188n6
Bousset, Wilhelm, 2, 19, 20, 26nn2, 3;
    111, 113n2
Bowie, Ewan, 140n38
Boyarin, Daniel, 37, 55nn44–46
Bréhier, Emile, 107n32
Briones, David E., 142n53
Brooke, G. J., 78, 87n97
Brookins, Timothy A., 142n56; 173n61
Bryan, Steven M., 14n14
Bujard, Walter, 114n11
Bultmann, Rudolf, 19, 20, 27n7;
    140n29; 142n58
Burkert, W., 175n87
Burney, C. F., 183–85; 191nn31, 33–34,
    37; 192n39
Byrne, B., 177n103

Cadwallader, H., 188n8

Campbell, Douglas A., 113, 113nn7–9; 116–17, 139n13; 168n2
Capes, David B., 60n95
Casey, Maurice, 42, 49, 57nn66, 74
Charles, R. H., 85n67
Charlesworth, J. H., 54n34
Chazon, E. G., 52n18
Chester, Andrew, 50n1; 113n1
Christiansen, Ellen Juhl, 13n13
Clifford, Richard J., 58n81
Clines, D. J. A., 26n1
Cohen, B., 143n67
Cohen, Samuel S., 50n1
Collange, J. F., 144n87; 145n98; 149n109
Collins, John J., 4, 14nn17, 19; 56n56; 68, 78, 82n21; 83nn40–42; 84n52; 87n89; 87–88n98; 88nn101–3, 106
Colpe, Carsten, 19–20; 27n4
Copenhaver, Adam K., 187nn1–4; 188n6
Cover, Michael, 118–20, 139n1; 140nn19–27, 31–36; 141n46; 144n83; 147n118
Cox, Ronald, 58nn81–82; 59nn83–84, 86, 88; 84nn52–53, 55; 93, 106nn16, 19–20, 23; 107nn33–35; 108nn45, 50; 109nn59, 61; 114n11; 191nn30, 36–37; 192nn39, 46
Cranfield, C. E. B., 168nn3–4; 169n6, 8–9, 12–13; 170nn24–25, 27–28; 171nn32, 35–36, 38–40; 173nn59, 65; 174nn67, 71; 175nn81–82, 84; 176n89; 177nn96, 102, 104
Crenshaw, J. L., 58n81
Curtis, Edward M., 80–81n3; 81nn5, 10–12

Dalton, W. J., 145n98
Daniélou, J., 107n32
Davidson, Maxwell J., 46, 52n23; 53n24; 59n91; 87n96
Davies, W. D., 191n35
Davila, James R., 12n6; 14n20; 64, 74, 82nn18, 22; 85n67; 86n71

Day, J., 51n8
DeMaris, Richard, 179, 188n7
Denis, Albert Marie, 66, 83n32
Dibelius, Martin, 180, 187n3; 188n6; 189n14
Dietzfelbinger, Christian, 28n26
Dijkstra, Meindert, 50n4; 51n5
Di Lella, Alexander A., 14n17; 56n56; 82nn25–26, 28
Dillon, John, 17nn57–58; 29n38; 59n86; 89–91, 93; 100–101; 104n2; 105nn4, 8–9, 11, 14; 106nn16, 20, 25; 107nn32, 34; 108nn37, 51; 109n60
Dimant, Devorah, 88n104
Donaldson, T. L., 6–7, 13n13; 15n33
Duff, Paul B., 116–18, 139nn8–16; 141n48; 143n66
Dunderberg, Ismo, 104n1
Dunn, J. D. G., 11–12n5; 15n24; 24–26, 29nn43–45; 29–30nn46; 30nn49, 52–53; 49, 139n17; 144n73; 148n128; 153, 164–65, 168nn1, 3–5; 169nn6–9, 13–14; 170nn24–25, 27–28; 171nn30, 33, 35–38, 40; 172n41; 173nn59, 63, 65; 174nn67, 71; 175nn81–82, 84; 176nn89, 91–94; 177nn95, 97–98, 100, 104; 180–81, 187nn2, 5; 188n9; 189nn17–18; 190nn20, 22–25, 27; 192nn46–47

Eco, Umberto, 7, 8, 16n39
Edsall, Benjamin, 114nn10–11
Elder, Nicholas, 174n68
Elgvin, T., 78, 88nn99, 101
Ellis, E. E., 55n43
Eltester, Friedrich-Wilhelm, 20, 27n9; 148n128; 192n46
Enermalm-Ogawa, A., 52n18
Engberg-Pedersen, Troels, 104nn1–2; 105nn3, 6; 172n43; 174nn73, 76
Eskola, Timo, 56n52
Esler, Philip F., 17n55
Evans, C. A., 16n40, 53; 187n5

Falk, D. K., 52n18

Author Index

Fee, Gordon D., 25–26, 29n43; 30nn27–28; 113n3; 114n11; 144n72; 147n124; 148n128
Feuillet, A., 146n109
Fiensy, D. A., 82n20
Firmage, E. B., 80n3
Fitzmyer, Joseph, 116, 139nn3, 17; 144n73; 153, 155, 168nn1, 4; 169nn6, 8, 13; 171nn32–33, 35–36, 38–39; 172nn43–47; 173nn59, 61, 63, 65; 174nn67, 71; 175n81; 176n89; 177n104
Fletcher-Louis, Crispin, 10, 11, 17n65; 29–30n46; 42–45, 50n1; 54n39; 56n53; 57n72; 57–58n75; 58nn76, 79–80; 75–76; 87nn84–85, 87, 91; 108n47
Fossum, J. E., 55n44
Foster, Paul, 16n53
Francis, Fred O., 179–80, 187–88n5; 188n9
Fraser, P. M., 107n32
Frede, Michael, 17n56; 46, 59n92; 90, 105n5
Fredriksen, Paula, 17n59; 32–33, 51nn12–14
Furnish, Victor P., 28n26; 140n27; 141nn44, 49; 142n51; 143nn67–68; 144n85; 145nn95–96, 100–101; 146n104; 147nn120, 126; 148n128

Gamble, Harry Y., 168n2
Garr, W. R., 80n3
Geffcken, J., 83nn40–41
Geertz, Clifford, 11n4
Georgi, Dieter, 116, 139n5; 140n27; 141n44
Gertz, Jan Christian, 81n8
Gieschen, Charles A., 54n39
Gnuse, Robert, 50n4; 51nn8–10
Goff, J., 78, 88nn98, 103, 105–6
Goldingay, John, 14n19
Goodenough, E. R., 107n32
Goodrich, John K., 175n83

Gordley, Matthew E., 11n3; 114nn10–11; 185; 191n30; 192nn41, 44, 46
Gorman, Michael, 197n2
Goulder, Michael D., 140n28
Green, Joel B. 28nn35, 41
Green, Thomas, 16n54
Griffioen, Sander, 11n4
Grindheim, Sigurd, 6–7, 12n9; 13n13; 15n34–36; 16n38
Gross, W., 80n3; 81n5
Guthrie, George H., 141n47; 142n51; 143n63

Habets, Augustinus C. J., 105n8
Hafemann, Scott J., 141n47; 143n63; 144nn74, 80, 87; 147n121
Halvorson, Martien A., 14n15
Hannah, Darrell D., 53n24; 54n39
Harrington, D. J., 83n39
Harris, Murray J., 28n26; 142nn51, 54; 143nn63, 67–68; 144nn75, 85–88; 145nn94–95, 97, 99–101; 146nn104, 107, 109–10; 147nn121, 123, 126
Hartman, Lars, 60n96
Hartman, Louis F., 14n17; 56n56
Hay, David M., 56n52
Hayman, Peter, 51n11
Hays, Richard B., 7–9, 16nn40–54; 113n5; 116, 131, 139nn1, 6–7; 141n45; 143nn61, 63, 65; 144nn74, 79, 82, 89; 145nn90–92, 94–96; 168–69n5; 177n101
Heckel, Theo K., 176n87
Hegermann, H., 59n89
Heiser, Michael, 59n90
Hengel, Martin, 27n4; 113n4
Henze, Matthias, 15nn25, 26
Heschel, Susannah, 26n2
Hiebert, Robert J. V., 175n83
Hill, Wesley, 48–50, 60n99–106
Hinschberger, R., 80n3
Hofius, Otfried, 172n46
Horbury, William, 33, 51n15
Huggins, R. V., 174n76
Hugedé, Norbert, 146n109

Hurtado, Larry W., 10, 11, 17nn60, 63; 26n2; 26–27n3; 27n16; 29nn43, 44; 30n53; 47–49, 50n1; 51n10; 51–52nn16–18; 52nn20–22; 53nn28–29; 54nn35, 38; 55nn43–44; 56nn49, 53, 55; 57n67; 58n75; 59nn88, 94; 60nn97–98; 114n10; 176n91; 188n9

Isaac, Ephraim, 66, 83nn30–31, 33

Jacob, Haley Goranson, 11n3
Janowski, B., 80n3
Jastrow, M., 146n115
Jervell, Jacob, 21, 27nn10–15; 148n127
Jewett, Robert, 168nn3–4; 169nn6–9, 12–13; 170nn24, 27; 171nn29, 33, 36–38; 172nn42–43; 173nn59, 64–65; 174nn71, 76, 78; 175nn81–82, 84, 86; 176n88; 177nn95–96, 100, 102, 104
Jipp, Joshua, 113n3; 192n45
Johnson, M. D., 58n76–77
Johnson, N. B., 52n18
Jonquiere, T. M., 52n18
Joüon, P., 81n13–14

Kaminsky, Joel, 13n13
Käsemann, Ernst, 20, 27n8; 141n47; 143n67; 175n84; 192n46
Keck, Leander E., 176n91
Kee, H. C., 85nn67–68
Keesmaat, Sylvia, 177n99
Kenney, John P., 59n94
Keyes, C. W., 142n59
Kiefer, Jörn, 14n14
Kim, C. H., 143n59
Kim, Seyoon, 22, 27n4; 28nn24, 26; 111, 113n3; 146n107
Korpel, Marjo C. A., 50n4
Kratz, Reinhard G., 51n8
Kugler, Chris, 171n34
Kugler, Robert, 14n14; 15n28
Kümmel, W. G., 156–57; 173nn54, 63
Kutsko, John F., 82n16

Lampe, G. W. H., 177n103

Lange, A., 78, 87n97; 88n101
Larsson, Edvin, 19, 20, 21, 27–28nn19–22
Lehmkühler, Karsten, 26n2
Levison, John, 58n77; 70, 82n28; 84nn46, 51; 85nn59–60, 62
Lichtenberger, Hermann, 174n73; 176n91
Lietzmann, Hans, 116, 139n3
Lightfoot, J. B., 188n6
Lincoln, Andrew, 179, 187n1
Litwa, M. David, 118, 134–37, 140n18; 146nn111–14, 116; 147nn117, 120, 122
Lohse, Eduard, 114n11; 175n84; 187n2; 188n6; 189n18; 190nn24, 26–27; 192n46
Longenecker, Richard, 168n4; 169n15; 171nn35, 39; 172n46
Lorenzen, Stefanie, 19, 22–23; 26n1; 28nn24, 27–33; 29n42; 107n32
Lossky, Vladimir, 82n19; 109n66
Luckmann, Thomas, 11n4

MacDonald, Nathan, 31–32, 49, 50n2–3; 60n103
Mach, Michael, 52n19; 53n24; 54nn35–36
Mack, Berton L. 59n89
Malherbe, Abraham, 104n1
Marchand, Suzanne L., 26n2
Marcus, Joel, 58nn76, 78; 84n49
Marcus, Ralph, 50n1
Margulies, M., 147n117
Markschies, C., 175–76nn87
Marques, Valdir, 19, 20, 22, 28n23
Marshall, Paul, 11n4
Martin, Dale B., 17n55
Martin, Ralph P., 140n28; 141n44; 142n58; 144n87
Martin, Troy, 187n4
Martin-Achard, Robert, 13n13
Martínez, García, 15n27
Martyn, J. L., 113n5
Maston, Jason, 172n47; 174nn76–78; 176n90

McGrath, James, 49
McKnight, Scot, 187n5; 188n8; 189nn12, 17–18; 190nn20, 22–26; 191n31; 192nn43, 46–47; 193n48
McLaren, James S., 13n13
McLay, Tim, 56–57nn59–60
McNamara, Martin J., 144nn76–78
Meeks, Wayne A., 16n55
Merrill, E. H., 81n5
Metzger, Bruce M., 14n16; 84n45; 142nn57–58; 146n103
Meyer, W., 58n76
Middleton, J. Richard, 81n5
Milgrom, Jacob, 81n7; 88n107
Milik, J. T., 83n31
Mitchell, Stephen, 46, 59nn93–94
Moffitt, David M., 55n40; 58n76
Mohr, Richard D., 106n16
Moo, Douglas, 168n4; 171n33; 172n48; 174nn68, 70, 72; 175n84; 191n31
Moule, C. F. D., 116, 139n3
Mouw, Richard, 11n4
Muraoka, T., 81nn13–14; 82n15
Murphy-O'Connor, Jerome, 139n4

Naugle, David, 11n4
Neusner, Jacob, 86n81
Newman, Carey, 22, 28nn24, 26; 111, 134; 146nn105–6
Newsom, Carol, 88n104
Nickelsburg, George W. E., 42, 57n73; 83nn30–31, 37
Niehoff, Maren R., 17n57
Novenson, Matthew V., 10, 17nn60–61; 152, 169n16; 170nn20, 22–24

Odeberg, Hugo, 55n45
Oeming, M., 51n8
Olyan, Saul, 53n24
Owen, Paul L., 57n67

Pao, David, 189n19; 190n27
Pearson, B. A., 59n89
Pedersen, Troels-Engberg, 89–90
Peuch, E., 86n80
Piotrowski, Nicholas G., 13n14

Popowic, M., 85n68
Porter, Stanley E., 145n96
Prümm, Karl, 143nn62, 67

Radice, Roberto, 107n32
Rainbow, Paul A., 50n1; 56n51
Räisänen, Heikki, 175n84
Ramsay, W. M., 180, 189n14
Rasimus, Tuomas, 104n1
Reitzenstein, Richard, 20, 27n5, 6
Reydams-Schils, Gretchen J., 106n16
Reynolds, Benjamin, 57n69
Rodríguez, Rafael, 151–52, 169n16; 170n18
Rowe, C. Kavin, 104n1
Rowland, Christopher, 42, 54n39; 55n44; 57n71; 187n5
Rowley, Harold H., 13n13
Runia, David, 107n32
Russell, Norman, 86n71

Sanders, E. P., 11–12nn5; 12n11; 14n17; 52n18
Sandmel, Samuel, 107n32
Sappington, T. J., 187n3
Schäfer, Peter, 53n24; 54n36
Schenck, Kenneth, 107n32
Schlatter, Adolf, 50n1; 192n45
Schmid, K., 51n8
Schmithals, Walter, 140n29
Schnelle, Udo, 28n26; 29n40; 60n98; 172n46
Schrage, Wolfgang, 60n98
Schreiner, Thomas R., 140n17; 153, 168nn3–4; 169nn5–6, 8, 12–15; 170n24; 171nn31, 33, 35–36, 38; 172n48; 173nn59, 62–63, 65; 174n79; 175nn81, 84; 176n89; 177nn98, 100, 102, 104
Schüle, Andreas, 62, 80n3; 81n9
Schulz, Siegfried, 116, 139n4
Schwanz, Peter, 21, 27nn17–18; 82n19
Schweizer, Eduard, 176n91; 188n7
Scott, James M., 13n14
Scroggs, R. 148n128

Segal, Alan F., 22, 28n24, 26, 37, 55n46; 57n69; 111
Sharpe, J. L., 85n61
Sim, David C., 13n13
Sire, J. W., 11n4
Skehan, Patrick W., 82nn25–26, 28
Smith, Daniel L, 177n99
Smith, Mark S., 51nn6, 8–9
Sohn, Seock-Tae, 13n13
Spieckermann, Hermann, 51n8
Staudt, Darina, 50n1
Steck, O. H., 13n14; 14–15n21
Stendahl, Krister, 172n43; 173nn51, 63
Sterling, Gregory, 70, 84nn52, 54; 91; 100–101; 104n1; 105nn3, 7–8, 14; 108nn45–46, 48, 50, 55–56; 109nn57–58
Stern, Ephraim, 50n4; 51n7
Stettler, Christian, 113, 114nn10, 12; 191n30; 192nn45–46
Stone, Michael E., 15n25; 58n76; 85n67
Stowers, Stanley K., 156–57, 170n21; 171n29; 172n49; 173nn50–58; 174nn73, 76
Strawbridge, Jennifer, 114nn10–11
Stuckenbruck, Loren, 34, 40, 53nn25–26; 54n35; 54–55nn39, 57nn61, 65, 68–70; 58n77; 83nn30–31, 34–37
Sullivan, Kevin P., 53n24; 54n39
Sumney, Jerry, 189n19

Taylor, A. E., 106n16
Taylor, C. C. W., 120, 140n39
Teixidor, J., 59n94
Theiler, Willy, 108n45
Theissen, Gerd, 160, 174nn73–74, 78
Thiessen, Matthew, 169n16
Thom, Johan C., 105n7
Thorsteinsson, Runar, 151–52, 169n16; 170nn19, 22–23
Thrall, Margaret, 28n26; 137, 141nn44, 48–50; 142nn50–51, 54, 58; 143nn59, 63, 67–68; 144nn85, 87–88; 145nn93, 95, 97, 99–101; 146nn104, 107, 109–10; 147nn120–26; 148n128
Tigchelaar, E. J. C., 15n27
Tilling, Chris, 10, 11, 17n65; 50n1; 56n53; 60n98
Tobin, Thomas H., 59n85; 174nn73, 76
Tooman, William A., 16n53
Tov, Emmanuel, 15n21; 56nn58–59
Trainor, Michael, 188n8
Trebilco, Paul, 188n8

van den Beld, A., 174n73
van der Horst, P. W., 86nn70–72, 76, 78
VanderKam, James C., 13n14, 42; 57n73
van Dülmen, A., 175n84
van Kooten, George H., 23–24, 26n3; 28nn34–41; 67, 74–78, 80n1; 82nn16, 26, 28; 83nn36, 38; 84n44; 85nn56–57, 60, 64–66, 68; 87nn82, 86, 88, 92; 88nn100, 102–3, 105–6; 100–101; 105–6n15; 106n19; 107nn32–33, 35; 108nn38, 40–41, 44; 109nn60, 64; 111, 113n2; 118, 120–23, 140nn18, 30, 37; 141nn44, 46; 169n7; 175n87; 196–97
van Nuffelen, P., 59n94
Völker, W., 107n32
Vollenweider, Samuel, 22, 28nn24, 26; 111
von der Osten-Sacken, P., 175n84
von Rad, Gerhard, 58n81
Vriezen, Karel J. H., 50n4
Vriezen, Theodorus C., 13n13

Wagner, J. Ross, 168n5; 177n101
Walten, John H., 81n4
Wassen, Cecilia, 53–54n31; 88n104
Wasserman, Emma, 172–73n49; 174n76
Weber, Reinhard, 172n46
Weiss, H. F., 59n89
Wenham, Gordon J., 81nn4, 11; 81–82n14
Wilkens, U., 59n89; 172n48; 175n84

Wilson, M., 188n9; 189nn16–18; 190nn20, 22–26; 192nn40, 47; 193n48
Wilson, Walter T., 86nn72, 74–76, 78
Windisch, Hans, 115–16, 139n2; 144n87
Winston, David, 84nn47–48, 51–53; 85nn56–57; 106n21
Winter, Bruce, 118, 120–24, 140nn18, 30, 37–38, 41; 141n44; 142nn52, 55–56
Witherington III, Ben, 144n72
Wittenberg, G., 81n5
Wold, B. G., 78, 87nn95–96; 88nn99, 101, 105
Wolff, Christian, 28n26
Wolfson, H. A., 107n32
Woyke, Johannes, 50n1; 60n98
Wright, Christopher J. H., 13n13
Wright, N. T., 3, 6–7, 10–11, 11–12n5; 12n9; 13–14nn12–15; 15nn29–32, 37; 17nn59–60, 62; 29nn43, 45; 29–30n46; 50n1; 53n29; 55n43; 59n89; 60n98; 85n58; 104n1; 104–5nn2–3; 105n7; 113n3; 116; 139n6; 141n45; 143nn64, 69; 146nn106, 109; 147n128; 153, 168nn1, 2–5; 170n25; 171nn29, 34, 39–40; 172n48; 173nn62, 65; 174nn67, 69–70, 72, 79; 176n91; 177nn95, 99; 183–85, 187n5; 189nn13, 18, 20; 190n20, 22–23; 191nn31, 33–35, 37; 192nn39, 45; 193n48

Xeravitis, Géza G., 87n92

Young, D., 86n70

Zetterholm, Magnus, 152, 169nn16–17; 170n18
Ziegler, Joseph, 84n48

Subject Index

Adam christology, 11nn1–2; 24–26; 138, 185–87, 195–97

Colossian heresy, 179–83

divine christology, definition of, 10–11
divine identity, 37–39

election, missiological construal of, 6–7, 12n9; 13n13; 15n37; 150–52
exile, continuing, 3–6, 13n12; 14–30, 161–62, 165–68

intermediary doctrine, 23–24, 92–104, 183–87
intertextuality, 7–9

Jewish monotheism, 47; and divine attributes, 45–46; and exalted patriarchs, 37–45; exclusive, 33; and idolatry, 31–32; and principal angel traditions, 33–37, 179–87

likeness to god, 93–94, 101–3
logos, 45–46, 95–98

Medea paradox, 160–63

philosophical traditions, definition of, 9–10
prepositional metaphysics, 98–101, 183–85

sophia, 4–5, 25–26, 45–46, 183–85

Two Powers Heresy, 37

wisdom christology, 11nn1–2; 24–26, 138, 163–65, 183–87, 195–97
worldview, 2–7; Worldview, The Jewish Narrative, 2–7, 3

Ancient Literature

GRECO-ROMAN LITERATURE

Alcinous

Didaskalikos
Ep. 9.3 99

Diodorus Siculus

Bibliotheca Historica
40.3.3–8 44

Epictetus

Discourses
1.16.15–20 150
2.8.11–13 105n15
2.26.1–2 4–5160

Lucian of Samasota

Essays in Portraiture Defended
28 94–95

Plato

Phaedrus
236D 123

Protagoras
313D–E 121, 123

Theaetetus
176B 93–94, 102–3, 196–97

Timaeus
28A–29B 92
31 92
92C 92

Plutarch

Themistocles
27.1–3 93

Uneducated Ruler
780E–F 94, 101–3

Seneca

Epistles
65.2 99
65.8 99

Strabo

Geography
14.673 120

OLD TESTAMENT LITERATURE

Genesis		2 Chronicles	
1.1	183–85	23.17	62
1.1–3	137		
1.26–28	22, 61–66, 68–79, 82n24; 96, 102–3, 111–12, 138	Nehemiah	
		9.6	38
2.7	68, 73–79	Esther	
3	156	(LXX) 7.4	70
(LXX) 3.13	158–59	(LXX) 8.1	70
(LXX) 3.15	159		
4	70	Job	
5.1	22, 63, 65, 79	1.646	
5.3	22, 61, 63–65, 67, 79		
6–9	67	Psalms	
6.4	67	33.6	70
7.1	67	82.1	46
9.6	22, 61, 63–65, 79, 96	89.27	106n22
(LXX) 15.6	155	110.1	39
Exodus		Proverbs	
(LXX) 8.25	159	8.22	45–46
31.18	126–27	8.22–31	183–85
32–34	115		
32.15	126–27	Isaiah	
33.11	135	6.139	
33.20	135, 137	40–44	32
34	116–17, 120, 130–34	40–55	166
(LXX) 34.34	132	44.24	38
Exodus 38.8		45.18	38
(LXX) 38.26	135	48.12–13	38
		55.12	166
Numbers			
12.6–8	135	Jeremiah	
33.52	62	31.33 (LXX 38.33)	126–27
Deuteronomy		Ezekiel	
9.10	126–27	1.26–28	41–42, 63, 75–76
Ruth		7.20	62
2.10	43	11.19	126–27
		16.17	62
2 Kings		23.14	62
11.18	62	36.26	126–27

Ancient Literature

Daniel
2	39
2.46	39
7	37, 39, 40–42
7.10	34

9.1–24	3–4

Amos
5.26	62

SECOND-TEMPLE JEWISH LITERATURE

Apocalypse of Abraham
7.10	38

Apocalypse of Sedrach
13.1–3	82n20

Apocalypse of Zephaniah
6.15	54n35

Ascension of Isaiah
7.21–22	54n35

Baruch
1–3.31	4–5
3.9–4.4	4–5, 26

2 Baruch
14.17	70
21.4	70
29.3	42

3 Baruch
4.8	70
4.16	65

Bel and the Dragon
5	38

1 Enoch
1–36	67
6	67
14.18–22	39
14.22	34
15.8–9	67
37–71	37, 42–43
45.3	39, 42
46.5	39, 42–43
48.2–7	42
48.5	39, 42–43
51.3	39, 42
55.4	39, 42
61.8	39, 42
62.2–5	39, 42
62.6	39, 42–43
62.9	39, 42–43
69.27	39, 42
106.1–10	66–67
106.10	64–66, 79
106.13–18	67

2 Enoch
20.3	39
22.8–10	67
44.1–3	72–73
47.3–4	38
65.2	64–65, 72–73, 79
66.4	38

4 Ezra
6.35–59	69
6.38	70
7.45–48.36	69
8.41	69
8.44	64–65, 68–69, 72, 79
11–12.39	5
13.25–32	42

Joseph and Aseneth
12.1–2	38
12.9	70
15.11–12	34

Jubilees		3.20–35	38
6.8	64–65, 79	8.266	64
10.8	70	8.375–376	38
12.3–5	38	8.402	64
12.4	70	Fragment 1.5–6	38
		Fragment 3	38
Latin Life of Adam and Eve		Fragment 5	38
10	64–65, 79		
12	64–65, 79	Sirach	
12.1–16.1	43–44, 71–72	1.4	45–46
13.3	73–75	1.9	45–46
33	64–65, 79	17.3	22, 64–65, 79
33.5	69	24	8–9, 45–46
35	64–65, 79	24.23–24	185
35.3	69	50	44
(Greek) Life of Adam and Eve		Synagogal Prayers	
10.2–3	72	7.34.6	82n20
15	70		
16	70	Testament of Abraham	
17	70	9.6	70
20.2	65		
21	70	Testament of Job	
33.5	72	2.4	38
		3.3	70
2 Maccabees		17.1	70
1.24–29	38	26.6	70
Prayer of Jacob		Testament of Levi	
1.1–3	35	5.5–6	34
Pseudo Philo's LAB		Testament of Naphtali	
3.11	64–65, 79	2.2–5	73–74
15.6	34	2.5	64–65, 75, 79
19.16	129	3.1	70
50.7	64–65, 67, 79	8.4	70
		8.6	70
Pseudo Phocylides			
1.100–106	74–75	Testament of Solomon	
1.106	64–65, 71, 79	15.11	70
Sibylline Oracles		Tobit	
1.23	64–65, 68, 79	11.14–15	34
3.8	64–65, 68, 79		
3.8–10	73–75	Wisdom	
3.10–34	68	2.22	71, 74

2.23–24	22, 44, 64–65, 69–71, 74–75, 79	11Q14 Fragment	
3.7–8	71, 75	1.1.2–6	34
7.22–28.1	45–46, 70, 92, 185		
7.26	22, 64–65, 69–71, 79, 92	**Josephus**	
9.1–2	45–46, 70	*Antiquities*	
9.10	164	10.211–212	39, 56n57
		11.331	44

Dead Sea Scrolls

Philo

CD
1.1–8	5	*On Agriculture*	
3.20	75–77	143	120

1QH

Allegorical Interpretation
4.14–15	75–77	3.96	95, 97
		3.101	136

1QS
4.22–23	75–77	*On Cherubim*	
		125	99

1Q19
Fragment 3	66	*On Confusion*	
		25	97
4Q204		144–147	65, 92
Fragment 5.1–2	66		
		On Creation	
4Q400		69	71, 74, 80
Fragment 2.1–9	34		
		On the Decalogue	
4Q403		72–74	101–3
Fragment			
1.1.31b–33a	34	*On Dreams*	
		1.239	97
4Q417			
Fragment		*On Flight*	
2.1.15–18	73–75, 77–78, 81n4	12	97
		68–69	81n4
4Q418		101	97
Fragment			
8.1.1–15	34	*Heir*	
		205–6	45–46, 59n87
4Q504		231	97
Fragment 8.1.4	73–77		

Life of Moses		Special Laws	
2.70	129	1.81	97
2.212	121	1.171	97
		1.327–329	96–97
On Names		3.83	97
30–31	81n4	3.207	97
Questions and Answers on Genesis		On Tongues	
2.62	96–97	97	97
		147	97

NEW TESTAMENT LITERATURE

John		5.12–17	154
1.1–3	48	5.13	158
1.1–18	112, 138	6.6–23	155
1.3	25, 98, 100–101, 184	7.6	127–28, 155, 161–62, 167
1.10	98, 100–101, 184		
1.14	92	7.7–13	157–59
1.18	92	7.11	128
		7.14–25	157, 159–63
Acts		7.15	156, 160–61, 168
1.24	47	7.17	156, 160–61, 168
18.24–28	119	7.19	160–61
22.16	47	7.21	161
		7.22	160, 168
Romans		7.23	166–67
1.16	149	7.25	156
1.17	149–50	8	196–97
1.18–32	150–51	8.1–3	163–65
1.25	101	8.3	167
1.28	150–51	8.14–21	165
2.9–10	149	8.19–21	163
2.11	151	8.28–30	164
2.12	118	8.29	20, 21, 25, 65, 79, 92, 97–98, 103–4, 111, 160, 167–68, 184, 186
2.17–24	150–53, 167		
2.25–29	152		
2.29	127–28		
3.1–4	152–53	8.38	36
3.1–8	149	10.4	131
3.9	152	10.9	47
3.21–24	153–55	11.36	98, 100–101
4	163	12.1–2	150–51
4.13	154–55, 165–66	13.8	162
5.12–14	163, 166–67	14.1–6	162

15.8a	149	10–13	115–17, 122–24, 138
16.18	159	10.10	124
16.20	159	10.12	122–23
		10.18	122–23
1 Corinthians		11.5–9	123–25, 138
6.11	47	11.6	124
8.6	24, 25, 47, 98–101, 103–4, 111, 138, 164, 184	11.22–23	123–25
		12.2–10	47
		12.11	122–23
11.7	65, 79	12.16	124
11.23–26	47		
12.3	47	Galatians	
15.49	20, 21, 65, 79, 112	3.27–28	112
15.56	128	4.4	164
16.22	47		
		Philippians	
2 Corinthians		2.5–11	47
2.17–3.1	115–16, 120–25, 134, 138, 160	2.6	21, 26
		2.10	36
3.2–3	126–27	2.11	47
3.4	127		
3.5–6	116, 127	Colossians	
3.6	126	1.13	101
3.6–11	128–30	1.15–16	20, 21, 25, 26, 36, 48, 65, 79, 92–93, 98–99, 111–12, 165, 183–87
3.7–18	116–18, 120, 122, 125, 127		
3.7	117–18, 127		
3.9	117–18	1.15–20	25, 47, 100–104, 138
3.11	127	2.8	179–83, 186–87
3.12	131, 133	2.11	179–83, 186–87
3.12–15	118, 130–33, 137	2.16	179–83, 186–87
3.16–17	132	2.18	35, 179–83, 186–87
3.18	20, 21, 65, 79, 97–98, 103–4, 111, 115, 125, 132–38, 186	2.20–23	182–83, 186–87
		3.9–11	21, 79, 112, 182, 186–87
4.1–3	116		
4.1–6	133–34	Ephesians	
4.2	121–22	1.20–21	36
4.3–4	133–34	3.16	162
4.4	20, 21, 65, 79, 131–34, 137–38	4.22–24	21, 82n24
4.6	137–38	1 Thessalonians	
4.16	162	3.11–13	47
5.12	122	5.23	24
6.4	122		

Hebrews
1–2   36
1.1–4   112, 138
1.2   25, 48, 98, 100–101, 184
1.6   92

James
3.9   82n24

1 Peter
3.22   36

1 John
3.2   109n63

Revelation
1.17–3.22   47
19.10   54n35
22.8–9   54n35

EARLY CHRISTIAN LITERATURE

Apology of Aristides
14   54n38

Clement of Alexandria

Protrepticus
12.122.4   102–3

Stromata
6.5.39   54n38

Epistle of Barnabas
6.12   81n4

Justin Martyr

Dialogue 62   81n4

Origin

Against Celsus
5.6   54n38

Commentary on John
13.17   54n38

RABBINIC LITERATURE

Babylonian Avodah Zarah
42b   36, 54n38

Babylonian Yoma
69a   44

Genesis Rabbah
1.1   185

Leviticus Rabbah
1.14   135–36

Mekhilta Exodus
20.4   36, 54n38

20.20   36, 54n38

Mishnah Hullin
2.8   36, 54n38

Pirke Avoth
3.14   64–65, 75, 79

Targum Pseudo Jonathan Exodus
20.20   36, 54n38

Tosefta Hullin
2.18   36, 54n38

About the Author

Chris Kugler (PhD) is Assistant Professor of Theology at Houston Baptist University in Houston, Texas.

www.ingramcontent.com/pod-product-compliance
Lightning Source LLC
Chambersburg PA
CBHW032128010526
44111CB00033B/218